The Growth of Firms in Less-Developed Countries

"This is one of those rare books that explore growth in the least developed of economies from the perspective of a firm. It is both empirically and theoretically relevant and digs new ground in this area. Crucially, it is about Kosovo, the least developed European economy about which we know very little."

—Slavo Radosevic, *Professor of Industry and Innovation Studies, University College London, UK*

"This book examines the processes of firms in Kosovo for the first time. Growth of firms leads to the growth of the economy, reduction in unemployment, poverty and many social problems. But as the author shows, growth of firms is constrained by poor business environment and a slow process of Schumpeterian creative destruction. This is the challenge facing policy makers. This book belongs on the reading lists of all universities' programmes in economics and business in Kosovo."

—Iraj Hashi MBE, *Emeritus Professor of Economics, Staffordshire University, UK*

Fadil Sahiti

The Growth of Firms in Less-Developed Countries

Lessons from Kosovo

palgrave
macmillan

Fadil Sahiti
Rochester Institute of Technology Kosovo
Prishtinë, Kosovo

ISBN 978-3-030-14820-1 ISBN 978-3-030-14821-8 (eBook)
https://doi.org/10.1007/978-3-030-14821-8

Library of Congress Control Number: 2019932975

This Palgrave Macmillan imprint is published by the registered company Springer Nature Switzerland AG
The registered company address is: Gewerbestrasse 11, 6330 Cham, Switzerland

I dedicate this book to my late dad and mom, who sadly did not see the fruits of my work

Acknowledgements

I want to thank several people for their support and encouragement while I was working on this book. First, I am very grateful to friends and colleagues for their support and reassurance during the process. All of them demonstrated active interest in my research by providing thoughtful comments and guidance.

I am particularly grateful to my family, who always believed in me and never stopped encouraging me to achieve something that, it is hope, will be valuable to many.

Contents

Abbreviations

BEEPS	Business Environment and Enterprise Performance Survey
BSCK	Business Support Centre of Kosovo
CBK	Central Bank of Kosovo
CIS	Commonwealth of Independent States
DEED	Diaspora Engagement for Economic Development
EBRD	European Bank for Reconstruction and Development
ECA	Europe and Central Asia
EIU	Economist Intelligence Unit
EU	European Union
FDI	Foreign Direct Investment
GD	Growth Diagnostics
GDP	Gross Domestic Product
GNI	Gross National Income
GNP	Gross National Product
ICJ	International Court of Justice
IFC	International Finance Corporation
IPA	Instrument for Pre-Accession Assistance
KBRA	Kosovo Business Registration Agency
KSA	Kosovo Statistics Agency
MNE	Multi-National Enterprise
MOI	Management, Organization and Innovation (survey)

NPL	Non-Performing Loans
OECD	Organisation for Economic Cooperation and Development
PAK	Privatization Agency of Kosovo
PICS	Productivity and Investment Climate Survey
PISA	Programme for International Student Assessment
RBT	Resource-Based Theory
ROE	Return on Equity
SAA	Stabilisation and Association Agreement
SBA	Small Business Act
SEE	South East Europe
SFRY	Socialist Federal Republic of Yugoslavia
SME	Small and Medium Sized Enterprises
SOE	Socially Owned Enterprise
TFP	Total Factor Productivity
UN	United Nations
UNDP	United Nations Development Programme
UNMIK	United Nations Mission in Kosovo
VAT	Value Added Tax
VET	Vocational Education and Training

List of Figures

List of Tables

1
Introduction

The aim of this book is to assess the dynamics and determinants of firm growth in less-developed countries, through the exploration of four important dimensions: firm creation, exit, and survival dynamics; firms inputs, firms' managerial practices and organizational capabilities; how external (environmental) factors affect firm growth, and how social conditions enable and/or constrain the capabilities of firms to innovate. Although the main focus in the book is the case of Kosovo, this economy is not treated as an isolated case; the findings are compared to a set of five reference countries. This positions the analysis between the body of microeconomic work on firm growth and the empirical literature on less-developed countries.

The book begins with a comprehensive introductory chapter, which discusses the inspiration for the book and implications for empirical analyses that emerge. It sets out an empirical research agenda and identifies some characteristics of the countries used as benchmarks.

F. Sahiti, *The Growth of Firms in Less-Developed Countries*,
https://doi.org/10.1007/978-3-030-14821-8_1

1.1 Motivation for the Book

The book addresses the important theme of which factors enable and constrain firm growth in less-developed economies. The empirical evidence used for the analysis is related to Kosovan firms, but the findings are presented in the wider context of development economies. However, the Kosovan context has some intrinsic merits since there is no other published book that addresses economic development in Kosovo specifically. Although Kosovo is a small country, it reached the international headlines in the context of its centrality in a major war in Europe. Its geopolitical importance and the unresolved nature of the conflict between Kosovo and Serbia, which could erupt again in Europe, mean that economic development and job creation in this country are issues deserving of more attention than they have received in the current scholarly literature.

Albeit from a low base, in the post-financial crisis period, Kosovo's economy has grown consistently and at a higher rate compared to other Western Balkans countries. In 2017, Kosovo's GDP per capita reached US$ 3902 from US$ 1088 in 2000 (World Bank 2018). The World Bank includes Kosovo in the group of countries with low-income per capita group. Its economy is dominated by Small and Medium-sized Enterprises (SMEs). According to the Kosovo Statistics Agency (KSA) these types of firms account for 99.78% of the total firm population.

Consequently, the analysis in this book focuses on SMEs. The empirical evidence suggests that this category of firms is of vital importance for sustainable economic growth in both high- and low-income economies (Ayyagari et al. 2011; OECD 2016). Governments and policy makers around the world recognize the strategic importance of SMEs and identification and implementation of policies to promote a conducive business environment are a deliberate goal of the governments in both advanced and less-developed countries (Smallbone and Welter 2001).

The following list of reasons why SMEs play such a pivotal role in economic growth is not exhaustive, but includes the most prominent ones:

- there is empirical evidence showing that SMEs are the dominant business firm type in the firm populations of many economies. Although accurate and up-to-date data on the structure of the firm population is not immediately accessible, according to Ayyagari et al. (2011) more than 95% of firms across the world are SMEs. This percentage varies across regions and countries, but in those market economies with the lowest shares their numbers are still high. For instance, among the industrialized countries, Japan has the highest proportion of SMEs and they account for more than 99% of total firm population (EIU 2010). The picture is similar for the Organisation of Economic Cooperation and Development (OECD) area countries where SMEs predominate and represent some 99% of all firms. They are the main source of firm employment in these countries, accounting for around 70% of jobs on average, and are major contributors to value creation, generating between 50 and 60% of value, added on average (OECD 2016). An IFC (2010) report indicates the number of micro, small and medium-sized enterprises in emerging markets as somewhere between 365–445 million, 25–30 million of which are formal SMEs and 55–70 million formal micro enterprises, with the remaining 285–345 million being informal enterprises and one-person firms.
  SMEs are known for their contribution to economic development, particularly in developing countries, although this varies substantially across countries. According to IFC (2010), SMEs contribute up to 33% of GDP in developing economies, although this is significantly higher if the contribution of firms operating in the informal sector is included. In a report prepared for the European Commission, Wymenga et al. (2011) argue that the contribution of SMEs to overall output is generally lower than that made by larger companies. This is because the former group tend to be more labour intensive, with the result that smaller firms, typically, are less productive;
- since SMEs are more labour intensive business entities, they provide a more substantial contribution to employment in national economies around the world. Higher labour intensity results in a lower capital cost of job creation in smaller compared to in larger firms,

which matters for developing countries and economies with high unemployment rates (Liedholm and Mead 1987; Schmitz 1995). The contribution of SMEs to total employment varies widely between countries and regions; there is some evidence that SME employment, which is important in all countries, is especially important in high-income countries. According to the OECD (2016), SMEs are the main employers in developed countries, accounting for around 70% of jobs, on average, while in emerging economies SMEs represent up to 45% of total employment. These figures confirm the finding in an earlier report, based on a World Bank survey of 47,745 businesses in 99 countries, which shows that firms with between 5 and 250 employees account for 66% of total permanent, full-time employment in these countries (Ayyagari et al. 2011). Figure 1.1 depicts the contribution of SMEs to employment in different country groups;

SMEs are responsible for a higher proportion of job creation than large enterprises. De Kok et al. (2011) argue that between 2002 and

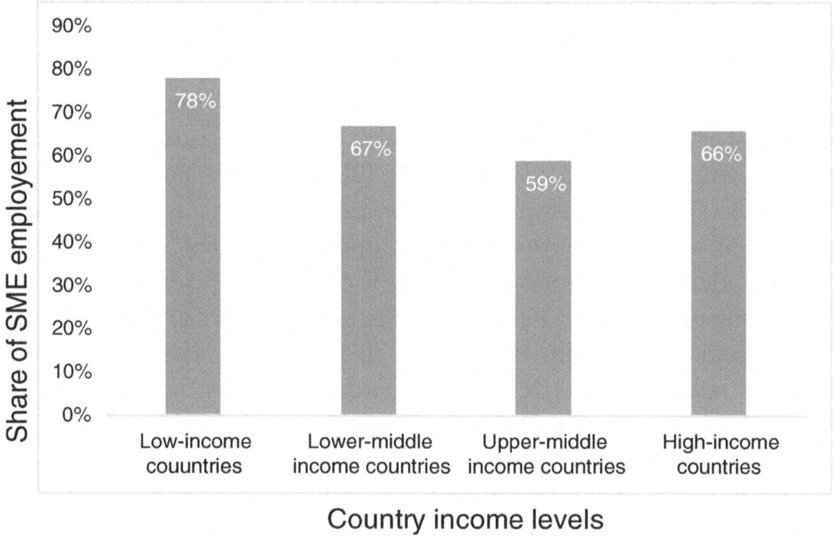

Fig. 1.1 Employment contribution of SMEs (*Source* Author of the book, using data from Ayyagari et al. [2011])

2010, 85% of total employment growth, on average, was attributable to SMEs. Ayyagari et al. (2011, p. 3) provide evidence showing that, across country income groups, while small firms may not employ large numbers, they generate the most new jobs. More specifically, they show that small firms with less than 20 employees generate 45.34% of new jobs and that, even in countries with aggregate net job loss, small firms (less than 20 employees) are the major job creators (36.54% of new jobs). Job creation is particularly important in countries plagued by high rates of unemployment such as Kosovo;

- SMEs are critical for innovation and productivity growth. The empirical evidence suggests that the SME sector makes a significant contribution to the invention and innovation diffusion processes and the establishment of competitive national innovation systems (Baumol 2002; Piech 2004; Radosevic and Mickiewicz 2003; Čučković and Bartlett 2007, p. 16). The further input of SMEs to national innovation activity has been boosted by the development of knowledge-based economies, increased non-technological innovation and the emergence of open or network-based modes of innovation (OECD 2010). Nevertheless, many SMEs find it difficult to identify and connect to appropriate knowledge partners and networks and develop appropriate skills and management practices to enable coordination and integration of external knowledge in in-house practices and innovation processes (OECD 2013). The impact of SMEs on innovation activity has increased in recent decades. Niche market demand has grown and technological changes have boosted the comparative advantage of SMEs and reduced the structural disadvantages stemming from resource constraints and limited ability to benefit from economies of scale (OECD 2010). While not all SMEs are innovative, new and small firms frequently are the driving force behind the sort of radical innovations that are important for economic growth (Baumol 2002). It seems that SMEs have the ability to work outside the dominant paradigm, exploit technological and commercial opportunities overlooked by more established companies and enable commercial application of knowledge that, otherwise, would remain in universities and research organizations (OECD 2010). For instance, SMEs in Europe account for about 20% of

- patents, which are a reliable measure of innovation, in biotechnology-related fields (Eurostat 2014). In addition, they create value by adopting innovations generated elsewhere and adapting them to different contexts through incremental changes, and supplying new or niche products to satisfy diverse customer needs (OECD 2010).

Although the SME sector has a fundamental positive influence on employment in developing countries, it is generally considered less productive than the large firm sector, which tenders its contribution to economic growth less evident (Ayyagari et al. 2011). Only a small proportion of SMEs achieve a rapid growth in employment or economic development (Schrör 2005). SMEs find such growth difficult and, despite the large amounts of evidence, generated by many research studies, little is known about what influences their growth (Nichter and Goldmark 2009; Storey and Greene 2010).

The so-called "barriers to growth" literature demonstrates that, while only a proportion of small businesses are growth-oriented, their ability to realize their growth potential is impeded by the external business environment (Hashi and Krasniqi 2011, p. 8). The most commonly explored aspects include the physical infrastructure, the legal and the financial systems, various micro and macro policy environmental factors such as taxation, regulation and macroeconomic stability, and social factors such as the levels of crime and corruption in the focal society (Hashi 2001; Bartlett and Bukvic 2001; Smallbone and Welter 2001; McMillan and Woodruff 2002; Pissarides et al. 2003; Clement et al. 2004).

When investigating the relationship between the business environment and firm growth, many studies tend to focus on the effect of difficulties related to accessing finance, based on firm type—especially firm size. The empirical evidence suggests that, in relation to access to external sources of finance, smaller firms are more constrained than larger companies are (Schiffer and Weder 2001; Love and Mylenko 2003). These constraints are related to factors such as, among others, the market for loans which is imperfect and of small size (even in developed countries) (Chilosi 2001; Beaver 2002); the information asymmetries in capital markets which render smaller firms more likely to be penalized by credit rationing (Stiglitz and Weiss 1981; Bratkowski et al. 2000); and the ability to provide collateral (Aghion et al. 2005).

Another business environment-related factor that has received attention in the literature is the institutional framework within which the firm operates. The main features characterizing the institutional environment are the rule of law, judiciary functioning and law enforcement agencies along with government related aspects such as level of organized crime and corruption in the focal society. There is a wealth of evidence indicating that an unfavourable institutional framework has an adverse impact on SME growth (Bartlett and Bukvic 2001, 2002; Hashi 2001; Pissarides et al. 2003; Giavazzi and Tabellini 2004, p. 2; Aidis and Estrin 2006; Smallbone and Welter 2001).

An unfavourable business environment can create a greater incentive for firms to evade the regulation, which can be accompanied by a partial or total move to working in the informal sector, and corruption (Johnson et al. 2000). All of these things can encourage development of an anti-competitive environment in which the market fails to allocate resources efficiently because some market players are operating outside the law while those operating within the legal system face increased costs of "doing business" legally (Hashi and Krasniqi 2011, 9).

Some empirical studies suggest that, in high-income economies, high levels of "dynamism" or high rates of firm entry and exit (or Schumpeterian "creative destruction"), are essential for economic growth (Bartelsman et al. 2004, 2009). The level of firm dynamics depends on the country's policy environment; an appropriate policy environment stimulates entrepreneurship. Factors, such as the legal and regulatory regimes, the speed and expense of the business registration process, flexibility of employment regulations and low corporate taxes (all characteristic of developed economies) typically lead higher levels of firm entry and exit (Klapper and Love 2011).

However, there are some studies that argue that overly high rates of firm formation might not be useful for or may be harmful to economic growth. For instance, Green et al. (2004) call for caution in evaluating the policy measures designed to increase business formation rates. According to Green and colleagues, building a competitive enterprise sector involves more than simply increasing firm formation rates; it also involves development of the preconditions for enterprise growth in terms of market share, innovation, technological progress, financial efficiency and sustainable employment levels. In other words, it could be argued that the quality of the new firms created is as important as their quantity. Bartlett and Bukvic (2001) point out that the creation of a competitive enterprise sector and removal of the constraints related to the expansion and growth of new firms can be more decisive. In any case, creation of a competitive enterprise sector is not easy process and these authors suggest that the difficulties are rooted in the fact that it is a complex structural process and involves more than removing the administrative barriers to the creation of new enterprises.

It is clear that a favourable business environment promotes SME growth. In addition, there is significant evidence arguing that firms in less-developed countries face a tougher business environment compared to their counterparts in the developed world. However, a less conducive business environment is probably not the only reason for lack of SMEs growth; many SMEs may be dependent on local demand and may be part of both the social and economic fabric of their economies. There is wide support for the positive impact on firm growth of internal factors such quality of human capital (education), quality of training and work experience (Koch and McGrath 1996; Schutjens and Wever 2000; Coff and Kryscynski 2011; Brown et al. 2005). Several authors suggest other factors that can enable or constrain firm growth including their business networking (Cao and Zhang 2011; Schiefer and Hartmann 2008; Ruben et al. 2006; Brown et al. 2005), team-working (Foss et al. 2008), marketing capabilities (Fowler et al. 2000), dynamic capabilities (Teece 2016), and corporate entrepreneurship (Zahra et al. 2006; Zahra and Covin 1995; Lee et al. 2001; Morrow et al. 2007). There is a stream of literature that focuses specifically on the role of management practices in firm growth (Bloom and Van Reenen 2007, 2010).

The analysis in this book builds on four particular approaches. The first is related to the role of firm dynamism on the growth of firms. There are studies that argue that high dynamism of firms is characteristic of healthy economies, and the higher the firm dynamism, the higher the growth of firms. The second approach is related to role of the business environment in firm growth. From this perspective, business environment factors are seen to be a key to firm growth. In that case, it can be assumed that, once any business environment barriers are alleviated or removed, firm growth will be automatic. The third approach is related to the internal factors that impede or enable firm growth. Again, it might be assumed that, once these internal factors are mitigated, firm growth will follow. The fourth approach places the focus on firms endowed with innovation capabilities as drivers of growth, emergence of which require specific social and economic conditions. The conventional approaches tend to distinguish between business environment factors and the internal dynamics related to building organizational capabilities. We argue in this book that the factors that constrain or enable firm growth cannot be explained adequately by either the approaches with focus on external factors, or/and approaches with focus on internal factors and that the explanatory factors are more complex. This is because firm growth is a function of several factors within these two dimensions.

Thus, the novelty and main theoretical contribution of this book is that it shows that the drivers of firm growth derive from the interactions among micro and macro factors. Firm growth is not a solely macro or micro issue; it is the interaction between these dimensions that enables or constrains firm growth.

In this context, the empirical starting point of this book, which represents the overarching research enquiry guiding the analysis, is firm growth in less-developed economies. Its analysis does not provide a definite answer, but does contribute some important insights which contribute to an answer.

1.2 Setting the Research Agenda: Firm Growth in Less-Developed Countries

The topic addressed in this book is part of a broader research agenda related to firm growth in general. Work in this area in relation to the developed economies has a fairly long history, but is less robust in the case of the less-developed countries. The conventional wisdom is that firm growth is primarily a function of the business environment.

The aim is to provide empirical evidence on the determinants of firm growth in less-developed countries and demonstrate the importance of a range of internal managerial, organizational and social factors rather than investigating only on environmental and institutional issues.

This, then, is the premise of the book: to assess those factors that, externally and internally, enable or/and constrain the growth of SMEs in less-developed economies.

To refine this somewhat broad field, the analysis involves the investigation of four components of firm growth: firm demography and dynamics; environmental and institutional factors; internal managerial and organizational capabilities that influence firm growth; and the social and economic institutions that promote or impede the emergence of firms with innovative capabilities. A large body of the firm growth literature (Bartelsman et al. 2009; Barney 1991; Barney et al. 2011; Hausmann et al. 2008; Lazonick 2013) acknowledges the importance of these four dimensions for firm growth. However, this literature does not provide conclusive empirical evidence on aspects and, particularly, for firms operating in less-developed countries. By using diverse theoretical perspectives, a broad spectrum of methodological approaches and unique primary data and secondary data, this book should add to our understanding of the factors that enable and constrain firm growth in less-developed economies. The approaches were chosen on the basis that, together, they provide a comprehensive framework to explain the micro and macro foundations to firm growth in a less-developed economic context.

While each approach is aimed at understanding what it is that affects firm growth, each has a different focus and addresses a specific aspect of firm growth. For example, the demographic and dynamics approach explores whether high rates of churn among firms influence their growth, while the environmental approach analyses the role of institutions. Within the overarching research topic are four sub-topics whose mutual interrelation and interrelation with the overarching topic are described in what follows.

The empirical evidence on developed economies shows that, typically, healthy market economies exhibit a high rate of firm dynamics, which is productivity enhancing as outputs and inputs are reallocated from less productive to more productive businesses (Ahn 2001; Bartelsman et al. 2009). These findings raise questions about whether differences in income levels across countries can be accounted for by differences in firm dynamics across countries.

On the one hand, there is considerable evidence linking entrepreneurial dynamism to economic growth in developed countries; on the other hand, there are few analyses of this relationship in less-developed economies. Using a new and unique dataset, which includes the all firms registered between 2010 and 2016, this study examines the business demography and dynamics in Kosovo and benchmarks the findings from this country against a set of countries with higher income levels. The investigation is based on analysing trends in newborn firms, firm death rates, the impact of firm dynamics on employment rates and rates of firm survival during this period. In this introductory chapter, is examined the determinants of firm survival among new firms. It is investigated whether such factors as economic sector, legal status and firm size affect the significant differences in new market entrants' survival rates. To analyse survival patterns, hazard models are used, which allow simultaneous exploration of the determinants of firm survival.

The findings reveal some striking differences in the patterns of firm survival for Kosovan compared to other countries' firms. First, large firm entry rates are much lower in Kosovo compared to other countries. Second, new firm survival rates are much higher than in developed countries. This leads to low churn, which is in line with the results for other transition economies (Bartelsman et al. 2009). However, this similarity is stronger for smaller firms compared to larger ones, where entry rates are significantly lower compared to other countries. The presence of low firm entry and exit rates, especially for larger firms, points to the existence of high barriers to entry, which translate into high exit barriers if re-entry is a possibility. Unfavourable business environment factors (poor infrastructure, limited human capital, high levels of corruption, crime, high customs rates, high taxes, high costs of finance) in developing countries may discourage firm entry (World Bank 2008). Previous empirical findings suggest absence of regulation and, more importantly, inadequate enforcement of regulation to protect investors can be effective barriers to new firm creation (Rajan and Zingales 2003). In addition, the cost of capital and inadequate supply of human capital can hinder the entry of large firms (Klapper et al. 2008). In this case, the issue may not be the supply of labour force per se, but rather supply of a labour force with adequate industry skills. Finally, Klapper and colleagues provide evidence of an inverted U-shaped relationship between risk of firm exit and both firm age and size.

The second sub-topic is related to the factors that externally affect the growth of firms. More specifically, in this part of the book we investigate the constraints binding private investment and entrepreneurship in less-developed economies. The analysis employs the growth diagnostics framework and methodology proposed by Hausmann et al. (2008). Growth diagnostics acknowledges that scarce firm resources in developing countries cause numerous and various types of constraints. However, not all of these constraints are equally restrictive. Therefore, the framework investigates which are disproportionately constraining and which, if relaxed, would deliver the biggest benefits. The aim of this part is to investigate the set of external factors that potentially constrain firm growth and to identify the most binding constraints, which have the largest negative effects on firm growth and whose alleviation would produce significant movement in the objective function (Hausmann et al. 2008). The empirical information used to test our hypotheses are from two different sources. The first is a set of international databases and information and the second is data based on a survey of 585 business firms operating in Kosovo, conducted in 2017. The findings show that firm growth in less-developed economies, such as Kosovo, is hampered by various factors, the most binding being the rule of law, financial constraints and inadequate human capital.

In the part of the book analysing internal growth factors, the aim is to discern those that differentiate high from low growth firms. Three types of conceptual frameworks are employed: the conventional approach, Resource-Based Theory (RBT) and managerial practices. Conventional approach argues that growth of firms is the function of resources/inputs, while RBT argues that organizational capabilities are the factors that most likely shape firm performance. The managerial practices framework is utilized to investigate those skills and practices applied by managers that influence performance variability among firms. We use a set of specific variables to identify managerial skills and practices deployed by firms, including operating practices, monitoring practices, skills drawn on when establishing business targets and the incentive practices deployed in business organizations. The survey, conducted by the author of this book, was administered in face-to-face interviews with managers of a set of selected manufacturing firms. The selection of firms was based on specific characteristics and a pairing technique. The pairing technique was aimed at establishing patterns of dichotomy between successful and less successful firms. The survey questionnaire resulted in 58 indicators and 185 variables—greatly exceeding the number of case study firms (100), which indicates that the survey was mostly explorative. These variables range from those aimed at investigating tangible resources (physical and financial), human resources (education, training, experience), organizational capabilities (entrepreneurial mindset, marketing, teamwork, networking, dynamic capabilities), to those examining management practices (operations, monitoring, targets, incentives). The ultimate aim is to investigate discriminating factors at the level of organizational capabilities and management practices that promote differences between successful and less successful firms. High growth firms employ more university graduates, provide more inhouse training and have more experienced founders. External business environment factors do not affect differences in growth performance, but managerial practices are crucial for explaining growth. In the context of organizational capabilities, differences in marketing and teamwork capabilities have little influence on growth, but differences in entrepreneurship and innovation capabilities and networking prove causal factors.

Special attention is paid to innovation capabilities. They stem from specific social and economic conditions, and achieved levels of strategic control, organizational integration and investment commitment. These have been described as "social" factors, but, in reality, are institutional or "business culture" factors. Social conditions at the national level are examined using diverse data and information from various national and international sources, while firm-level social conditions are analysed using firm-level data obtained from a survey conducted in 2017/2018. The findings indicate that the social conditions in less-developed countries, such as Kosovo, provide few incentives for firms to innovate.

While Kosovo has managed to establish a business institutional framework, which, largely, is compatible to the institutional frameworks of developed countries, its implementation has been problematic. The number of Kosovan firms endowed with the social conditions conducive to innovation is very low.

1.3 Selection of Comparator Countries

Although this book analyses firms operating in Kosovo's economy, it does not treat it as an isolated case. The findings are benchmarked against five European Union (EU) countries. We are interested in whether certain regulations and institutions in different countries affect the business demography or/and firm growth more generally. We are interested, also, in identifying similarities and differences among firms operating in diverse economic settings and to capture this diversity within a common framework.

The criteria for the selection of countries for the benchmarking are, first, geographical proximity (Croatia and Slovenia as ex-Yugoslav countries) and similar economic structure (all former socialist countries); and second, similar-sized populations. It could be argued that the differences between the economies of Kosovo and the reference countries are significant. Although the Baltic countries may display larger geographical and historical differences, similarities to Croatia and Slovenia are more evident since, for almost a century, they were part of ex-Yugoslavia. However, despite being part of the same state for so long, there are stark differences in economic development between Kosovo and these two countries. For instance, in terms of per capita Gross National Product (GNP), in 1990 the respective figures for Croatia and Slovenia were 65 and 200 respectively compared to 24 for Kosovo, and in terms of unemployment, the differences were 21.1% for Croatia and 5.1% for Slovenia, compared to 38.8% for Kosovo.[1]

---

[1]Štiblar, F. (2013). *Economic growth and development in post Yugoslav countries*. https://www.wilsoncenter.org/sites/default/files/Franjo_Stiblar_WWICS.docx.pdf.

It is conceivable that there will always be differences among even the most advanced market-based economies. However, there are some common economic features—which are reminiscent of their socialist past—that distinguish ex-socialist from western economies.

Although all the comparator countries are now EU members, ex-socialist economies, including Kosovo, had relatively similar recent economic histories before joining the EU. All had to go through a substantial transition stage before becoming full members. Many relevant institutions believe that these countries have completed the monumental task of transition from a state-controlled, socialist or communist system of economic governance to a system governed by the mechanisms of competitive and open markets (Stephan 2011). However, we do not know whether the selected countries provide would-be entrepreneurs with similar framework conditions for economic activity to those in the kind of competitive environment, with its opportunities and constraints that prevail in western European countries. While their existing economic opportunities and activities appear to meet the criteria related to a market-type economy, there are persisting strong differences between east and west Europe, which provide a somewhat different portrait from that promoted by the most relevant institutions related to the transition process (Stephan 2011).

In addition to being a developing country, Kosovo is also a European country with aspirations for EU membership. Kosovo has signed the European Stabilisation and Association Agreement (SAA) and is involved in the EU Instrument for Pre-Accession Assistance (IPA) programme to develop institutions compatible with eventual EU membership and create a functioning market economy.

Table 1.1 provides an overview of the social and economic indicators for Kosovo and the comparator countries. The differences are important for the task facing these countries in terms of levels of economic development in general and income per capita in particular. According to the World Bank, Kosovo is in the group of low-income countries with annual Gross National Income (GNI) per capita of US$ 3950 while the reference countries belong to the group of economies with a high level of income per capita. It is clear that, apart from its population size, which is similar to the population sizes in the reference countries, the other indicators differ significantly.

Table 1.1 Comparison of socio-economic indicators between Kosovo and reference countries

	Est	Cro	Lat	Lit	Slo	Kos
Population	1.3	4.2	1.9	2.9	2.1	1.8
GNI	18,480	12,690	14,900	15,000	22,610	3950
GDP	23,338	50,715	27,573	42,739	44,709	6650
Business economy-firms in number*	50,748	108,401	73,324	54,341	66,507	29,412
Firm/population ratio	3.9	2.6	3.9	1.9	3.2	1.6

Source EUROSTAT and KAS
*Subject of analysis is population of firms in business economy, and only employer firms. Firms with zero employees are omitted from analysis

1.4 Structure of the Book

The book includes eight chapters. Following this introduction, Chapter 2 describes the macroeconomic environment in Kosovo in some detail. Chapter 3 reviews the literature on firm growth and related current challenges. Chapter 4 investigates firm demography and survival in Kosovo and compares their patterns with the selected reference countries. Chapter 4 addresses similarities and differences in the populations of active firms and newly established firms, and firms' exits and survival rates. It discusses business environment factors and their impact on firm demography and survival, and the determinants of firm survival in Kosovo.

Chapter 5 investigates the environmental and the institutional factors that influence private investment and entrepreneurship in less-developed countries such as Kosovo. Chapter 5 compares the outcomes with the reference countries. The resulting set of significant factors are both informative in themselves and should be of use to policy makers in terms of which are the most binding.

Chapter 6 reviews internal factors related to firm growth and, specifically, the empirical results on inputs, organizational capabilities and managerial practices among manufacturing firms in Kosovo's economy. Chapter 7 analyses social and economic factors, such as form of government, employment and investment institutions at macro level, as well as form of strategic control, organizational integration and investment commitment at micro level that determine the emergence of firms with innovation capabilities.

Chapter 8 concludes the book. It summarizes the findings from each chapter and also provides a comprehensive picture of what determines firm growth in a less-developed economy by combining all of the findings. It provides a brief discussion of possible avenues for further research to analyse both external and internal business factors that might constrain or enable firm growth. Finally, it highlights some caveats and limitations related to the approaches employed and what they might imply for the future research agenda.

References

Aghion, P., Howitt, P., & Mayer-Foulkes, D. (2005). The effect of financial development on convergence: Theory and evidence. *Quarterly Journal of Economics, 120*(1), 173–222.

Ahn, S. (2001). *Firm dynamics and productivity growth: A review of micro evidence from OECD countries* (OECD Economics Department Working Paper 297). Paris: OECD.

Aidis, R., & Estrin, S. (2006). *Institutions, networks and entrepreneurship development in Russia: An exploration* (Institute for Study of Labour-IZA, Discussion Paper, 2161). Bonn.

Ayyagari, M., Demirgüç-Kunt, A., & Maksimovic, V. (2011). *Small vs. young firms across the world—Contribution to employment, job creation, and growth* (Policy Research Working Paper 5631). The World Bank Development Research Group.

Barney, J. B. (1991). Firm resources and sustained competitive advantage. *Journal of Management, 17*, 99–120.

Barney, J. B., Ketchen, D. J., & Wright, M. (2011). The future of Resource-based Theory: Revitalization or decline. *Journal of Management, 37*(5), 1299–1315.

Bartelsman, E., Haltiwanger, J., & Scarpetta, S. (2004). *Microeconomic evidence of creative destruction in industrial and developing countries* (The World Bank Policy Research Working Paper Series 3464).

Bartelsman, E., Haltiwanger, J., & Scarpetta, S. (2009). Measuring and analyzing cross-country differences in firm dynamics. In T. Dunne, J. B. Jensen, & M. J. Roberts (Eds.), *Producer Dynamics*. Chicago, IL: University of Chicago Press for the NBER.

Bartlett, W., & Bukvic, B. (2001). Barriers to SME growth in Slovenia. *Most Economic Policy in Transition Economies, 11*(2), 177–195.

Bartlett, W., & Bukvič, V. (2002). What are the main barriers to SME growth and development in South-East Europe. In W. Bartlett, M. Bateman, & M. Vehovec (Eds.), *Small enterprise development in South-East Europe: Policies for sustainable growth* (pp. 17–38). Boston: Kluwer.

Baumol, W. (2002). *The free-market innovation machine: Analyzing the growth miracle of capitalism*. Princeton: Princeton University Press.

Beaver, G. (2002). *Small business, entrepreneurship and enterprise development*. London: Pearson Education.

Bloom, N., & Van Reenen, J. (2007). Measuring and explaining management practices across firms and countries. *Quarterly Journal of Economics, 122*(4), 1351–1408.

Bloom, N., & Van Reenen, J. (2010). Why do management practices differ across firms and countries? *Journal of Economic Perspectives, 24*(1), 203–224.

Bratkowski, A., Grosfeld, I., & Rostowski, J. (2000). Investment and finance in de novo private firms: Empirical evidence from the Czech Republic, Hungary and Poland. *Economics of Transition, 8*(1), 101–116.

Brown, M. E., Trevino, L. K., & Harrison, D. A. (2005). Ethical leadership: A social learning perspective for construct development and testing. *Organizational Behaviour and Human Decision Processes, 97*, 117–134.

Cao, M., & Zhang, Q. (2011). Supply chain collaboration: Impact on collaborative advantage and firm performance. *Journal of Operations Management, 29*(3), 163–180.

Chilosi, A. (2001). Entrepreneurship and transition. *Economic Policy in Transitional Economies, 11*(4), 327–357.

Clement, K., Wang, K., & Ang, B. (2004). Determinants of venture performance in Singapore. *Journal of Small Business Management, 42*(4), 347–363.

Coff, R., & Kryscynski, D. (2011). Drilling for microfoundations of human capital-based competitive advantage. *Journal of Management, 37*(5), 1429–1443.

Čučković, N., & Bartlett, W. (2007). Entrepreneurship and competitiveness: The Europeanization of small and medium-sized enterprise policy in Croatia. *Southeast European and Black Sea Studies, 7*(1), 37–56.

De Kok, J. M. P., Vroonhof, P., Verhoeven, W., Timmermans, N., Kwaak, T., Snijders, J., et al. (2011). *Do SMEs create more and better jobs?* (Report prepared by EIM for the European Commission DG Enterprise and industry). Brussels: European Commission.

EIU Economist Intelligence Unit. (2010). SMEs in Japan: A new growth driver. *The Economist*. http://viewswire.eiu.com/report_dl.asp?mode=fi&fi=1227698307.PDF.

Eurostat. (2014). *Patent statistics at Eurostat: Mapping the contribution of SMEs in EU patenting*. Luxembourg: Eurostat Manuals and Guidelines. http://ec.europa.eu/eurostat/documents/3859598/6064260/KS-GQ-14-009-EN-N.pdf/caa6f467-11f8-43f9-ba76-eb3ccb6fab6d.

Foss, N. J., Klein, P. G., Kor, Y. Y., & Mahoney, J. T. (2008). Entrepreneurship, subjectivism, and the resource based view: Toward a new synthesis. *Strategic Entrepreneurship Journal, 2,* 73–94.

Fowler, S. W., Wilcox King, A., Marsh, S. W., & Victor, B. (2000). Beyond products: New strategic imperatives for developing competencies in dynamic environments. *Journal of Engineering and Technology Management, 17*(3–4), 357–377.

Giavazzi, F., & Tabellini, G. (2004). Economic and political liberalizations (NBER working paper No. 10657).

Greene, F. J., Mole, K. F., & Storey, D. J. (2004). Does more mean worse? Three decades of enterprise policy in the Tees Valley. *Urban Studies, 41*(7), 1207–1228.

Hashi, I. (2001). Financial and institutional barriers to SME growth in Albania: Results of an enterprise survey. *MOST: Economic Policy in Transitional Economies, 11*(3), 221–238.

Hashi, I., & Krasniqi, B. (2011). Entrepreneurship and SME growth in transition: Evidence from advanced and laggard transition economies. *International Journal of Entrepreneurial Behaviour & Research, 17*(5), 456–487.

Hausmann, R., Klinger, B., & Wagner, R. (2008). *Doing growth diagnostics in practice: A mindbook* (Harvard University Centre for International Development Working Paper 177).

IFC. (2010). *The SME banking knowledge guide*. Washington, DC: IFC.

Johnson, S., Kaufmann, D., McMillan, J., & Woodruff, C. (2000). Why do firms hide? Bribes and unofficial activity after communism. *Journal of Public Economics, 76*(3), 495–520.

Klapper, L., Amit, R., Guillén, M. F., & Quesada, J. M. (2008). *Entrepreneurship and firm formation across countries* (The World Bank Policy Research Working Paper 4313).
Klapper, L., & Love, I. (2011). The impact of the financial crisis on new firm registration. *Economics Letters, 113,* 1–4.
Koch, M. J., & McGrath, R. G. (1996). Improving labour productivity: Human resource management policies do matter. *Strategic Management Journal, 17,* 335–354.
Lazonick, W. (2013). The theory of innovative enterprise: Methodology, ideology, and institutions. In Jamee K. Moudud, Cyrus Bina, & Patrick L. Mason (Eds.), *Alternative theories of competition: Challenges to the orthodoxy* (pp. 127–159). London and New York: Routledge.
Lee, C., Lee, K., & Pennings, J. M. (2001). Internal capabilities, external networks, and performance: A study on technology-based ventures. *Strategic Management Journal, 22,* 615–640.
Liedholm, C., & Mead, D. (1987). *Small scale industries in developing countries: Empirical evidence and policy implications* (MSU International Development Paper No. 9, 1978). East Lansing: Department of Agricultural Economics, Michigan State University.
Love, I., & Mylenko, N. (2003). *Credit reporting and financing constraints* (World Bank Policy Research Working Paper 3142).
McMillan, J., & Woodruff, C. (2002). The central role of entrepreneurs in transition economies. *Journal of Economic Perspectives, 16*(3), 153–170.
Morrow, J. L., Sirmon, D. G., Hitt, M. A., & Holcomb, T. R. (2007). Creating value in the face of declining performance: Firm strategies and organisational recovery. *Strategic Management Journal, 28,* 271–283.
Nichter, S., & Goldmark, L. (2009). Small firm growth in developing countries. *World Development, 37*(9), 1453–1464.
OECD. (2010). *SMEs, entrepreneurship and innovation.* Paris: OECD Publishing.
OECD. (2013). *Skills development and training in SMEs.* Paris: OECD Publishing.
OECD. (2016, June 1–2). *The productivity-inclusiveness Nexus, meeting of the OECD Council at ministerial level* (C/MIN(2016)3). Paris.
Piech, K. (2004). *The knowledge-based economy in transition countries: Selected issue.* London: University College London, School of Slavonic and East European Studies.
Pissarides, F., Singer, M., & Svenjar, J. (2003). Objectives and constraints of entrepreneurs: Evidence from small and medium-sized enterprises in Russia and Bulgaria. *Journal of Comparative Economics, 31*(3), 503–531.

Radosevic, S., & Mickiewicz, T. (2003). *Innovation capabilities in seven candidate countries: An assessment* (Vol. 2.8). Brussels: Enterprise Directorate General, CEC.

Rajan, R., & Zingales, L. (2003). The great reversal: The politics of financial development in the 20th century. *Journal of Financial Economics, 69*(1), 5–50.

Ruben, R., Slingerland, M., & Nijhoff, H. (2006). Agro-food chains and networks for development: Issues, approaches and strategies. In R. Ruben, M. Slingerland, & H. Nijhoff (Eds.), *Agro-food chains and networks for development*. The Netherlands: Springer.

Schiefer, J., & Hartmann, M. (2008). Determinants of competitive advantage for German food processors. *Agribusiness, 24*(3), 306–319.

Schiffer, M. & Weder, B. (2001). *Firm size and the business environment: Worldwide survey results* (IFC Discussion Paper No. 43).

Schmitz, H. (1995). Collective efficiency: Growth path for small scale industry. *Journal of Development Studies, 31*(4), 529–666.

Schrör, H. (2005). *Business demography in Europe: Results from 1997 to 2002, Eurostat statistics in focus: Industry* (Trade and Services, 36/2005). Luxembourg: Eurostat.

Schutjens, A., & Wever, E. (2000). Determinants of new firm success. *Papers in Regional Science, 79*(2), 135–159.

Smallbone, D., & Welter, F. (2001). The role of government in SME development in transition economies. *International Small Business Journal, 19*(4), 63–76.

Stephan, J. (2011). The role of human capital and managerial skills in explaining productivity gaps between East and West. *Eastern European Economics, 46*(6), 5–24.

Stiglitz, J., & Weiss, A. (1981). Credit rationing in markets with imperfect information. *American Economic Review, 71*(3), 393–409.

Storey D. J., & Greene, F. J. (2010). *Small business and entrepreneurship*. New York: Prentice Hall.

Teece, D. J. (2016). Dynamic capabilities and entrepreneurial management in large organizations: Toward a theory of the (entrepreneurial) firm. *European Economic Review, 86*, 202–216.

World Bank. (2008). *Unleashing Prosperity Productivity Growth in Eastern Europe and the Former Soviet Union*. http://siteresources.worldbank.org/ECAEXT/Resources/publications/UnleashingProsperity.pdf.

World Bank. (2018). *Country snapshot*. http://pubdocs.worldbank.org/en/423771524155944422/Kosovo-Snapshot-Spring2018.pdf.

Wymenga, P., Spanikova, V., Derbyshire, J., & Barker, A. (2011). *Are EU SMEs recovering from the Crisis? Annual Report on EU small and medium-sized enterprises 2010/11* (Report for the European Commission).
Zahra, S. A., & Covin, J. G. (1995). Contextual influences on the corporate entrepreneurship performance relationship: A longitudinal analysis. *Journal of Business Venturing, 10*(1), 43–58.
Zahra, S. A., Sapienza, H. J., & Davidsson, P. (2006). Entrepreneurship and dynamic capabilities: A review, model and research agenda. *Journal of Management Studies, 43*(4), 917–955.

2

Economic Profile of Kosovo: Problems and Challenges

This chapter provides a short historical overview of the macroeconomic environment of Kosovo. It is organized in three sections: the macroeconomic environment in Kosovo before 1999; the period 1999–2008; and the period since the declaration of an independent state (2008 to the present).

2.1 Economic Environment Before 1999

Kosovo was an Autonomous Province of the Socialist Federal Republic of Yugoslavia (SFRY). Under the 1974 constitution, it was one of the eight constitutive elements in the federation, although, nominally, it was part of the Republic of Serbia. As an autonomous province, Kosovo enjoyed a large degree of political and economic freedom. Despite its economic potential, rich natural resources base and fertile agricultural land, Kosovo has always been the least developed and poorest region in the federation (European Commission and the World Bank 1999). It was the least economically developed part of the federation with the highest unemployment rates, the worst infrastructure, the lowest levels of education and the fastest growing population (Woodward 1995; Ramet 2006).

F. Sahiti, *The Growth of Firms in Less-Developed Countries*,
https://doi.org/10.1007/978-3-030-14821-8_2

Until 1955, Kosovo was not a priority for the Yugoslav federation authorities (Ramet 2006). After that time, the economy of Kosovo started to receive desperately needed financial support. However, the federation budget allocated to Kosovo was significantly lower relative to the monies allocated to other parts of the federation (Dallago and Uvalic 1998). A World Bank (1999) report demonstrates the huge development disparity among the regions in the SFRY. It shows that average Gross National Product (GNP) per capita in Kosovo was only 45% of GNP in the underdeveloped republics (Montenegro, Macedonia and Bosnia and Herzegovina).

Funds allocated by the federal authorities for the development of Kosovo's economy during the decades of so-called 'general federal growth' in the 1960s and 1970s, were concentrated predominantly on heavy industry rather than on labour-intensive industries and agriculture (Ramet 2006, pp. 270–275; Petiffer 2002, pp. 4–7). In the 1970s and 1980s, economic activity was centred increasingly on mining, production of raw materials and semi-finished products such as lead, coal, zinc and some textiles. There were four main industrial activities, all related to mining and the raw materials industries (European Commission and the World Bank 1999):

- lead and zinc mining, ore concentration plants, lead smelting and refinery plants, a zinc refinery, a sulphuric acid plant and a fertilizer and battery plant in and around the town of Mitrovica;
- lignite open cast mines, a lignite drying plant, a gasification plant, two thermo power plants, a steam power plant and a nitrogen fertilizer plant located in and around the town of Obiliq;
- ferro-nickel mines and a metallurgical industry located around the town of Drenas (Gllogovc); and
- limestone quarries and a cement factory in the town of Elez Han.

It would seem that federal investment was aimed primarily at the heavy industry, especially mining and power production to serve other parts of the country. It is estimated that two-thirds of the power produced by Kosovo's industrial capacity was sold to other regions at very low prices, which were determined by the federal authorities (UNDP 2007, p. 6). Certainly, during this period (1970–1980), the economy of Kosovo started to grow in absolute terms, but in relative terms, economic growth remained well below that in other republics, with all sectors operating below capacity (Ramet 2006).

The firm institutional and regulatory environment was based on SFRY-style state and social ownership: heavy industry was largely state and socially owned (European Commission and the World Bank 1999). At that time, commercial criteria played almost no part in decision-making about business activities. Most decisions about resource allocation and the location of industry were political (World Bank 1999).

Over this same period, the share of industry and mining in overall output in Kosovo, increased from one-third to one-half, while the share of agriculture fell from almost one-third to one-fifth (World Bank 1999). More than 60% of the pre-conflict population lived in rural areas, with the result that the main economic activity at that time was agriculture (World Bank 1999). The land was nearly all privately owned. Before 1989, there were some signs of transformation from a predominantly rural society to a more urban one (European Commission and the World Bank 1999). The proportion of population engaged in agriculture fell at that time to about 26%.

Though signs of economic crisis in Yugoslavia were apparent before Tito died in 1980, it seems that his death deepened the crisis (Medjad 2004). The consequences of this crisis had significant effects for Kosovo. It encouraged nationalism and introduced a regime that was conducive to corruption and mismanagement (Palairet 2001). The 1980s marked the end of the Yugoslav type of socialist economic management (Bartlett 1985).

The crisis culminated in 1989 when Kosovo's autonomous status in the federal constitution since 1974, was abrogated. As a result of the so-called 'enforcement measures' implemented by the Serbian authorities, the majority of ethnic Albanian employees lost their jobs. It is estimated that 145,000 people were fired from posts in the civil administration, public services and economic enterprises (Hoti 2004).

The new circumstances triggered the setting up by the Albanian population of a parallel (though underground and illegal) government, health care and education system. This culminated in an economy within the economy (Pula 2004).

It was in this period that the informal economy grew rapidly and a large majority of the population became dependent on it. Many of those who had lost their jobs found alternative income sources in SMEs—both formal and informal. Though there are no official figures on the number of firms that were operational at that time or their levels of productivity, it is believed that, in 1996, the private sector contributed 47% of GDP and played an overwhelming role in the agriculture, construction and trade sectors—and survived better than did public enterprises (World Bank 1999).

A large number of Kosovar Albanians migrated to western countries, while others who had been sacked from their jobs in state enterprises returned to rural areas or worked in the informal sector. The agricultural sector was always important for local food production, but also contributed one-third of GDP in 1995 (European Commission and the World Bank 1999). In 1998, though based largely on small family farms with low productivity, agricultural activities accounted for some 60% of employment and played a key role in food security at the household-level (European Commission and the World Bank 1999). Agribusiness activities provided about half of domestic income, the other half coming from remittances and off-farm incomes (World Bank 1999).

The installation of an 'apartheid' regime by the Serbian government authorities during the 1990s was followed by the imposition of a discriminatory process of privatization of socially owned enterprises (SOEs) (Perritt 2005). Along with large scale dismissal of the workforce from their jobs, the Serbian authorities introduced a discriminatory process of takeover of Kosovo's companies and their merger with Serbian enterprises, and sale of companies all of which excluded Kosovar Albanians and other potential foreign investors from participation in the privatization process. The 1998 and 1999 war dealt another severe blow to the economy of Kosovo.

The SME policy and institutional framework before 1999 should be considered in light of the above described political and economic context. Legally, Kosovo was part of the Federal Republic of Yugoslavia which included Serbia and Montenegro. The majority of firms operating in Kosovo were informal and, consequently, would not have been eligible to benefit from any programmes designed to support SMEs; however, federal government did not implement any forms of support for the development of SMEs (Kutlaca 2002). There were some initial institutional attempts made after the outbreak of the Kosovo war in 2000, that is, after Kosovo became a United Nations (UN) protectorate. However, before this period, that is, during the period 1992–1999, federal government had introduced some support to improve the economic environment for the development of SMEs including introducing an appropriate policy for the regulation and fostering of SMEs; identifying the main problems in the SME sector; organizing training activities for entrepreneurs and SME employees, etc. (Kutlaca 2002).

Several other laws were adopted as part of the institutional framework, aimed at fostering SME growth. These included: the foreign investors law (introduced in 1994 and amended in 1996); the law on privatization and ownership changes (introduced in 1992 and amended in 1996, 1997, 1998, and 1999); the law on enterprises (introduced in 1996 and amended in 1997, 1998, and 1999) (Kutlaca 2002). However, these measures had limited, if any, effects on firms operating in Kosovo.

2.2 Economic Environment in Kosovo Between 1999 and 2008

The war took a heavy toll on Kosovo's economy. The post-war economy in Kosovo consisted of three groups of firms. First, a large number of privately owned firms, engaged predominantly in trade and service activities. Second, a substantial number of firms operating outside the regulatory framework which were difficult to distinguish from former registered private firms. Third, a finite population of SOEs and publicly owned companies operating in all sectors of the economy (European Commission and the World Bank 1999). The first and second groups of firms were not involved in industrial production or processing activities. Almost all of the few production firms that were active before the war were damaged significantly during the war (World Bank 1999). In addition, after the war there were no operational financial institutions and no regulatory framework in place.

According to Security Council Resolution 1244, the United Nations Mission in Kosovo (UNMIK) administered Kosovo, with the aim of establishing effective and accountable institutions and a market economy. In parallel with the process of institution building, the international administration sought to opportunities for faster economic development and reconstruction of the country. The transfer of the public sector into private hands was seen as one method to boost the recovery process (World Bank 1999).

Kosovo had inherited around 600 SOEs and 60–70 publicly owned companies, which represented a decent starting point for the country's economic development (Hethy 2002). A Riinvest Institute (2001) study reported that the fixed assets value of 192 large and medium-sized SEOs was 4.5 billion German marks, while the losses caused by the wartime destruction reached 1.3 billion German marks. According to a Kosovo Trust Agency (2004) report, the value of the SOEs was even greater and 75% were deemed operational.[1]

Based on the Social Capital Act, Kosovo's privatization process started in 1989 (Riinvest 2001). However, the number of companies that completed this process was very small. As a result of the imposition of emergency measures and abolition of Kosovo's autonomy by the Serbian government in 1989, the newly introduced privatization process soon ended.

[1]The EU-led Pillar IV responsible for economic reconstruction and development had established Kosovo Trust Agency (KTA) as the only body which has the role of direct administration of SOEs and not only their supervision. This administration included electing managerial and leading structures, appointing supervisory boards, financial management policies and financial control (Article 2) in all SOEs (Riinvest 2001). The KTA's 'Draft strategy' study cites 450 confirmed SOEs and another 180 with unclear status.

Following the war in 1999, there were some short-term pre-privatization experiments undertaken by UNMIK one of which was described as 'commercialization'. The aim was to transfer SOE ownership to private sector investors via 10-year leases to avoid difficult questions about ownership and claims from creditors (Riinvest 2001). However, the process was soon abandoned since it proved cumbersome and complex. In addition, it was considered too slow, too limited, as entailing high transaction costs and providing potential investors with few incentives (Medjad 2004).

SOE privatization started with the establishment of the Kosovo Trust Agency in 2002. From the start, the process was characterized by dilemmas and controversies, which were reflected in the delays that occurred in the process. There were some major breaks: first, during the fourth quarters of 2003 and 2004, after which the process was smoother until a major slow down during 2008 (Forum 2008, 2009). Second, after declaration of independence, administration of the process of privatization was taken over by the Privatization Agency of Kosovo (PAK).

There was a specific privatization method applied during the process. It consisted of selling to the highest bidder (a regular spin-off), a method not commonly employed by successor countries of former Yugoslavia (Riinvest 2004). In the case of some large companies, investment commitments or the so-called special spin-off method (Riinvest 2004) was employed. In general, only SOEs' assets and current liabilities (defined generally as the last three months of unpaid accounts payable and the last year of unpaid VAT) were sold, other liabilities being left to the privatization proceeds, which were held in an escrow account (KTA 2004).

The privatization process in Kosovo is now in its final phase, leaving some 10% of SOEs still to be privatized (PAK 2015). The figures published by different agencies and institutions differ in terms of the total number of SEOs and the total number of privatized companies. A PAK report, published in January 2015, states that the total number of the SOEs identified by the KTA in Kosovo was 604 (PAK 2015, p. 5). The number of the SEOs that were privatized by KTA and PAK was 518. Since the beginning of the privatization process, these 518 enterprises have yielded 769 new firms. The accumulated proceeds from the privatized assets sale reached over €600 million or around 15% of Kosovo's GDP. However, these funds remained in foreign financial institutions, which attracted considerable criticism. The isolation of these monies from Kosovo's economy was shown to have 'a negative effect on the economic growth of the country' (Forum 2009).

The process of privatization received mixed reactions from Kosovan society. Some saw it as a failure, while others—taking account of Kosovo's political and economic circumstances—saw it as being successful. A Forum 2015 (2009) report states that among 103 selected privatized companies, a third were 'not functioning' and the rest achieved 'significantly smaller turnover' than comparable private sector companies.

The trend towards new firm formation after the war in 1999 was impressive. According to the Kosovo Business Registration Agency (KBRA), the process of firm registration in Kosovo evolved through two phases. The first phase began in the post-war period, that is, 2000–2003, when firm registration was considered provisional. The second phase began in 2003. According to KBRA, until 2003, there was a confusion over what were considered provisional and what were considered permanent firm registrations. Finally, after coordination among several bodies, including UNMIK structures, the tax administration, customs, KBRA and the Kosovo Statistical Institution, after 2003 all registrations were considered permanent. The number of firms almost doubled from a total of 56,572 registered firms in 2003 to almost 70,000 in 2008.

2.3 The Economic Environment in Kosovo Since 2008

Kosovo is the youngest independent country in Europe. It declared independence on 17 February 2008. In July 2010, the International Court of Justice (ICJ) confirmed that Kosovo's declaration of independence did not breach international law.[2] The country's total area is 10,908 km^2, populated by 1.8 million inhabitants.

[2]http://www.icj-cij.org/search/index.php?pg=1&p2=2&op=0&str=Report+on+Kosovo&lg=0&op=1.

2.3.1 Main Macroeconomic Indicators

The World Bank classifies Kosovo in the group of lower-middle-income economies—with GNI per capita between $US1,006 and $US3,987. According to Kosovo's statistics agency, the average monthly private sector gross salary ranged from euro 272 to euro 359 in 2008–2016.[3] Table 2.1 presents economic indicators that show the trend of economic growth in Kosovo is driven primarily by government spending, especially on infrastructure. Net exports provided a positive contribution to growth, based on exports large quantities of metals. The supply side of GDP shows encouraging broad-based growth, driven mainly by the construction, trade and financial sectors, while public administration and other service activities decreased sharply (IMF 2018). In general, Kosovo's production capacities are considered underdeveloped and the economy remains reliant on consumption, investment in infrastructure and, especially, remittances. Table 2.1 shows that remittances are an important source of revenue for many Kosovo households and represent around 11% of the total current account balance. The level of remittances, which come predominantly from Kosovars living in Germany, Switzerland and the Scandinavian countries, is the highest in the region (World Bank 2014). The country's public debt has remained relatively low, at 16.4% of GDP in 2017; however, it is expected to increase in the future following the first issue in August 2017 of a bond with a seven-year maturity.

Despite its recent positive growth performance, structural weaknesses constrain Kosovo's long-term development. As a result of the small size of its economy, Kosovo has relatively weak international integration and limited Foreign Direct Investment (FDIs). The poor FDI performance and international integration are the results, also, of a difficult business environment and poor infrastructure. Domestic investment continues to be hampered by problems related to accessing finance,

[3]Kosovo Agency for Statistics, http://ask.rks-gov.net/media/3821/results-of-the-structural-business-survey-2016.pdf.

Table 2.1 Main macroeconomic indicators of Kosovo, 2015–2020

	2014	2015	2016	2017e	2018f	2019f	2020f
Real GDP growth (%)	1.2	4.1	4.1	4.4	4.8	4.8	4.8
Composition (percentage points)							
Consumption	5.5	2.5	3.9	0.4	2.3	2.2	2.2
Investment	−1.3	3	2.1	3	3.4	3.5	3.3
Net exports	−2.9	−1.4	−1.9	1.1	−0.9	−1	−0.7
Exports	1.4	0.4	1.6	3.6	2.2	2.2	2.1
Imports (−)	4.3	1.8	3.5	2.6	3.1	3.2	2.9
Consumer price inflation (%, period average)	0.4	−0.5	0.3	1.5	1.7	1.7	1.9
Public debt (% of GDP)	10.4	12.7	14.1	15.8	16.6	18.6	20.9
Goods exports (% of GDP)	5.8	5.6	5.1	6	6.2	6.4	6.6
Goods imports (% of GDP)	42.8	41.9	42.8	44.9	45.4	46.1	46.4
Trade balance (% of GDP)	−28.7	−28.5	−27.6	−26.8	−26.3	−26.2	−25.6
Remittance inflows (% of GDP)	9.9	10.5	10.5	11.2	11.4	11.8	12.1
Foreign direct investment inflows (% of GDP)	2.2	4.7	2.9	3.6	4	4.7	5.3
Unemployment rate (%, period average)	35.3	32.9	27.5	30.4	n.a.	n.a.	n.a.
GDP per capita (current US$)	4055	3745	3699	3902	4075	4393	4575

Sources World Bank (2018)

and government interference in the private sector (OECD 2016). In addition, limited implementation of the rule of law and high levels of corruption further constrain economic development and investment (European Commission 2018). The informal economy accounts for 39% of GDP, although regular attempts have been made to combat the grey economy (OECD 2016).

Kosovo's export basket is one of the least diverse in the region and is dominated mainly by low added-value products, such as base metals and mineral products, which make up 65% of total export value. Exports of goods and services are stagnating in Kosovo and stood at 19.6% of GDP in 2014 (World Bank 2015).

Economic growth has not been sufficient to significantly reduce the high rates of unemployment. Kosovo has one of the highest unemployment rates in South East Europe (SEE), ranging between 30 and 35%. The youth unemployment rate reached 61% in 2015 (World Bank 2015). At the same time, Kosovo has the youngest population in Europe, with 38% of its population aged under 19 years. Combined with Kosovo's weak training capacity and underdeveloped consultancy services, the high unemployment rate suggests that brain drain poses a major threat to its sustainable development, with a high number of Kosovars trying to migrate to achieve better economic prospects in 2015 (OECD 2016).

2.3.2 Education System in Kosovo

Education has long been viewed as a driver of economic development. There is empirical evidence showing that education has a triple impact on economic growth. First, education can increase the human capital in the labour force, which in turn increases labour productivity and, thus, transition to a higher equilibrium level of output (Mankiw et al. 1992). Second, education can increase the economies capacity for innovation, while knowledge about new technologies, products and processes promotes growth (Lucas 1988; Aghion and Howitt 1998). Third, education facilitates the diffusion and transmission of knowledge needed to understand and process new information and successfully implement new technologies devised by others, which promotes economic growth (Nelson and Phelps 1966; Benhabib and Spiegel 1994).

As the economy of Kosovo emerges from its state of backwardness, policy interest in the crucial role of education and, particularly, workforce skills is increasing. Policy makers are positioning education and training at the centre of the drive for competitiveness and jobs.[4] However, the quality and availability of skilled labour in Kosovo continues to hamper growth. More specifically, there are concerns over education programmes and labour market needs, which are resulting in low employability of graduates and a significant skills premium (European Commission 2018). Public spending on education and training is broadly in line with that in middle-income countries—at around 4.6% of GDP. However, taking into consideration the relatively large student enrolment, Kosovo is spending considerably less than some reference countries, for instance Slovenia at 6.6% and Latvia at 8.8%. A major concern is that this spending is being managed sufficiently efficiently to provide good quality education to the comparatively large number of Kosovo's young population. The quality of the education system in the country continues to be problematic at all levels. According to the 2015 OECD Programme for International Student Assessment (PISA), Kosovo is ranked third from the bottom of the list of over 70 systems tested. Although the number of students enrolled in higher education is nearly double the EU average compared to the size of its population, completion rates are low and there are high unemployment rates among university degree holders—25% (European Commission 2018).

Based on a KSA (2015) report, 5.8% of the population has no formal education and 3.8% of the population is illiterate. Almost 80% of the illiterate are females. Only 8.2% of the population, of which 3% are females, have a university degree (KSA 2015), compared to an average of 34% in the EU-27 countries, 23% in Croatia and 17% in Macedonia (OECD 2013). One of the major problems with human capital and the education system, in particular, is the structure. The majority of students enrolled in tertiary education are studying social rather than technical sciences (OECD 2013). For example, at the University of Pristina, the biggest university in the country, 5.6% of enrolled students are studying natural and mathematical sciences and

[4]In July 2017, government adopted its strategic plan on education for 2017–2021. The strategy covers participation and inclusion, management of the education system, quality assurance, teacher development, early and preschool education, vocational education and training, higher education and adult education.

3.4% electrical and computer engineering. By contrast, in the Former Yugoslav Republic of Macedonia, 11.6% of students are studying sciences and 7.7% are enrolled in fields related to engineering, manufacturing and construction, while in Croatia the figures are 7.8% (sciences) and 12.2% (engineering, manufacturing and construction) (UNESCO 2012). Therefore, the shift in the structure towards technical sciences remains a major problem.

The internship system widely applied in developed countries is applied either on a small scale or not at all (OECD 2013). Therefore, due to the old system of teaching (rote learning of facts and theories rather than application of knowledge and critical thinking), there is a general view among firms that students that graduate from both private and public universities, lack applied skills (OECD 2013).

Entrepreneurial learning is considered essential to build the skills required for a more entrepreneurial culture (European Commission 2018).[5] Consistent address of entrepreneurial learning activities in the school and university systems is one of the major challenge (European Commission 2018). It will require all students across all disciplines to have an opportunity for entrepreneurial learning (European Commission 2018). One way to assess how well a country is managing to build a system that allows accumulation of the skills required for an entrepreneurial culture is incorporation in vocational and training programmes. In the case of Kosovo, a Vocational Education and Training (VET) system is in place. However, the programmes implemented do not include practical and applied courses and with only a few are accredited by the National Qualifications Authority (European Commission 2018). Enrolment of the younger generation in vocational training is low; around half of upper secondary education students choose vocational education compared to 71% in Croatia and 61%

[5]Entrepreneurial learning is defined as 'all forms of education and training, formal and non-formal, which contribute to entrepreneurial spirit or behaviour with or without a commercial objective'. In this definition, the notion of entrepreneurship is not a purely business phenomenon with a specific focus on start-up training; it also considers entrepreneurship as a key competence, comprising both cognitive and behavioural traits required to translate ideas into action (European Commission 2006).

in Macedonia (OECD 2013). The education system and labour market requirements are not coordinated and students following vocational education in schools and universities are not acquiring skills and competences aligned to labour market needs (OECD 2013). The VET system in Kosovo lacks a tracking mechanism to determine the positioning of vocational graduates in the labour market and, particularly, whether in self-employment or start-ups.

SMEs and innovative entrepreneurship are important in the context of innovation (Kostoff 2003). The structure of firms in Kosovo is dominated by SMEs, which, in principle, are seen as having a lower propensity to innovate. However, public support could facilitate their development and commercialization of innovations (Audretsch 1995). In Kosovo, public support is almost non-existent with current public spending on research and innovation is at only 0.1% of GDP compared to 2 and 1% of GDP in Slovenia and Estonia respectively of GDP (European Commission 2018). Added to this, Kosovo has a poor record of using even its small budget and, often, spends only half of it.

2.3.3 SMEs in Kosovo—Institutional, Regulatory and Operational Environment

The economy of Kosovo is small, consumption-driven, dominated by a service sector (wholesale and retail 57.4%) and a large agricultural sector (World Bank 2015). Kosovo's legislation distinguishes between micro, small and medium-sized firms according to the 2013 Law on Foreign Investment. The criterion used is employment size, which is in line with EU definitions (Table 2.2).

According to KSA data, in 2016, small and medium-sized firms represented 99.78% of all active firms and accounted for 74.9% of total employment. In the case of new firms, the official statistics show that the number of SMEs is increasing annually by some 10,000 per year (Fig. 2.1).[6]

[6]Republic of Kosovo (2016) *Statistical Repertoire of Enterprises in Kosovo Q42015*, http://ask.rks-gov.net/ENG/bussinesstatistics/publications.

Table 2.2 Definition of micro, small and medium-sized enterprises in Kosovo

	EU definition	Law on Foreign Investment 2013
Micro	<10 employees EUR 2 million turnover or balance sheet	<10 employees
Small	<50 employees ≤EUR 10 million turnover or balance sheet	<50 employees
Medium-sized	<250 employees ≤EUR 50 million turnover ≤EUR 43 million balance sheet	<250 employees

Source Republic of Kosovo (2013), 'Ligj per investimet e huaja' (Law on Foreign Investment), Law No. 04/L-220, Republic of Kosovo (available at www.kuvendikosoves.org/common/docs/ligjet/04-L-220percent20sh.pdf), page 3, paragraph 1.21

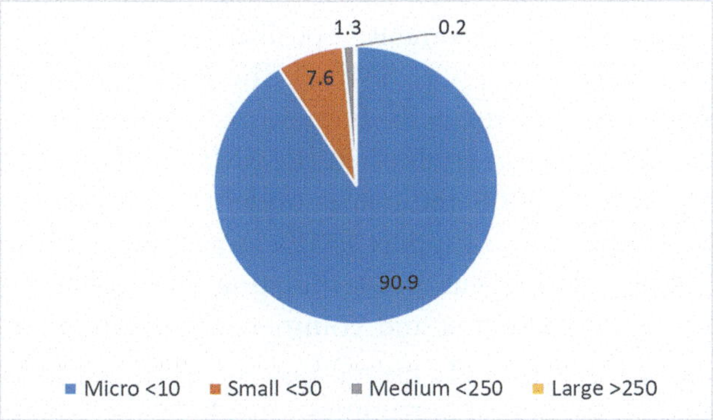

Fig. 2.1 Structure of firms by size (*Source* KAS)

The majority of Kosovo's firms operate in the wholesale and retail trade sectors (47.7%), accounting for 34.9% of total employment. Firms in manufacturing sector accounts for 15.6% of employment and only 13.5% of total enterprises. Kosovo's business owners tend to be young, with a notable 18% of firms owned by under 30-year-olds in 2014 according to a national survey. Another 32% of business firms are owned by individuals aged between 30 and 39 years, while only 20% have owners aged over 50.[7] Most firms are located in the capital, Pristina (23.9%), followed by Peja (7.4%), Prizren (7.1%), and Ferizaj (6.5%), etc. Sole proprietors typically register as individual businesses, while Limited Liability Company is the most popular registration type for non-sole proprietors. Foreign ownership among SMEs is rare, with less than 5% of new enterprises in the fourth quarter of 2015 with any foreign ownership (Table 2.3).

Although measures to improve the business environment have been put in place, the provision of critical infrastructure and, especially, the distribution of electricity to businesses and households, remain a major difficulty. Kosovo has an out-dated power system that is inadequate and unreliable and poses significant challenges to economic growth; frequent outages hamper investment and disrupt manufacturing, education and health services (World Bank 2018). Water supply conditions are similar.

Kosovo has taken some major steps towards building an institutional framework for SME development. Specifically, in 2008, government passed a specific law to support SMEs.[8] The goal was to provide institutional, regulatory and financial framework, conducive to the development of SMEs. The law established the SME Support Agency, which became operational in 2008 and comes under the Ministry of Trade and Industry. Its objective is: to support SMEs in gaining access to loans and credit; compiling, analysing and disseminating statistics and other useful information on the economic and commercial environment; encouraging private sector investment; preventing and reducing the barriers to business; opening trading opportunities outside of the country; creating policies and legislative instruments to provide SMEs with more flexible employee legislation; and facilitating communication among SMEs,

[7]KOSME (2014) *Report on SMEs in Kosovo 2014*, http://www.eciks.org/repository/docs/Report_on_State_of_SMEs_in_Kosovo_2014_99378.pdf.

[8]*Law No. 03/L-031 on Amendment and Supplementation of the Law No. 02/L-5 on Supporting the Small and Medium Enterprises*, Article 3, available at http://www.kuvendikosoves.org/common/docs/ligjet/2008_03-L-031_en.pdf.

Table 2.3 Structure of enterprises according to economic section for the years 2008–2016

Section	Description of the economic section	2008	2009	2010	2011	2012	2013	2014	2015	2016
B	Mining and quarrying	0.5	0.5	0.5	0.5	0.5	0.5	0.5	0.5	0.5
C	Manufacturing	9.9	9.7	10.0	10.3	11.0	12.9	12.7	13.5	13.5
D	Electricity, gas, steam and air conditioning supply	0.1	0.1	0.2	0.1	0.2	0.1	0.1	0.2	0.1
E	Water supply, sewerage, waste management and land revitalization activities	3.4	3.4	4.6	3.7	4.0	0.5	0.4	0.4	0.5
F	Construction	5.7	5.8	6.2	6.5	7.3	7.2	6.7	7.9	7.6
G	Wholesale and retail trade, repair of motor vehicles, motorcycles	50.6	50.2	48.2	47.8	49.1	55.4	50.6	50.6	47.7
H	Transportation and storage	3.0	2.9	2.8	2.8	2.8	4.0	3.7	3.6	3.7
I	Accommodation and food service activities	8.5	8.5	8.2	8.4	8.9	10.8	10.5	11.1	10.4
J	Information and communication	8.8	8.8	9.1	8.9	8.5	2.2	2.2	2.6	2.4
L, M, N, R, S	Other service activities	9.5	10.0	10.3	11.0	7.6	6.5	12.6	9.6	13.6
	Total	100	100	100	100	100	100	100	100	100

Source KSA

larger enterprises and other relevant private professionals to enhance capacities and expertise.[9] In addition, the Support Agency aims to provide training and consultancy schemes for entrepreneurs; develop business incubators; and develop SME support programmes and schemes.[10] The first of this Agency's SME strategies was implemented in 2010.[11] The importance of SME development for Kosovo is reflected, also, in the government's Private Sector Development Strategy 2013–2017.[12]

The World Bank's doing business scale for 2018 ranks Kosova 40th, while the OECD (2016) scoring of Kosovo's regulatory framework for SME policy making was 3.01 out of 5, which is below most of the other countries in the region except Bosnia and Herzegovina. There has been improvement in two indicators: resolving insolvency and enforcing contracts. By introducing a legal framework for corporate insolvency, Kosovo has made insolvency resolution easier and given access to liquidation and reorganization procedures to debtors and creditors. In the case of contract enforcement, a private bailiff system has been implemented, which, it is expected, should improve contract enforcement efficiency. The country is ranked 10th for ease of starting a business; it involves three procedures and 5.5 business days on average, compared to 5.2 procedures and 10.1 days in Europe and Central Asia, on average. The indicators with the worst ranking include negotiating construction permits (122), electricity supply (106) and protecting minority investors (89).

Kosovo's business tax rates are relatively low. According to the 2018 Doing Business report, the total tax and contribution rate in Kosovo is 15.2 versus 34.8% on average in Europe and Central Asia. The same report ranks Kosovo 40th for ease of paying taxes. The number of hours

---

[9] *Law No. 02/L-5 on Supporting the Small and Medium Enterprises*, Article 5, available at http://www.kuvendikosoves.org/common/docs/ligjet/2005_02-L5_en.pdf.

[10] *Law No. 03/L-031 on Amendment and Supplementation of the Law No. 02/L-5 on Supporting the Small and Medium Enterprises*, Article 5, available at http://www.kuvendikosoves.org/common/docs/ligjet/2008_03-L-031_en.pdf.

[11] 'SME Development Strategy 2012–2016', http://gapmonitor.org/data/Image/SMEstrategy.pdf.

[12] http://www.mti-ks.org/repository/docs/2013_MTI_Strategjia_ZHSP_Eng_115534_268412.pdf.

involved in tax payments per year is 155 versus 50 in Estonia; as a result, tax avoidance is rampant, with businesses frequently keeping separate sets of books for the tax authorities and for lenders.

Despite good progress in establishing an operational environment conducive to SMEs, Kosovo's performance in the 2016 Small Business Act (SBA) is generally below the regional level (OECD 2016).[13] For instance, for provision of business services, the national policy framework established by government is considered poor. According to OECD (2016), measures related to business support services in the SME strategy are broad and do not have clear targets. In particular, services related to start-ups are limited and depend heavily on donor support. The major constraints in the SME policy and the institutional framework include those related to government institutional support services and government financial support services for innovative SMEs (OECD 2016).

2.3.4 Financial Services

In 2002, Kosovo unilaterally adopted the euro as its official currency. On the one hand, this has provided a strong monetary anchor and, generally, has been positive for the economy; on the other hand, it makes fiscal policy the main instrument for domestic demand management and imposes limitations on the central bank's ability to act as the lender of last resort (IMF 2018).

Financial institutions in Kosovo are well capitalized and characterized by relatively high levels of liquidity (see Table 2.4). The Non-Performing Loan (NPL) rate is among the lowest in the region, indicating relatively high quality of loan portfolios in the banking sector. However, lending to SMEs remains constrained, not least due to high levels of informality, low-quality loan applications by small

[13]The Small Business Act (SBA) is an overarching framework for the EU policy on SMEs. It aims to improve the approach to entrepreneurship in Europe, simplify the regulatory and policy environment for SMEs, and remove the remaining barriers to their development (OECD 2016). https://europa.ba/wp-content/uploads/2016/06/SME-Policy-Index-Western-Balkans-and-Turkey-2016.pdf.

companies and difficult and lengthy enforcement procedures in the case of default (OECD 2016). To promote lending, Kosovo launched a credit guarantee scheme primarily for agricultural producers and small businesses in the non-agriculture sector. There are alternative sources of lending, such as microfinance institutions, though their capacity is limited.

The country's financial system is considered a success story, at least in terms of its soundness (IMF 2018). The system is dominated, generally, by banks. The banking system includes 10 banks, which account for more than 75% of total financial system assets. Eight of these banks are locally incorporated and two are foreign branches. The three largest locally incorporated banks are subsidiaries of European banks and, together, account for more than 70% of bank assets. Despite the widespread presence of microfinance institutions, (there are 14), their capitalization is relatively low and many continue to rely on international donor support. Other sources of non-bank finance are largely underdeveloped and lack diversification. Leasing operations are gradually being developed and there is a legal framework for their activities, but in the absence of data on penetration, it is difficult to ascertain uptake among SMEs. There is availability of factoring services, despite absence of a specific legal framework. Kosovo's venture capital ecosystem is in its infancy and Kosovo has amended the legal framework to allow for venture capital activities. Although there are no government-supported venture capital schemes, there is an active private business angels network and, also, individual business angels, often involving the Kosovar diaspora. These business angels provide alternative funding for entrepreneurs in Kosovo.

Table 2.4 shows that, following several years of weak lending, credit has increased in recent years. However, credit penetration and lending to the productive sectors remains at a low level. They are driven by plummeting interest rates (thanks to increased competition), healthier bank balance sheets, excess liquidity and reforms to strengthen contract enforcement and low-risk aversion among EU subsidiaries' parent banks. Nevertheless, at 38% of GDP, credit depth was low in 2016 relative to comparator countries such as Estonia at 71.9%, Croatia at 61.2%, and Latvia at 67.6%.

Table 2.4 Kosovo: selected financial soundness indicators, 2012–2017

	2013	2014	2015	2016	2017
Structure					
Number of banks	9	9	10	10	10
Foreign	7	7	8	8	8
Share of total assets (%)	89.6	90.2	89.9	88.7	88.1
Domestic	2	2	2	2	2
Share of total assets (%)	10.4	9.8	10.1	11.3	11.9
Net foreign assets		534	536	598	446
Assets		716	740	775	663
Liabilities		−182	−204	−177	−217
Asset quality					
NPL to total loans 3/	8.7	8.3	6.2	4.9	3.4
NPL net of provisions to capital	7.8	4.7	3	2.2	1.3
Credit to private sector		1881	2018	2227	2460
Deposits of the private sector		2378	2550	2773	2987
Deposits of the private sector (% of GDP)		42.7	43.9	45.7	46.6
Credit to the private sector (% of GDP)		33.8	34.8	36.7	38.3
Sectoral breakdown of loans					
Agriculture	2.6	2.4	3	2.7	2.3
Manufacturing	9.7	10	10	10	9.8
Trade	36.9	35.8	34.9	34.3	32.3
Other services	12.4	12.8	13.3	11.7	13.2
Construction	6.6	6	4.9	4.6	5.2
Households	31.8	33	34	35.8	36.5
Liquidity					
Liquid assets to total assets 4/	37.8	38.3	37.8	36	32.4
Deposits to loans	130.8	129.4	130.4	125.8	117.5
Liquid assets to short-term liabilities 5/	47.1	41	37.3	41.5	36.3

Source Central Bank of Kosovo (CBK)

Business interest rates have declined rapidly in recent years, dropping to below 8% from over 12%, on average, before 2013. Time duration of loans, appear to be sufficient and are often more than 7 years for SMEs. Collateral requirements are the biggest barrier to firm borrowing, specifically SMEs, since banks continue to employ conservative collateral practices.

In an attempt to enhance access to finance for SMEs, in 2016 Kosovo established a national SME credit guarantee fund. The objective was to support entrepreneurship development by providing credit guarantees for small firms and share credit risks with financial institutions. Loans guaranteed by the fund total between euro 10,000 and euro 100,000.

References

Aghion, P., & Howitt, P. (1998). *Endogenous growth theory*. Cambridge: MIT Press.

Audretsch, D. B. (1995). Innovation, growth and survival. *International Journal of Industrial Organization, 13,* 441–457.

Bartlett, W. (1985). Social services and local democracy in Yugoslavia. *Community Development Journal, 20*(1), 18–23.

Benhabib, J., & Spiegel, M. M. (1994). The role of human capital in economic development: Evidence from aggregate cross-country data. *Journal of Monetary Economics, 34*(2), 143–174.

Dallago, B., & Uvalic, M. (1998). The distributive consequences of nationalism: The case of former Yugoslavia. *Europe-Asia Studies, 50*(1), 519–543.

European Commission. (2006, February). *Communication from the Commission to the Council, the European Parliament, the European Economic and Social Committee and the Committee of the Regions—Implementing the Community Lisbon Programme: Fostering entrepreneurial mindsets through education and learning*. Brussels: European Commission.

European Commission. (2018). *Kosovo 2018 report*. Commission staff Working Document. Strasburg. https://ec.europa.eu/neighbourhood-enlargement/sites/near/files/20180417-kosovo-report.pdf.

European Commission and the World Bank. (1999, November 3). *Toward stability and prosperity*. Pristina. https://reliefweb.int/sites/reliefweb.int/files/resources/7DC58861A1B9C11685256824006EE9FF-ecwb-kosovo.pdf.

Forum 2015. (2008). *Privatization and post-privatization in Kosova: glass half empty of half full?* Pristina: Riinvest Institute.

Forum 2015. (2009). *Dilemmas and backwards in a fast track: Privatization of POEs in Kosovo*. Pristina. http://kfos.org/wp-content/uploads/2011/10/Privatization_ENG.pdf.

Hethy, L. (2002). Labour law for Kosovo South East Europe. *Review for Labour and Social Affairs, 5*(3), 65–77.

Hoti, A. (2004). *Human capital and unemployment in transition: The case of Kosova*. Pristina: Riinvest.

IMF. (2018). *Republic of Kosovo; Selected issues* (IMF Country Report No. 18/31).

Kosovo Statistics Agency (KSA). (2015). *Statistical yearbook of the Republic of Kosovo*. Pristina. http://ask.rks-gov.net/media/1303/statistical-yearbook-of-the-republic-of-kosovo-2015-08102015.pdf.

Kosovo Trust Agency (KTA). (2004). *Draft strategy of the privatisation department of the Kosovo Trust Agency*. https://www.esiweb.org/pdf/bridges/kosovo/11/1.pdf.

Kostoff, R. N. (2003). Stimulating innovation. In L. V. Shavinina (Eds.), *The international handbook on innovation* (pp. 388–400). London: Pergamon.

Kutlaca, D. (2002). Small and medium sized enterprises in Yugoslavia: A driving force in the catching-up process. *Small Firms and Entrepreneurship in Central and Eastern Europe, 14,* 157–178.

Lucas, R. E. (1988). On the mechanics of economic development. *Journal of Monetary Economics, 22,* 3–42.

Mankiw, N. G., Romer, D., & Weil, D. (1992). A contribution to the empirics of economic growth. *Quarterly Journal of Economics, 107*(2), 407–437.

Medjad, K. (2004). The fate of the Yugoslav model: A case against legal conformity. *The American Journal of Comparative Law, 52*(1), 287–319.

Nelson, R. R., & Phelps, E. (1966). Investment in humans, technology diffusion and economic growth. *American Economic Review, 56*(2), 69–75.

OECD. (2013, March). *Assessment of the Kosovo innovation system*. RCI Project Paper, OECD Development.

OECD. (2016). Overview: 2016 Small Business Act assessment of the Western Balkans and Turkey. In *SME Policy Index: Western Balkans and Turkey 2016: Assessing the implementation of the Small Business Act for Europe*. Paris: OECD Publishing. https://doi.org/10.1787/9789264254473-4-en.

PAK. (2015). *Annual activity report of Privatization Agency of Kosovo*. http://www.pak-ks.org/repository/docs/150130_FINANCIAL_STATEMENTS_OF_KOSOVO_BUDGET_Jan_-_Dec_2014_ENG.compressed.PDF.

Palairet, M. (2001). The economic consequences of Slobodan Milosevic. *Europe-Asia Studies, 53*(6), 309–323.

Perritt, H. (2005). Resolving claims when countries disintegrate: The challenge of Kosovo. *Chicago-Kent Law Review, 80*(119). https://scholarship.kentlaw.iit.edu/cklawreview/vol80/iss1/8.

Pettifer, J. (2002, January). *Kosovo economy and society after 1945—Some observations*. Conflict Studies Research Centre, Royal Military Academy, Surrey.

Pula, B. (2004). The emergence of the Kosovo parallel state 1988–1992. *Nationalities Papers, 32*(4), 79–91.
Ramet, S. P. (2006). *The three Yugoslavias: State-building and legitimating, 1918–2005*. Washington, DC: The Woodrow Wilson Centre Press; Bloomington: Indiana University Press.
Riinvest. (2001). SOEs and their privatization/transformation, in cooperation with Centre for International Private Enterprise. Washington, supported by the United States Agency for International Development (USAID), Pristina.
Riinvest. (2004). *Privatization in Kosova: Forwards and backwards*. Pristina.
UNESCO. (2012). *Data Centre, UNESCO Institute for Statistics website*. http://stats.uis.unesco.org/unesco/TableViewer/document.aspx?ReportId=136&IF_Language=eng&BR_Topic=0. Accessed 25 November 2012.
United Nations Development Programme (UNDP). (2007). *Energy for development: Kosovo human development report*. Pristina.
Woodward, S. (1995). *Socialist unemployment: The political economy of Yugoslavia, 1945–1990*. Princeton, NJ: Princeton University Press.
World Bank. (1999). *Kosovo—Building peace through sustainable growth: The economic and social policy agenda*. Washington, DC: World Bank.
World Bank. (2014). *Country snapshot on Kosovo*. http://www.worldbank.org/content/dam/Worldbank/document/eca/Kosovo-Snapshot.pdf.
World Bank. (2015). *World Bank national accounts data* (database). http://data.worldbank.org/. Accessed 26 June 2015.
World Bank. (2018). *Country snapshot*. http://pubdocs.worldbank.org/en/423771524155944422/Kosovo-Snapshot-Spring2018.pdf.

3

Firm Growth Factors: A State of the Art Review and Research Issues

3.1 Introduction

Factors that enable and constrain firm growth are one of most widely studied topics in the economic literature. The impact of firm growth on economic development, employment and innovation activities is the main reason why it is of such crucial interest.

The literature addressing the determinants of the business environment is large and provides numerous important insights into the role of institutions on firm growth. While there is a large body of work on firm dynamics and their influence on growth for firms in developed economies, the evidence for less-developed economies is scarce. This review of literature shows that the evidence is particularly scant in relation to explaining the role of firms' internal capabilities on firm growth in the context of less-developed countries. In addition, although the effect of social conditions on the emergence of innovative firms is relatively new, few academic works explore the social conditions needed to enable the emergence of firms with innovation capabilities.

F. Sahiti, *The Growth of Firms in Less-Developed Countries*,
https://doi.org/10.1007/978-3-030-14821-8_3

This chapter is structured as follows. Section 3.2 reviews the literature on firm demographics and firm dynamics and discusses how these studies relate firm demography and dynamics to firm growth. Section 3.3 examines the different approaches to analysing the impact of business environment factors on firm growth and Sect. 3.4 discusses how the literature explains the link between internal capabilities and firm growth. In addition, Sect. 3.4 reviews the evidence obtained from various research studies on the relationship between managerial practices and firm growth and Sect. 3.5 provides a short overview of the literature that aims to explain relationship between social conditions and the emergence of innovative firms. In Sect. 3.6, which concludes this chapter, research on firm growth is reviewed to identify areas where there are gaps and to highlight 'what is known' and 'what is not known' according to the extant academic literature.

3.2 Firm Demographics, Dynamics and Growth

There is a growing stream of work on business dynamics patterns and their impact on firm growth. This set of studies argues that a substantial part of firm growth can be attributed to churn (entries and exits) and the reallocation of resources from shrinking/exiting firms to expanding/new entry firms (Ahn 2001). The importance of firm dynamics to firm growth is acknowledged in many empirical studies, the majority of which build on Schumpeter's (1934) growth theory. Over the past 25 years, growth theory has developed into an integrated framework to explain both macroeconomic and microeconomic issues related to firm growth (Aghion et al. 2014). However, most of this work is confined to a focus on the manufacturing sectors in developed countries such as the US, Canada and the EU with comparatively few investigating less-developed economies.

Different studies use different variables to explain the pattern of firm dynamics. The most frequently used variables fall into four groups: firm-specific variables, industry-specific variables, spatial or geographic factors and variables related to the business environment.

Firm-specific factors include individual firm properties such as legal structure, age, size, adaptation to new technology, etc. Work on firm entry and post-entry performance emphasizes the importance of firm age and firm size for explaining firm survival. Firm age, in particular, is most often found to be an important determinant of firm survival. For instance, Stinchcombe (1965) points to the existence of 'liability of newness', that is, the fact that newly established firms suffer a greater risk of failure than their older counterparts. This is because younger firms cannot know whether they have the characteristics required to adapt to the competitive environment and to survive. As firms age, they learn about their fitness to survive—a characteristic underlined by passive learning models (Jovanovic 1982). A large number of empirical studies report a negative relationship between firm age and the probability of failure (Mata and Portugal 1994; Geroski 1995; Bartelsman et al. 2009); others suggest a different relationship between age and the probability of exit. The 'liability of adolescence' predicts an inverted U-shaped relationship between firm failure and age (Brüderl and Schussler 1990). New organizations are able to survive for a certain length of time, with little risk of failure, by drawing on their initial, founding stock of endowments (e.g., venture capital funding, bank loans). However, failure rates reach a peak at the exhaustion of these initial resources and then decrease with only the fittest firms remaining in the market.

The influence of firm size on the survival probability has been explored widely in the industrial organization literature, also. Empirical work on entry and post-entry performance shows that small firms suffer a significantly higher risk of exit compared to larger firms (Dunne et al. 1988). Some authors argue that large firms are close to the minimum efficient scale and have better access to external funds in addition to, generally, being more diversified than smaller firms (Audretsch and Mahmood 1994; Zingales 1998; Geroski et al. 2012). All these factors improve the firm's survival prospects by reducing the risk of failure. Finally, there is some evidence suggesting that larger firms benefit from better organizational capabilities and managerial practices, which, again, add to their chances of survival (Bloom and Van Reenen 2007, 2010; Geroski et al. 2012). In a young and developing economy such as Kosovo, institutional and regulatory factors shape the effects of firm age and size on survival. These factors are discussed in more detail in the succeeding sections.

The impact of the legal and ownership structures on firms' survival prospects has also been investigated (Brüderl et al. 1992; Mata and Portugal 2002). In general, it is expected, theoretically, that limited liability and foreign-owned firms will be more likely to survive. Stiglitz and Weiss (1981) show that in the case of limited liability firms, entrepreneurs undertake projects with relatively higher expected returns and lower risks of failure. Thus, it can be predicted that the legal and ownership structure will have a significant influence on the likelihood of firm survival. Some studies investigate the impact of foreign ownership on the risk of firm failure. For instance, Li and Guisinger (1991) hypothesize that foreign firms owned by Multi-National Enterprises (MNEs) will be more likely to survive than those with foreign ownership; however, their data do not provide much support for this prediction. Mata and Portugal (2002) suggest that foreign-owned firms have greater survival probabilities compared to firms with domestic ownership. However, after controlling for other factors, the impact of foreign ownership vanishes, mainly because foreign firms are larger, employ a larger proportion of university graduates, have more formal legal structures and own a larger number of plants. Moreover, compared to domestic-owned firms, the industries they tend to enter are more concentrated, have greater economies of scale, experience fewer new firm entries and have a larger share of employment in foreign firms.

There is another strand of work on the relationship between firm survival and the economic sectors in which firms operate (Geroski 1995; Audretsch et al. 2000; Arbia et al. 2015; Resende et al. 2015). These studies argue that survival conditions may differ across sectors. The literature links the factors driving survival to traditional market structure variables such as economies of scale, incumbent firms' cost advantages and rate of growth of sector-specific demand (Audretsch and Mahmood 1994; Mata and Portugal 1994). These results lead us to expect different survival probabilities across different industries.

Finally, empirical studies of firm dynamics provide evidence that spatial factors also shape survival probabilities. Their findings suggest that, compared to their counterparts in other parts of the country, new firms located in proximity to a metropolitan area, exhibit higher survival rates (Baldwin et al. 2000; Fotopoulos and Louri 2000). This is because, operating close to a metropolis allows the firm to benefit from external economies of scale (Marshallian economies) arising from proximity to a larger number of and higher quality suppliers, knowledge spillovers and specialized labour. The firm may benefit, also, from higher levels of demand based on location in a more heavily populated area. However, greater firm concentration could increase the competition among firms and increase congestion costs, which could have a negative effect in relation to firm survival. The empirical evidence shows a positive effect of agglomeration on firm survival, suggesting that the positive effects outweigh the negative effects of tougher competition and higher congestion costs (Berglund and Brännäs 1996). There is some more recent evidence that suggests that the location choice affects the survival prospects of entrants to firms in the manufacturing sector (Dunne et al. 2005; Pe'er and Vertinsky 2006).

Several research studies use various macroeconomic indicators to explain the pattern of firm dynamics. The most commonly used economic indicators include unemployment rate, interest rate, exchange rate, GDP level, income levels, etc. For instance, Audretsch and Mahmood (1994) and Holmes et al. (2000), investigate the impact of unemployment rates and interest rate levels on the firm survival. They find that high unemployment rates and high interest rates are expected to have a negative impact on survival prospects. On the other hand, Baldwin et al. (2000) suggest that high levels of GDP growth have a positive impact on the survival of new firms. Berglund and Brännäs (2001) provide evidence suggesting that, due to the greater purchasing power in regions with higher incomes, firms in these regions are less likely to fail. Using firm-level data on the OECD countries, Scarpetta et al. (2002) find that stricter product market and labour regulations are correlated negatively to entry of small and medium-sized firms in these countries. Klapper et al. (2008) use World Bank Group

Entrepreneurship Survey data for 2008 to show the presence of a strong and statistically significant relationship between firm entry and a better business environment. For instance, they show ease of establishing a business and better governance that are associated with higher levels of firm entry. In addition, their findings indicate that a quick, efficient and cost-effective business registration process is vital for fostering formal sector entrepreneurship. In a 2012 paper, Geroski et al. provide evidence suggesting that firms born in growing (boom) economic conditions are more likely to have almost permanent high survival rates, all other things being equal; they show that and survival rates are higher during times when the economy is growing rapidly compared to when it is declining.

Using a comprehensive database of firms in Western and Eastern Europe, Klapper et al. (2004) show how the country's business environment drives the creation of new firms. They focus on business environment factors, such as government regulation, level of development of the financial sector, level of specialization of the labour force, strong enforcement of intellectual property rights and strict labour laws. They find that entry-specific regulation hampers entry and they find lower levels of firm entry in countries with less sophisticated financial institutions. They find, also, that the availability of skilled labour enhances entry and, particularly, in industries that require high-skilled labour.

There is a specific stream of literature that considers pull and push factors as drivers of firm formation and exit (Feldman and Balino 2000; Carter et al. 2003; Bosma et al. 2008). While pull factors, related to firm creation, derive predominantly from market opportunities, push factors derive from necessity. These push (necessity) factors are considered significant determinants of firm formation—especially in poor countries (Naudé 2010a, b, 2012). The distinction between pull and push factors may, perhaps, be seen as ambiguous since business opportunities depend on the context in which firms are born and operate. Thus, the opportunities available to firms operating in a developing country environment differ from those available in high-income countries. Business environment differences depend on education level, organizational capabilities, resources and financial capital (Caballero 2006). Low levels of these attributes add to problems related to a weak institutional framework;

therefore, in developing country economic settings, a large proportion of firms operate in the informal sector and are survivors (Naudé 2007). Most such firms are single owner firms or involve very small numbers of (often casual) employees (Banerjee and Duflo 2007). These firms, which De Soto (1989) calls as survivalist firms, operate in business environments with weak institutions and unclear or non-existent rules of the game, and in a context of 'destructive uncertainty' (Berner et al. 2008). A weak institutional environment promotes informality and survivalist firms (De Soto 1989). Although important in developing countries (Banerjee and Duflo 2007), many of the firms in the informal sector exist in the market, but are unproductive and are unable to grow (Baumol 1990).

The growing body of work on firm dynamics since the mid-1990s, suggests the existence of large firm heterogeneity across different interrelated dimensions such as size, growth, market share, life cycle, etc. Certain patterns have been identified and become stylized facts. For example, Geroski (1995) suggests some stylized facts to explain the drivers of firm entry and the effects on the market of new firms. He argues, *first*, that market entry of new firms annually is common; however, the percentage that manage to penetrate the market (survive and grow) is small. One of the reasons for this is the small size of new entrants; small firms find it difficult to grow to match incumbents. According to Geroski (1995), it is a stylized fact that small-scale compared to large-scale entry is relatively easy (Geroski 1995). Geroski's *second* stylized fact refers to the fact that firm entry differences among industries do not persist and most of the variation in entry across industries and over time is 'within' rather than 'between' industry variation. The *third* stylized fact refers to the positive correlation between entry and exit rates, with net entry rates a small fraction of gross entry rates and survival. Entries increase with increased profit in the sector and, correspondingly, decrease when profits turn negative. In summary, entries and exits are part of a process of change involving large numbers of new firms displacing large numbers of older firms, resulting in the total number of operating firms remaining stable (Geroski 1995, p. 424). The *fourth* stylized fact refers to the low survival rate of new entrants; even successful entrants can take a decade or more to achieve a size that is comparable to that of the average incumbent. The displacement mechanism affects young firms especially severely. Geroski's (1995) findings suggest, further, that experience is a crucial determinant of survival, but that the acquisition of experience takes time. The *fifth* stylized fact refers to the greater frequency of de novo firms, although these are, in general, less successful than those that enter as part of a diversification strategy. In other words, firms that benefit from the financial backing of a corporate parent operating in a different market, have an advantage over other types of new entrant. The *sixth* stylized fact refers to the variation in entry rates over time (the shakeout process); firm entry tends to occur in waves, with different waves including different types of entrant. This type of entry often reaches a peak in the early lives of many markets. Geroski's final stylized fact is related to the cost of adjustment. He argues adjustment costs seem to penalize large-scale initial entry and encourage very rapid post-entry penetration rates. This *seventh* stylized fact helps to explain the fourth stylized fact, which in turn explains why it can take successful entrants more than ten years to achieve a size comparable to that of the average incumbent. It should be noted that many of these stylized facts have been confirmed by several subsequent empirical studies.

The empirical work conducted by Bartelsman et al. (2004, 2009) confirms most of Geroski's (1995) stylized facts. These authors show that the population of firms undergoes significant changes over time, through both resources reallocations among existing firms and the firm entry and exit process. Bartelsman et al. note, also, that the efficiency with which the economy deals with the reallocation process affects both productivity and labour market dynamics and unemployment in particular issues. Finally, they argue that there is significant heterogeneity of firms in each market and country, which is manifested in the large disparities in firm size, firm growth and firm productivity.

The main stylized facts they propose are:

- the average size of incumbent firms varies widely across sectors and countries. The variety in firm size is driven, largely, by within-sector differences, although in some countries sectoral specialization also plays a significant role. Bartelsman and colleagues find that smaller countries tend to have a size distribution that is skewed towards smaller firms, but that the average size and dispersion of firms within and across countries, do not map precisely with the dimensions of the domestic market overall;

- there is evidence that firm churn (firm entry and exit) is substantial. They add that gross firm turnover 10 and 20% of all firms in the industrialized countries with the percentage slightly higher in the transition economies. Newly born firms and exiting firms tend to be small, thus, firm flows affect only around 5–10% of total employment, suggesting entry of small firms is relatively easier than entry of larger firms, but that small firm survival is more difficult and many small new-comer firms fail to achieve an efficient production scale;
- Bartelsman and colleagues provide empirical evidence which suggests that entry and exit rates are part of the same process (in line with Geroski's third stylized fact) and, in most of the countries investigated, entry and exit rates are correlated across industries. Their findings confirm that, although the total number of firms in the market at each point in time remains mostly unaffected, there are a large number of new firms which displace a large number of obsolete firms. The authors argue, also, that in transition economies and some emerging countries these correlations are weaker as a result of the greater structural changes in their economies due to declining traditional sectors and expanding modern sectors;
- Bartelsman and colleagues propose another stylized fact related to market selection; they provide evidence that some 20–40% of new entrants fail within two years. They also provide evidence supporting previous findings on firm size and growth (Klepper and Simons 1993; Geroski 1995), showing that failure rates decline with duration. That is, that conditional on surviving for a few years, the probability of survival increases. However, they show that only some 40–50% of new entrants in a given cohort of firms survive beyond year seven;
- survivor firms tend to expand rapidly; they are both relatively larger and grow rapidly. Bartelsman et al. argue that the combined effect of exits being concentrated among the smallest units, and growth of survivors, allows the average size in a given cohort increase rapidly towards an efficient scale;

- Bartelsman et al. point out that the notion of creative destruction is relevant to productivity growth. Restructuring and upgrading by incumbents is crucial for improving aggregate productivity, but the part played by firm dynamics related to new firm entry and exit of obsolete units is also essential to this process. This is particularly evident in the case of high-tech industries, which are more able to exploit new technologies;
- according to these authors, the creative destruction model promotes not only aggregate productivity but also market contestability, primarily by stimulating the use of productivity-enhancing strategies by incumbents. They find some preliminary evidence of significant correlation between firm turnover rates and incumbent productivity growth, across industries and countries. They also find significant correlation between the contribution to productivity of net firm entry and incumbents' productivity growth; that is, growth is attributable to the incumbents based on pressure from newcomers, but these newcomers do not necessarily grow;
- this would seem to confirm that higher firm turnover rates are associated to higher productivity growth among incumbents and that the more effective the process of creative destruction for productivity, the more it stimulates incumbent growth.

Bartelsman et al. (2009) suggest that the process of creative destruction has a greater impact in the five central and eastern European transition countries. They found that the process of creative destruction, manifested by firm creation and destruction, generally has been more pronounced in the transition countries compared to developed countries, because of the many new, small firms that have replaced obsolete larger units inherited from the central plan period. The business opportunities available to smaller firms consist of chances to establish new market niches, especially in the early years of transition when competition is lower and survival rates are higher. However, due to the effects of market forces, transition economies reach some level of stabilization and equilibration in entry and exit rates, and failure of new firms. Bartelsman and colleagues find, also, that the resources reallocation process by shifting resources to new, but also more productive firms, becomes increasingly effective during the transition stage.

Several researchers have tried to establish a broad theorizing and mapping agenda in relation to empirical work in this area through the use of different theoretical frameworks. For instance, Ahn (2001) reviews the three most frequent theoretical frameworks, commonly used to explain the link between firm dynamics and firm growth.

Schumpeter's (1934) theory of firm growth and, specifically, his concept of creative destruction, are the references used to establish these theoretical framework models. Schumpeter's model is seen as vital for the continued dynamism of the modern economy (Klapper and Richmond 2009). Ahn (2001, p. 5) offers the following explanation of the model of creative destruction:

> a new innovator enters a market with new technology and competes with incumbents with conventional technology. If the innovation is successful, the entrants will be able to replace the incumbents. If not, they will fail to survive. Competition weeds out the unsuccessful firms and nurtures the successful ones. When incumbents who have already accumulated substantial experience with conventional technology are less enthusiastic about taking risks of adopting new technology, new entrants aggressively experimenting with new technology can be a driving force of innovations. Aggregate productivity evolves with successive innovations through entry and exit, while this process reallocates resources from losers to winners.

As a result of this competitive process, there is a reallocation of resources from losers to winners. This process is considered an essential component of productivity growth, which governs the pace at which the potential offered by new technologies can be exploited (Nelson and Phelps 1966). Schumpeter's theory is distinguished by its recognition of the heterogeneity of firms and the essential nature of firm dynamics (based on firm entry, exit, expansion and contraction) for developing and creating new processes, products and markets (Bartelsman et al. 2004).

Another theoretical model shaping firm dynamics and heterogeneity is the experimentation under competition and uncertainty framework (Foster et al. 2002). The rationale underlying this framework is that, uncertainty about the demand for new products or the cost-effectiveness of alternative technologies, encourages firms to experiment with different technologies, goods and production facilities

(Roberts and Weitzman 1981). Experimentation, in its turn, generates differences in outcomes (Jovanovic 1982; Ericson and Pakes 1989). In order to achieve an optimal position to face possible future circumstances and to compensate for lack of incentive to engage in experimentation, firms are encouraged by uncertainty about future costs and demand conditions, to differentiate their products and services (Lambson 1991). This model is consistent with Geroski's second stylized fact, which states that a higher percentage of newborn firms are small firms. This is likely because of entrepreneurs' uncertainty about future demand, which provides an incentive to expand, based on thorough experimentation to forecast future profit. Operating under uncertain conditions, enables entrepreneurs to learn about the business environment in which they are operating and about the capabilities they possess or need to develop to cope with future challenges. The learning process involved could be passive or active. The passive learning model, according to Jovanovic (1982), involves new firms that enter a market with no *ex ante* information about potential profitability. It is only after they start their business operations that they are able to estimate potential profits, based, primarily, on the profits realized. This knowledge enables decisions about whether to expand, contract or exit the market. This framework explains why many young firms decide to exit the market—sometimes almost immediately after entry—and predicts that smaller and younger firms will demonstrate higher and more variable growth rates. This model explains Geroski's fourth stylized fact, which predicts that failure rates decline with firm duration and that older firm age increases the survival probability.

In contrast, the active learning framework (Ericson and Pakes 1995) maintains that firms explore their economic environment actively, and invest to enhance their capability to earn profits in the face of competitive pressure from within and outside the industry (Ahn 2001). Their profits and business potential evolve over time, mainly as a product of their investments, but also as a result of their responses to the reactions of other actors operating in the same market. Consequently, if the firm is able to manage this process successfully, it will grow; if it is unable to respond adequately to market demands, it will contract or exit the market.

To summarize, according to the passive learning model, a firm enters a specific market with no previous knowledge on profitability; this information is gleaned from 'noisy' information on profits realized. To make decisions about the future, the firm needs to update this learning continually (Jovanovic 1982). In contrast, an active learning firm is a firm that responds to competitive pressure by actively exploring its economic environment and investing to enhance its capability to earn profits (Ericson and Pakes 1995).

Ahn's (2001) third theoretical model is the technology and product-cycle framework. In this model, firm dynamics are influenced by the technological environment, for example, in a product-cycle framework. The technology and product-cycle framework is linked to the introduction of a new product; in other words, when a successful new product appears, the market grows rapidly and a large number of new firms enter. The situation is reversed in the context of a mature market. In this case, demand decelerates and economies of scale assume great importance and, as a result, the number of firms in these new industries initially grows then declines sharply before levelling-off. This suggests that, during the unsettled stages in the product-cycle framework, it is relatively easier to enter, but is particularly difficult to survive during the next stage when the number of firms experiences a sharp decline. According to Mata et al.'s (1995) interpretation of Gort and Klepper (1982), high firm turnover rates (i.e., high levels of entry and exit) are observed in the earlier stages of the product-cycle framework.

An example that explains the pattern of firm shakeout as product markets mature, is represented by the model proposed by Jovanovic and MacDonald (1994). According to their model, initially, all firms use the same technology. Over time, new technologies emerge, which enable lower costs and higher levels of output per firm. The process of changing from the old to the new technology causes shakeout of the first generation of firms, resulting in the survival of a smaller number of firms which employ the new technology (Bartelsman et al. 2004). Assuming some capital market imperfections and sales inertia, larger firms will invest more in the fixed costs of product innovation and, over time, will tend to displace smaller firms generating further shakeout (Klepper 2001).

3.3 Business Environment and Firm Growth

To analyse the effects of business environment factors on firm growth, most studies use three different sources of evidence. The first is based on cross-country growth regressions, which, basically, are derived from the average or typical response of the economy to various environment factors. The second is based on the subjective assessments of managers; it draws on the business environment constraints from the manager's point of view. The third source is based on the findings from case studies of the history of the focal country and similar relevant countries (Carlin and Seabright 2007). Each source provides various—sometimes contradictory empirical evidence—on the most binding constraints on firm growth. The following sub-sections describe the main characteristics of each of these sources of evidence.

3.3.1 Empirical Research Based on Cross-County Regressions

Cross-country regression approaches exploit the relationship between two or more variables to explain regional or country growth rates, using one or more independent (explanatory) variables and an explanatory or dependent variable. These models try to show the causal association between (some of) these variables and average country growth. The following formula can be applied to measure this growth:

$$gt = \alpha \; \log(Y_{t-1}) + \beta_1 x_1 + \beta_2 x_2 + \cdots \beta_n x_n$$

This formula estimates the marginal contribution of each factor to growth β, assuming that this contribution is the same for all countries, in all sub-periods in the sample. There are several similar regressions using a range of geographic, institutional, demographic and financial explanatory variables (Sala-i-Martin 1997).

Many researchers are baffled by why some countries grow faster than others do. Most argue that institutions play a major part in wealth and long-term growth (Acemoglu et al. 2001). In other words, countries that managed to establish better political and economic institutions in the past are richer today. Along similar lines, Djankov et al. (2006) study the relationship between business regulations and firm growth. These authors use the Doing Business dataset for 135 countries, to measure how the regulation in seven regulatory areas helps or hinders business performance. Their findings suggest that government business regulations have a major impact on firm growth. In particular, they find that improved business regulations (from the worst (first) to the best (fourth) quartile) imply a 2.3 percentage points increase in average annual growth. However, if compared to the influence of other variables, such as primary schooling, the effect is smaller (moving from the second worst to the best quartile of countries for primary school enrolment is associated to a 0.9 percentage points increase in growth rates). The effect of improved secondary education, inflation and government consumption are also significantly less than the effect of business regulation (Djankov et al. 2006). Djankov et al. provide evidence, also, of a consistent and positive correlation between the business regulation index and growth. According to them, countries with less onerous business regulation grow faster.

There is a specific stream of analytical work on the impact of financial intermediation on firm growth. Aghion et al. (2005) pick up this theme and, using a sample of 71 countries, analyse the role of financial intermediation in firm performance. They test the Schumpeterian model, which implies that growth rates in all countries, above some critical level of financial development, should converge and that, in these countries, financial development has a positive, but eventually vanishing effect on steady-state GDP (Aghion et al. 2005). In addition, drawing on the contributions of other authors, they show that Schumpeterian growth theory provides a framework for analysing various forces that contribute to non-convergence. The empirical evidence they provide suggests that financial development is one of the most powerful of these forces, especially since education attainment, initial relative output and a large number of other variables, have no analogous effects when included in the regressions that also include financial development (Aghion et al. 2005).

Along similar lines, in an exploration of the effects of society's other institutions, Bardhan (2005) discusses how, in some countries, in the initial stages of industrialization, the state can play a crucial catalytic role in coordinating development (and providing appropriate positive and negative incentives) and, particularly, in relation to obtaining long-term finance for industrial development. Bardhan provides evidence that the governments in some countries are unsuccessful in this regard due to poor institutional capacity and inability to withstand inevitable political and rent-seeking pressures. He points out that the failure of the state in some of these countries, to address the coordination problems in financial markets, is part of a more general failure to resolve other collective action problems related to the provision of public goods and the social infrastructure. Their lack of provision, frequently, is a strategic outcome of fundamental distributive conflicts in society. He states, also, that initial inequality can result in the persistence of dysfunctional institutions and, especially, in many poor countries. Bardhan (2005) concludes that state antiquity (including among countries that were not former European colonies) predicts the security of property rights and, for some aspects of development, such as literacy, an index of participatory rights and democratic accountability is a better explanatory variable than property rights institutions.

Rodrik et al. (2004) study three clusters of the 'factors' of economic growth: institutions, integration and geography. Based on a sample of 80 countries, they repeat the 'traditional regression' using a larger set of instruments. Their results indicate that, based on these three factors, institutional quality is the most important. They argue that after controlling for the impact of institutions, conventional measures of geography have at the most, weak direct effects on incomes, although their influence on the quality of institutions is strong and direct. Similarly, after controlling for institutional quality, the impact of trade is almost always insignificant and often enters the income equation with a negative sign (Rodrik et al. 2004). The authors point out that, despite institutions taking primacy over other factors, this result is not very significant because the main indicator of institutional quality remains 'investor' ratings of the institutional environment. The quality of the institutions is related to the likelihood that: investors will retain the fruits of their investments, the state will expropriate them and the legal system will protect their property rights. Rodrik et al.'s findings indicate that if investors believe that their property rights are protected, the economy ends up richer. However, this is not to imply that this is due only to strong property rights. The authors illustrate this, using the cases of Russia, where there is system of property rights in place, and China, which still retains a socialist legal system. It seems that entrepreneurs in China feel sufficiently secure to make large investments, resulting in China having one of the world's fastest growing economies. By contrast, in Russia, investors feel insecure and private investments are at a low level. This could be understood as meaning that the existence on paper of a property rights system is not sufficient to attract foreign investments. However, credible signals of reasonably strong property rights protection seems to be more important than their enactment in law as a formal property rights regime (Rodrik et al. 2004).

Using a large dataset of 121 countries for the years 1960–2000, Calderon and Serven (2004) provide an empirical evaluation of the impact of infrastructure development on economic growth and income distribution. They find that the volume of infrastructure stocks has a significant positive effect on long-run economic growth, and that this finding is robust to different measures of infrastructure. They argue that the extent and quality of the infrastructure have a robust negative impact on income inequality. They find that income inequality declines not only with more extensive infrastructure but also with better quality infrastructure services. Some separate experiments (using a reduced sample) show that improved access to safe water has an additional positive impact on income equality. Another important result from this study is related to the impact of infrastructure on poverty. The authors find evidence suggesting that infrastructure both increases growth and reduces income inequality, which implies that infrastructure development may be the win-win ingredient for reducing poverty. In addition to raising the level of income in society, it increases the incomes of the poor more than proportionately (Calderon and Serven 2004). Calderon and Serven believe that development of the infrastructure should be at the top of the poverty reduction agenda.

There is a set of studies that provide empirical evidence on the effects of and interactions between economic and political liberalization. Based on a sample that includes 140 developed and developing countries, spanning the years 1960–2000, Giavazzi and Tabellini (2004) analyse the role of government quality in national economic growth.

They argue that bad economic policy is the result not of random policy mistakes, but rather systematic economic failures in several dimensions. Conversely, countries ruled by 'good' governments enact bundles of sound economic policies. The fact that studies occasionally observe comprehensive and rapid policy improvements or deteriorations, suggests that the government quality is not determined entirely by history (Giavazzi and Tabellini 2004, p. 2). Which should come first, economic or political liberalization? Are there interaction effects between these two types? Giavazzi and Tabellini show that countries that first liberalize their economies and then become democracies do much better, in almost all dimensions, than countries that reverse this sequence. The authors justify their claims using the Chinese and Russian cases. So, Russia became a democracy and then tried to open up its economy. Most of the countries in their sample followed this pattern. However, the practical results show that the economic payoffs are much higher for countries that adopted the reverse pattern, namely who open up the economy while still being autocracies, and later become democracies (Giavazzi and Tabellini 2004). Numerous empirical studies consider the impact of political and economic liberalization on economic development. For instance, Glaeser et al. (2004) investigate whether political institutions cause economic growth or whether growth and human capital accumulation lead to institutional improvements. The literature includes two approaches to resolving this dilemma. The first supports the idea that countries need to start by becoming a democracy and develop sound institutions; their establishment then should lead to investments in human and physical capital and to economic growth. The second approach emphasizes the need for human and physical capital accumulation to start the process. It is based on the idea that even pro-market dictators can secure property rights, for instance, as a policy choice. From the vantage point of poor countries, democracy and other institutional improvements are considered the consequence not the cause of increased education and wealth (Glaeser et al. 2004, p. 2). The authors provide additional evidence that: (a) human capital is a more basic source of growth than institutions; (b) poor countries escape poverty via good policies, often pursued by dictators; and (c) poor countries improve their political institutions at a later date.

Various studies support the argument of a positive relationship between per capita income and governance quality. For example, Kaufmann et al. (2007) distinguish strong positive causal effects of better governance and higher per capita incomes, and identify a weak or even negative causal effect running in the opposite direction. They use a dataset of 175 countries for the period 1996–2005. Their main findings suggest that causality runs from governance to per capita GDP. They find no evidence of virtuous circles, in which higher incomes lead to further governance improvements.

Another business environment factor widely discussed in the literature is corruption. Many researchers argue that malfunctioning of government institutions constitutes a severe obstacle to increased private investment. It would seem generally to be accepted that corruption happens and exists all over the world and is more frequent in poorer economies. In debate over the impact of corruption on the growth process, researchers are undecided about whether corruption greases or sands the wheels of economic growth (Bardhan 1997; Aidt 2011). Supporters of the 'greasing hypothesis' base their argument on the idea that corruption facilitates trade and, moreover, promotes efficiency by allowing private agents to circumvent cumbersome bureaucracy and regulation (Méon and Weill 2010). On the other hand, opponents of this view have constructed a solid theoretical rebuttal, arguing that the greasing hypothesis may be only a second-best option in a bad institutional setting. There is abundant empirical evidence supporting this latter view. For instance, a widely cited paper is Mauro (1995), which uses data on 68 countries during the period 1980–1983. Maoro argues that corruption reduces investment across developing countries, thereby, negatively affecting growth. Later, two consecutive research studies (Reinikka and Svensson 2004) find that corruption has detrimental effects on human capital accumulation. However, the empirical evidence on the economic consequences of corruption remains inconclusive (Svensson 2005). There are some studies that support the greasing-the-wheels hypothesis of a positive correlation between corruption and growth in a number of fairly successful Asian economies including China (Rock and Bonnett 2004; Li and Wu 2010).

Despite its usefulness and advantages, empirical research on growth constraints based on a cross-country regression approach, seems to fall short of providing a comprehensive framework to effectively diagnose and identify the constraints that might be affecting firm growth in specific economic settings and at particular points in time. This is because this approach does not consider that different countries may have different characteristics and, therefore, that the patterns derived from the analysis may not be applicable to all of them (Hausmann et al. 2008). Others point to other deficiencies in this approach. For instance, Carlin and Seabright (2007, p. 8) note that cross-country regression analysis does not reveal which institutions or elements of the business environment matter for long-run development, for the following reasons:

- it fails to provide correlations between the proxies used to characterize them;
- there are problems related to measurement of the business environment variables;
- institutions are persistent over time;
- many samples include on a small number of countries;
- frequently, these studies are characterized by a paucity of credible instruments to deal with the problems of reverse causality, measurement error and omitted correlated variables.

In summary, based on these limitations, those studies that seem to identify one particular aspect of the business environment, derived from cross-country analysis, should be treated with some scepticism. Just as epidemiologists are sceptical about new research claiming to have found a foodstuff (say, broccoli this year and dairy products last year) that raises or lowers the risk of breast cancer, economists should be sceptical of claims that the key dimension of the business environment can be derived from a cross-country study (Carlin and Seabright 2007, p. 8).

3.3.2 Empirical Research Based on Firm-Level Regressions

Some empirical studies are based on subjective measures and produce different and, quite often, contradictory outcomes regarding the relationship between business environment factors and firm performance. This type of evidence is collected by asking firm managers what they consider to be the biggest barriers to their firms' operations and growth. Along these lines, Dollar et al. (2005) used investment climate surveys to measure how institutional and policy weaknesses affect the performance of firms in four developing countries. The study focuses on the garment industry and uses city averages to measure the quality of the business environment by including five business climate measures. It is remarkable that, among those five independent variables, the most binding constraint identified by managers was delay in obtaining a phone line, followed by customs delays and power outages. Overdraft facilities and number of government official inspections—the fourth and fifth factors—were not considered as binding. The findings are interesting because, a subsequent survey (i.e., Carlin et al. 2006) that covered the same countries (i.e., the Business Environment and Enterprise Performance Survey—BEEPS), the constraints related to the telecommunication infrastructure were never recorded as of above average importance. As Carlin et al. (2006) argue, there could be other possible explanations for the discrepancy between the regression results and the low reported costs of the constraints related to the raw data. One of these is reverse causality—that is, countries (or cities in Dollar et al.'s analysis) that prosper for a variety of other reasons for which it is not feasible to control econometrically, but which higher level telecoms services; another reason could be the presence of network externalities (Carlin et al. 2006).

There is an important study, e.g., Ayyagari et al. (2006) who also highlights interpretation issues, that deal with the role of business climate factors for promoting and restraining firm growth. This study reports firms identifying many obstacles to growth, not all of which are equally constraining. Some of the constraints affect firm growth—either indirectly via their influence on other obstacles. On the basis of a regression analysis, the authors report that only obstacles related to access to external finance, crime and political instability directly affect firm growth rates. More specifically, they argue that, among these three, access to finance is the most binding constraint, with political instability and crime less robust to the exclusion of transition and African countries, where it might be expected they would be the most problematic for business growth. Thus, these results have important policy implications for prioritization of reform efforts. Finally, the authors argue that maintaining political stability, keeping crime under control and undertaking financial sector reforms to relax financing constraints are likely to be the most effective means of promoting firm growth (Ayyagari et al. 2006, p. 29). When discussing the role of finance in firm growth, the authors emphasize the impact of high interest rates as a constraining factor. In addition to high interest rates, other related factors such as collateral and amounts of paperwork are reported as hampering firm growth. However, other studies (e.g., Carlin et al. 2006), which include these same countries in their samples, identify issues, such as taxes and regulation, as important.

The study by Commander and Svejnar (2007) raises a number of issues in relation to the regression analysis between business environment factors and firm performance. They conduct regression analysis on BEEPS data for 26 transition economies, to assess the effects on performance of firm ownership, competition, export orientation and the firm's business environment. They provide evidence suggesting that ownership and competition affect performance, but the results do not support earlier findings that foreign firm ownership compared to domestic private ownership has a positive effect on performance (Commander and Svejnar 2007, p. 34). They argue, further, that the firm's export orientation has a positive effect on performance in simple specifications, but that the effect disappears when firm ownership is taken into account (Commander and Svejnar 2007, p. 34). According to their findings, firm-level variations in the country's business environment seem not to be important. This is because firms can get around these constraints at relatively low cost and, therefore, the effect is not detectable in the data, or managers of firms facing severe constraints compensate for their presence by reporting a lower severity than the reality (Commander and Svejnar 2007). This confirms the idea of the business environment being a country-level characteristic (Carlin and Seabright 2007). Commander and Svejnar (2007) also highlight that, based on their sample of only 26 countries, regression analysis is unable to distinguish which elements of the business environment matter most—or indeed distinguish between business environment and other country characteristics.

Based on the relative importance of different constraints on growth and how these vary across countries and firm types, Carlin et al. (2006) report some interesting patterns. Firstly, physical infrastructure is rarely identified as a strong constraint by the sample countries. Land access is mentioned by some African countries, transport by some poor or war-torn economies such as Sri Lanka, Kosovo and Ireland. The telecoms infrastructure was not identified as a barrier, which contrasts with Dollar et al.'s (2005) findings. Electricity is identified by some African countries and two transition countries (Albania and Kosovo). Secondly, limitations related to licensing and customs are mentioned as especially severe in Commonwealth of Independent States (CIS) countries, where tax administration is also a particular concern. Thirdly, crime and/or corruption were identified as severe constraints by almost all countries except the OECD group: crime was identified by 25% of countries and corruption by 70% (Carlin et al. 2006). Fourthly, among the various restrictions on growth, firms in all the countries included in the sample, singled out seven as of greater than average importance: anti-competitive practices; tax rates and tax administration; access to and cost of finance; and policy uncertainty and macroeconomic stability. The burden imposed by taxes was common to all firms in all countries. The South East European countries see policy uncertainty as the most severe limitation. Fifthly, labour regulation is a major limitation only for prosperous economies. Another part of the survey findings shows that more efficient firms are especially restricted by poorly functioning customs regulation and legal system inadequacies, and that private rather than state-owned firms are the most likely beneficiaries of improvements to macroeconomic stability and policy predictability, better legal system and reduced corruption and crime rates (Carlin et al. 2006, p. 31).

3.3.3 Regional and Country Studies Related to Business Environment Factors

As already stated, when analysing the relationship between business environment factors and firm growth, researchers draw on three sources of evidence, one of which is regional and country-level studies. The cross-country regression methodology relies on the assumption of a common technology, which transforms inputs, including the business environment, into outputs (Carlin and Seabright 2007). The outcome of this methodology is the average—a model based on an average score. According to this methodology, countries that perform worse than the average, should try to improve their business environment factors to promote firm growth. However, the methodology does not identify whether the average score is related to the specific conditions in some countries. This issue can be addressed, in part, by evidence collected from a survey of managers. Carlin and Seabright (2007, p. 24) point out that, regional and country-level studies can be useful for suggesting causal hypotheses, but are not good at testing them since there is usually almost no basis for evaluating hypotheses other than a general inclination or disinclination to accept the author's finding. Different researchers can focus on similar variables, but reach different and incompatible conclusions, which can cause confusion.

There are many research studies of regions and individual countries. Among the regional studies, we would highlight the work by Bartlett and Bukvic (2002) which investigates the impact of business environment factors on firm growth in South East Europe, focusing on Bosnia, Macedonia and Slovenia. The research was designed to reveal the extent to which small and medium-sized firm policies in Bosnia, Macedonia and Slovenia deal with the barriers to growth. The study findings show that, in these three countries, survey respondents consider financial barriers to be extremely important. The high cost of credit was perceived to be the most important barrier to growth. Other finance related aspects, such as requirement for high levels of collateral, were prioritized over other barriers. In the context of the regulatory framework in which firms interact with customers, government can influence firm growth.

Other constraints to growth identified in this study include complex laws, rules and regulations concerning small firms, tax-related barriers, social capital, trust and network ties among firms. The research outcomes for these countries include increased uncertainty and high cost of doing business. The main barrier was late payment of bills, which caused a chain of reactions giving rise to a generalized liquidity crisis. When added to an inefficient judicial system, especially in Bosnia and Macedonia, it is not difficult to understand why firms rank late payments as a major barrier to growth.

There is a stream of literature that discusses the state and the impact of business environment factors in transition economies. Access to external finance is among the most important aspects discussed by this literature (Richter and Schaffer 1996; Lizal and Svejnar 2002; Filatotchev and Mickiewicz 2006).

Institutional constraints on the firm activity in the transition economies were highlighted first by Baumol (1990) and have been explored further by a number of researchers including McMillan and Woodruff (1999, 2002), De Soto (2000), Djankov et al. (2006), and Sobel (2008). They argue that several institutional aspects affect firm growth including strength of legal enforcement, administrative barriers to entry, prevalence of extra-legal payments and lack of market-supporting institutions. Johnson et al. (2000), in their study, find that the entrepreneur's lack of faith in the court's ability to enforce contracts efficiently, has a negative effect on employment growth, though this effect is not significant with respect to sales growth. Similarly, Djankov et al. (2003) finds evidence that Russian entrepreneurs have less confidence than non-entrepreneurs in the efficiency of the court system. According to Svejnar (2002), the legal and institutional system underlying the market economy is immature in most transition economies; in many of these countries it was introduced post-1990. There is a difference between the countries of central and Eastern Europe and those of the former Soviet Union. As Estrin et al. (2009) point out, the central and eastern European economies, for the most part, inherited stronger legal, institutional and cultural frameworks from the perspective of operating a successful market economy. According to Estrin and colleagues, this is in part because many of these countries had thriving capitalist economies in the nineteenth century and during interwar period. In their study, Bevan and Estrin (2004) stress that this initial advantage gave these countries easier access to the EU and resulted in their adopting EU legal codes and institutions. In contrast, as Mickiewicz (2005) suggests, the rule of law in ex-Soviet countries was poor and, therefore, it was difficult to enforce voluntary contracts related to customers paying for the goods they had purchased and firms paying for workers their contracted wages.

Taxes are a limitation for all firms worldwide (Rosen 2005). In the transition economies, tax issues often are related to the costs created by inefficient, inconsistent and/or corrupt tax collection systems, which can add substantially to the cost of operations (Aidis and Mickiewicz 2006).

Human capital is an important variable in firm growth (Davidsson and Honig 2003). There is evidence that transition countries fare relatively well in terms of formal measures of education and the central and east European economies continue to invest a high proportion of their GDP in education, outperforming some west European countries (Barr et al. 2005). Estrin et al. (2009) also found that transition economies typically have a high proportion of students enrolled in the 'hard' sciences, mathematics and engineering.

Corruption is an interesting institutional characteristic that is likely to have a significant impact on firm growth and entrepreneurship in general (McMillan and Woodruff 2002). According to Aidis and Mickiewicz (2006), corruption has damaging effects on entrepreneurial activity and firm expansion because it increases the level of uncertainty and reduces entrepreneurial gains. Corruption is often seen as one of the key outcome variables reflecting the institutional weaknesses in an economic setting (Treisman 2007; Aidt 2009) and, as Tanzi (1998) points out, it can be used to proxy for overall institutional quality. Evidence provided by Aidis and Mickiewicz (2006) shows that corruption has been an important obstacle to business expansion in the transition economies.

Among individual country studies, the most relevant are those focused on Kosovo's economy. It should be noted that some research studies report contradictory outcomes in relation to obstacles to firm growth. The findings from several surveys conducted by different institutions contradict those from international surveys such as PICS, BEEPS, etc.

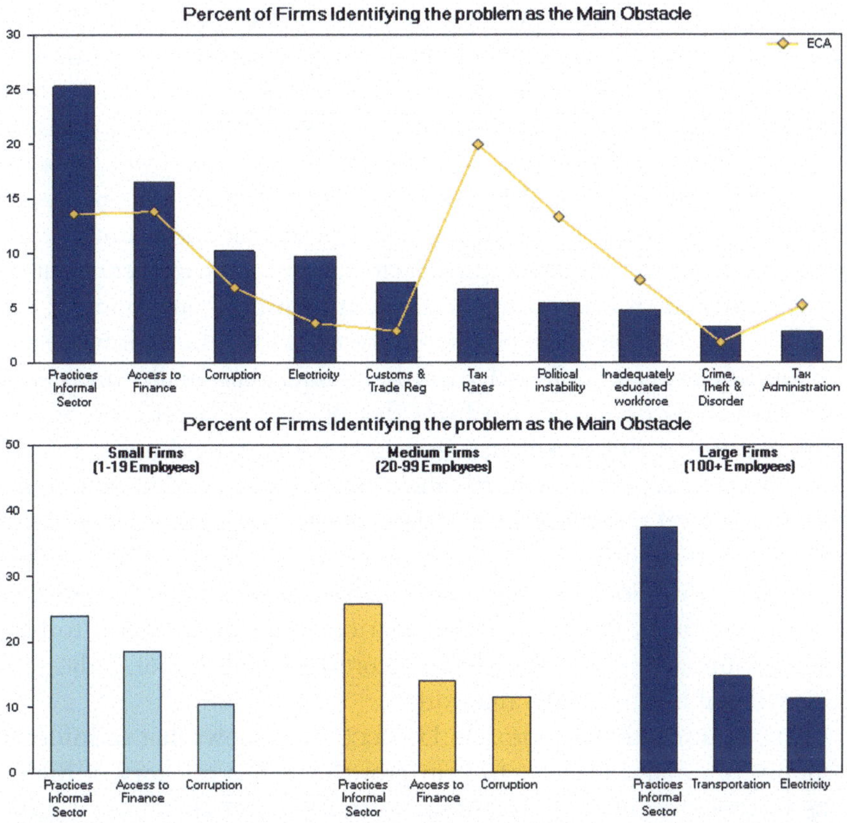

Fig. 3.1 Firms' perceptions of the constraints to firm growth in Kosovo (*Source* Enterprise survey 2013)

The most recent survey conducted in Kosovo was published by the World Bank in 2013. Figure 3.1 depicts the growth constraints broken down by large, medium and small enterprises operating in Kosovo.

Research focused on Kosovo sometimes provides contradictory outcomes in relation to firm growth constraints. In his study based on surveys conducted by the Riinvest Institute, Krasniqi (2007) identifies three main constraints to the growth of small and medium-sized firms: tax burden, unfair competition and access to finance. According to his findings, the tax burden slows firm growth through the cost of regulation, whereas unfair competition is caused mainly by corruption and the presence of the informal sector which increases the costs of doing business. Access to external finance is identified as limitation based on its high costs, which have negative consequences for growth for smaller firms. In a subsequent study, Krasniqi (2012) uses a larger dataset from the same institute to investigate the determinants of firm growth. He employs an econometric approach and considers four aspects that affect firm growth: firm-related factors, human capital factors, firm's management strategy and entrepreneurial orientation, and external business environment factors. In relation to the first type, the author argues that both firm size and firm location are crucial. In other words, he finds that smaller firms grow faster than larger ones, and that firms that operate in larger areas, specifically in a capital city, experience faster and higher growth rates. In relation to human capital factors, the main obstacles to growth are training related. The level of education and skills of the managers surveyed seem to influence their firms' growth. An interesting finding is that employees' level of education does not seem to affect growth rates. For external growth constraints, this study shows that only corruption seems to have a negative impact on growth, which, according to the author, indicates a weak national institutional framework.

Using an institutional approach, Hoxha (2009) shows that an informal economy is a major obstacle to firm growth. In this category of limitations to growth, unfair competition, corruption and an informal economy are the most critical. The author suggests that the reason why firms do not identify any formal constraints to growth is related probably to the post-war period, which has been characterized by an institutional vacuum and lack of basic economic laws that would provide equal opportunities for all players in the marketplace. What is striking in both these research studies is that power outages are not identified as a problem, although the PICS and BEEPS surveys highlight outages as important.

In an investigation of the impact of informal and formal growth constraints for companies that operate internationally, Kutllovci et al. (2012) find that both have a significant influence on firm growth. Among formal barriers, they report high taxes, fiscal policy, the general business environment, and the approach in regional and international markets are considered the most serious restrictions on the growth of these types of firms. Specifically, they note that authorization issues, licences, certification by various institutions can take time and often are unclear. Obtaining the documentation required to trade internationally can be time-consuming because the relevant institutions have no clear systems and processes in place. In terms of informal constraints, the authors report that, among the most frequent obstacles mentioned by respondents, are low levels of professionalism and ethics among officials in the respective institutions and poor enforcement of regulations.

Sen and Kirkpatrick (2009) in their study, seek to provide a more comprehensive view of Kosovo's economic prospects. To identify the most severe constraints on economic growth and job creation, the authors use a 'diagnostics' analytical framework. Their study should be considered in the context of the relationship between business environment factors and firm performance. In other words, using a growth diagnostics methodology, the authors tried to identify the most significant limitation on firm growth. They conclude that limited access to finance, particularly for the smallholder agricultural sector, and poor provision of rural infrastructure, are the main obstacles to the growth of SMEs.

3.4 Resource-Based View and Management Practices

This section provides an updated review of the work on firm resources, organizational capabilities and management practice approaches. It is organized as follows: the first part reviews the literature on organizational capabilities and the literature on managerial practices. The findings from these two streams of work are summarized and presented in light of the succeeding chapters in this book.

The resource-based view was proposed originally by Edith Penrose (1959). Her basic argument was that a firm consists of a collection of productive resources, which can contribute to its competitive advantage to the extent that they are exploited in such a manner that their potentially valuable services are made available to the firm. However, the resource-based view tends to be associated now with the work of Prahalad and Hamel (1990), Rumelt (1991), Barney (1991), Grant (1991), and Peteraf (1993).

A seminal article related to resource-based theory was written by Barney (1991) and is entitled 'Firm resources and sustained competitive advantage'. The arguments put forward in this article build on two assumptions. *First*, firms operating in the same industry are heterogeneous in terms of the strategic resources they control and, *second*, these resources are not perfectly mobile across firms, which can tender this heterogeneity long-lasting. Special emphasis is given to the impact of these assumptions on the identification of the firm's internal resources, which lead to the creation of sustained competitive advantage. Barney (1991) believes that firms cannot expect to achieve sustainable competitive advantage if strategic resources are distributed evenly across all firms and when these resources are highly mobile. He points out, also, that sustained competitive advantage cannot be purchased on the open market; it must be created internally and depends, primarily, on the existence of rare, imperfectly imitable and non-substitutable resources which are controlled by the firm.

The essential question in the context of resource-based theory is related to the specific resources that enable some firms to achieve superior performance relative to others. Many studies have attempted to investigate and articulate the specific resources associated to competitive advantage. Early empirical research associates certain factors to competitive advantage with internal differences across firms such as founding conditions, and historical or chance events (Helfat and Leaberman 2002). As stated above, it was Barney (1991) who argued that superior performance originated from heterogeneous resources endowments, which can lower the costs of production and service provision or increase the willingness to pay more. Building on this, Leiblein (2011) suggests that only firms endowed with heterogeneous resources are able to obtain competitive advantage (relative willingness to pay minus costs), which, essentially, is based on the relative productivity of a binding, scarce resource. He notes, also, that it is not scarcity per se, but rather the capability underlying the resource that enables those controlling the more functionally productive resources to capture value.

Grant (2002) categorizes firm resources into three main groups: tangible capital resources, human capital resources and intangible capital resources (organizational capabilities). Tangible resources embed physical attributes—physical capital resources and financial resources. According to Barney (1991), physical capital resources, such as physical technology, geographic location and access to raw materials, are not imperfectly imitable assets since they can be duplicated by competitors. In order to gain competitive advantage relative to competitors, firms need to develop capabilities that are idiosyncratic and distinctive and are very difficult for other firms to reproduce (Barney 1991).

3.4.1 Human Capital Resources

In trying to identify the most valuable resources that shape firm performance, several studies converge on human capital as perhaps the most universally valuable and imperfectly imitable resource (Kogut and Zander 1996; Grant 1991, 1996; Barney et al. 2011). Human capital refers to the knowledge, skills and abilities embodied in the workforce (Coff and Kryscynski 2011).

Human capital includes not only explicit knowledge, skills and abilities but also tacit knowledge, skills and abilities which are not easily articulated (Polanyi 1962). The literature argues that these variables, along with the education, training and experiences of managers and employees, are key drivers of superior performance.

Frequently, education is seen as an influential factor in business success because it can enhance the entrepreneur's psychological confidence, knowledge and skills. In this context, Brush and Hisrich (1991) note that length of an entrepreneur's formal education before they start a business, has a positive effect on firm performance. In a study of firms in Oklahoma, USA, Box et al. (1993) find a positive relationship between a high education level among entrepreneurs and the performance of manufacturing firms. In small businesses, the entrepreneur's education level can be a critical success factor for firm survival, especially in difficult conditions, and business profitability (Yusuf 1995). Schutjens and Wever (2000) suggest that entrepreneurs with a reasonable level of education are better able to deal with complicated business activities.

Recent empirical work reaches similar conclusions. For instance, using data on 208 organizations, Youndt et al. (2004) find that investments in human capital and education are more effective than investment in other forms of capital. Similarly, Griffith et al. (2004), in an investigation of the determinants of productivity growth for a panel of industries in 12 OECD countries, find that human capital and, more specifically, education stimulate growth directly through innovation and indirectly through technology transfer. Using data on human capital and levels of automation in manufacturing across US cities, Lewis (2005) provides further evidence on the link between education and technology adoption. He shows that cities with lower levels of human capital (due to low-skilled immigration) have lower levels of automation even within narrowly defined industries. Similar results are provided by Switzer and Huang (2007), who found that the performance of mutual funds (from a Canadian sample) was related directly to managerial human capital characteristics.

Training for managers and workers is crucial to upgrade and update their expertise, knowledge and skills. This is particularly important in the case of leadership positions, whose holders can enhance firm performance. Specific-firm training can increase the competence of managers and workers transforming it into a 'strategic asset' (Winter 1987). The benefits of training accumulated in the past forms 'bundles' of routines, which can be difficult to understand and imitate (Koch and McGrath 1996) and which can improve competitive advantage and, consequently, lead to superior performance.

Working experience is a prerequisite for starting an entrepreneurial business and is an influential factor in firm performance (Cooper 1981). There is evidence indicating that prior experience provides human resources with both general and specific knowledge and skills and, consequently, can be a source of sustainable competitive advantage (Yusuf 1995). Box et al. (1993) in a study of 300 manufacturing firms in Tulsa, Oklahoma, USA, indicate that the length of prior experience of entrepreneurs is correlated significantly to performance. Experience accumulates know-how through learning by doing and on-the-job training, both of which play crucial roles in the performance of firms (Bishop 1991; Castanias and Helfat 1991).

Thus, it can be expected that human capital resources and formal education, training activities and work experience are factors that differentiate high-performing and low-performing firms operating in less-developed countries such as Kosovo.

3.4.2 Tangible Capital Resources

Tangible resources contain physical attributes—physical capital resources and financial resources. According to Barney (1991), physical capital resources include the physical technology used in the firm including its plant and equipment, geographic location and access to raw materials. Barney does not deny the relevance of physical resources, but points out that complex physical technology is not an imperfectly imitable asset since it can be duplicated easily by competitors. For instance, if a firm is able to purchase a certain physical technology and implement it using a particular strategy, other firms should be able also to do this. It is the way these resources are used and exploited that makes the difference. Two firms can possess the same physical technology, but only one may have the knowledge, social relations, culture and tradition to enable its full exploitation and the implementation of strategies that other firms will find difficult to duplicate (Barney 1991). Consequently, firms need to develop idiosyncratic capabilities that make it distinctive and are difficult for other firms to duplicate. These capabilities refer to managers and firm employees who are able to deploy knowledge, skills and abilities in distinctive ways (Drucker 1993). Several studies highlight the relationship between technology sophistication and superior performance (Steiner and Solem 1988; Storey 1994).

Financial capital resources include availability of financial funds used by firms to finance their business activities (cash balance, debtors, creditors, etc.). A few works study the impact of internal finance on firm performance. Most focus on the impact of access to external funds on firm growth. However, an appropriate financing strategy is crucial to business success (Storey 1985). Hitt and Ireland (1985) found that finance activities are associated positively to performance. Also, some studies argue that the availability of financial resources can bolster the firm's capacity to support its innovative activities (Lee et al. 2001; Harris and Trainor 1995), while lack of financial funds can limit its innovation activity (Baysinger and Hoskisson 1989; Teece and Pisano 1994; Helfat 1994). According to transaction cost economics and agency literatures, internally (firm) generated funds are more conducive to R&D activities and investments compared to external funds. This is primarily because of the information asymmetries between the firm and the external capital market (e.g., competitors obtain information on R&D projects; firms lose control over their innovations). Tangible resources represented by the implementation of new technology and financial resources can influence performance variability among firms that operate in poor economic environments.

3.4.3 Organizational Capabilities as a Unique Resource

There is a large body of work on the role of organizational capabilities as unique resources, which enable achievement of sustained competitive advantage. For instance, Teece (2000, 2014, 2016) notes that superior performance depends on the firm's ability to defend and use its intangible assets. Hitt et al. (2001) point out that strategically intangible resources are especially important because they allow the firm to create the prerequisites for generating sustainable advantage in the marketplace.

Barney (1991) argues that, while the existence of resources is crucial, their existence per se does not confer sustained competitive advantage on the firm. A critical task for management is to how to use capabilities to produce goods and provide services that customers need, but have not yet imagined (Prahalad and Hamel 1990). Drawing on the above insights from the literature, below we describe a set of organizational capabilities that, potentially, affect performance variability among firms.

Corporate entrepreneurship is an organizational capability, which, for long, was considered a core constituent of capitalism dynamics and a driving force of the whole market system (Mises 1949; Baumol 1993). In trying to gain competitive advantage and create value, firms need to manage their resources and build unique capabilities (Sirmon et al. 2007).

In this context, corporate entrepreneurship is regarded as a critical organizational capability, embedded in the enterprise's culture, which contributes to building and renewing the firm's competitive advantage (Zahra and Covin 1995; Lee et al. 2001; Morrow et al. 2007).

In line with resource-based theory, corporate entrepreneurship refers to articulation of a long-term vision by the firm with the aim of achieving higher growth through the introduction of innovative products, technologies and processes (Foss et al. 2008). It is generally related to the development of new business ideas and opportunities (Birkenshaw 2003). Many research studies discuss corporate entrepreneurship in the context of a firm-level entrepreneurial orientation, reflected by three dimensions: the firm's orientation to innovation, risk-taking and pro-activeness.

In general, innovation is related to the creation of new products, services, processes, technologies and business models (Morris and Kuratko 2002). For some authors, this definition of innovation is too narrow to capture the whole range of activities related to an entrepreneurial mindset. Hence, for Kreiser et al. (2002), innovation refers to the firm's capability and willingness to support creativity and experimentation and to solve recurring customer problems. For these authors, innovation means not only generating creative ideas but also the commercialization and implementation of and modification to existing products, systems and resources. In other words, innovativeness in the context of an entrepreneurial mind-set, allows firms to develop unique sets of internal competencies, which differentiate them from competitor firms (Kreiser et al. 2002; Hashi and Stojcic 2010).

Risk-taking is another component of corporate entrepreneurship and is linked to the ability of the firm to use resources effectively, exploit new opportunities and launch projects with uncertain outcomes and uncertain projected returns on investment (Scheepers et al. 2008). Risks can be minimized by the extent of the firm's knowledge or its unique capabilities and networks, which allow it to exploit opportunities (Morris and Kuratko 2002). Risk can be minimized by firms conducting experiments to test the markets, which allows them, over time, to assimilate risk-taking capabilities that render them more successful compared to other firms (Scheepers et al. 2008). It is clear that when implementing projects, firms can make mistakes, but these failures will ensure more sustainable long-run success (Morris and Kuratko 2002). Morrow et al. (2007) stress that managers need to take risks to change existing resource portfolios and the firm's capabilities; they need to be motivated. Research into corporate entrepreneurship notes that certain internal factors, such as compensation practices (e.g., manager option incentives) can encourage managers to take moderate and calculated risks (Wright et al. 2005).

Pro-activeness describes the actions of management in pushing the firm to achieve its objectives through aggressive and follow-up actions (Kreiser et al. 2002, p. 78), assertiveness and unconventional tactics (Knight 1997) and a forceful approach to competition (Covin and Slevin 1988). In other words, pro-activeness, as a critical element of entrepreneurship, is associated to several attributes such as the firm's disposition towards its competitors, organizational pursuit of favourable business opportunities, being a pioneer or fast follower and high regard for the initiatives of employees (Stevenson and Jarillo 1990; Lumpkin and Dess 1996; Knight 1997).

In sum, firms endowed with an entrepreneurial mind-set are searching constantly for new opportunities by anticipating future demand and developing products and services to satisfy customer needs (Kreiser et al. 2002).

The concept of dynamic capabilities evolved from the resource-based view of the firm. It was proposed, first, by Teece et al. (1997) and has been discussed at some length by many scholars. For Teece et al. (1997), dynamic capabilities refer to the firm's ability to integrate, build and reconfigure internal and external competences to address rapidly changing environments. The theoretical aim of the dynamic capabilities approach is to understand how firms can sustain a competitive advantage by responding to and creating environmental change (Teece 2007).

Empirical research views dynamic capabilities as something that can be built internally rather than purchased on the open market (Makadok 2001). These capabilities are considered to be as organizational processes (Helfat et al. 2007) or routines (Zollo and Winter 2002) that become embedded in the firm over time. In the most general sense, dynamic capabilities are employed to reconfigure the firm's resource base by obliterating obsolete resources or recombining old resources in new ways (Sirmon et al. 2007). Since resources are shaped by the decisions made by the firm throughout its history (Eisenhardt and Martin 2000; Zollo and Winter 2002), this implies that dynamic capabilities are essentially a function of path dependency (Dierickx and Cool 1989). Path dependency 'not only defines what choices are open to the firm today, but…also puts bounds around what its internal repertoire is likely to be in the future' (Teece et al. 1997, p. 515).

Teece (2012, 2014, 2016) argues that dynamic capabilities can be grouped into three clusters of activities and adjustments: (1) identifying and assessing new opportunities (sensing); (2) mobilizing resources to address an opportunity and to capture value (seizing); and (3) continued renewal (transforming). Teece (2012, p. 11) states further that these three variables are necessary for the firm to be sustainable as markets and technologies change.

The variable sensing, for Teece (2012, p. 11) is an 'inherently entrepreneurial set of capabilities that involves exploring technological opportunities, probing markets, and listening to customers, along with scanning the other elements of the business ecosystem'. He believes that deployment of this variable requires management to build and test; hypotheses related to market and technological evolutions, including recognition of latent demand.

In the case of seizing capabilities, Teece (2012) notes that these capabilities include design of business models to satisfy customers, securing access to capital and the necessary human resources, and establishing strong relationships with suppliers, complementors, etc. He adds, also, that good inventive design is a necessary, but not sufficient condition for superior performance in this area.

In discussing transforming capabilities, Teece (2012) states that they are needed, mostly, when new opportunities emerge for the firm. However, he notes that they are needed, from time to time, to soften the rigidities that develop as a result of asset accumulation, standard operating procedures and insider misappropriation of rents. He emphasizes the need for the firm's assets to be aligned to achieve the best strategic 'fit'—between firm and ecosystem, between firm structure and strategy and between the firm's various assets.

Marketing capabilities refer to the firm's ability to develop and maintain lasting customer relationships (Moorman and Slotegraaf 1999). Fowler et al. (2000) suggest that if firms develop adequate marketing competencies, they are better able to understand and satisfy the current and future needs of their customers and reach new customers, and are able to assess their competitors and the competition more accurately. Thus, marketing-related competences are considered an important driver of superior performance (Day 1994). In addition, adequate marketing capabilities allow easier identification and selection of markets distribution channels, allowing the firm to position its products and prices relative to competitors (Kotler 2004).

Because marketing capabilities are not transferable, they are a source of sustained competitive advantage (Capron and Hulland 1999) and are imperfectly imitable (Bharadwaj et al. 1993) and non-substitutable (Moorman and Rust 1999). Many empirical studies find a direct link between market orientation and superior business performance.

Teamwork capability is regarded as a key variable in competitive advantage because it has an influence on socialization within the firm and affects the ability to imitate the complex interactions comprising teamwork (Nonaka 1991; Nonaka and Takeuchi 1995). Penrose (1959, p. 46) points out that an organizational team is 'something more than a collection of individuals; it is a collection of individuals who have had experience in working together, for only in this way can teamwork be developed' (original emphasis). When working together, team members learn to exchange ideas, challenge one another's views and make decisions collectively (Foss et al. 2008).

Barney (1995) notes that, due to the social complexity of the processes supporting team entrepreneurship (e.g., the processes feeding cognitive diversity and positive team dynamics), imitating the idiosyncratic creativity of a team can be difficult. Also, these team processes may be the most causally ambiguous source of heterogeneity, which allows the creation of sustained competitive advantage.

There is empirical evidence associating firm performance to teamwork capabilities. The reasons proposed are that it involves collective activity, positive synergies, complementary skills and individual and mutual responsibility (Robbins 1996). Senge et al. (1994, 1999) argue that firms that encourage cohesive teams, whose members act together to pursue a common goal, achieve higher performance. Moreover, firm employees who prefer to work in a team usually achieve greater job satisfaction and perform better in their jobs (Cummings 1981).

Network capability is another component of organizational capabilities and is considered important for attaining sustained competitive advantage. The main focus is on establishing network relationships with stakeholders (customers, suppliers, banks, etc.) that enable better and easier access to new resources, reduce transaction costs, provide information on customers, guarantee the quality and safety of raw materials and improve performance (Cao and Zhang 2011; Schiefer and Hartmann 2008; Ruben et al. 2006).

Several works find that network capabilities help firms to know their customers and other agents better (Day 2000; Lee et al. 2011). Networking helps to establish a good level of communication along the chain and this improves the flows of information, useful for marketing activities (Lee et al. 2011). Networking is considered not just as pure transaction but also as a variable that leverages information sharing and market knowledge creation for sustained competitive advantage (Cao and Zhang 2011). Establishing network relationships based upon trust and communication boosts innovation capability (Grunert et al. 2008; Wei and Wang 2011). Often, innovation does not depend on solitary R&D activities, but involves cooperation programmes, aimed at realizing inventions based on collaboration along the chain, and knowledge and expertise sharing and creation (Ruben et al. 2006).

In sum, it can be expected that organizational capabilities are a significant differentiating factor distinguishing high- and low-performing firms. More specifically, organizational capabilities in the form of corporate entrepreneurship, dynamic capabilities, marketing capabilities, teamwork orientation and ability to create adequate and sustainable business networks allow distinctions among firms that operate in undeveloped countries such as Kosovo.

3.4.4 Management Practices as Specific-Firm Capabilities

Many empirical studies recognize the role of management practices as crucial for generating higher rents (Penrose 1959; Barney 1991; Mahoney 1995). The fundamental argument is that management competences, represented by technical, human and conceptual skills, provide the foundations for sustained competitive advantage (Down 1999; Greenbank 2000; O'Dwyer and Ryan 2002; Kelliher and Henderson 2006). In the most recent decade, a stream of literature has emerged, based on an innovative survey methodology that investigates the relationship between management practices and firm performance (Bloom and Van Reenen 2007). Proponents of this relationship find compelling evidence that management quality and practices are significantly correlated to firm performance. The indicators used to measure the impact of management practices on firm performance include productivity, sales growth, assets growth, etc.

Supports of this managerial practices approach, embrace the fact that technology or capital has a strong influence on the different performance of firms. However, as Greenwald (2004) points out, the decision to apply new technology and other factors of production, in a systematic way, is primarily a management function. Greenwald argues that most operating efficiency improvements are attributable to incremental benefits derived from day-to-day management intervention rather than to dramatic technological innovations or capital investments.

A seminal article related to this approach is Bloom and Van Reenen (2007). These authors developed a new survey methodology to measure 18 key management practices, grounded in use of an interview-based evaluation tool and a one ('worst practice') to five ('best practice') scoring system. This methodology and the survey tool utilized enable them to explain statistically the correlation between management practices and firm performance and growth. The authors point out that there is no one management practice that explains the statistical correlation between management practice and performance. They discuss the average score for 18 types of management practices which are grouped into four areas: operations (3 practices); monitoring (5 practices); targets (5 practices); and incentives (5 practices). Their findings indicate that these practices have a direct impact on the performance of the observed firms and that, firms with superior management practices are associated to higher productivity, higher returns on equity and greater market capitalization.

The findings from a follow-up study, conducted by Bloom and Van Reenen in 2007, reinforce the earlier evidence. Their results confirm that business firms with superior management practices show higher and superior performance.

In a study of 6000 medium-sized manufacturing firms across Asia, Europe and North and South America, Bloom and Van Reenen (2010), again, find a robust impact of management practices on firm performance. They also found large differences in management practices across both firms and countries. These differences in management practices are correlated to firm-level productivity and other performance measures such as profitability and survival rates. They show that there are larger differences in management practices among firms in the same country than among firms across countries. They point out that the empirical results suggest that firm-specific factors and sector-specific factors are at least as important as the general business environment for shaping managerial performance. Management differences are correlated to competition, labour market flexibility, education and ownership structure, with dispersed ownership associated to better performance compared to state or family ownership (Bloom and Van Reenen 2010).

Bloom and Van Reenen (2010) examine the correlation between management practices and firm performance in terms of productivity, profitability, growth rates, survival rates and market value, and find that higher management scores are related strongly to better performance. Drawing on the three consecutive studies cited above, the authors identify 20 basic management practices patterns.

First, their empirical evidence shows that firms with 'better' management practices tend to show better performance, demonstrated in their higher productivity, faster growth, size and better survival rates. Second, they find that management practices differ and vary considerably across firms and countries. They show that most of the difference in a country's average management score is due to the size of the long tail of very badly managed firms. They find fewer very badly managed firms in the US compared to the numerous badly managed companies while in some developing countries, such as Brazil and India, where they identify a long tail. Third, they show that different countries favour different management styles. For instance, US firms score much higher than Swedish firms for incentives, but score less than Swedish firms for monitoring. Fourth, Bloom and Van Reenen (2010) show that strong product market competition appears to boost average management practices through the combined effect of eliminating the tail of badly managed firms and pushing incumbents to improve their practices. The fifth pattern is related to multinational structure; they found that, in general, multinational firms are well managed in all countries. This might be because firms impose headquarters management styles on their foreign subsidiaries. For instance, they show that US multinationals with operations in the UK offer better incentives for management, but have less efficient management practices than Swedish multinationals with UK subsidiaries. Sixth, it seems that firms that export (but do not produce overseas) are better managed than domestic non-exporters. However, these firms appear to be less well-managed than multinationals. Seven, family ownership has an effect: inherited family-owned firms and those that appoint a family member (especially the eldest son) as chief executive officer, are more badly managed on average. Eighth, government-owned firms tend to be extremely badly managed, while public listed and private equity firms tend to be well-managed. The ninth pattern shows that those firms with more intensive use of human capital, measured by the number of higher educated workers, tend to have better management practices. Finally, the tenth pattern shows that, at the country level, relatively lighter labour market regulation is associated to more productive use of incentives by management.

A question frequently raised in the management practice literature is which factors influence the adoption of better management practices. In this context, product market competition is seen as having a robust influence on management practice quality. The evidence shows that, in a context of less intense market competition, some low-productivity firms manage to survive (Syverson 2004; Bloom and Van Reenen 2010). Bloom et al. (2009a) provide similar evidence, demonstrating that tougher competition increases the quality of average management practices. Another influence on management practices is labour market regulation, which is linked to managers' ability to hire, fire, pay and promote employees. Strict labour market regulation is significantly negatively correlated to management scores for incentives, but not significantly correlated to management practices in other dimensions such as monitoring and targets (Bloom and Van Reenen 2010). Ownership and meritocratic selection of the CEO also induce differences in management practices. For instance, there is empirical evidence showing that family-owned and family-managed (internal CEO) firms tend to be less well-managed, while family-owned firms with a non-family CEO are regarded differently by shareholders (Bloom and Van Reenen 2010). Private equity firms tend to be well-managed and, in particular, compared to family-owned and government-owned firms (Bloom et al. 2009b). Other variables that influence the quality of management practices are multinational status and exporting status. The findings in the literature show that the ability to transfer good management practices abroad allows multinational firms to show better management practices (Burstein and Monge-Naranjo 2009). Also, firms that export show better management practices than those that do not (Helpman et al. 2004). Education is strongly correlated to management scores—in the case of both executives and managers and, also, workers. Bloom and Van Reenen (2010) argue that more highly educated managers and workers may find it easier to implement many management practices.

Most studies of managerial practices focus on developed and developing economies. Apart from a few studies that suggest that low levels of productivity in firms in the transition countries are due to the lack of appropriate skills (Estrin et al. 2009; Brown et al. 2006; Zelenyuk and Zheka 2006; Yudaeva et al. 2003), data on management practices on other than developed economies is almost non-existent. Using data from the European Bank for Reconstruction and Development (EBRD) Management, Organization and Innovation (MOI) survey, Bloom et al. (2011) investigated management practices in several less-developed countries and found some striking results. They found widespread variation in management practices—both within and across countries. For instance, there is a solid evidence suggesting that firms in Central Asian transition countries, such as Uzbekistan and Kazakhstan, often have extremely poor management practices. On average, the management of the firms in these countries is worse than developing countries such as Brazil, China and India. On the other hand, Bloom and co-authors found that the management practices in firms in some central European transition countries, such as Poland and Lithuania, and are fairly similar to those in the UK, France and Germany. They found, also, that, in transition countries, good management is linked strongly to better firm performance and, based on this finding, suggest that poor management practices may be impeding the development of Central Asian transition countries. When they examined the factors affecting management quality, they found that the same factors matter in both transition and non-transition countries. They point out that factors such as stronger product market competition, higher levels of multinational ownership and higher levels of employee education are all strongly correlated to better management. Similar to the evidence for developed countries, Bloom et al. (2011) find that higher levels of private ownership are correlated strongly to better management and suggest that being exposed to both domestic and foreign competition, privatization of state-owned and socially owned firms and increased workforce education should promote better management and, ultimately, higher national productivity.

There are some interesting outcomes for individual countries, related to management practices. For instance, Friebel and Schweiger (2012) investigated whether management quality explains firm performance in Russia. Controlling for type of firm ownership, they investigated the factors that influence management quality in Russian regions, that is, the Far East region and the rest of Russia. Their study found no strong positive correlations between management practice quality and firm performance for the case of manufacturing firms in Russia, they found weak evidence that management practices affect the performance of manufacturing firms in the Far East, but not in the rest of Russia.

3.5 Social Conditions and Innovation

The next body of work includes recent research and findings related to the link between external/internal factors and innovation activities in the context of SMEs. The evidence suggests that, in the case of SMEs, there is a strong positive relationship between exporting and innovation activity (Golovko and Valentini 2011). SMEs with innovation capabilities are more likely to export and more likely to grow based on exporting, compared to non-innovating firms (Love and Roper 2013; Melkas and Pekkarinen 2016; Shapira et al. 2011). In addition, the findings from this literature indicate that exporting SMEs are three times more likely to introduce products or services that are new to their sector, than firms with only a domestic orientation (European Commission 2010).

Various studies discuss the strengths and weaknesses of small firms relative to larger ones, in terms of innovation and exporting. Their findings suggest that smaller firms are more able to make fast decisions, take risks and respond flexibly to new market opportunities, whereas larger firms benefit from advantages linked to scale and availability of specialist resources (Love and Roper 2013; Murphree et al. 2016). There is evidence, also, that the relative strengths of large businesses are predominantly material, that is, they are related to economies of scale and scope, financial and technological resources, etc. while small firms reap the benefits of behavioural strengths related, for example, to entrepreneurial dynamism, flexibility, efficiency, proximity to the market and motivation (Vossen 1998).

To investigate the internal enablers of firm innovation/exporting, researchers use a range of variables such as workforce skills, managerial and marketing skills, education and workforce diversity, capital investment, business strategy, internal finance, R&D, ownership, etc. There is a broad agreement that firms require distinct skills to become successful innovators and exporters (Barney 1991; Leiponen 2005; Freel 2005; Bloom and Van Reenen 2007; Herrmann and Peine 2011). The empirical literature emphasizes the importance for innovation, also, of the national 'skills ecosystem' and related legal, vocational education and industrial relations systems (Cooney 2010). It has been suggested that partnering and collaborative working in the context of innovation provide access to external skills and help to overcome internal skills shortages (Love and Roper 2013). Some studies find a positive relationship between innovation and workforce education differences (Østergaard et al. 2011); others investigate the relationship between ownership structure and the innovation process (Love et al. 2009).

Some research finds a positive link between fixed capital investment and innovation. For example, Pellegrino et al. (2009) show that small firms' machinery and equipment purchases are important for innovative outputs. A number of studies investigate the role of internal financing on innovation activities and find that internal funding for innovation is more important for small rather than larger companies, which is likely a reflection of the stronger constraints on access to external finance experienced by small firms (Ughetto 2008). Several works focus on the effect of business strategy on innovation, and the role of ownership (e.g., family ownership) on innovation activities. Current findings related to the link between business strategies and innovation include conflicting theoretical predictions, persisting knowledge gaps and theoretical inconsistencies (Keupp et al. 2012). Some empirical works cast doubt on the existence of a positive link between innovation and family ownership; there is some evidence that family ownership is related positively to the firm's ability to recognize innovation opportunities and to innovate (Bresciani et al. 2013; Lichtenthaler and Muethel 2012; Classen et al. 2012).

In the context of the effect of external factors/enablers on firm innovation capabilities, they seem to fall into two main categories. First category is related to external factors that enhance or augment the firm's knowledge base and, hence, provide a basis for innovation. The second category is related to resource augmenting factors that can help the firm to overcome internal resources constraints (Kanter 2000; Hausmann et al. 2008; Love and Roper 2013; Rodríguez et al. 2014). There is some fairly recent research that distinguishes three main channels that allow the firm to obtain external knowledge that can contribute to its innovation activity. These three channels include local knowledge or information flows mediated by social contacts or labour market linkages; formal partnering with other organizations, aimed at accessing technical knowledge or gaining market understanding; and knowledge gained through exporting activity (Freeman et al. 2012; He and Wong 2012; Gust-Bardon 2014). There is some specific evidence explaining how certain external linkages have a greater impact on firm's innovation and exporting, which emphasizes, in particular, the link between the firm's clients and suppliers. For example, a study involving 1500 European SMEs conducted by Brunswicker and Vanhaverbeke (2011) found that customers can be a valuable source of innovation inputs. Collaborative relationships between firms and other research organizations can also be useful for reducing the resource constraints of small firms. In this context, central government's facilitating role through the provision of public sector grants or loans is emphasized (Hewitt-Dundas and Roper 2009).

3.6 Main Findings and Conclusions

The aim of this literature review was threefold: to examine the current status of the research related to firm growth; to identify gaps in this literature; and to see where the theory on firm dynamics needs augmenting.

Drawing on above, the findings from this literature can be summarized as follows:

- the empirical evidence on firm dynamics strongly supports the view that the formation of new firms and the decline of unproductive ones are fundamental to overall economic dynamics. The evidence suggests significant correlations between the rate of firm turnover and incumbents' productivity growth, across industries and countries, and between the net contribution to productivity of new entrants and incumbents. Based on the stylized facts, the literature suggests that growth emerges, basically, from incumbent firms pressurized by new entrants, which latter do not necessarily grow;
- firm-specific variables, such as size, age, legal structure and adaptability to new technology, explain differences in firm survival. The literature suggests, also, that industry specifics, generally represented by variables such as stage of growth of the specific industry, average firm

size in the industry and type of industry in which the firm operates, play a crucial role in firm survival. Finally, the empirical evidence highlights that the location/region in which the firm operates is likely to be related to its survival. Several studies show that macroeconomic factors and factors related to internal characteristics (organizational capabilities, managerial practices) have a significant impact on firm survival;

- various researchers have suggested stylized facts to enable a theorizing and mapping agenda for empirical work. One of the less controversial stylized facts, based mostly on empirical research, states that large numbers of firms enter and exit the market annually and that most are involved in search rather than competing against rivals in the market (Bartelsman et al. 2004). The second stylized fact states that firm entry is more likely to affect smaller firm-size classes. This is due, primarily, to the fact that firms are uncertain about future profitability and, therefore, prefer to enter on a relatively small scale to minimize potential exit costs. A widely accepted stylized fact states that small firms grow faster than large firms and that exit rates decline with size (Bartelsman et al. 2004, 2009);
- the literature argues that the model of creative destruction is important for promoting productivity growth, which occurs through a process of restructuring and upgrading by incumbents, combined with the entry of new firms and exit of obsolete units. The creative destruction model promotes aggregate productivity and market contestability, primarily by motivating incumbents to employ productivity-enhancing strategies. The empirical evidence shows that growth is driven, foremost, by incumbents under pressure from the creative destruction process and that the effects of new entries are, de facto, secondary (World Bank 2008);
- despite the growing empirical evidence related to the impact of firm dynamics on productivity growth, this body of work has some limitations. First, although there is evidence of a link between firm dynamics and firm growth in developed countries, in the case of undeveloped countries, the evidence is insufficient (Caves 1998; Klapper and Richmond 2009). Second, there are few findings on the impact of business constraints on productivity growth, and the

literature on the relative productivity of entrants and the learning and selection processes that affect post-entry productivity dynamics is scant (Brown and Earle 2008). Third, there have been attempts to study the relative productivity of entrants, and the learning and selection processes that affect post-entry productivity dynamics. However, there are problems related to the accurate measurement of entry and post-entry dynamics in the data, and time series, usually, are short and contain gaps, which mean that cohorts of entrants are not followed over time (Brown and Earle 2008).

It is clear that firm dynamics-related topics have received considerable attention. Most studies are interested in finding evidence to explain the impact of firm dynamics on firm productivity growth and the majority focus on developed economies. The amount of similar evidence for developing countries is much smaller. Drawing on the findings from the literature reviewed, the aim is to identify further evidence on the pattern of firm dynamics in developing economy settings, to contribute to the firm dynamics literature.

With regard to the literature on business environment factors, it is apparent that the findings vary and, often, are contradictory, due, perhaps, to the questions addressed by researchers or the different methodologies used. Nevertheless, studies using the same approach and methodology also provide different results. Research based on regressions tends to test hypotheses related to the importance of a particular set of institutions, against the null hypotheses that no institutions are important, rather than against predictions about the importance of different institutions (Carlin and Seabright 2007). In this sense, in the context of relative importance, surveys based on managers' assessments are more informative. Some authors, such as Carlin and Seabright (2007), propose to treat the findings derived from regressions as preliminary and complementary rather than as substitutes or as definitive and contradictory. According to Carlin and Seabright, regression methodologies establish that institutions matter, but not how, and they point out that conjectures about causal channels need to be defined. This is akin to saying that 'medical studies have established that diet is important for health, but we have no idea which is the best diet' (Carlin and Seabright 2007, p. 27).

With the aim of identifying factors that constrain firm growth, researchers have identified a range of culprits, using a range of methodologies. Some scholars insist that researchers should avoid acting as categorical advocates for specific approaches to growth (Rodrik 2010). They should, instead, act as diagnosticians and adapt approaches and methodologies that are not substitutes, but rather complement each other. Above all, this research suggests use of models that enable navigation through varying contexts and realities. The growth diagnostics approach claims to offer a more systematic process to contextualize the research, which, in turn, leads to the identification of binding constraints to growth in a specific economic setting. The growth diagnostics approach is based on a simple theory combined with suggestive empirics (Rodrik 2010). In the following sections, we analyse the main elements of the growth diagnostics approach, including its limitations, and propose a theoretical framework to analyse the impact of business environment factors on firm growth.

Most research studies that employ a resource-based view organizing framework to study internal firm resources that enable superior firm performance, focus on developed economies. There is little evidence on the impact of inputs, organizational capabilities and management practices on firm growth in less-developed countries. This might be expected since the capabilities approach is aimed at understanding the cause of firm heterogeneity. It is assumed that, almost by definition, firms in less-developed economies will be less differentiated since they use standard technologies and lack unique organizational and technological capabilities. By extending this framework to the context of less-developed economies, this book tries to provide new empirical evidence to show that high performance is not just a function of resources such as equipment. Firm growth is a function of both resources, such as technology, and organizational capabilities and managerial practices, which play important roles in achievement of good performance.

In summary, despite the fact that, over the last decades, advances have been made in our understanding of the internal and external enablers of and/or constraints to firm growth and innovation, the evidence is inconsistent or limited in some areas. For instance, the majority of papers focus on developed countries and large firms. There is little consensus about what needs to be done and which approaches to employ to obtain a better understanding of the dynamic interactions between the external and internal factors influencing firm growth and innovation in developing countries and low-income countries, in particular, as well as SMEs. Firms—especially SMEs—are complex entities, which do not grow and innovate automatically once external constraints are removed and internal capabilities improved, as growth diagnostics and resource-based theory and managerial practice approaches might suggest. None of these theories considers firm innovation and growth capabilities in a dynamic way. There would seem to be a need for a perspective that integrates both of these aspects in a single theoretical framework, which perhaps would enable a better understanding of the dynamic interaction between the organizational conditions and institutional environments in which firms operate.

References

Acemoglu, D., Johnson, S., & Robinson, J. A. (2001). The colonial origins of comparative development: An empirical investigation. *American Economic Review, 91*(5), 1369–1401.

Aghion, P., Akcigit, U., & Howitt, P. (2014). What do we learn from Schumpeterian growth theory? In *Handbook of economic growth* (1st ed., Vol. 2, Chapter 1, pp. 515–563). Amsterdam: Elsevier.

Aghion, P., Howitt, P., & Mayer-Foulkes, D. (2005). The effect of financial development on convergence: Theory and evidence. *Quarterly Journal of Economics, 120*(1), 173–222.

Ahn, S. (2001). *Firm dynamics and productivity growth: A review of micro evidence from OECD countries* (OECD Economics Department Working Paper 297). Paris: OECD.

Aidis, R., & Mickiewicz, T. (2006). Entrepreneurs, expectations and business expansion: Lessons from Lithuania. *Europe-Asia Studies, 58*, 855–880.

Aidt, T. (2009). Corruption, institutions, and economic growth. *Oxford Review of Economic Policy, 25*(2), 271–291.

Aidt, T. (2011). Corruption and sustainable development. In S. Rose-Ackerman & T. Søreide (Eds.), *International handbook on the economics of corruption* (Vol. 2). Cheltenham, UK: Edward.

Arbia, G., Cella, P., Espa, G., & Giuliani, D. (2015). A micro spatial analysis of firm demography: The case of food stores in the area of Trento (Italy). *Empirical Economics, 48*(3), 923–937.

Audretsch, D. B., & Mahmood, T. (1994). The rate of hazard confronting new firms and plants in US manufacturing. *Review of Industrial Organization, 9*, 41–56.

Audretsch, D. B., Houweling, P., & Thurik, A. R. (2000). Firm survival in the Netherlands. *Review of Industrial Organization, 16*, 1–11.

Ayyagari, M., Demirgüç-Kunt, A., & Maksimovic, V. (2006). *How important are financing constraints? The role of finance in the business environment* (World Bank Policy Research Working Paper, WPS3820).

Baldwin, J., Bian, L., Dupuy, R., & Galletly, G. (2000). *Failure rates of new Canadian firms: New perspectives on entry and exit.* Ottawa: Statistics Canada.

Banerjee, A. V., & Duflo, E. (2007). The economic lives of the poor. *Journal of Economic Perspectives, 21*(1), 141–167.

Bardhan, P. (1997). Corruption and development: A review of issues. *Journal of Economic Literature, 35*, 1320–1346.

Bardhan, P. (2005). *Scarcity, conflicts, and cooperation: Essays in political and institutional economics of development.* Cambridge: MIT Press.

Barney, J. B. (1991). Firm resources and sustained competitive advantage. *Journal of Management, 17*, 99–120.

Barney, J. B. (1995). Looking inside for competitive advantage. *Academy of Management Executive, 9*(4), 49–61.

Barney, J. B., Ketchen, D. J., & Wright, M. (2011). The future of resource-based theory: Revitalization or decline. *Journal of Management, 37*(5), 1299–1315.

Barr, H., Koppel, I., Reeves, S., Hammick, M., & Freeth, D. (2005). *Effective inter-professional education: Assumption, argument and evidence.* London: Blackwell.

Bartelsman, E., Haltiwanger, J., & Scarpetta, S. (2004). *Microeconomic evidence of creative destruction in industrial and developing countries* (The World Bank Policy Research Working Paper Series 3464).

Bartelsman, E., Haltiwanger, J., & Scarpetta, S. (2009). Measuring and analyzing cross-country differences in firm dynamics. In T. Dunne, J. B. Jensen, & M. J. Roberts (Eds.), *Producer dynamics.* Chicago, IL: University of Chicago Press for the NBER.

Bartlett, W., & Bukvič, V. (2002). What are the main barriers to SME growth and development in South-East Europe. In W. Bartlett, M. Bateman, & M. Vehovec (Eds.), *Small enterprise development in South-East Europe: Policies for sustainable growth* (pp. 17–38). Boston: Kluwer.

Baumol, W. J. (1990). Entrepreneurship: Productive, unproductive and destructive. *Journal of Political Economy, 98*, 893–921.

Baumol, W. J. (1993). Formal entrepreneurship theory in economics: Existence and bounds. *Journal of Business Venturing, 3,* 197–210.

Baysinger, B. D., & Hoskisson, R. E. (1989). Diversification strategy and R&D intensity in large multi-product firms. *Academy of Management Journal, 32,* 310–332.

Berglund, E., & Brännäs, K. (1996). Entry and exit of plants: A study based on Swedish panel count data for municipalities. In *Yearbook of the Finnish statistical society 1995* (pp. 95–111). Helsinki: Springer.

Berglund, E., & Brännäs, K. (2001). Plants' entry and exit in Swedish municipalities. *The Annals of Regional Studies, 35,* 431–448.

Berner, E., Gomez, G., & Knorringa, P. (2008). *Helping a large number of people becoming a little less poor: The logic of survival entrepreneurs.* Helsinki, Finland: UNU-WIDER Workshop on Entrepreneurship and Economic Development.

Bevan, A., & Estrin, S. (2004). The determinants of foreign direct investment into European transition economies. *Journal of Comparative Economics, 32*(4), 775–787.

Bharadwaj, S. G., Varadarajan, R. P., & Fahy, J. (1993). Sustainable competitive advantage in service industries: A conceptual model and research propositions. *Journal of Marketing, 57*(10), 83–99.

Birkinshaw, J. (2003). The paradox of corporate entrepreneurship. *Strategy and Business, 30,* 46–57.

Bishop, J. H. (1991). *The impact of previous training in schools and on job on productivity, require OJT, and turnover of new hires* (Unpublished manuscript). Centre for Advanced Human Resource Studies, Cornell University (cited in Cappelli and Singh, 1992).

Bloom, N., & Van Reenen, J. (2007). Measuring and explaining management practices across firms and countries. *Quarterly Journal of Economics, 122*(4), 1351–1408.

Bloom, N., & Van Reenen, J. (2010). Why do management practices differ across firms and countries? *Journal of Economic Perspectives, 24*(1), 203–224.

Bloom, N., Raffaella, S., & Van Reenen, J. (2009a). *The organization of firms across countries* (National Bureau of Economic Research Working Paper Series No. 15129). Retrieved from http://www.nber.org/papers/w15129.pdf.

Bloom, N., Sadun, R., & Van Reenen, J. (2009b). Do private equity-owned firms have better management practices? In A. Gurung & J. Lerner (Eds.), *The global economic impact of private equity report 2009* (pp. 1–23). Geneva, Switzerland: World Economic Forum. Available from http://www.weforum.org/pdf/cgi/pe/Full_Report2.pdf.

Bloom, N., Schweiger, H., & Van Reenen, J. (2011). *The land that lean manufacturing forgot? Management practices in transition countries* (National Bureau of Economic Research Working Paper Series No. 17231).

Bosma, N. S., Jones, K., Autio, E., & Levie, J. (2008). *Global entrepreneurship monitor 2007 executive report.* London: Global Entrepreneurship Research Association.

Box, T. M., White, M. A., & Barr, S. H. (1993). A contingency model of new manufacturing firm performance. *Entrepreneurship Theory and Practice, 18*(2), 31–45.

Bresciani, S., Thrassou, A., & Vrontis, D. (2013). Change through innovation in family businesses: Evidence from an Italian sample. *World Review of Entrepreneurship, Management and Sustainable Development, 9*(2), 195–215.

Brown, J. D., & Earle, J. S. (2008). *Understanding the contributions of reallocation to productivity growth: Lessons from a comparative firm-level analysis* (Upjohn Institute Staff Working Paper, No. 08-141).

Brown, J., Earle, S., & Telegdy, A. (2006). The productivity effects of privatization: Longitudinal estimates from Hungary, Romania, Russia, and Ukraine. *Journal of Political Economy, 114*(1), 61–99.

Brüderl, J., & Schussler, R. (1990). Organizational mortality: The liabilities of newness and adolescence. *Administrative Science Quarterly, 35,* 530–547.

Brüderl, J., Preisendorfer, P., & Ziegler, R. (1992). Survival chances of newly founded business organizations. *American Sociological Review, 57*(2), 227–242.

Brunswicker, S., & Vanhaverbeke, W. (2011). Beyond open innovation in large enterprises: How do small and medium-sized enterprises (SMEs) open up to external innovation sources? https://papers.ssrn.com/sol3/papers.cfm?abstract_id=1925185.

Brush, C. G., & Hisrish, R. D. (1991). Antecedent influences on women-owned businesses. *Journal of Management Psychology, 6*(2), 9–16.

Burstein, A., & Monge-Naranjo, A. (2009). Foreign know-how, firm control, and the income of developing countries. *Quarterly Journal of Economics, 124*(1), 149–195.

Caballero, R. (2006). *The macroeconomics of specificity and restructuring.* Cambridge: The MIT Press.

Calderón, C., & Servén, L. (2004). *The effects of infrastructure development on growth and income distribution* (Working Papers No. 270). Central Bank of Chile.

Cao, M., & Zhang, Q. (2011). Supply chain collaboration: Impact on collaborative advantage and firm performance. *Journal of Operations Management, 29*(3), 163–180.

Capron, L., & Hulland, J. (1999). Redeployment of brands, sales forces, and general marketing management expertise following horizontal acquisitions: A resource-based view. *Journal of Marketing, 63*(2), 41–54.

Carlin, W., & Seabright, P. (2007). *Bring me sunshine: Which parts of the business climate should public policy try to fix?* (Unpublished manuscript). Available at http://www.worldbank.org.

Carlin, W., Schaffer, M., & Seabright, P. (2006). *Where are the real bottlenecks? A Lagrangian approach to identifying constraints on growth from subjective survey data* (CEPR Discussion Paper 5719).

Carter, N. M., William, B., Gatwoood, E. J., & Shaver, K. G. (2003). The career reasons of nascent entrepreneurs. *Journal of Business Venturing, 18*(1), 13–39.

Castanias, R. P., & Helfat, C. E. (1991). Managerial resources and rents. *Journal of Management, 17*(1), 155–177.

Caves, R. E. (1998). Industrial organization and new findings on the turnover and mobility of firms. *Journal of Economic Literature, 36*(4), 1947–1982.

Classen, N., Van Gils, A., Bammens, Y., & Carree, M. (2012). Accessing resources from innovation partners: The search breadth of family SMEs. *Journal of Small Business Management, 50*(2), 191–215.

Coff, R., & Kryscynski, D. (2011). Drilling for microfoundations of human capital-based competitive advantage. *Journal of Management, 37*(5), 1429–1443.

Commander, S., & Svejnar, J. (2007). *Do institutions, ownership, exporting and competition explain firm performance. Evidence from 26 transition countries* (Discussion Paper 2637). Institute for the Study of Labour (IZA).

Cooney, R. (2010). Exploring skill ecosystems in the Australian meat processing industry: Unions, employers and institutional change. *Economic and Labour Relations Review, 21*(2), 121–138.

Cooper, A. C. (1981). Strategic management: New ventures and business performance. *Long Range Planning, 14*(5), 39–45.

Covin, J. G., & Slevin, D. P. (1988). The influence of organization structure on the utility of an entrepreneurial top management style. *Journal of Management Studies, 25,* 217–234.

Cummings, T. G. (1981). Self-regulating work groups: A sociotechnical synthesis. *Academy of Management Review, 3*(3), 625–634.

Davidsson, P., & Honig, B. (2003). The role of social and human capital among nascent entrepreneurs. *Journal of Business Venturing, 18,* 301–331.

Day, G. S. (1994). The capabilities of market driven organizations. *Journal of Marketing, 58,* 37–52.

Day, D. V. (2000). Leadership development: A review in context. *Leadership Quarterly, 11,* 581–613.

De Soto, H. (1989). *The other path: The invisible revolution in the Third World.* New York: Harper Row.

De Soto, H. (2000). *The mystery of capital: Why capitalism triumphs in the West and fails everywhere else.* New York: Harper & Row.

Dierickx, I., & Cool, K. (1989). Asset stock accumulation and sustainability of competitive advantage. *Management Science, 35*(12), 1504–1511.

Djankov, S., La Porta, R., Lopez-de-Silanes, F., & Shleifer, A. (2003). Courts. *Quarterly Journal of Economics, 118,* 453–518.

Djankov, S., La Porta, R., Lopez-de-Silanes, F., & Shleifer, A. (2006). *The law and economics of self-dealing* (Working paper). World Bank.

Dollar, D., Hallward-Driemeier, M., & Mengistae, T. (2005). Investment climate and firm performance in developing economies. *Economic Development and Cultural Change, 54,* 1–31.

Down, S. (1999). Owner-manager learning in small firms. *Journal of Small Business and Enterprise Development, 6*(3), 267–280.

Drucker, P. F. (1993). *Postcapitalist society.* New York: HarperCollins Publishers.

Dunne, T., Roberts, M., & Samuelson, L. (1988). Patterns of firm entry and exit in US manufacturing industries. *Journal of Economics, 19*(4), 495–515.

Dunne, T., Klimek, S., & Roberts, M. J. (2005). Exit from regional manufacturing markets: The role of entrant experience. *International Journal of Industrial Organization, 23,* 399–421.

Eisenhardt, K. M., & Martin, J. A. (2000). Dynamic capabilities: What are they? *Strategic Management Journal, 21*(10–11), 1105–1121. Special Issue.

Ericson, R., & Pakes, A. (1989). *An alternative theory of firm and industry dynamics* (Discussion Paper No. 445). New York: Columbia University.

Ericson, R., & Pakes, A. (1995). Markov-perfect industry dynamics: A framework for empirical work. *The Review of Economic Studies, 62*(1), 53–82.

Estrin, S., Hanousek, J., Kočenda, E., & Svejnar, J. (2009). Effects of privatization and ownership in transition economies. *Journal of Economic Literature, 47*(3), 699–728.

European Commission (EC). (2010). *Internationalisation of European SMEs.* Directorate-General for Enterprise and Industry, *Brussels* [Online]. http://www.ec.europa.eu/enterprise/policies/sme/market-access/files/internationalisation_of_european_smes_final_en.pdf. Accessed 12 July 2012.

Feldman, D. C., & Bolino, M. C. (2000). Career patterns of the self-employed: Career motivations and career outcomes. *Journal of Small Business Management, 38*(3), 53–67.

Filatotchev, I., & Mickiewicz, T. (2006). Private benefits of control and debt financing. In T. Mickiewicz (Ed.), *Corporate governance and finance in Poland and Russia* (pp. 159–176). Houndmills: Palgrave Macmillan.

Foss, N. J., Klein, P. G., Kor, Y. Y., & Mahoney, J. T. (2008). Entrepreneurship, subjectivism, and the resource based view: Toward a new synthesis. *Strategic Entrepreneurship Journal, 2,* 73–94.

Foster, L., Haltiwanger, J., & Krizan C. J. (2002). *The link between aggregate and micro productivity growth: Evidence from retail trade* (NBER Working Paper).

Fotopoulos, G., & Louri, H. (2000). Location and survival of new entry. *Small Business Economics, 14*(4), 311–321.

Fowler, S. W., Wilcox King, A., Marsh, S. W., & Victor, B. (2000). Beyond products: New strategic imperatives for developing competencies in dynamic environments. *Journal of Engineering and Technology Management, 17*(3–4), 357–377.

Freel, M. S. (2005). Patterns of innovation and skills in small firms. *Technovation, 25*(4), 123–134.

Freeman, J., Styles, C., & Lawley, M. (2012). Does firm location make a difference to the export performance of SMEs? *International Marketing Review, 29*(1), 88–113.

Friebel, G., & Schweiger, H. (2012). *Management quality, firm performance, and market pressure in Russia* (European Bank for Reconstruction and Development Working Papers, 144), 1–29.

Geroski, P. (1995). What do we know about entry? *International Journal of Industrial Organization, 13,* 421–440.

Geroski, P. A., Mata, J., & Portugal, P. (2012). Founding conditions and the survival of new firms. *Strategic Management Journal, 31*(5), 510–529.

Giavazzi, F., & Tabellini, G. (2004). *Economic and political liberalizations* (NBER Working Paper No. 10657).

Glaeser, E. L., LaPorta, R., Lopez-de-Silanes, F., & Shleifer, A. (2004). Do institutions cause growth? *Journal of Economic Growth, 9*(3), 271–303.

Golovko, E., & Valentini, G. (2011). Exploring the complementarity between innovation and export for SMEs' growth. *Journal of International Business Studies, 42*(3), 362–380.

Gort, M., & Klepper, S. (1982). Time paths in the diffusion of product innovations. *Economics Journal, 92*(3), 153–158.

Grant, R. M. (1991). The resource-based theory of competitive advantage: Implications for strategy formulation. *California Management Review, 33*(3), 114–135.

Grant, R. M. (1996). Toward a knowledge-based theory of the firm. *Strategic Management Journal, 17,* 109–122.

Grant, R. M. (2002). *Contemporary strategy analysis: Concepts, techniques, applications* (4th ed.). Malden, MA: Blackwell.

Greenbank, P. (2000). Training micro-business owner-managers: A challenge to current approaches. *Journal of European Industrial Training, 24*(7), 403.

Greenwald, B. (2004). The good life: How managers made the modern world. *Hermes*. Retrieved from 18 March 2008, http://www2.gsb.columbia.edu/hermes/winter2004/article_greenwald.cfm.

Griffith, R., Redding, S., & Van Reenen, J. (2004). Mapping the two faces of R&D: Productivity growth in a panel of OECD industries. *Review of Economics and Statistics, 86*(4), 883–895.

Grunert, K. G., Jensen, B. B., Sonne, A. M., Brunsø, K., Byrne, D. V., Clausen, C., et al. (2008). User-oriented innovation in the food sector: Relevant streams of research and an agenda or future work. *Trends in Food Science and Technology, 19*, 590–602.

Gust-Bardon, N. I. (2014). Regional development in the context of an innovation processes. *International Journal of Innovation and Regional Development, 5*(4/5), 349–366.

Harris, R., & Trainor, M. (1995). Innovations and R&D in Northern Ireland manufacturing: A Schumpeterian approach. *Regional Studies, 29*(7), 593–604.

Hashi, I., & Stojcic, N. (2010). The impact of innovation activities on firm performance using a multi-stage model: Evidence from the Community Innovation Survey 4. *Research Policy, 42*(4), 353–366.

Hausmann, R., Klinger, B., & Wagner, R. (2008). *Doing growth diagnostics in practice: A mindbook* (Harvard University Centre for International Development Working Paper 177).

He, Z. L., & Wong, P. K. (2012). Reaching out and reaching within: A study of the relationship between innovation collaboration and innovation performance. *Industry and Innovation, 19*(7), 539–561.

Helfat, C. E. (1994). Firm specificity in corporate applied R&D. *Organization Science, 5*(2), 173–184.

Helfat, C. E., & Lieberman, M. B. (2002). The birth of capabilities: Market entry and the importance of pre-history. *Industrial and Corporate Change, 11*(4), 725–760.

Helfat, C., Finkelstein, S., Mitchell, W., Peteraf, M., Singh, H., Teece, D., & Winter, S. (2007). *Dynamic capabilities: Understanding strategic change in organisations*. Malden: Blackwell Publishing.

Helpman, E., Marc, J., & Stephen, R. (2004). Export versus FDI with heterogeneous firms. *American Economic Review, 94*(1), 300–316.

Herrmann, A. M., & Peine, A. (2011). When 'national innovation system' meet 'varieties of capitalism' arguments on labour qualifications: On the skill types and scientific knowledge needed for radical and incremental product innovations. *Research Policy, 40*(5), 687–701.

Hewitt-Dundas, N., & Roper, S. (2009). Output additionality of public support for innovation: Evidence for Irish manufacturing plants. *European Planning Studies, 18*(1), 107–122.

Hitt, M. A., & Ireland, R. D. (1985). Corporate distinctive competence, strategy, industry and performance. *Strategic Management Journal, 6*(3), 273–293.

Hitt, M. A., Bierman, L., Shimizu, K., & Kochhar, R. (2001). Direct and moderating effects of human capital on strategy and performance in professional service firms: A resource-based perspective. *Academy of Management Journal, 44,* 13–28.

Holmes, P., Stone, I., & Braidford, P. (2000). New firm survival: An analysis of UK firms using hazard function. In *Proceedings: The Royal Economic Society 2000 Conference*. St Andrews, Scotland: University of St Andrews.

Hoxha, D. (2009). The performance of micro firms in Kosova: Size, age and educational implications. *International Journal of Globalisation and Small Business, 3*(1). https://doi.org/10.1504/ijgsb.2009.021568.

Johnson, S., Kaufmann, D., McMillan, J., & Woodruff, C. (2000). Why do firms hide? Bribes and unofficial activity after communism. *Journal of Public Economics, 76*(3), 495–520.

Jovanovic, B. (1982). Selection and the evolution of industry. *Econometrica, 50*(3), 649–670.

Jovanovic, B., & MacDonald, G. (1994). The life cycle of a competitive industry. *Journal of Political Economy, 102*(2), 322–347.

Kanter, R. M. (2000). When a thousand flowers bloom: Structural, collective, and social conditions for innovation in organizations. In B. Staw & R. Sutton (Eds.), *Research in organizational behavior* (Vol. 22). Amsterdam, The Netherlands: Elsevier Science.

Kaufmann, D., Aart, K., & Mastruzzi, M. (2007). *Governance matters VI: Aggregate and individual governance indicators for 1996–2006* (World Bank Policy Research Working Paper No. 4280). Washington, DC.

Kelliher, F., & Henderson, J. B. (2006). A learning framework for the small business environment. *Journal of European Industrial Training, 30*(7), 512–528.

Keupp, M. M., Palmié, M., & Gassmann, O. (2012). The strategic management of innovation: A systematic review and paths for future research. *International Journal of Management Reviews, 14*(4), 367–390.

Klapper, L., & Richmond, C. (2009) *Patterns of business creation, survival, and growth: Evidence from a developing country.* Development Research Group, World Bank, Washington, DC and Anderson School of Management, University of California, Los Angeles.

Klapper, L., Laeven, L., & Rajan, R. (2004). *Business environment and firm entry: Evidence from international data* (Working Paper No. 10380). Cambridge, MA: NBER.

Klapper, L., Amit, R., Guillén, M. F., & Quesada, J. M. (2008). *Entrepreneurship and firm formation across countries* (The World Bank Policy Research Working Paper 4313).

Klepper, S. (2001). Employee start-ups in high-tech industries. *Industrial and Corporate Change, 10*(3), 639–674.

Klepper, S., & Simons K. L. (1993). *Technological change and industry shakeouts.* Carnegie Mellon University (mimeo).

Knight, G. A. (1997). Cross-cultural reliability and validity of a scale to measure firm entrepreneurial orientation. *Journal of Business Venturing, 12*(3), 213–225.

Koch, M. J., & McGrath, R. G. (1996). Improving labour productivity: Human resource management policies do matter. *Strategic Management Journal, 17,* 335–354.

Kogut, B., & Zander, U. (1996). What firms do? Coordination, identify, and learning. *Organization Science, 7,* 502–518.

Kotler, A. (2004). *Principles of marketing.* Hoboken, NJ: Pearson Education.

Krasniqi, B. (2007). Barriers to entrepreneurship and SME growth in transition: Case of Kosova. *Journal of Developmental Entrepreneurship, 12*(1), 71–94.

Krasniqi, B. (2012). Building an expanded small firm growth model in a transitional economy: Evidence on fast growing firms. *Journal of East West Business, 18*(3), 231–273.

Kreiser, P. M., Marino, L. D., & Weaver, K. M. (2002). Assessing the psychometric properties of the entrepreneurial orientation scale: A multi-country analysis. *Entrepreneurship Theory and Practice, 26,* 71–94.

Kutllovci, E., Shala, V., & Troni, B. (2012). *Business strategy, the key determinants of SME growth in Kosovo* [Data file]. Retrieved 15 June 2013, from the University of Prishtina site www.managementjournal.info.
Lambson, V. (1991). Industry evolution with sunk costs and uncertain market conditions. *International Journal of Industrial Organization, 9*(2), 171–196.
Lee, C., Lee, K., & Pennings, J. M. (2001). Internal capabilities, external networks, and performance: A study on technology-based ventures. *Strategic Management Journal, 22,* 615–640.
Lee, R. P., Naylor, G., & Chen, Q. (2011). Linking customer resources to firm success: The role of marketing program implementation. *Journal of Business Research, 64,* 394–400.
Leiblein, M. J. (2011). What do resource and capability theories propose? *Journal of Management, 37*(4), 909–932.
Leiponen, A. (2005). Skills and innovation. *International Journal of Industrial Organization, 23*(5/6), 303–323.
Lewis, E. G. (2005, May). *Immigration, skill mix, and the choice of technique* (Federal Reserve Bank of Philadelphia Working Paper No. 05-8).
Li, A., & Guisinger, P. (1991) Comparative business failures of foreign-controlled firms in the United States. *Journal of International Business Studies, 22*(2), 209–224.
Li, S., & Wu, J. (2010). Why some countries thrive despite corruption: The role of trust in the corruption-efficiency relationship. *Review of International Political Economy, 17*(1), 129–154.
Lichtenthaler, U., & Muethel, M. (2012). The impact of family involvement on dynamic innovation capabilities: Evidence from German manufacturing firms. *Entrepreneurship Theory and Practice, 36*(6), 1235–1253.
Lizal, L., & Svejnar, J. (2002). Investment, credit rationing, and the soft budget constraint: Evidence from Czech panel data. *The Review of Economics and Statistics, 84*(2), 353–370.
Love, J., & Roper, S. (2013). *SME innovation, exporting and growth, enterprise research center* (White Paper No. 5).
Love, J. H., Roper, S., & Du, J. (2009). Innovation, ownership and profitability. *International Journal of Industrial Organization, 27*(3), 424–434.
Lumpkin, G. T., & Dess, G. G. (1996). Clarifying entrepreneurial orientation construct and linking it to performance. *Academy of Management Review, 2*(1), 135–172.
Mahoney, J. T. (1995). The management of resources and the resource of management. *Journal of Business Research, 33,* 91–101.

Makadok, R. (2001). Toward a synthesis of the resource-based and dynamic-capability views of rent creation. *Strategic Management Journal, 22*(5), 387–401.

Mata, J., & Portugal, P. (1994). Life duration of new firms. *Journal of Industrial Economics, 42*(3), 227–245.

Mata, J., & Portugal, P. (2002). The survival of new domestic and foreign-owned firms. *Strategic Management Journal, 23*(4), 323–343.

Mata, J., Portugal, P., & Guimaraes, P. (1995). The survival of new plants: Start-up conditions and post-entry evolution. *International Journal of Industrial Organization, 13,* 459–481.

Mauro, P. (1995). Corruption and growth. *Quarterly Journal of Economics, 110*(3), 681–712.

McMillan, J., & Woodruff, C. (1999). Inter-firm relationships and informal credit in Vietnam. *Quarterly Journal of Economics, 114*(4), 1285–1320.

McMillan, J., & Woodruff, C. (2002). The central role of entrepreneurs in transition economies. *Journal of Economic Perspectives, 16*(3), 153–170.

Melkas, H., & Pekkarinen, S. (2016). SMEs and regional design services for innovation: Experienced and expected impacts on users and non-users. *International Journal of Innovation and Regional Development, 7*(3), 222–236.

Méon, P. G., & Weill, L. (2010). Is corruption an efficient grease? A cross-country aggregate analysis. *World Development, 38*(3), 244–259.

Mickiewicz, T. (2005). *Economic transition in Central Europe and the Commonwealth of Independent States.* Houndmills: Palgrave Macmillan.

Mises, L. V. (1949). *Human action: A treatise on economics.* New Haven, CT: Yale University Press.

Moorman, C., & Rust, R. T. (1999). The role of marketing. *Journal of Marketing, 63,* 180–197.

Moorman, C., & Slotegraaf, R. J. (1999). The contingency value of complementary capabilities in product development. *Journal of Marketing Research, 36*(2), 239–257.

Morris, M. H., & Kuratko, D. F. (2002). *Corporate entrepreneurship.* Mason, OH: South-Western College Publishers.

Morrow, J. L., Sirmon, D. G., Hitt, M. A., & Holcomb, T. R. (2007). Creating value in the face of declining performance: Firm strategies and organisational recovery. *Strategic Management Journal, 28,* 271–283.

Murphree, M., Tang, L., & Breznitz, D. (2016). Tacit local alliance and SME innovation in China. *International Journal of Innovation and Regional Development, 7*(3), 184–202.

Naudé, W. A. (2007). *Peace, prosperity, and pro-growth entrepreneurship* (WIDER Discussion Paper 2007/02). UNU-WIDER: Helsinki.
Naudé, W. A. (2010a). *Entrepreneurship and economic development.* Basingstoke: Palgrave Macmillan.
Naudé, W. A. (2010b). Entrepreneurship is not a binding constraint on growth and development in the poorest countries. *World Development, 39*(1), 33–44.
Naudé, W. A. (2012). *Entrepreneurship and economic development: Theory, evidence and policy* (Discussion Paper No. 7507). Bonn, Germany: University of Maastricht.
Nelson, R. R., & Phelps, E. (1966). Investment in humans, technology diffusion and economic growth. *American Economic Review, 56*(2), 69–75.
Nonaka, I. (1991). The knowledge-creating company. *Harvard Business Review, 69*(6), 96–104.
Nonaka, I., & Takeuchi, H. (1995). *The knowledge-creating company.* New York: Oxford University Press.
O'Dwyer, M., & Ryan, E. (2002). Management development—A model for retail business. *Journal of European Industrial Training, 26*(9), 420–429.
Østergaard, C. R., Timmermans, B., & Kristinsson, K. (2011). Does a different view create something new? The effect of employee diversity on innovation. *Research Policy, 40*(3), 500–509.
Pe'er, A., & Vertinsky, F. (2006). *The survival value of clusters* (Tuck Business School at Dartmouth Working Paper).
Pellegrino, G., Piva, M., & Vivarelli, M. (2009). *How do young companies innovate?* (Discussion Paper IZA DP No. 4301) [Online]. http://www.ftp.iza.org/dp4301.pdf. Accessed 12 April 2013.
Penrose, E. T. (1959). *The growth of the firm.* New York: Wiley.
Peteraf, M. (1993). The cornerstones of competitive advantage: A resource-based view. *Strategic Management Journal, 14*(3), 179–191.
Polanyi, M. (1962). *Personal knowledge—Towards a post-critical philosophy.* London: Routledge and Kegan Paul.
Prahalad, C. K., & Hamel, G. (1990). The core competence of the corporation. *Harvard Business Review, 68*(3), 79–91.
Reinikka, R., & Svensson, J. (2004). Local capture: Evidence from a central government transfer program in Uganda. *The Quarterly Journal of Economics, 119*(2), 679–705.
Resende, M., Cardoso, V., & Façanha, L. O. (2015). Determinants of survival of newly created SMEs in the Brazilian manufacturing industry: An econometric study. *Empirical Economics, 50*(4), 1255–1274.

Richter, A., & Schaffer, M. (1996). The performance of De Novo private firms in Russian manufacturing. In S. Commander, Q. Fan, & M. Schaffer (Eds.), *Enterprise restructuring economic policy in Russia*. Washington, DC: EDI/The World Bank.

Robbins, V. K. (1996). *Exploring the texture of the texts: A guide to socio-rhetorical interpretation*. Harrisburg, PA: Trinity Press International.

Roberts, K., & Weitzman, M. L. (1981). Funding criteria for research, development, and exploration projects. *Econometrica, 49*(5), 1261–1288.

Rock, M. T., & Bonnet, H. (2004). The comparative politics of corruption: Accounting for the East Asian paradox in empirical studies of corruption, growth and investment. *World Development, 32*, 999–1017.

Rodríguez, J. C., Navarro-Chávez, L., & Gómez, M. (2014). Regional innovation systems in emerging economies: Evidence of system failures for innovation. *International Journal of Innovation and Regional Development, 5*(4/5), 384–404.

Rodrik, D. (2010). Diagnostics before prescription. *Journal of Economic Perspectives, 24*(3), 33–44.

Rodrik, D., Subramanian, A., & Trebbi, F. (2004). Institutions rule: The primacy of institutions over geography and integration in economic development. *Journal of Economic Growth, 9*(2), 131–165.

Rosen, H. S. (2005). *Public finance*. New York: McGraw-Hill/Irwin.

Ruben, R., Slingerland, M., & Nijhoff, H. (2006). Agro-food chains and networks for development—Issues, approaches and strategies. In R. Ruben, M. Slingerland, & H. Nijhoff (Eds.), *Agro-food chains and networks for development*. Dordrecht, The Netherlands: Springer.

Rumelt, R. (1991). How much does industry matter? *Strategic Management Journal, 12*, 167–185.

Sala-i-Martin, X. (1997). I just ran two million regressions. *American Economic Review, 87*, 178–183.

Scarpetta, S., Hemmings, P., Tressel, T., & Woo, J. (2002). *The role of policy and institutions from productivity and firm dynamics: Evidence from micro and industry data* (OECD Economics Department Working Papers 329).

Scheepers, M. J., Hough, J., & Bloom, J. Z. (2008). Nurturing the corporate entrepreneurship capability. *Southern African Business Review, 12*(3), 50–75.

Schiefer, J., & Hartmann, M. (2008). Determinants of competitive advantage for German food processors. *Agribusiness, 24*(3), 306–319.

Schumpeter, J. (1934). *Theory of economic development*. Cambridge: Harvard University Press.

Schutjens, A., & Wever, E. (2000). Determinants of new firm success. *Papers in Regional Science, 79*(2), 135–159.
Sen, K., & Kirkpatrick, C. (2009). A diagnostic approach to economic growth and employment policy in low income economies: The case of Kosovo. *Journal of International Development, 23*(1), 132–154.
Senge, P., Roberts, C., Ross, R., Smith, B. J., & Kleiner, A. (1994). *The fifth discipline fieldbook*. London: Century.
Senge, P., Kleiner, A., Roberts, C., Roth, G., & Ross, R. (1999) *The dance of change: The challenges of sustaining the learning organization*. New York, NY: Doubleday.
Shapira, P., Youtie, J., & Kay, K. (2011). Building capabilities for innovation in SMEs: A cross-country comparison of technology extension policies and programmes. *International Journal of Innovation and Regional Development, 3*(3/4), 254–272.
Sirmon, D. G., Hitt, M. A., & Ireland, R. D. (2007). Managing firm resources in dynamic environments to create value: Looking inside the black box. *Academy of Management Review, 32*(1), 273–292.
Sobel, R. (2008). Testing Baumol: Institutional quality and the productivity of entrepreneurship. *Journal of Business Venturing, 23,* 641–655.
Steiner, M. P., & Solem, O. (1988). Factors for success in small manufacturing firms. *Journal of Small Business Management, 26*(1), 51–56.
Stevenson, H., & Jarillo, J. (1990). A paradigm of entrepreneurship: Entrepreneurial management. *Strategic Management Journal, 11,* 17–27. Special Issue.
Stiglitz, J., & Weiss, A. (1981). Credit rationing in markets with imperfect information. *American Economic Review, 71*(3), 393–409.
Stinchcombe, A. L. (1965). Social structure and organizations. In J. G. March (Ed.), *Handbook of organizations* (pp. 142–193). Chicago: Rand McNally & Co.
Storey, D. J. (1985). Problems facing new firms. *Journal of Management Studies, 22*(3), 327–345.
Storey, D. J. (1994). *Understanding the small business sector*. London: Routledge.
Svejnar, J. (2002). Transition economies: Performance and challenges. *Journal of Economic Perspectives, 16*(1), 3–28.
Svensson, J. (2005). Eight questions about corruption. *Journal of Economic Perspectives, 19*(3), 19–42.

Switzer, L., & Huang, Y. (2007). How does human capital affect the performance of small and mid-cap mutual funds? *Journal of Intellectual Capital, 8*(4), 666–681.

Syverson, C. (2004). Product substitutability and productivity dispersion. *Review of Economics and Statistics, 86*(2), 534–550.

Tanzi, V. (1998) Corruption around the world: Causes, consequences, scope, and cures. *IMF Staff Papers, 45*(4), 559–594. Republished in V. Tanzi (2000), *Policies, institutions and the dark side of economics*. Chellenham: Edward Elgar and in G. T. Abed and S. Gupta (Eds.) (2002), *Governance, corruption and economic performance*. Washington, DC: The International Monetary Fund.

Teece, D. J. (2000). *Managing intellectual capital: Organizational, strategic, and policy dimensions*. Oxford: Oxford University Press.

Teece, D. J. (2007). Explicating dynamic capabilities: The nature and microfundations of (sustainable) enterprise performance. *Strategic Management Journal, 28*(13), 1319–1350.

Teece, D. J. (2012). Dynamic capabilities: Routines versus entrepreneurial action. *Journal of Management Studies, 49*(8), 1395–1401.

Teece, D. J. (2014). The foundations of enterprise performance: Dynamic and ordinary capabilities in an (economic) theory of firms. *Academy of Management Perspectives, 28*(4), 328–352.

Teece, D. J. (2016). Dynamic capabilities and entrepreneurial management in large organizations: Toward a theory of the (entrepreneurial) firm. *European Economic Review, 86*, 202–216.

Teece, D. J., & Pisano, G. (1994). The dynamic capabilities of firms: An introduction. *Industrial and Corporate Change, 3*(3), 537–556.

Teece, D. J., Pisano, G., & Shuen, A. (1997). Dynamic capabilities and strategic management. *Strategic Management Journal, 18*(7), 509–533.

Treisman, D. (2007). What have we learned about the causes of corruption from ten years of cross-national empirical research? *Annual Review of Political Science, 10*, 211–244.

Ughetto, E. (2008). Does internal finance matter for R&D? New evidence from a panel of Italian firms. *Cambridge Journal of Economics, 32*(6), 907–925.

Vossen, R. W. (1998). Relative strengths and weaknesses of small firms in innovation. *International Small Business Journal, 16*(3), 88–95.

Wei, Y., & Wang, Q. (2011). Making sense of a market information system for superior performance: The roles of organizational responsiveness and innovation strategy. *Industrial Marketing Management, 40*(2), 267–277.

Winter, S. (1987). Knowledge and competence as strategic assets. In D. J. Teece (Ed.), *The competitive challenge*. Cambridge, MA: Ballinger.

World Bank. (2008). *Unleashing prosperity productivity growth in Eastern Europe and the former Soviet Union.* http://siteresources.worldbank.org/ECAEXT/Resources/publications/UnleashingProsperity.pdf.

Wright, M., Filatotchev, I., Hoskisson, R. E., & Peng, M. W. (2005). Strategy research in emerging economies: Challenging the conventional wisdom. *Journal of Management Studies, 42,* 1–33.

Youndt, M., Subramaniam, M., & Snell, S. A. (2004). Intellectual capital profiles: An examination of investments and returns. *Journal of Management Studies, 2,* 335–361.

Yudaeva, K., Melentieva, N., & Ponomareva, N. (2003). Does foreign ownership matter? The Russian experience. *Economics of Transition, 11*(3), 383–409.

Yusuf, A. (1995). Critical success factors for small business: Perceptions of South Pacific entrepreneurs. *Journal of Small Business Management, 32*(3), 68–73.

Zahra, S. A., & Covin, J. G. (1995). Contextual influences on the corporate entrepreneurship performance relationship: A longitudinal analysis. *Journal of Business Venturing, 10*(1), 43–58.

Zelenyuk, V., & Zheka, V. (2006). Corporate governance and firms efficiency: The case of transitional country, Ukraine. *Journal of Productivity Analysis, 25*(1), 143–169.

Zingales, L. (1998). Survival of the fittest or the fattest? Exit and financing in the trucking industry. *Journal of Finance, 53*(3), 905–938.

Zollo, M., & Winter, S. (2002). Deliberate learning and the evolution of dynamic capabilities. *Organization Science, 13*(3), 339.

4

Measuring Business Dynamics in Kosovo: Cross-Country Comparison and Analysis

4.1 Introduction

This chapter analyzes the business dynamics in Kosovo. The patterns that emerge are compared with those for five reference countries (Estonia, Croatia, Lithuania, Latvia, and Slovenia). Most of the data on the reference countries come from official statistics provided by national statistical institutes to Eurostat. Data for Kosovo are from the Kosovo Statistical Agency (KSA) and Kosovo Business Registration Agency (KBRA).

Data on business demography are sourced mainly from the respective national business registers which include information on firms' names and addresses, type of economic activities and employment levels. Based on this information, we can derive statistics related to number, type and size of firms and analyse a range of variables for specific subpopulations in various economic sectors, for example, ownership (legal form) and size (numbers of employees). The business demographics measured in this chapter refer to the active firm population and how it has changed over time. We consider the number of new firms and firm closures (firm births and deaths) and firm survival rates during the period 2010–2015. We are, especially, interested in tracking cohorts of

F. Sahiti, *The Growth of Firms in Less-Developed Countries*,
https://doi.org/10.1007/978-3-030-14821-8_4

newly born enterprises over the five-year period. The focus of analysis is on SMEs in the NACE rev. 2 business economy category; we exclude those companies categorized as K64.2. This chapter is organized as follows. Section 4.2 discusses the reasons why the national dynamics is important, while Sect. 4.3 provides the contribution of this chapter. In Sect. 4.4 is provided the theoretical perspective used to analyse the patterns of firms in Kosovo, followed by Sect. 4.5 which provides data description and methodology used in the study. The data analysis is carried out in Sect. 4.6 where the dynamism of active firms is explored, while in Sect. 4.7 flow of firm entry and exit is analyzed; and finally in Sect. 4.8 firm survival pattern in Kosovo were examined, and the same are compared with reference countries. Section 4.9 investigates how countries' institutional characteristics are associated to firm creation and survival over time. In Sect. 4.10 are examined determinants of firm survival in Kosovo. The final section provides a synthesis of our findings and make some proposals for their use by experts and policy makers.

4.2 Why National Business Dynamics?

Since the late 1990s, the ex-socialist countries have experienced a dramatic change in the sectoral composition of their economies. Policy makers concerned about sustaining economic development and employment growth are relying progressively less on large-scale industrial complexes and favouring support for local entrepreneurship, which, usually, initially is a small business (Chatterji et al. 2013). Policy attention on the SME sector, in this context, derives from the expectation that new enterprises will generate growth by fostering employment and productivity (Birch 1979, 1981; Romer 1986). There is empirical evidence suggesting that young and small firms contribute substantially to employment growth (Neumark et al. 2011; Haltiwanger et al. 2010; Criscuolo et al. 2014). This empirical evidence applies, particular, to young and small firms in developed economies; typically, healthy market economies exhibit high rates of churn and changes in inputs and outputs (Caves 1998; Bartelsman and Doms 2000; Ahn 2001; Foster et al. 2001). The evidence shows, also, that these changes are productivity enhancing since they allow inputs to be reallocated from less productive to more productive businesses (Bartelsman et al. 2009). These findings raise questions about whether differences in economic performance across countries can be attributed to differences in the firm dynamics across countries.

Most countries experience a disproportionate share of new firms and related employment growth (OECD 2014). Some of the economic theory literature attributes heterogeneous spatial distribution of entrepreneurial activity to differences in entry costs, input factors and talent across regions (Glaeser et al. 2010; Guiso and Schivardi 2011). In addition, clusters can emerge and prosper, based on social and cultural factors with a strong local component (Becattini 1990). The uneven distribution of firm dynamics across countries is enhanced by the agglomeration dynamics associated to productive clusters (Krugman 1991). The presence of an incumbent firm can be a catalyst for entrepreneurial business and is associated to higher rates of firm survival and positive cross-industry spillovers (Delgado et al. 2010, 2014). This agglomeration trait is explained, in part, by the capacity of clusters to lower entry costs, provide access to better intermediate inputs and enlarge the pool of workers with similar skills (Overman and Puga 2010; Delgado et al. 2010, 2014). Also, the effects of entrepreneurship on employment may be mediated by a substantial regional component; business quality can differ endogenously across regions and benefit from inter-regional spillovers (Fritsch and Mueller 2004; Fritsch 2008). Therefore, entrepreneurial dynamics at the national level are important to inform policy making and the design of policies tailored to local circumstances and suited to sustaining long-term growth.

4.3 What This Study Offers

This chapter contributes in three ways. *First*, it provides an analysis of the business demography (active firms, and firm births, deaths and survival rates) in a low-income economy and compares the analytical findings to a set of EU countries across a five-year time span (2010–2015). Note, that, it examines business demographics following the entry of populations of newborn firms rather than a firm sample. The analysis includes several, not just one cohort of entrants in a developing and relatively young economy, which has received sparse research attention so far. In addition, wherever available, this chapter provides data on employment indicators related to active firms, which includes survivor firms, new firms and existing firms. *Second*, the relatively scarce previous empirical work on the determinants of firm survival in low-income countries, mainly examine the role of financial variables in firm survival. The analysis in this chapter examines the impact of firm size, age, location and legal structure on the probability of firm survival, which is the approach generally adopted in the industrial organization literature. *Third*, the analysis in this chapter contributes to the development of a comparative methodology to measure business activity from an international perspective. The findings obtained for Kosovo are compared to data on five EU benchmark countries, to measure business demography indicators at the national level. The analysis in this chapter is based on enterprise indicators. An enterprise approach enables a sounder measurement of real firm dynamics in the sense that it measures firm births and deaths accurately and consistently and does not include new plants/subsidiaries belonging to already existing businesses. In addition, business demography statistics at the enterprise level have achieved a substantial degree of international comparability.

4.4 Theoretical Perspective

To construct the theoretical framework used to investigate the specifics of the business demography in Kosovo, this chapter draws on Schumpeter's (1934) growth theory. There are several models based on this theory that attempt to shed light on firm growth processes.[1] This study uses the firm dynamics model, which can generate predictions

[1]Aghion et al. (2014) discuss 4 aspects where this theory make distinct predictions: (i) the role of competition and market structure; (ii) firm dynamics; (iii) the relationship between growth and development with the notion of appropriate growth institutions; and (iv) the emergence and impact of long-term technological waves.

about firm dynamics (entry, exit and survival and reallocation of resources) and explain how these patterns shape the overall growth process (Aghion et al. 2014).

A concept that is fundamental to this model is the notion of 'creative destruction'. Creative destruction accounts for the weeding out by the competition of unsuccessful firms and the nurturing of successful ones. Evidence, in the form of stylized facts, suggests that the impact of creative destruction on firm growth in developed countries is significant (World Bank 2008). It suggests that a healthy market economy is characterized by a high pace of firm churn and the reallocation of outputs and inputs across firms (Bartelsman et al. 2009). This churn rate influences productivity growth which comes, mainly, from incumbent firms.

To explain the impact of firm dynamics on firm growth, the literature identifies three fundamental factors: firm entry, exit and survival. The empirical evidence on firm dynamics suggests that these factors are influenced by variables related to firm specifics, industry specifics, business environment factors and spatial factors (Mata and Portugal 2002; Audretsch and Mahmood 1994; Audretsch et al. 1999; Pe'er and Vertinsky 2006). Thus, on this basis, we would suggest that the firm dynamics in less-developed countries is also a function of firm-specific and industry-specific variables, and macroeconomic and spatial factors. Each of these variables has specific properties. For instance, firm specific variables reflect individual firm properties such as firm size, age, legal structure, adaptability to new technology, organizational capabilities, managerial practices, etc. Industry-specific variables refer to industry characteristics such as stage of growth of a specific industry, average firm size in the industry, type of sector/subsector in which the firm operates, level of competition (concentration) in the industry, etc. Business environment variables include level of economic and political stability, unemployment rate, interest rate, exchange rate, GDP level, income levels, etc. Spatial variables refer to firm location, level of competition in the region and agglomeration economies.

The following explanatory variables are used investigate the impact of firm-specific properties on firm dynamics in Kosovo: firm size and legal structure, economic sector and spatial factors. Firm size is used to investigate patterns of firm entry, exit and survival in the industry and business sectors. Legal structure investigates whether governance factors have an impact on firm survival rates. The industry specifics examined include the industry, services and construction sectors as explanatory variables to investigate variation in firm survival. Finally, spatial factors—location/region in which the firm operates—are used to explain differences in survival patterns.

Although the analysis focuses on Kosovo's economy, we do not study Kosovan firm demographics as an isolated case. The findings for Kosovo's economy are compared to other countries with higher income levels. To allow comparison of the differences in patterns of firm dynamics, we use countries income levels as the independent/explanatory variable. Overall, the perspective adopted is built on three elements: Schumpeterian theory of creative destruction, stylized facts based on the empirical evidence and the firm dynamics of the reference countries.

Using these variables, the theoretical framework can be adapted to show that the potential growth of firms in Kosovo is a function of firm turbulence and the interaction of this turbulence with incumbent firm growth. This interaction is enabled by a process of creative destruction, which is shaped by a variety of firm and industry specifics, local factors and income levels as conditional independent variables.

4.5 The Database Used for the Empirical Analysis

This section describes the data and methodology used to analyse business demography patterns in Kosovo and the five reference countries. The analysis is conducted on KSA data, which cover a group of variables that explain business demography characteristics and patterns.

The dataset relies on business register information to compile business demography indicators, and originates from administrative sources such as tax administration records and compulsory registers of legal entities operating in certain towns and cities. KSA and KBRA business register data are superior to survey data because they provide complete information on the population of firms operating in a given country. The data cover firms that active firms and firms that entered and exited the market during 2010–2015.

To maximize international comparability, Kosovo's business demography pattern is compared with business demography patterns for five selected EU countries, and the indicators are from Eurostat. Eurostat's Manual of Business Demography Statistics provides methodological guidelines and indicators to allow production of internationally comparable business demography outcomes (see Eurostat/OECD 2008). As a result of compliance with these guidelines, the national data used for this study have been harmonized *ex ante*.

4.5.1 Data Description

The data used to analyse business demography for Kosovo and the chosen reference countries, include indicators to explain the features and demography of the business population. The unit of analysis is the firm not the plant or subsidiary. That is, a firm with several active plants is considered as a single observation. The definition of firm is essentially the same as the definition of enterprises and conforms to the Eurostat/OECD (2008, p. 12) definition. The target population is the private sector economy. The methodology employed for this study enables production of data on active firms, firm birth, death and survival rates, and related employment indicators.

The firm sectors included (NACE Rev. 2) include those in industry sections B to E construction (section F) and services (sections G to N) and excludes holding companies and agriculture, forestry and fishing (section A) and public sector and non-market activities (sections O to U).

Also, to achieve greater international comparability, the subject of analysis is the employer enterprise or an enterprise with a positive number of employees in any part of the year. Single owner firms are excluded.

The main indicators used for the analysis include: stock of active firms, number of newborn firms, number of firm deaths, distribution of firms in terms of size, variables for employment, and dynamics of firm survival for to five years. These indicators allow us to derive measures for firm birth rates, exit rates, survival and hazard rates, and employment shares.

4.5.2 Definition of a Business Statistical Unit

What is meant by the term business demography? In the analysis in this chapter it refers to a group of variables that explain the features and demography of the business population in Kosovo's economy. The creation of new enterprises and the closure of unproductive businesses can be seen as contributing significantly to the business dynamism (Ahn 2001; Bartelsman et al. 2009). In addition to studying firm births and deaths, we look at the counts and characteristics of the population of active firms. Special attention is paid to the impact of these demographic events on employment. To obtain information on the impact of firm births and examine their growth and survival, we follow new firms for six years on the case of Kosovo and five years for the reference countries.

In the case of Kosovo, the business demography indicators presented in this chapter are based on data from national statistical offices. Data for the reference countries are from Eurostat's country business demography database (see Table 4.1). The timeframe spans 2010–2015. A breakdown of the indicators used is based on the firm's sector of economic activity (1 digit NACE Rev. 2). The size-class breakdown distinguishes micro firms (1–9 employees) and larger firms (10 or more employees). The indicators include number of active firms, firm births and deaths, and the number of firms surviving for five years.

Table 4.1 Data sources and country breakdown

Country	Years	Sector breakdown	Size class breakdown	Non-employer separate	Source
EU	2008–2015	Yes	Yes	Yes	Eurostat
Estonia	2008–2015	Yes	Yes	Yes	Eurostat
Croatia	2013–2015	Yes	Yes	Yes	Eurostat
Lithuania	2008–2015	Yes	Yes	Yes	Eurostat
Latvia	2008–2015	Yes	Yes	Yes	Eurostat
Slovenia	2008–2015	Yes	Yes	Yes	Eurostat
Kosovo	2008–2016	Yes	Yes	Yes	KSA

Source Eurostat and KSA

The definition of these demographic events follows standard international guidelines on the development of business demography statistics (Eurostat/OECD 2008). The data include some indicators for employment in business (employment in active firms new firms, exiting firms and surviving firms). Births/new firms, deaths, survivals and active firms are defined as follows:

Enterprises: An enterprise or firm is defined by Eurostat/OECD (2008, p. 12), as the 'smallest combination of legal units producing goods or services, which benefits from a certain degree of autonomy in decision-making, especially for the allocation of its current resources. An enterprise carries out one or more activities at one or more locations'. It defines local units as 'enterprises or parts thereof (e.g. a workshop, factory, warehouse, office, etc.) situated in a geographically identified place. At or from this place economic activity is carried out for which—save for certain exceptions—one or more persons work (even if only part-time) for one and the same enterprise' (Eurostat/OECD 2008, p. 86). An enterprise can control multiple establishments, which, in turn, may operate across different economic sectors or geographical areas.

Value and employment thresholds for inclusion in the registers: KSA use production value or legal form to distinguish firms that must be included in the statistical business register and indicators. This study defines an active firm as a company with a positive payroll at some period during the year or with at least one employee.

Selection of economic sectors: Business registers differ in their scope. Some sectors, such as private households, are excluded from business registers. When harmonizing indicators across countries, it is necessary to ensure a consistent definition of the business population in order to build indicators with equivalent sectoral scope. It is necessary, also, to ensure comparability across sectoral classification systems—in our case indicators are based on the NACE Rev. 2 classification.

Employment: Employment can be measured by headcounts or full-time equivalents. The distinction is important because employment thresholds can affect the inclusion of firms in registers. Also, it affects the measurement of employment, whether generated or destroyed by entrepreneurial activity. According to Eurostat/OECD (2008, p. 41) guidelines, full-time equivalent is more precise since headcounts can overestimate the amount of work produced; for example, it would include part-time employees. However, for some countries, full-time equivalents are not available so using headcounts maximizes the amount of data available.

Following the adoption of regulation related to business registers for statistical purposes, business demography data for Kosovo are largely comparable to EU standards. Therefore, the definitions are generally consistent with the Eurostat/OECD (2008) framework. The following paragraphs describe the guidelines related to recording the main demographic events that affect firms.

Births and entries: The definition of firm birth is strongly related to the definition of a business. However, while firm births can be considered businesses that are created from scratch, entries refer to the appearance in business registers of enterprises already active in the previous period(s) (Ahmad 2008). The definition of firm birth is in line with Eurostat/OECD (2008, p. 77). A birth amounts to the creation of a combination of production factors with the restriction that no other enterprises are involved in the event. Births do not include entries into the population due to mergers, break-ups, split-off or restructuring of a set of enterprises. It does not include entries into a sub-population resulting only from a change of activity. A birth occurs when an enterprise starts from scratch and actually starts activity. An enterprise creation can be considered an enterprise birth if new production factors, in particular new jobs, is created. If a dormant unit is reactivated within two years, this event is not considered a birth. Within this type of firms are those firms that have at least one paid employee in its birth year.

Deaths: This demographic event relates to the dissolution of the firm's legal entity and, its definition in the case of a firm closure, is likely to be relatively consistent and comparable across EU countries. However, deaths encompasses exits in the form of a change to the firm's legal form (merger/break-up/split-off), internal restructuring, change of ownership, take-over, joint venture and reactivation. Again, these events, in principle, should be excluded from birth/death statistics (Eurostat/OECD 2008, p. 52). Overall, the definition of a business death is consistent across countries in terms of both enterprise and establishment indicators. According to Eurostat/OECD (2008, p. 77), a death occurs with the dissolution of a combination of production factors with the restriction that no other enterprises are involved in the event. Deaths do not include exits from the population due to mergers, take-overs, break-ups or restructuring of a set of enterprises. It does not include exits from a sub-population resulting only from a change of activity. An enterprise is included in the count of deaths only if it is not reactivated within two years. Equally, a reactivation within two years is not counted as a birth'.

Survival: An enterprise is considered as surviving if it was included in the business register in the previous continuous time periods and is included in the current one. The Eurostat/OECD (2008, p. 45) framework defines as survivors as 'An enterprise born in year xx or having survived to year xx from a previous year is considered to have survived in year xx+1 if it is active in terms of turnover and/or employment in any part of year xx+1 (= survival without changes)'.

Activity: Activity is defined as turnover and/or employment in the period 1st January–31st December in a given year. This definition is in line with the concept of activity in the Business Registers glossary.

Growth: Firm growth can be defined according to an increase in employment or turnover in a given time period with respect to the previous period. However, high-growth might be defined differently in terms of both thresholds and time span over which it is calculated. The Eurostat/OECD (2008, p. 63) guidelines define as high-growth those enterprises where employment or turnover experienced average annualized growth of more than 20% per annum over a three-year period. Gazelles are defined as high-growth enterprises that have existed for at least five years (Eurostat/OECD 2008, p. 63) although Eurostat's regional database defines high-growth as enterprises with average annualized growth in numbers of employees of greater than 10% per year over a three-year period ($t-3$ to t) from an initial employee base of at least ten employees ($t-3$).

Time: The time frame is a year: firms are considered active, if they have been active at any point in a given year.

Size-class breakdown: Firms are classified into three size classes according to the number of their employees: micro-enterprise (1–5); small-enterprise (5–9); and large firm (10+). This classification is available for most of the countries in our analysis, although not necessarily for all indicators.

Sectoral breakdown: The sectoral classifications in the original data sources have been harmonized to make them comparable to the ISIC Rev. 4 one-digit classification. The firms are classified as: industry (NACE sections C to E), construction (NACE section F) and services (NACE sections G to K).

The method used is comparative analysis. The findings for Kosovo's business demography are compared to a set of reference countries. The comparative method is used widely in all sciences and in social sciences it role is prominent (Lijphart 1971, 1975; Ragin 1987; Collier 1998). The comparative analysis in this chapter identifies and assesses similarities and differences in the business demographics of Kosovo and the five reference countries. Bartelsman et al. (2009, p. 1) point out that comparative analysis can be particularly useful to test hypotheses about market structure and institutional differences across countries affecting the observed magnitude, nature and efficiency of the creative destruction process. However, these 'meta analyses' or ex-post country study comparisons are inherently difficult given differences in measurements and methodologies across studies (Bartelsman et al. 2009).

4.6 Population of Active Firms in Kosovo (2010–2015)

The following three sections provide a general overview of the business firm population in Kosovo in the six-year period 2010–2015. It begins by looking at the stock of active firms in the whole of the business sector and subsectors. The analysis uses aggregate data for industry (NACE sections B to E), construction (NACE section F) and services (NACE sections G to S). In addition to a sectoral and sub-sectoral examination, the analysis focuses on the distribution of firms by size, firm entries and exits and the impact on employment. The overall aim is a cross-country comparison. For the statistical comparison, patterns of firm demography for Kosovo's economy are compared to the patterns for the aggregate EU and for the five selected countries—Estonia, Croatia, Latvia, Lithuania, and Slovenia. The reasons for choosing these countries are set out in Chapter 1.

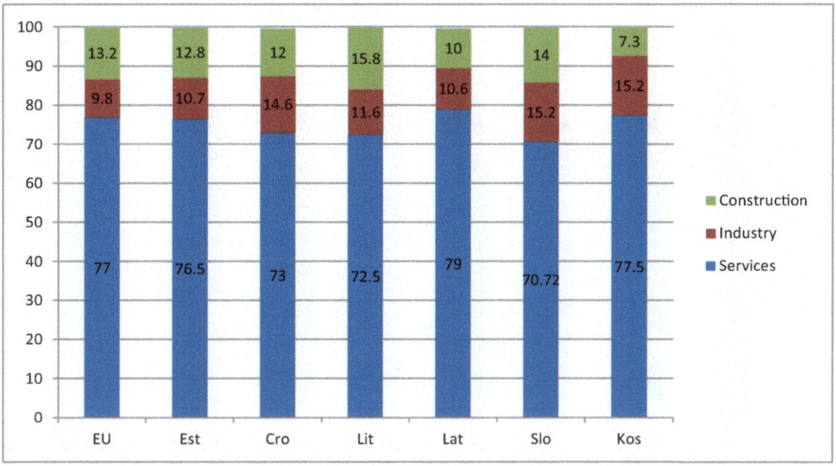

Fig. 4.1 Structure of active enterprises by sector, business economy, 2015 (percentages) (*Source* Eurostat and KSA)

The findings suggest that the population of active firms in Kosovo is dominated by service firms. On average, more than three quarters (77.7%) of the firm population is active in the service sector (NACE G to S) and account for 66.6% of total employment. These outcomes are comparable with those for the reference countries. For instance, at the EU level, three-quarters (75.8%) of all active firms in the business economy are in services and provide 67.7% of total employment. Similarly, services accounts for some 70.72% of firms in the business economy in Slovenia and 76.5% of firms in Estonia. In terms of its contribution to employment, services account for 55.54% of the workforce in Slovenia and 67.8% in Latvia (see Fig. 4.1).

In contrast, Kosovo's industry sector accounts for 15.2% of active firms and 24.0% of total employment. In the aggregate EU, 9.8% of active firms are in industry, but this small percentage accounts for 23.5% of total employment. In Slovenia, industry accounts for 15.2% of all enterprises in the business economy and in Estonia it accounts for 10.7% of the total. However, for contribution to employment, the industry sector accounts for 34.9% of

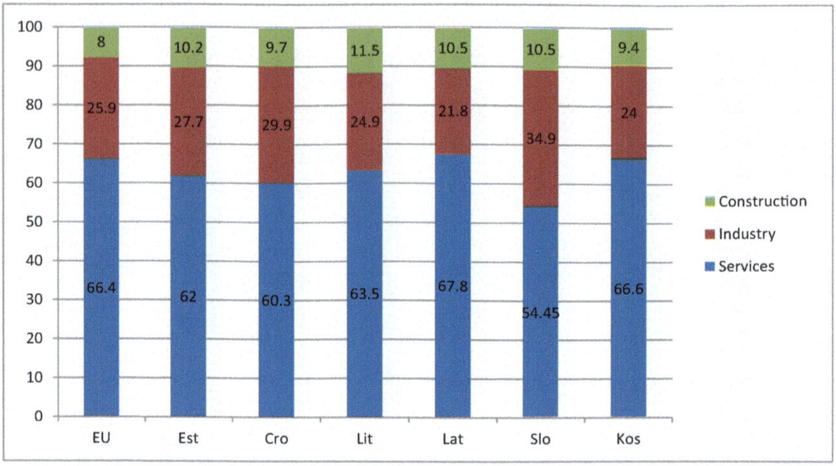

Fig. 4.2 Structure of employment by sector, business economy, 2015 (percentages) (*Source* Eurostat data for the reference countries and KSA for Kosovo)

the workforce in Slovenia and only 21.9% in Latvia. The difference among these shares is evidence that the average size of industry firms (as in terms of number of persons employed) is considerably higher than services firms. Across the EU-28 countries, industrial firms employ an average of 13 persons, compared to five persons for services. The average employment in construction is the lowest at three persons per enterprise.

The number of active construction firms in Kosovo is 7.5%, accounting for 9.2% of total employment. In the EU, the proportion of active firms in construction is 13.2%—almost twice as high—but the contribution to employment is only 8%. Among the reference countries, the highest proportion of employment in construction is in Lithuania and Slovenia with 15.8% and 14% respectively and employment of 11.5% and 10.5% respectively (Figs. 4.2, 4.3, and 4.4).

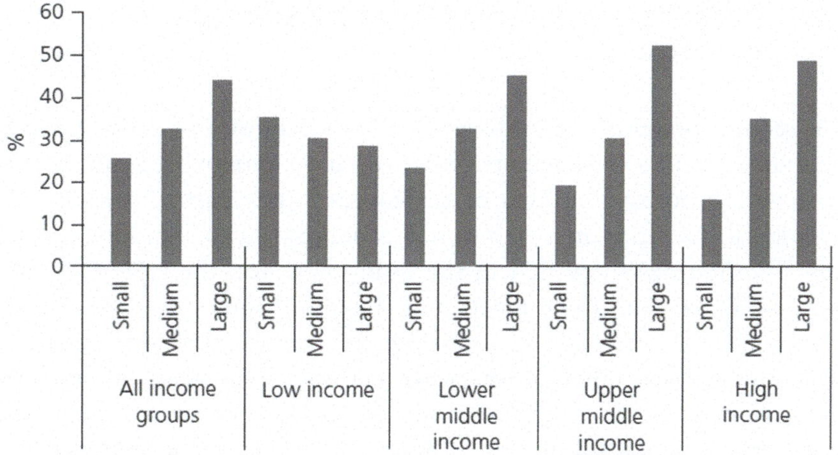

Fig. 4.3 Share of employment based on national income levels (*Source* IFC [2013] Enterprise surveys, *Note* small firms 5–19, medium firms 20–99, large firms 100+)

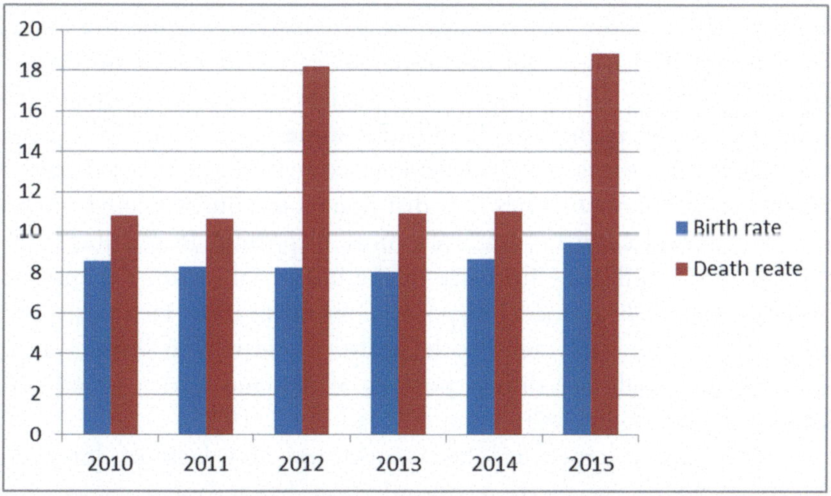

Fig. 4.4 Entry and exit rates in Kosovo, 2010–2015 (*Source* KSA)

4.6.1 Population of Active Firms by Subsectors in Kosovo

This section presents the findings on the distribution of active firms in the industry and service sectors. We focused on employing firms, that is, those with a positive number of employees in any part of the year. We include all the firms in the business economy except holding companies. The findings show that in the industry sector, the largest number of firms is engaged in manufacturing. Table 4.2 shows that this subsector accounts for 92% of all industrial firms, and 51.9% of industrial employment. Two other sectors with relatively high shares of firms are mining and quarrying which accounts for 3.7%, and water supply, sewerage, etc. which accounts for 3.0% of all firms in the industrial sector. With regard to employment, mining and quarrying represents 4.9% of the total industrial workforce and water supply, sewerage, etc. accounts for 8.6 of total employment. These findings indicate that active firm structure within the industrial sector in Kosovo's economy is comparable to that in the reference countries. However, they underline the relatively small average size of firms operating in Kosovo's economy compared to the other countries. For instance, while the average size of a manufacturing firm operating in the EU is 13, in Kosovo it is only 4 on average. This pattern is repeated in most other industry subsectors except electricity which includes some larger firms. The pervasiveness of small firms in less-developed countries can be explained by various factors. Some features that distinguish the business environment in less-developed countries are even more important in relation to factors that might influence firm size in the industrial sector. For instance, public goods, such as roads, airports, communication facilities, power and access to safe water, tend to be relatively limited in less-developed countries. So, small and diffuse pockets of demand lead to small-scale, localized production (Liedholm and Mead 1987, 1995).

In addition, a large unskilled workforce and lack of long-term finance create incentives to economize on fixed capital. Since most machinery and equipment has to be imported, the trade regime and lack of local technical support can further militate against factory production in small markets (Liedholm and Mead 1995). In the presence

Table 4.2 Share of active firms, employment and average size in the industrial sector, 2015

	Share of the number of enterprises (%)							Share of the number of persons employed (%)							Average number of persons employed per enterprise (units)						
	EU	Est	Cr	Lv	Lt	SI	Kos	EU	Est	Cr	Lv	Lt	SI	Kos	EU	Est	Cr	Lv	Lt	SI	Kos
Industry	1.00	1.00	1.00	1.00	1.00	1.00	1.00	1.00	1.00	1.00	1.00	1.00	1.00	1.00	13	14	14	12	12	10	5
Mining and quarrying	0.9	1.6	1.1	2.2	0.60	0.5	3.7	1.7	3.9	4.0	2.3	1.2	1.1	4.8	24	34	53	12	24	24	6
Manufacturing	89.1	92.2	92.2	90.0	90.2	90.3	92.0	88.9	89.1	83.5	84.4	86.8	90.1	84.1	13	14	13	11	11	10	4
Electricity, gas, steam and air conditioning supply	6.4	2.7	2.7	4.6	7.2	7.2	1.3	4.6	4.2	4.9	7.9	5.6	4.2	2.5	8	23	26	21	9	6	9
Water supply, sewerage, etc.	3.6	3.5	4.0	3.2	2.0	2.0	3.0	4.8	2.8	7.6	5.3	6.4	4.6	8.6	16	11	27	21	37	23	12

Source KSA

of wage rigidities, abundant labour and scarce capital can also mean that formal sector jobs are rationed; workers unable to find employment in the formal sector may set up micro-enterprises in order to survive (Berner et al. 2008).

Finally, an unstable regulatory and macroeconomic business environment discourages mass production techniques, which require long-term investment in assets, which, in turn, involves long-term commitment to particular products and production volumes (Liedholm and Mead 1995). In a context of uncertainty about future demand for these products, it makes sense to choose production techniques that rely more heavily on labour (Brunetti et al. 1997). In sum, uncertainty about policies and demand conditions, weak rule of law and corruption are the areas that, in qualitative surveys, managers identify as the most problematic (Brunetti et al. 1997).

In the service sector, more than a half of all active firms are active in either wholesale and retail (57.4%)—see Table 4.3. These two sub-sectors together, account for 48.3% of total services sector employment. This sector is the largest business economic sector among the references countries, whose levels range from 23.6% in Latvia to 35.2% in Lithuania. Most service sector firms report average employment of less than five people. The lowest values are for other services (1.2), retail trade (1.5), and transportation and storage (1.5). However, some other subsectors report a significantly higher average number of employees per firm, for example, public administration and defence (5.3). If we extend the analysis to other service subsectors, the percentage of firms is significantly lower in Kosovo compared to the reference countries. One of the most striking patterns that emerged was for professional, scientific and technical activities. This subsector includes firms that specialize in providing professional, scientific and technical services to clients in a variety of industries.[2] In Kosovo, the proportion of firms in this subsector is 6.5%, but ranges between 16% in Latvia and 26% in Slovenia.

[2]These activities include: legal advice and representation; accounting, bookkeeping and payroll services; architectural, engineering and specialized design services; computer services; consulting services; research services; advertising services; photographic services; translation and interpretation services; veterinary services; and other professional, scientific and technical services.

Table 4.3 Share of active firms, employment and average size in the service sector, 2015

	Share of the number of enterprises (%)							Share of the number of persons employed (%)							Average number of persons employed per enterprise (units)						
	EU	Est	Cr	Lv	Lt	Sl	Kos	EU	Est	Cr	Lv	Lt	Sl	Kos	EU	Est	Cr	Lv	Lt	Sl	Kos
Service sector total	1.00	1.00	1.00	1.00	1.00	1.00	1.00	1.00	1.00	1.00	1.00	1.00	1.00	1.00	5	4	6	4	5	3	3
Wholesale and retail trade; repair of motor vehicles and motorcycles	34.4	25.7	30.4	23.6	35.2	21.9	57.4	34.0	30.4	33.6	31.6	32.6	29.3	48.7	5	5	6	6	4	4	2
Transportation and storage	6.5	10.3	7.0	5.5	7.1	7.1	4.2	11.2	13.7	12.5	15.4	14.2	11.9	5.1	8	6	10	11	9	5	4
Accommodation and food service activities	10.6	4.1	16.1	5.2	3.5	9.2	12.5	11.5	8.0	14.3	6.8	5.8	9.4	12.9	5	8	5	9	8	3	3
Information and communication	7.1	6.7	5.2	5.2	5.1	7.0	3.2	6.7	7.0	5.8	5.7	4.2	6.5	5.4	5	4	6	5	6	3	5
Financial and insurance activities	3.5	1.3	0.8	1.5	0.5	1.6	0.511	5.9	3.2	5.8	3.6	2.2	5.7	3.05	9	11	38	10	23	11	17
Real estate activities	7.1	8.2	3.2	11	7.4	2.2	1.052	3	3.8	1.7	6.2	3.3	1.2	0.76	2	2	3	2	2	2	2
Professional, scientific and technical activities	24	19	19	16	16.1	26	6.463	13	9.7	11	9.2	8.5	14	7.02	3	2	3	2	2	2	3
Administrative and support service activities	8.5	6.7	5.3	5.7	4.2	5.9	2.225	14	12	7.3	7.6	7	9.3	4.75	8	7	8	6	8	5	6
Education	n/a	2.3	1.2	2.8	4.8	4.0	1.626	n/a	1.3	1.2	2	6.1	1.7	4.19	n/a	2	5	3	5	1	7

(continued)

Table 4.3 (continued)

	Share of the number of enterprises (%)							Share of the number of persons employed (%)							Average number of persons employed per enterprise (units)						
	EU	Est	Cr	Lv	Lt	Sl	Kos	EU	Est	Cr	Lv	Lt	Sl	Kos	EU	Est	Cr	Lv	Lt	Sl	Kos
Human health and social work activities	n/a	2.6	4.5	4.8	2.2	3.4	3.541	n/a	6	3.1	4	11	4.7	3.89	n/a	10	4	4	24	4	3
Arts, entertainment and recreation	n/a	4.6	1.5	3.4	4.8	5.8	1.28	n/a	2.1	1.8	2.3	2.2	2.7	2.05	n/a	2	7	3	2	1	5
Other service activities	n/a	8.2	5.5	17	9.4	6.3	6.095	n/a	3.1	2.5	5.6	3	3.2	2.2	n/a	2	2	1	2	2	1

Source KSA

4.6.2 Distribution of Active Firms by Size in the Total Economy: Cross-Country Comparisons

This section provides an overview of the distribution of active firms in terms of size. Why is firm size important in a firm dynamics analysis? The literature on firm dynamics suggests that smaller firms are more subject to churning, but also show greater potential for growth (Sutton 1997). According to Bartelsman et al. (2009) a size distribution that favours small size implies higher entry and exit figures, but greater post-entry expansion among successful/survivor firms. These authors emphasize that, in some countries, this might signify sectoral specialization towards new industries, where churn rates are higher, and more firms experimenting with new technologies. Other factors that influence the churn rate are related to institutional factors (for instance, small firms may be subject to less strict labour regulation), since it is easier for firms in countries with weak enforcement of the regulation to avoid its implementation. Furthermore, the firm size distribution is likely to be influenced by the overall size of the internal market and the business environment in which the firms operate, and this can discourage firm expansion (Bartelsman et al. 2009).

Tables 4.4 and 4.5 compare share of firms to associated employment for Kosovo, as a low-income country, and the five reference countries. Firms are compared according to two firm sizes: less than 10 employees (Table 4.4) and 10+ employees (Table 4.5). The evidence suggests that the firm population in all the countries is dominated by micro and small units. While in most of the reference countries, smaller firms (fewer than 10 employees) account for 80% of average of the total population, their share in the employment level is much lower. Their share in total employment ranges from 21.6% at EU as a whole, and 24.5% for some countries (e.g., Estonia and Slovenia).

The share of micro firms in the total economy in Kosovo does not show any significant differences to the reference countries. The outcomes are similar for both manufacturing and services. However, the share of total employment accounted for by micro firms is higher in Kosovo; it is almost double that in the reference countries. The share of

Table 4.4 Share of micro firms in the total firm population and in total employment (Firms with fewer than 10 employees as a percentage of the total)

	Share of number of firms			Share of employment		
	Total economy	Manufacturing	Service	Total economy	Manufacturing	Service
EU	93.9	84.5	94.9	20.6	8.5	29.3
Estonia	91.7	79.1	93.7	25.4	10.9	23.2
Croatia	91.5	83.4	93.4	24.5	13.4	29.9
Lithuania	91.1	83.2	92.4	21.3	8.3	27.1
Latvia	92.1	82.9	93.9	23.2	12.1	26.9
Slovenia	94.9	88.9	96.2	25.4	11.9	31.8
Kosovo	91.5	86.9	92.2	41.3	32.9	30.6

Source Eurostat data for the reference countries and KSA for Kosovo

Table 4.5 Share of small firms in the total firm population and in total employment (Firms with 10+employees as a percentage of the total)

	Share of number of firms			Share of employment		
	Total economy	Manufacturing	Service	Total economy	Manufacturing	Service
EU	6.1	15.5	5.1	79.4	91.5	76.8
Estonia	8.3	20.9	6.3	74.6	89.1	70.7
Croatia	8.5	16.6	6.6	75.5	86.6	70.1
Lithuania	8.9	16.8	7.6	78.7	91.7	72.9
Latvia	7.8	17.1	6.1	76.8	87.9	73.1
Slovenia	5.1	11	3.8	74.6	88.1	68.2
Kosovo	8.9	13.1	7.8	58.7	67.1	69.4

Source Eurostat data for reference countries and KSA for Kosovo

micro firms in total employment in the reference countries ranges from 20.6 in the EU as a whole, to 25.5% in both Estonia and Slovenia. In manufacturing, Kosovo's share of employment is almost triple that of the other countries, while in services, with the exception of Slovenia where employment share is slightly higher, employment by micro firms is similar to the other reference countries.

Among firms that employ more than 10 people, we found that the share of these types of firms in the total population of firms in Kosovo is relatively comparable to the other countries. More specifically, the share of firms with 10+ employees (in the total population of firms) is 6.1 in the EU as a whole, 5.1% in Slovenia, with the share of these firms in Kosovo comparable to Lithuania, Estonia, and Croatia.

Again, in services, Kosovo's share of employment is similar to the reference countries, while the percentage of firms with 10+ employees in the total economy and manufacturing sector is significantly lower than in the reference countries. For instance, the contribution of firms with 10+ employees in total employment in Kosovo is 58.7%, which is around 20%, on average, lower than in the reference countries. This implies that majority of firms in both the total economy and in manufacturing in Kosovo are small firms, employing fewer than 10 employees. There are many reasons why firms in less-developed countries tend to remain small, for example, institutional factors, which push firms either to remain small or to expand (Bartelsman et al. 2009), and factors related to internal resources (Barney 1991; Bloom and Van Reenen 2010).

4.6.3 Size Class Breakdown in Business Economy

While almost 8 in 10 enterprises (76.4%) in the business economy have fewer than five employees, this sub-population of enterprises accounts for less than a quarter of total employment (24.5%)—see Table 4.5. The proportion of very small enterprises with fewer than five employees is highest in Slovenia at 77.6% of the total, while the proportion of small firms in Lithuania is the lowest—at 55.4%. Note, also, that the lower half of Table 4.5 refers to persons employed, while size-class thresholds are given in terms of employees. In the calculation, we include only employer firms; enterprises with zero employees are excluded.

Table 4.6 Breakdown by size-class of the number of enterprises and the number of persons employed in the business economy, 2015

	Estonia	Croatia	Latvia	Lithuania	Slovenia	Kosovo
Active enterprises: proportion of each size-class in total (%)						
1–4	73.5	75.8	70.7	55.4	77.6	81.1
5–9	13	12.8	13.4	22.1	11.6	10.1
10+	13.5	11.4	15.9	22.5	10.8	8.8
Persons employed: proportion of each size-class in total (%)						
1–4	15.2	17.5	18.5	9.6	18	24.5
5–9	10.2	9.2	9.1	11.2	9.3	12.9
10+	74.6	73.3	72.4	79.2	72.7	62.6

Source Eurostat data for reference countries and KSA for Kosovo

Some 89.4% of those employed in the EU's business economy work in enterprises with 10 or more employees, while this same subpopulation represents only 13.6% of total enterprises. Across countries, 62.6% of those employed in Kosovo's business economy work in an enterprise with 10 or more employees, a significantly lower share compared to the reference countries where the figures range from 72.7% in Slovenia and 79.3% in Croatia (Table 4.6).

Similarly, some studies suggest that SMEs account for around 45% of formal employment in the world economy, while in the developing economies it is around 50% or more of total employment (Ayyagari et al. 2003).[3] The variation in the contribution of employment in terms of firm size becomes clearer when analyzed in the context of national income levels. Figure 4.5 shows that, in low-income countries, small firms have the highest share of employment, followed by medium and larger firms, while in high-income countries large firms have the highest share of employment, followed by medium-sized firms, and small firms with the lowest share (IFC 2013).

[3]The Financial Inclusion Experts Group (2010) puts the number at up to 48%.

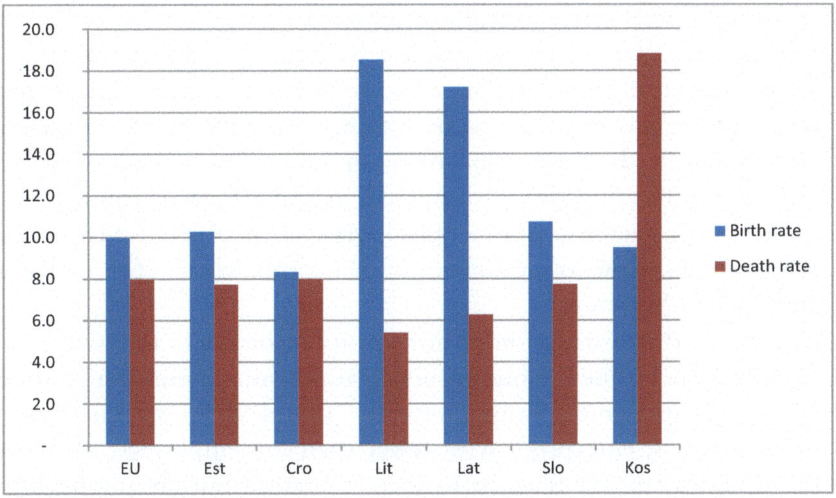

Fig. 4.5 Entry and exit rates in the business economy, 2015 (*Source* Eurostat and KSA)

4.6.4 Main Findings

Below, are some of the main findings for the population of active firms:

- In all countries, including Kosovo, the vast majority of firms operate in service sector—77.5% in Kosovo and 79% in Latvia. Similarly, the service sector in Kosovo provides 66.6% of total employment, while in other countries the contribution of service sector to total employment ranges between 54.5% in Slovenia and 67.8% in Latvia.
- In terms of distribution of industry firms, some interesting patterns emerged. In all countries, the vast majority of enterprises—90% in Latvia, 92.0% in Kosovo and 92.2% in Estonia—operate in the manufacturing sector. However, these figures hide the relatively small average size of firms operating in Kosovo's economy compared to the other countries. While the average size in Estonia is 14, in Kosovo it is only 4 on average. Some significant differences between Kosovo

and the comparator countries arise, also, in the service subsectors. For instance, Kosovo's service sector is dominated by wholesale and retail, accounting for 54.5%, while in other countries this proportion ranges between 25.7% in Estonia and 35.2% in Lithuania. Consequently, the proportion of other subsectors in Kosovo's economy is significantly lower compared to the reference countries. In professional, scientific and technical services the difference is particularly striking: Kosovo registers only 6% compared to 16% in Latvia and 26% in Slovenia.

- Analysis of the distribution of firms in terms of size in the total economy and the business economy also reveals some interesting patterns. In all countries, most firms (between 70 and 95%) are micro-businesses, that is, enterprises with fewer than ten employees. However, the findings suggest that, in Kosovo, the contribution among firms employing 1–4 employees is 41% in the total economy and 32.4% in manufacturing sector compared to around have as much on both counts in the reference countries. The results are similar for the business economy.

4.7 Firm Entry and Exit Flows in Kosovo

Firm creation, death and survival differ substantially across countries (OECD 2016b). Entrepreneurship has been highlighted as a determinant in the economic literature and by policy makers. Newborn firms are considered to play a significant role in the economic growth and competitiveness (Ahn 2001; Bartelsman et al. 2004, 2009; Geroski et al. 2012) and it is believed that they increase competitive pressure on incumbent firms, forcing them to become more efficient (Fritsch and Mueller 2004; Fritsch 2008). In this perspective, newborn firms influence innovation and facilitate the adoption of new technologies. By helping to increase the overall productivity within the economy, newborn firms promote a shift among resources from less to more productive activities (Bartlesman et al. 2009; Aghion et al. 2014). This process was described by Schumpeter (1934, 1943) as a process of 'creative destruction' and is a fundamental aspect of capitalist market economies. Newborn firms enter the market with new technology, and compete with incumbents using conventional technology. If the new technology proves successful, these new entrants will replace the incumbents, if not, they will not survive. Competition weeds out unsuccessful firms and nurtures successful ones.

A firm birth can be the result of several different factors. From a theoretical perspective, the main motivation of the firm founder is to make a profit, in which case, it would be reasonable to expect higher rates of firm birth in sectors where profits are expected to be consistent and high and to expect more firm deaths in consistent loss-making sectors. The literature discusses several factors that might constrain or facilitate firm creation and survival. Firm creation can be affected by market conditions or the presence of public finance initiatives, and the level of domestic demand. It can be affected, also, by business environment factors such as ease of access to finance, availability of a skilled workforce, adequate infrastructure, presence of supporting industries, etc. Entrepreneurship can be promoted by a positive business development environment, national sympathy towards entrepreneurship, a tradition of management and a competitive market.

Understanding the scale, heterogeneity and determinants of business creation is particularly important for policy makers because it can promote policies that encourage firm creation and survival. These could include initiatives to support firms directly via financial support, or indirectly through the creation of a business environment and a favourable fiscal policy or a good education system.

As already stated above, in this study a firm birth is seen as 'the creation of a combination of production factors with the restriction that no other enterprises are involved in the event'. Within the population of new born firms are many that do not enter the market because, for instance, of a merger, break-up, split-off or restructuring of a set of enterprises. This sub-population is not included in the analysis.

4.7.1 Within-Country Distribution of Business Births and Deaths

Firm birth rates, defined as the number of new business opening in a given year as a fraction of total active firms, can be considered a measure of the firm dynamics in a specific economy. Firm dynamics differs substantially among countries. While, on average, the proportion of newly created businesses as a share of active firms is around 10%, some countries, such as transition economies, display much higher rates than the country average (Bartelsman et al. 2009). The firm dynamism associated to higher than average entry is often accompanied by a high number of firm exits. Business death rates exceed 10% per year in many countries (OECD 2017).

The following section provides a general overview of firm birth and death rates in Kosovo's economy during 2010–2015. It considers aggregate data for industry, construction and services and provides evidence of firm entry and death based on firm size. It should be noted, that the analysis focuses on employer enterprises, that is, firms with a positive number of employees in any part of the year. In the first part of analysis, the magnitude and characteristics of firm creation and destruction are analyzed; in the second part, the findings for Kosovo's economy are compared to the reference countries. A short overview of the economic conditions in Kosovo during the period analyzed is provided in Fig. 4.4.

Many firms enter the market each year. Bartelsman et al. (2009) suggest that transition economies are characterized by high rates of entry—over 10% per year. However, contrary to our expectations for Kosovo (see Fig. 4.6), we found that entry rates fell short of 10% during the period analyzed. However, we found very high exit rates, suggesting a high level of firm turbulence (Geroski 1995).

With regard to economic sectors, the results show that the industrial sector has the highest entry rates among the three sectors. The average entry rate during the last four consecutive years was 10.5%, with the highest rate -at 11.9%—reported in 2010. In that same year, exit rates in the industrial sector reached 14.7%. Two other sectors show low average rates. In services, the entry rate was 13.4% (exit rate around 15%) and in construction the entry rate was 12.9% and an exit rate of less than 12%.

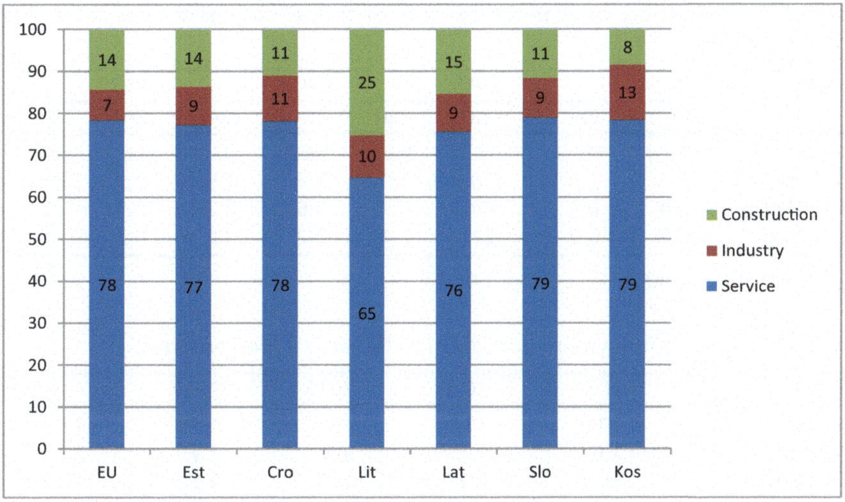

Fig. 4.6 Proportion of enterprise births by sector, 2015 (*Source* Eurostat and KSA)

In terms of firm size, the results indicate that there is a clear correlation between entry and exit relates and firm size. A closer look shows that, in consecutive years, micro firms (few than 5 employees) were the majority (around 97%) of entry firms during that period. Similarly, micro firms dominate among exits, which is evidence of the high level of correlation between entry and exit rates (Table 4.7).

By focusing on the entire population of firms with at least one employee, we find that slightly higher than 8% of employment, on average, is involved in a process of firm creation and destruction. The findings indicate that, from a firm churn perspective, the highest contributor to employment is the industry sector, with an annual average growth rate in terms of employment levels of 12.8%, followed by construction, which accounted for 9.6% on average. The results show that there is a significant difference between these two sectors and the service sector. The rate growth of employment in the service sector is 2.1% on average (Table 4.8).

Table 4.7 Proportion of firm births and exits for each size class 2014–2017 (percentages)

Years	2014		2015		2016		2017	
	Entry	Exit	Entry	Exit	Entry	Exit	Entry	Exit
1–4 empl.	97.0	97.3	97.3	96	96.7	97.7	96.2	97.4
5–9 empl.	2.2	2.0	2.0	3.0	2.3	1.9	2.5	2.1
10–19 empl.	0.4	0.4	0.4	0.7	0.6	0.2	0.5	0.5
20+ empl.	0.2	0.2	0.2	0.4	0.2	0.2	0.2	0.1

Source KBRA and KSA

Table 4.8 Gross employment contribution by sectors (percentages)

Years	2014	2015	2016	2017	Average
Industry	13.3	11.9	13.5	12.6	12.8
Service	1.6	1.2	2.8	2.7	2.1
Construction	10.1	8.1	10.6	9.5	11.1
Average	8.3	7.1	9.0	8.3	**10.2**

Source KSA

4.7.2 Entry and Exit Flows of Firms: Cross-Country Comparisons

This section compares the findings for flows of firm entries and exits in Kosovo's economy with the findings for the reference countries. The data sources provide rich national information for five EU countries. Finally, we analyse how countries' institutional characteristics are associated to firm creation and survival over time.

The indicators in this section have been harmonized and combined with data from Eurostat's country business demography database. The time frame covers the years 2010–2015. The indicators are developed according to the firm sector of economic activity (NACE Rev. 2, 1-digit). They include the number of active firms, firm births and deaths, and the number of five-year survivors. Definitions of these demographic events follow the standard international guidelines on the development of business demography statistics (Eurostat/OECD 2008).

As mentioned above, firm creation, death and survival differ substantially across countries (OECD 2016b). This cross-country variation in entry as well as exit and survival could, in part, be associated to fixed factors, such as geography or availability of natural resources, or may be a function of institutional factors, such as availability of finance, education levels in the population, and quality of local governments and institutions, all of which are known to differ widely across regions (OECD 2016c).

The evidence suggests, that in industrialized countries, entry rates are lower compared to transition countries where entry rates mostly exceed 10% (Bartelsman et al. 2009). The empirical findings for industrialized countries indicate, also, that firm dynamism is often accompanied by a high number of firm closures. This suggests high levels of turbulence in all industrial countries with many firms entering and exiting most markets every year (Geroski 1995).

Figure 4.7 depicts entry and exit rates for the business economy; it shows that firm entry in Kosovo is similar to the reference countries. However, while EU firm entries and exits are almost equal, in Kosovo, exit is significantly higher than firm entry. This is evidence of the higher dynamism often associated to industrialized countries, where firm turbulence and creative destruction are functions of innovation and advanced technologies and market demand (Duranton and Puga 2001). On the other hand, these differences might reflect differences in the sectoral composition of the business population in industrial countries (Ahn 2001; Bartelsman et al. 2009).

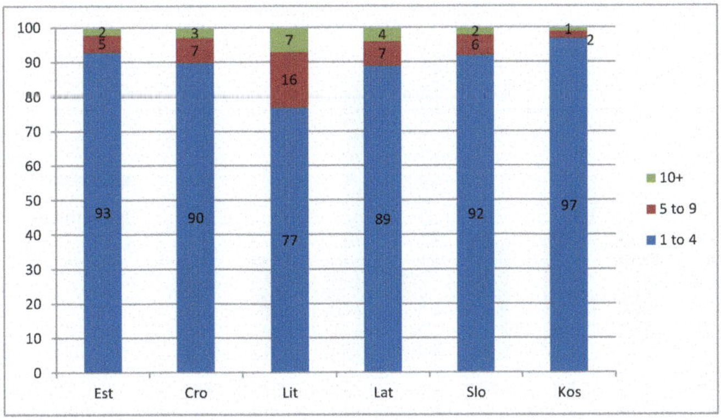

Fig. 4.7 Proportion of firm births in the business economy by size, 2015 (*Source* Eurostat and KSA)

In the context of the proportion of firm creation across the three main economic sectors, Kosovo is fairly similar to the five reference countries. In all of them, the highest proportion of newborn firms is consistent in the services sector. On average, three out of every four new enterprises in the business economies of these six countries in 2015 were operating in the service sector (75%). The only difference is in the industry sector; in the case of Kosovo the proportion is 13% while in the other countries it was 9% on average. Kosovo has the lowest proportion of firm entry in the construction sector (8%) compared to the other countries (15%).

Figures 4.7 and 4.8 show there are no major differences in firm entry/exit rates or the sectoral structure of newborn firms in Kosovo's economy compared to the reference countries. An alternative way to measure the flow of firms is to look at the number of newborn firms in terms of size. The previous evidence suggests that, in most of the developed countries, newborn firms are dominated by companies employing between 1 and 4 employees. In other words, the share of small firms that enter the market is 90%. However, Fig. 4.9 shows that the share of small firms in total firms in Kosovo's economy is significantly higher—reaching 97%. In all countries, around 90% of newborn enterprises in 2015 had fewer

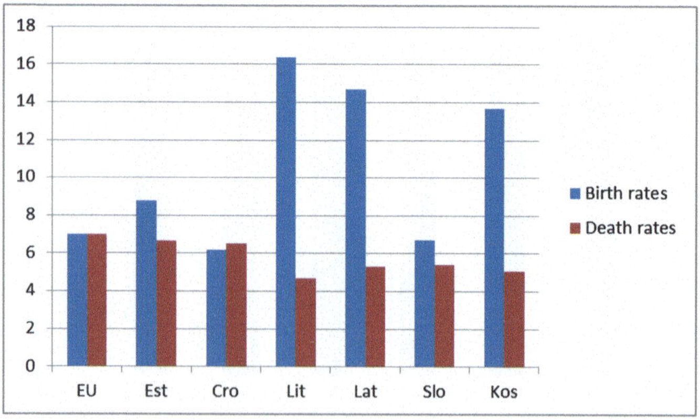

Fig. 4.8 Entry and exit rates in the industrial sector, 2015 (*Source* Eurostat data for reference countries and KSA)

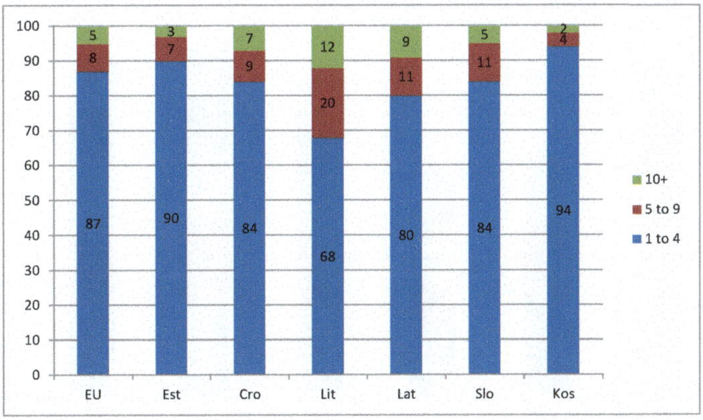

Fig. 4.9 Proportion of firm births in the industry sector size, 2015 (*Source* Eurostat data for reference countries and KSA)

than five employees. However, there are some deviations from these general trends. For example, in Estonia the share of newborn enterprises with 1–4 employees reached 93% while their share was only 77% in Lithuania and 89% in Latvia. These differences might be attributable, in part, to the different structures of the national business economies and their relative specialization in certain activities (OECD 2016c). The characteristics of the labour market can also have an effect on new entrant size in the form of average personnel costs, flexibility of employment protection legislation and incidence of false self-employment or form registration as self-employed, focused on a single client, over the long term, thus, resembling dependent employees (Geroski 1995; Bartelsman et al. 2009; Mata and Portugal 2012) (Fig. 4.10).

Firm entry and exit is another dimension we could examine to identify differences in firm dynamics between Kosovo and the reference countries. Sectoral variations among countries reflect a rich mix of the technological, cost and demand factors driving firm dynamics and national market structures and institutions (Overman and Puga 2010). Figure 4.11 depicts the proportion of newborn firms, based on size, in the industrial sector in 2015. It shows that the share of smaller firms in total firms in Kosovo's economy is significantly higher than in the reference countries.

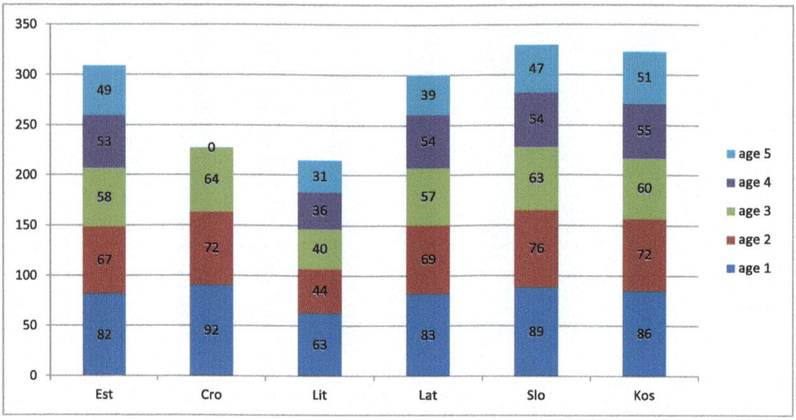

Fig. 4.10 Firm survival in the business economy excluding holding companies' activities: firm age 1–5 (*Source* Eurostat and KSA, *Note* Survival rates for Croatia are for 3 years of age)

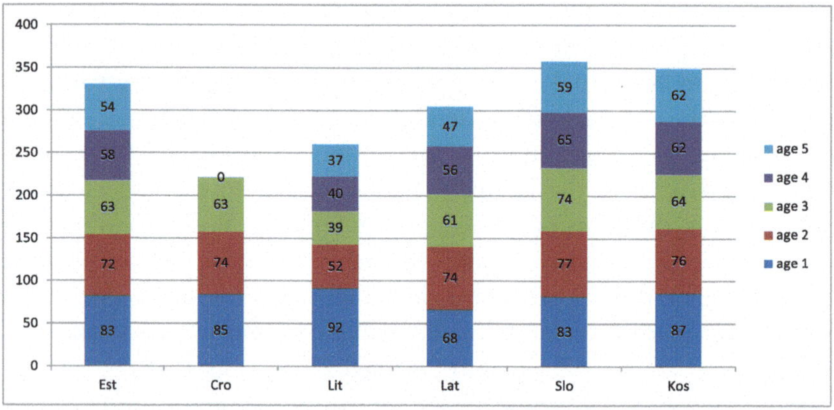

Fig. 4.11 Firm survivals in industry, age 1–5 (*Source* Eurostat and KSA, *Note* Survival rates for Croatia are for up to year 3)

While in all the reference countries for which data are available, around 80% of newborn enterprises in 2015 had fewer than five employees; in the case of Kosovo, this proportion is 94%. For example, in Lithuania the share of newly born enterprises between 1 and 4 employees reached 64%, in Estonia 91%, and in Slovenia 84%.

4.7.3 Main Findings

The firm birth rate in Kosovo is comparable to that in the reference countries. Kosovo has experienced a steady firm birth rate since 2010. Most new employer enterprises in the business economy are created with between one and four employees. The average number of employees in a new employer enterprise is typically higher in industry than in services, reflecting economies of scale. Across the reference countries, the average size of employer enterprise births is broadly similar in the services sector, but differences are more significant in industry. While in Kosovo 94% of firms have between on and four employees is this ranges between 68% in Lithuania and 90% in Estonia. In terms of firm deaths, the results point to similarities between Kosovo and the reference countries except in 2015, where the rate of firm deaths was significantly higher in Kosovo than in the comparator countries.

4.8 Firm Survival Over Time

Another way to understand firm dynamics is to examine post-entry firm performance. If entrepreneurship is to drive economic growth, then a new firm needs to be able to overcome the difficulties that emerge in its early post-entry years, expand its activities and maintain employment numbers over time (Klapper et al. 2008). To understand firm dynamics we need to observe the firm after market entry. In addition, post-entry performance sheds light on the market selection process that separates successful entrants that survive and prosper from firms that stagnate and, eventually, exit (Bartelsman et al. 2009).

We conduct an analysis of the life cycle of newly born firms and the probability that they will survive. The data used allow newly born firms to be tracked over time to trace how many survive from one year to the next. The main aim is to study survival rates through to the fifth year in the market. We have relevant data for the cohort of firms that were born in 2010 and survived to 2015. A firm born in year t is considered to have survived in year t + 1 if it is active in terms of turnover and/or employment in any part of year t + 1.

Figures 4.12 to 4.14 compare survival rates in Kosovo with the reference countries, for the business economy and the three main economic sectors: industry (NACE sections C to E), construction (NACE section F) and services (NACE sections G to K). Specifically, Fig. 4.12 presents non-parametric (graphic) estimates of survival rates for firms operating in the business economy. These survival rates indicate the

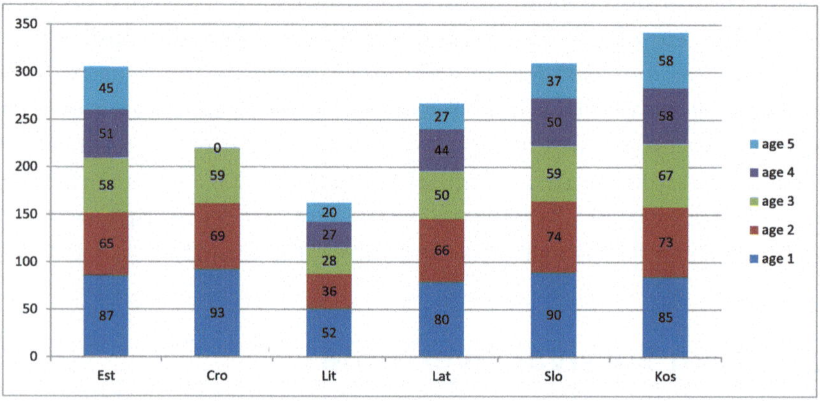

Fig. 4.12 Firm survival in the construction sector, age 1–5 (*Source* Eurostat and KSA, *Note* Survival rates for Croatia are for up to year 3)

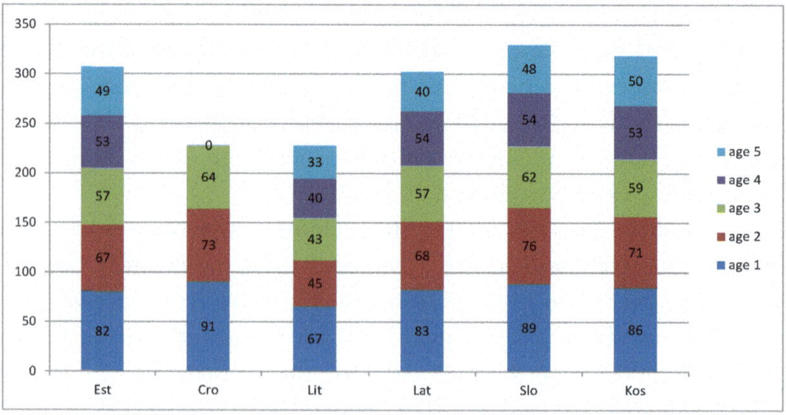

Fig. 4.13 Firm survivals in the service sector, age 1–5 (*Source* Eurostat and KSA, *Note* Survival rates for Croatia are up to 3 age)

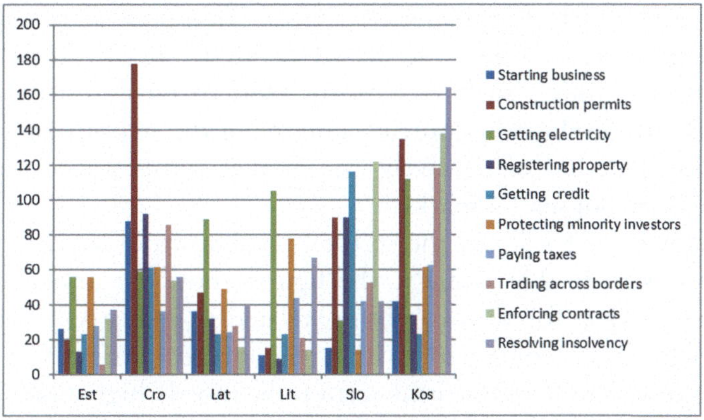

Fig. 4.14 Doing business indicators for Kosovo and the reference countries, 2015 (*Source* Doing business 2015, World Bank)

proportion of firms from a cohort of entrants that were still operating in the fifth year. The results show that survival rates for one-year-old to four-year-old firms in Kosovo are comparable to the reference countries, except Lithuania, which reports fairly low survival rates compared to the other countries. In the case of Kosovo, after one year of business operations, about 14% of firms exit the market compared to 11% in Slovenia and 8% in Croatia, while survival rates in the Baltic countries range from 63% in Lithuania to 83% in Latvia.

It appears that the probability of survival for firms in Kosovo is quite strong after five years. So, conditional on survival through the initial four years, the prospects for firm survival in Kosovo improve in the subsequent period. For firms that are still in the market after the fourth year, the survival probability does not change significantly, so that, about 55% of firms in Kosovo survive after year four, relative to 36% in Lithuania and 54% in Slovenia and Latvia. After year five, around 51% of firms can be expected to survive, a pattern that is comparable to Estonia with 49%, and significantly higher relative to Lithuania and Latvia where survival rates are around 31% and 39% respectively. These differences may be due, also, to the different market orientation of the firms and the environment in which they operate (Ahn 2001; Klapper et al. 2008). This pattern confirms one of Bartelsman et al.'s (2009) stylized facts that rate of exit of firms in transition economies, such as Kosovo, tend to be significantly lower than those in developed countries, endorsing the hypothesis that new firms enjoy a period of relatively low market competition—especially in new, lightly populated markets.

Figures 4.11–4.13 depict the sectoral breakdown of survival rates for enterprises born in 2010–2015. The figures show the deviation in the pattern of survival for Kosovo's firms, related to industry, construction and services firms, compared to the reference countries. The survival prospects of industry sector firms seem to be mostly higher compared to the reference countries with the exception of Latvia, where the survival rate is 68%. The survival rate for the industry in the other countries is 87% in year 1 in Kosovo and between 83% (in Estonia and Slovenia) and 92% (in Lithuania) in the reference countries. Similar to the patterns for the business economy, the survival rate pattern in Kosovo resembles that in the other countries for the first four years. Then, from year five, the survival rate of industry firms in Kosovo is relatively higher than in the other countries at 62% with Slovenia the next highest at 59%. The highest survival rates for industry are considerably above the average rates achieved by Lithuania and Latvia—at least 25 percentage points higher in the first case and 15 percentage points higher in the second.

In construction, survival rates are similar to those for industry firms. If firms manage to survive to year 4, after that their prospects for survival are greater. Survival rates in years 4 and 5 are 58% in Kosovo and, in the other countries, in year 5, are significantly lower, between 20% in Lithuania and 45% in Estonia.

In the service sector, five-year survival rates to 2015 are more than twice as high as in the business economy for firms born in 2010—see Table 4.11. A breakdown of survival rates by years shows that Kosovan firms have higher survival prospects compared to the reference countries. The survival rates at five years for firms in the service sector are similar to the reference countries except Lithuania, whose rate is significantly lower rate—33% in year 5.

4.8.1 Main Findings

The findings show that the survival prospects for one-year-old to four-year-old firms in Kosovo are comparable to those in four of the reference countries (except Lithuania). They show, also, probability of survival for firms in Kosovo improves significantly after five years. Therefore, provided these firms manage to survive to year 4, the prospects of survival improve in the subsequent period. For firms that remain in the market after year 4, the survival probability increases significantly relative to the reference countries (except Slovenia). About 55% of firms in Kosovo survives after year 4 compared to 36% in Lithuania and 39% in Latvia. In the industrial sector, where production tends to be more capital-intensive and larger firms can exploit increasing returns to scale, firms show fairly consistently higher levels of survival than in other sectors. The survival rates of firms in the industrial sector in Kosovo (62%) are relatively higher than in the reference countries; at least 25 percentage points higher than Lithuania and 15 percentage points higher than Latvia. This difference increases in the construction sector, where the difference after year 4 is 28% higher than in Lithuania and 21% higher than in Latvia. The results for the service sector are similar.

4.9 The Role of Business Environment Factors on Firm Demography

The empirical evidence related to business demography indicates that there are several macroeconomic indicators which explain the pattern of firm dynamics. Klapper et al. (2008), using data from the 2008 World Bank Group Entrepreneurship Survey, find a very strong and statistically significant relationship between firm entry and a better business environment. For instance, they suggest that ease of starting a business and stronger governance are associated to higher rates of firm entry. They suggest, also, that a quick, efficient and cost-effective business registration process is important for encouraging formal sector entrepreneurship. Geroski et al. (2012) suggest that firms that are born in growing economic conditions are more likely to have almost continuously higher survival rates, other things being equal, than in those in which the economy is declining. The next section investigates the association between countries' institutional characteristics and firm creation and survival over time.

4.9.1 Ease of Doing Business and Firm Dynamics

This section considers those economic activities that require sensible rules to encourage start-ups and growth and avoid market distortions. The analysis uses the World Bank 'doing business' indicators for 2015. Doing business information includes two types of indicators: those that measure the complexity and costliness of the country's regulatory process, and those that measure the strength of legal institutions such as courts and credit information systems. Regulations determine how straightforward it is to establish or close a firm, efficiency of business contract enforcement, the procedures involved in obtaining permits for electricity, the bureaucracy related to importing and exporting activities, the ease of obtaining credit and the taxation system. Thus, regulation has a direct influence on the decision to start a business.

Empirical work suggests that an efficient and inclusive business environment can boost firm entry rates while a poor business environment discourages entrepreneurs from starting businesses. It has been argued that, at all stages of the business cycle including entry, investment, expansion, transfer and exit, an effective and transparent institutional and regulatory environment is crucial for business development (OECD 2017). A number of cross-country studies highlight that excessive regulation and burdensome legal procedures related to firm start up can constrain the entry of new firms. In the case of low-income countries, we know less about the effects of the regulatory burden or entry regulations and how much they differ from those in high-income countries.

It has been suggested that the various obstacles and the high costs imposed by inefficient firm registration systems deter individuals with business ideas from embarking on formal entrepreneurship. For instance, Bripi (2013) provides evidence that the regulatory burden matters for start-up creation, and Audretsch et al. (2014) offer similar findings. In general, institutional efficiency in relation to firm registration is seen as necessary for a healthy economy (De Sotto 2000). Among the indicators for registry efficiency, the most important include: a comprehensive electronic database; a 'one-stop shop' system' and an online platform to accomplish business registration. Doing business data show that Kosovo is ranked among the best economies for registry efficiency and has an efficient online business register system. It is ranked higher than some of the reference countries, for example, Croatia and Latvia—see Fig. 4.14. However, apart from starting a business and obtaining credit, for all other business indicators Kosovo is significantly behind the reference countries. We found that newly formed firms have to go undergo an onerous bureaucratic procedure to obtain permission to build a warehouse, and acquire a permanent electricity connection and permanent supply of electricity for a standardized warehouse.

There are three dimensions of the doing business indicators in which Kosovo performs very poorly relative to the reference countries: trade across borders; contract enforcement; and resolution of insolvency. The last two are linked to the firm birth, death and survival rates. Contract enforcement is associated to contract freedom, that is, the power of the contracting parties freely to determine the content of an agreement without interference from government or other individuals (Stam et al. 2006). The logical question that arises is why is enforcement of contracts so important for economic growth and efficiency? The answer is that its unrestricted exercise by parties with equal bargaining power and good knowledge of market conditions can promote the most efficient allocation of resources in the marketplace (Edwards 2009). In addition, enforcement of contracts contributes to the establishment of functional economies in which practicability is prized (DiMatteo and Rich 2006) while an effective judicial system provides a structured, timely and orderly framework for resolving disputes. It also fosters economic stability and growth (Audretsch et al. 2014).

The last doing business indicator where Kosovo performs poorly is resolving insolvency. The firm dynamics literature relates insolvency laws and their enforcement in practice to firm birth, death and survival rates. The empirical evidence suggests that individuals, from a range of social and demographic groups, consider the possibility of bankruptcy as the greatest barrier to starting a business and rank it above irregular income and lack of job security (European Commission 2012). It would seem that firm exists are a necessary condition for economic growth, and efficient exit rules could encourage more new firm creation (Cirmizi et al. 2010). It has been argued, also, that businesses started by previous failed entrepreneurs grow faster than those established by first time entrepreneurs (Araujo et al. 2012). Insolvency laws can improve predictability for both creditors and entrepreneurs and enable entrepreneurs to determine the maximum risk associated with failure (Lee et al. 2007). Thus, a transparent and enforceable legal framework for resolving insolvency would allow policy makers to promote entrepreneurship and new firm creation.

4.9.2 Access to Finance and Firm Dynamics

Typically, SMEs are more likely to rely on bank debt for their external financing and are more likely than large firms to be credit constrained (Kuntchev et al. 2012). Although access to finance for SMEs has generally improved, financing gaps persist—especially for young firms, start-ups, micro-enterprises and fast-growing innovative ventures (Djankov et al. 2008). Lack of comparable cross-country information on credit to firms makes it difficult to measure the cross-country dimension of credit constraints. However, it is possible to build proxies for the differences in credit constraints across countries for some indicators.

While data on business loans are collected directly by the Central Bank of Kosovo from the commercial banks, the information provided is not sufficiently fine grained to derive data on SMEs directly. Therefore, our information on SME loans in Kosovo comes from financial accounting data and reports from other monetary and financial institutions. The data on Kosovo is compared to other countries wherever appropriate data are available (see the Table 4.9).

Table 4.9 Scoreboard for Kosovo and the reference countries, 2015

	Unit	Kosovo	Estonia	Latvia	Sllovenia
Interest rates, SMEs	%	8	3.04	4.5	3.5
NPL SMEs	%	8.3	2.79	5.7	n/a
Share of SME outstanding loans	%	46.5	24.56	76.05	41.01
Government loan guarantees, SMEs	EUR million	n/a	44	n/a	552
Venture capital investments	EUR million	n/a	14	51.98	n/a
Leasing and hire purchases	EUR million	10	543	932	n/a
Factoring and invoice discounting	EUR million	n/a	2239	152	n/a

Source CBK and Financing SME and Entrepreneurs (OECD 2017)

Kosovo has established a reasonably well developed regulatory framework, which supports lending to the business sector including SMEs. Most of the Basel core principles have been implemented (OECD 2016a). The central bank credit registry covers 95.2% of the adult population (World Bank 2015). Banks and other financial institutions in Kosovo are well capitalized and are characterized by relatively high levels of liquidity. The non-performing loans rate is among the lowest in the region, indicating relatively high quality of loan portfolios in the banking sector. However, lending to SMEs remains constrained, not least because of their high level of informality, low-quality loan applications from small companies and difficult and lengthy enforcement procedures in the case of default (OECD 2016a).

SMEs' demands for finance are predominantly in the form of loans. A 2013 World Bank Enterprise Survey of Kosovo showed that 66.8% of firms have loans or credit lines, which is almost double the average for Eastern Europe and Central Asia. However, demand for equity is low for two reasons. First, the majority of SMEs operating in Kosovo are family owned and, second there is no financial equity market.

Other sources of non-bank finance remain largely underdeveloped. For instance, leasing products offered by banks seem not to be widely utilized by SMEs. There is a legal framework for leasing operations, but, in the absence of data on penetration, it is difficult to ascertain uptake among SMEs. However, the bank provides factoring services, although there is no specific legal framework (OECD 2016a).

Credit conditions have improved significantly in recent years. Interest rates on SME borrowing have declined from 14% in 2011 to 8% in 2015. However, these rates remain relatively high compared to interest rates in most other Euro zone countries, for example, interest rates for SMEs in Slovenia in 2015 were 3.5%, and in Estonia were 3.04% (see the Table 4.9).

Other sources of non-bank finance remain largely underdeveloped and undiversified (OECD 2016a). Direct loans are provided, mostly, by international banks such as EBRD or KfW Banking Group, but not by government, which is the loan provider in some of the reference countries such as Slovenia or Estonia.[4] A major problem related to financial support for SMEs is lack of equity finance and venture capital. There seem to be no examples of institutional equity investments in Kosovo apart from the regional Enterprise Expansion Fund and EBRD. Kosovo's venture capital ecosystem is in its infancy. There are no government supported venture capital schemes, but there is an active private business angels network and there are several individual business angels that provide support—many of which belong to the Kosovar diaspora.[5]

---

[4]Slovenia has established specific direct loan institutions, such as Slovenian Investment and Development Bank (SID), and public funds, such as the Slovene Enterprise Fund (SEF), the Slovenian Regional Development Fund and the Housing Fund. In Estonia, there is KredEx, which provides credit loan guarantees for start-up companies.

[5]The Kosovo Diaspora Investment Fund, established through the UNDP (UN Development Programme) DEED (Diaspora Engagement for Economic Development) project, is intended to encourage the Kosovo diaspora to invest in Kosovo. Since its establishment as a legal entity in 2014, it has failed to attract any investment funding (OECD 2016a).

4.9.3 The Importance of Human Capital: Education and Firm Dynamics

An adequate level of human capital is considered crucial for entrepreneurship because, for many firms, one of the most important production inputs is labour. Overman and Puga (2010) argue that the availability of a local pool of adequately skilled workers is a source of agglomeration and reduces new firms' search costs. In addition, training and education of workers can produce positive spillover effects in the form of knowledge-sharing (Fritsch and Aamoucke 2013). This is particularly evident in high-tech sectors that rely relatively more on workers with tertiary education. Differences in the supply of high skilled workers can give rise to productivity differences (Moretti 2004). The skills and education of the workforce are expected, also, to influence the choice to start a business and the feasibility of this activity.

Innovation and research are essential for entrepreneurship and (local) economic growth. The presence of universities and the quality of the research activities contribute to the creation of new enterprises (Audretsch et al. 2005). Pre-existing research activity and investment can stimulate entrepreneurship. Similarly, existing clusters of innovation-reliant business sectors are conducive to the creation of new firms as entrepreneurs can benefit from both knowledge spillovers and availability of an experienced and well-trained workforce (Chatterji et al. 2013).

There is a lack of data on education outcomes in Kosovo. However, benchmarking tertiary education attainment in Kosovo against the reference countries shows that Kosovo is lagging. For instance, according to OECD (2013), in 2011 only 40% of the population held an upper secondary degree and only just over a third were females—see Table 4.10. In 2011, 8% of the overall population had a university degree compared to an average of 20% in Croatia and 33% in Latvia. Almost 70% of tertiary degree holders in Kosovo are male and 10% of the population (75% of which are female) has received no formal education (OECD 2013).

Table 4.10 Educational attainment and expenditure on education and innovation

	Secondary education attainment as a % of population	Tertiary education attainment as a % of population	Public expenditure on education as a % of GDP	Share of budget on research and innovation as % of GDP
Est	50	33	6.1	1.49
Cro	60	20	4.8	0.84
Lat	56	28	5.9	0.63
Lit	53	33	5.4	1.04
Slo	56	27	5.5	2.2
Kos	40[a]	8[a]	4.6[b]	0.1[b]

Source EUROSTAT for comparator, 2015
http://appsso.eurostat.ec.europa.eu/nui/submitViewTableAction.do
http://ec.europa.eu/eurostat/tgm/table.do?tab=table&init=1&language=en&p-code=t2020_20&plugin=1
[a]OECD (2013), Assessment of the Kosovo Innovation System (accessed 10 May 2018) https://www.oecd.org/south-east-europe/programme/Kosovo%20Innovation%20Report%20English%20Version.pdf
[b]European commission (2018), https://ec.europa.eu/neighbourhood-enlargement/sites/near/files/20180417-kosovo-report.pdf

Upper secondary education includes general and vocational education. In Kosovo, 43% of students entered vocational schools in 2009/2010, a low number compared to 71% in Croatia. The education sector is not aligned to labour market needs, resulting in low employability of graduates and a significant skills premium (OECD 2013).

Public spending on education is fairly modest compared to the reference countries. Public spending in 2016 was 4.6% of GDP, which is broadly in line with middle-income countries with similar age profiles. Spending on innovation and research is virtually non-existent: government spending on research and innovation in 2016 was 0.1% of GDP. The research capacities of universities and research institutes in Kosovo re weak and there are no links between academic institutions and the private sector (European Commission 2018). The number of university staff engaged on research is small and there is almost no commercialization of research or patenting activity (OECD 2013).

4.10 The Determinants of Newly Born Firm Survival in Kosovo

This section explores the determinants of post-entry performance of Kosovo firms by examining survival patterns and the determinants of firm survival. It provides a brief overview of survival methods followed by discussion of the non-parametric and regression results.

4.10.1 Methods Used to Estimate Firm Survival

Survival methods focus on the conditional probability of suffering an event (firm failure) at time *t*, provided the firm has survived up to that period. Survival methods allow us to account for whether and when an event takes place and to control for the evolution of the risk of exit over time. This contrasts with traditional cross-section (ordinary least squares) methods that focus on average duration or unconditional average probability of occurrence of an event during the sample period (e.g., logit and probit). Second, the survival method used allows control for right censoring, that is, if the firm is still active at the end of the observation period. Third, they are also suitable to control for the presence of unobserved firm heterogeneity that could lead to biased inferences.

The empirical analysis is based on multivariate analysis of the hazard rate and its determinants to examine the effect of each explanatory variable, after controlling for other variables which could affect the conditional risk of firm failure. That is, in the regression analysis, the dependent variable is the hazard rate. Kalbfleisch and Prentice (1980) define hazard rate as the probability that the firm exits the market in a moment *t* conditional upon survival up to that time *t*, and conditional on a vector of the covariates *X*, which might include both time-varying and time-constant variables:

$$h(t; X_i(t)) = \lim_{\mathrm{dt}\to 0} \frac{\Pr\left[t \leq T < t + \mathrm{dt} \backslash T \geq t, X_i(t)\right]}{\mathrm{dt}} \quad (4.1)$$

where T is a non-negative random variable (duration, i.e., survival time since birth), which, initially, we assume to be continuous. The hazard rate is conditioned on a number of explanatory variables such as firm size, legal structure, geographic location and industry sector. Thus, the aim of analysis is to investigate whether or not and how a specific variable shapes the risk of firm failure (or, alternatively, its survival). Every firm i has a corresponding (latent) duration that is observable only if the event takes place during the observation window. If the event does not occur, the observation is right-censored. Assuming that the censoring mechanism is non-informative, that is, independent of the drivers of firm failure, survival methods can handle right-censoring.

The analysis begins with the estimation of the semi-parametric proportional hazards survival model proposed by Cox (1975). This model allows us to measure the relationship between the dependent variable, that is, the hazard function or the risk the firm will exit the market, and the set of explanatory variables. The estimation equation can be written as:

$$h_i(t) = h_0(t) \exp\left(\sum_{i=1}^{p} \beta_i X_i'\right) \tag{4.2}$$

where h_0 (t) is the baseline hazard that captures the common risk faced by all firms of a particular age (i.e., when $X_i = 0$). We do not specify, that is, we do not assume any particular parametric form. Therefore, the hazard (risk of failure) that an individual firm faces is some function of the hazard (risk of failure) that every firm of a particular age faces (the baseline hazard h_0), modified by a set of explanatory variables X_i, which proportionally shift the baseline function. The relationship between the explanatory variables and survival depends on some vector of the parameters β (Landau and Everitt 2004). In this model, the effect of each variable is a parallel constant shift in the baseline hazard, which is estimated for all those firms that survive up to a particular period. In the empirical specification, we include year dummies to control for the overall evolution of risk over time (i.e., to control for the effect of business cycle). The parameters are estimated consistently using the partial likelihood estimation method (Cox 1975).

Also, the analysis uses discrete survival methods given the nature of the dataset. In particular, although firm exit may occur at any particular instant in time (the stochastic process occurs in continuous time), the dataset provides yearly information. Hence, survival times are grouped into discrete one-year time intervals (interval-censored data).I In order to assess the effect of the explanatory variables, we estimate a complementary log-log (cloglog) model, a discrete time version of the Cox proportional hazard model.[6] In particular, assuming that the discrete hazard rate follows a complementary log-log distribution (Prentice and Gloeckler 1978) and allowing for unobserved individual heterogeneity, the estimation equation takes the following form:

$$\begin{aligned} c \log \log \left[1 - h_j(X|\nu)\right] &\equiv \log\left(-\log\left[1 - h_j(X|\nu)\right]\right) \\ &= \beta' X + \gamma_j + u \end{aligned} \tag{4.3}$$

where γ_j is the interval baseline hazard and summarizes the pattern of duration dependence (i.e., firm age). The analysis also incorporates firm-level random effects by means of an error term $u = \log(\nu)$ that is assumed to be normally distributed with zero mean and variance σ^2. This is the so-called frailty term and allows us to control for unobserved individual heterogeneity.[7] In the empirical analysis, we test whether the variance of the frailty term is statistically different from zero: if this variance is not statistically different from zero, then a non-frailty model would be the preferred specification. To obtain efficient estimators and unbiased standard errors, we apply the Huber-White sandwich or robust estimator.

[6]See Jenkins (2005) for an excellent overview of complementary log-log and proportional hazards models.

[7]The lack of control for unobserved heterogeneity may lead to over-estimation of the degree of negative duration dependence in the hazard as a result of a selection process, which, as time passes, leaves alive a higher proportion of 'well-suited to survive' firms. A second effect of neglecting individual unobserved heterogeneity is under-estimation of the true proportional response of the hazard to a change in an explanatory variable.

4.10.2 Regression Results

Table 4.11 presents the results of the estimations of the three reduced-form models. Column (1) reports the result of a semi-parametric Cox proportional hazards model specified by Eq. (4.3). Columns (2) and (3) show the results of the cloglog model with and without unobserved heterogeneity, respectively. Before turning to the main results, it is worth commenting on some issues related to the model specification and interpretation of the reported coefficients. First, to control for the presence of firm-level unobserved heterogeneity (related to unobserved firm organizational capabilities, access to specific assets, etc., which can affect firm survival chances), we estimate frailty survival models (column [3]). The null hypothesis of no unobserved individual heterogeneity cannot be rejected at the 1% significance level. Hence, non-frailty models are the appropriate models to estimate. Therefore, the preferred models are (1) and (2). Second, the preferred specification corresponds to the cloglog model with no unobserved heterogeneity (column [2]) because: (i) it is a discrete-time model, which overcomes a limitation of the Cox model when there is high incidence of 'ties', that is, a larger number of firms fail at the same age and (ii) it includes age-dummies, which account explicitly for the effect of firm age. The results of the Cox model are consistent under general conditions and provide a benchmark for comparison. Third, the reported coefficients are hazard ratios. Therefore, a unit change in a variable leads to a proportional shift in the conditional probability of exit. A hazard ratio smaller (greater) than 1 means a negative (positive) effect of the explanatory variable on the hazard rate. That is, if the hazard ratio is smaller (greater) than 1, the effect of the corresponding covariate is to decrease (increase) the hazard rate. Fourth, the covariates are included as a set of dummy variables to facilitate interpretation and, also, to account for possible nonlinearities in the effect of the explanatory variables.

The results in column (2) reveal an inverted U-shaped relationship between the hazard rate (i.e., conditional risk of firm failure) and firm age and size. For age, the hazard rate reaches a peak in the second year of the firm's life, and decreases thereafter.[8] The results

[8]The hazard rates for firms age 1 and age 3 are not statistically different.

Table 4.11 New firm survivals in Kosovo—regression results

Dependent variable: hazard rate	[1]	[2]	[3]
	Cox proportion hazard model	Cloglog model (discrete-time equiv. to [1])	Clog frailty model
Firm size (one employee omitted)			
[2–5]	1.09***	1.10***	1.10***
	[0.002]	[0.001]	[0.001]
[6–9]	1.46***	1.48***	1.48***
	[0.001]	[0.000]	[0.000]
[10–19]	0.85	0.85	0.85
	[0.343]	[0.331]	[0.331]
[20+]	0.81	0.8	0.81
	[0.361]	[0.351]	[0.366]
Ownership (limited liability omitted)			
Sole proprietorship	3.67***	3.74***	3.73***
	[0.000]	[0.000]	[0.000]
General partnership	4.11***	4.23***	4.24***
	[0.001]	[0.000]	[0.000]
Foreign company	2.07	2.11	2.06
	[0.000]	[0.000]	[0.000]
Sector (Industry omitted)			
Service	1.37***	1.42***	1.32***
	[0.000]	[0.000]	[0.000]
Construction	0.78***	0.76***	0.78***
	[0.045]	[0.043]	[0.043]
Region (Prishtina omitted)			
Prizren	1.40***	1.41***	1.41***
	[0.000]	[0.000]	[0.000]
Gjilan	0.92***	0.92***	0.92***
	[0.031]	[0.029]	[0.028]
Peja	1.66***	1.69***	1.69***
	[0.000]	[0.000]	[0.000]
Mitrovica	1.30***	1.31***	1.31***
	[0.000]	[0.000]	[0.000]

(continued)

Table 4.11 (continued)

Dependent variable: hazard rate	[1]	[2]	[3]
	Cox proportion hazard model	Cloglog model (discrete-time equiv. to [1])	Clog frailty model
Year dummies (year 2010 omitted)			
Year 2011	1.27***	1.28***	1.28***
	[0.001]	[0.001]	[0.001]
Year 2012	1.17***	1.17***	1.17***
	[0.022]	[0.024]	[0.022]
Year 2013	1.30***	1.29***	1.29***
	[0.000]	[0.000]	[0.000]
Year 2014	1.21***	1.22***	1.22***
	[0.003]	[0.004]	[0.005]
Year 2015	1.30***	1.31***	1.31***
	[0.000]	[0.000]	[0.000]
Firm age dummies (no omission)	NO		
One year old		0.007***	0.007***
		[0.000]	[0.000]
Two years old		0.010***	0.010***
		[0.000]	[0.000]
Three years old		0.007***	0.007***
		[0.000]	[0.000]
Four years old		0.004***	0.004***
		[0.000]	[0.000]
Five years old		0.003***	0.003***
		[0.000]	[0.000]
Six years old		0.002***	0.002***
	[0.000]	[0.000]	[0.000]
Log Likelihood	−65821.35	−25,821.45	−25,821.45
No of firms	40,138	40,138	40,138
No of observations	146,846	146,846	146,846

Source KBRA and KSA
p-values using standard errors in brackets
$^{***}p<0.01$, $^{**}p<0.05$, $^{*}p<0.1$

are in line with the 'liability of adolescence' hypothesis (Brüderl and Schussler 1990; Fichman and Levinthal 1991). That is, new organizations can survive for a time by drawing on their initial endowments. After that, failure rates reach peak with the exhaustion of these initial resources and decrease as only the fittest firms remain in the market. With respect to size, we found that single-employee firms face a lower risk of failure than firms with between two and nine employees. The risk of failure seems to be especially high for firms with six to nine employees; larger firms are the most likely to survive. However, the hazard rate is not statistically different from that for firms with only one employee. The high survival rate of single-employee new firms is consistent with the view of self-employment as an alternative for survival in an economy with a high unemployment rate. One explanation for why larger firms enjoy higher survival rates may be the financial commitment involved. Before launching a large firm, it is likely that a considerable amount of market research will have been conducted and lengthy discussions held with potential investors or organizations that might lend the capital required for the start-up (Kuntchev et al. 2012). On the other hand, a sole proprietor who decides to set up a business with no employees will have very low initial costs, which translates into a lower level of risk.

The results highlight that the new firm's legal structure is correlated to survival. In particular, after controlling for other factors, limited liability firms face much lower exit risks than their counterparts, including foreign-owned companies. These findings might be related to their better organizational capabilities, managerial skills and/or access to external finance (Storey 1994; Bloom and Van Reenen 2007, 2011). Also, foreign-owned firms have a lower risk of failure than firms of the other two ownership types (i.e., sole proprietors and general partnerships). The empirical evidence on the effect of foreign ownership on survival is mixed. On the one hand, Görg and Strobl (2003) and Bernard and Sjöholm (2003) report higher failure risks for Irish majority foreign-owned plants and foreign Indonesian firms, respectively. On the other hand, Li and Gusinger (1991), Mata and Portugal (2002) and Geroski et al. (2012) find that domestic newly formed firms are much more likely to exit than foreign-owned ones. Our findings fall between these results since we find an intermediate exit risk for newly created foreign-owned companies in Kosovo.

Sector of activity also influences new firms; survival prospects. In particular, compared to construction, the risk of failure is lower in the industry sector and higher in serviced, and the differences are statistically significant at conventional levels. A possible explanation for why industry firms have higher chances of survival might be related to their better organizational capabilities, managerial skills and/or access to external finance. Previous studies point to the existence of differences in hazard rates across sectors and relate them to traditional market structure variables such as the economies of scale, cost advantages of incumbent firms and rate of growth of sector specific demand (Audretsch and Mahmood 1994; Mata and Portugal 1994).

The results presented in Table 4.11 show that the firm's region affects its survival chances after entry. In particular, the lowest firm failure risk is for firms located in the capital, Prishtina, and Gjilan and is highest for firms in Peja, Prizren and, especially, Mitrovica. These findings are in line with previous studies which predict higher survival rates for firms located near metropolitan areas (Baldwin et al. 2000; Fotopoulos and Louri 2000), and are related to some cost and demand side advantages of agglomeration (Dunne et al. 2005; Pe'er and Vertinsky 2006a). On the cost side, firms can exploit external economies arising from the proximity to specialized suppliers, knowledge spillovers and the development of specialized labour markets. On the demand side, firms have access to larger potential demand for their products. Both forces are mutually reinforcing.

Finally, the year dummies account for the evolution of the risk of firm failure over time, which is common to all firms existing in a particular year. These variables capture the phase of the business cycle.

4.11 Conclusions

This chapter presented an analysis of business demography in Kosovo and compared the findings with the patterns in five selected EU countries. Based on data derived from official statistics, provided by national statistical institutes, we measured and discussed patterns in the active firm populations and their transformations over time, of flows of newly born firms (firm births), closures (enterprise deaths) and survival rates during the period 2010–2015. We focused, especially, on tracking cohorts of newly born enterprises over a five-year period. This is of interest in the context of a relatively undeveloped economy, given that successful entrepreneurship and successful firms are crucial for boosting productivity, increasing employment, enhancing economic growth and improving societal welfare.

Comparing patterns in the population of active firms, we found that, while there are similarities between Kosovo and the comparator countries in terms of sectoral structure, there are significant differences in the sizes of firms. Our findings suggest that the population of active firms in Kosovo is dominated by a smaller average size of active firms compared to the reference countries. They suggest that, in Kosovo, the contribution of firms to employment by firms with between one and four employees is significantly higher at 24.5%, while in the comparator countries this contribution varies between 9.6 and 17.5%. We found an important difference related to subsectors. Kosovo's economy is dominated by wholesale and retail, which account for more than 55% of total firms in the service sector, while the wholesale and retail subsectors in the reference countries are below 35%.

While the firm birth rate in Kosovo is comparable to the reference countries, most new employer enterprises in the business economy are created with between one and four employees. The average number of persons employed in employer enterprise births is typically higher in industry than in services, reflecting economies of scale. Across the reference countries, the average size of employer enterprise births is broadly similar in the services sector, but there are more significant differences in industry. In the context of firm deaths, the results point to similarities between Kosovo and the reference countries except in 2015, when the firm death rate in Kosovo was significantly higher.

In this chapter, we used both non-parametric and semi-parametric survival methods to examine survival patterns and the determinants of firm survival. The data comprise the population of new-born firms during the period 2010–2015. This analysis was complemented by a comparison of firm churn patterns in other referenced developed countries. Kosovo has two main distinguishing features. On the one hand, the entry rate of large firms is lower than in other reference countries. On the other hand, firm failure rates are lower in Kosovo, particularly after year four and especially for very small firms. The survival prospects of one-employee firms are not significantly different from the survival prospects of large firms. Thus, the firm churn rate is relatively low in Kosovo.

The findings in this chapter reveal some features specific to the functioning of the Kosovo economy. In particular, market selection forces, leading to high turnover, that is, high entry and exit, are less significant than in the reference countries. Firm turnover has been identified out as an important driver of innovation, productivity improvements and growth. The relatively soft market selection may be related to some distinctive features of the Kosovan economy. In particular, the prevalence of one-employee firms and their high survival chances seems to be related more to necessity in the presence of low job opportunities than to a high level of entrepreneurship. Furthermore, the results point, also, to the existence of important constraints (i.e., barriers to firm entry and exit) on economic activity in a context of high uncertainty. The combination of these two factors leads to low turbulence. They are related to unfair competition, limited rule of law, high level of corruption and low enforcement of regulation to protect investors, high cost of finance, poor infrastructure and, especially, low level of human capital. In this context, the low entry rates of large firms and higher incidence of small firm entry and low exit rates are consistent with the view that new firm entry is driven more by a search process to establish the potential firm's fitness to survive in the market in a context of high uncertainty. Large-scale entry involves large commitments (e.g., high sunk entry costs) in a context of high uncertainty and relatively small market. Thus, high entry barriers reduce both entry and exit.

These findings have several implications for policy makers. In particular, they suggest that, in addition to improving the physical infrastructure, it is essential to improve the functioning of market selection forces. Adequate enforcement of laws and regulations to protect investors and higher quality financial and education systems would result in high payoffs in terms of business dynamics, productivity and economic growth.

References

Aghion, P., Akcigit, U., & Howitt, P. (2014). What do we learn from Schumpeterian growth theory? In *Handbook of economic growth* (1st ed., Vol. 2, Chapter 1, pp. 515–563). Oxford: Elsevier.

Ahmad, N. (2008). A proposed framework for business demography statistics. *Measuring entrepreneurship* (pp. 113–174). New York: Springer.

Ahn, S. (2001). *Firm dynamics and productivity growth: A review of micro evidence from OECD countries* (OECD Economics Department Working Paper 297). Paris: OECD.

Araujo, A., Rafael, V., & Funchal, B. (2012). The Brazilian Bankruptcy law experience. *Journal of Corporate Finance, 18*(4), 994–1004.

Audretsch, D., & Mahmood, T. (1994). The rate of hazard confronting new firms and plants in US manufacturing. *Review of Industrial Organization, 9,* 41–56.

Audretsch, D. B., Santarelli, E., & Vivarelli, M. (1999). Start-up and industrial dynamics: Some evidence from Italian manufacturing. *International Journal of Industrial Organization, 17,* 965–983.

Audretsch, D. B., Lehmann, E., & Warning, S. (2005). University spillovers and new firm location. *Research Policy, 34,* 1113–1122.

Audretsch, D., Belitski, M., & Desai, S. (2014, February 20–21). *Multidimensional business environment and entrepreneurship in European cities.* Paper presented at the conference, Doing Business: Past, present and future of business regulations. Washington, DC.

Ayyagari, M., Beck, T., & Demirgüç-Kunt, A. (2003). *Small and medium enterprises across the globe: A new database* (Policy Research Working Paper 3127). Washington, DC: World Bank Publications.

Baldwin, J., Bian, L., Dupuy, R., & Galletly, G. (2000). *Failure rates of new Canadian firms: New perspectives on entry and exit.* Ottawa: Statistics Canada.

Barney, J. B. (1991). Firm resources and sustained competitive advantage. *Journal of Management, 17,* 99–120.
Bartelsman, E. J., & Doms, M. (2000). Understanding productivity: Lessons from longitudinal microdata. *Journal of Economic Literature, 38,* 569–594.
Bartelsman, E., Haltiwanger, J., & Scarpetta, S. (2004). *Microeconomic evidence of creative destruction in industrial and developing countries* (The World Bank Policy Research Working Paper Series 3464). Washington, DC: The World Bank.
Bartelsman, E., Haltiwanger, J., & Scarpetta, S. (2009). Measuring and analyzing cross-country differences in firm dynamics. In T. Dunne, J. B. Jensen, & M. J. Roberts (Eds.), *Producer Dynamics.* Chicago, IL: University of Chicago Press for the NBER.
Becattini, G. (1990). The Marshallian industrial districts as a socio-economic notion. In F. Pyke, et al. (Eds.), *Industrial districts and inter-firm co-operation in Italy* (pp. 37–51). Geneva: International Institute for Labour Studies.
Bernard, A. B., & Sjöholm, F. (2003). *Foreign owners and plant survival* (NBER Working Paper 10039). Cambridge, MA: National Bureau of Economic Research, Inc.
Berner, E., Gomez, G., & Knorringa, P. (2008). *Helping a large number of people becoming a little less poor: The logic of survival entrepreneurs.* UNU-WIDER Workshop on Entrepreneurship and Economic Development, Helsinki, Finland.
Birch, D. L. (1979). *The job generation process.* Cambridge, MA: MIT Program on Neighborhood and Regional Change, mimeo.
Birch, D. L. (1981). Who creates jobs? *The Public Interest, 65,* 3.
Bloom, N., & Van Reenen, J. (2007). Measuring and explaining management practices across firms and countries. *Quarterly Journal of Economics, 122*(4), 1351–1408.
Bloom, N., & Van Reenen, J. (2010). Why do management practices differ across firms and countries? *Journal of Economic Perspectives, 24*(1), 203–224.
Bloom, N., & Van Reenen, J. (2011). Human resource management and productivity. In O. Ashenfelter & D. Card (Eds.), *Handbook of Labor Economics* (Vol. 4B, Chapter 19, pp. 1697–1769). San Diego, CA: Elsevier.
Bripi, F. (2013). *The role of regulations on entry: Evidence from the Italian provinces* (Working Paper 932). Rome: Bank of Italy.
Brüderl, J., & Schussler, R. (1990). Organizational mortality: The liabilities of newness and adolescence. *Administrative Science Quarterly, 35,* 530–547.

Brunetti, A., Kisunko, G., & Weder, B. (1997). *Institutional obstacles to doing business: Region-by-region results from a worldwide survey of the private sector* (World Bank PRD Working Paper 1759). Washington, DC: World Bank.

Caves, R. E. (1998). Industrial organization and new findings on the turnover and mobility of firms. *Journal of Economic Literature, 36*(4), 1947–1982.

Chatterji, A., Glaeser, E. L., & Kerr, W. R. (2013). *Clusters of entrepreneurship and innovation* (NBER Working Paper Series, No. 19013). Cambridge, MA: National Bureau of Economic Research. www.nber.org/papers/w19013.pdf.

Cirmizi, E., Klapper, L., & Uttamchandani, M. (2010). *The challenges of bankruptcy reform* (Policy Research Working Paper 5448). Washington, DC: World Bank.

Collier, D. (1998). Comparative method in the 1990s. *American Political Science Association–Comparative, 9*(1), 1–2, 4–5.

Cox, D. R. (1975). Partial likelihood. *Biometrica, 60,* 269–276.

Criscuolo, C., Gal, P. N., & Menon, C. (2014). *The dynamics of employment growth: New evidence from 18 countries* (OECD Science, Technology and Industry Policy Papers, No. 14). Paris: OECD Publishing. http://dx.doi.org/10.1787/5jz417hj6hg6-e.

Delgado, M., Porter, M. E., & Stern, S. (2010). Clusters and entrepreneurship. *Journal of Economic Geography, 10*(4), 495–518.

Delgado, M., Porter, M. E., & Stern, S. (2014). Clusters, convergence, and economic performance. *Research Policy, 43*(10), 1785–1799. https://doi.org/10.1016/j.respol.2014.05.007.

De Soto, H. (2000). *The mystery of capital: Why capitalism triumphs in the west and fails everywhere else.* New York: Harper & Row.

DiMatteo, L., & Rich, B. (2006). A consent theory of unconscionability: An empirical study of law in action. *Florida University Law Review, 33,* 1067–1118.

Djankov, S., Hart, O., McLiesh, C., & Shleifer, A. (2008). Debt enforcement around the world. *Journal of Political Economy, 116* (6), 1105–1149.

Dunne, T., Klimek, S., & Roberts, M. J. (2005). Exit from regional manufacturing markets: The role of entrant experience. *International Journal of Industrial Organization, 23,* 399–421.

Duranton, G., & Diego, P. (2001). Nursery cities: Urban diversity, process innovation, and the life cycle of products. *American Economic Review, 91*(5), 1454–1477.

Edwards, C. (2009). Freedom of contract and fundamental fairness for individual parties: The tug of war continues. *University of Kentucky Law Review, 77,* 569–646.

European Commission. (2012). *Entrepreneurship in the EU and beyond* (Flesh Eurobarometer 354). Brussels: European Commission. http://ec.europa.eu/public_opinion/flesh/fl_354_en.pdf.

European Commission. (2018). *Kosovo 2018 Report* (Commission Staff Working Document). Strasburg. https://ec.europa.eu/neighbourhood-enlargement/sites/near/files/20180417-kosovo-report.pdf.

Eurostat/OECD. (2008). *Manual on business demography statistics*. http://ec.europa.eu/eurostat/ramon/statmanuals/files/KS-RA-07-010-EN.pdf.

Fichman, M., & Levinthal, D. (1991). Honeymoons and the liability of adolescence: A new perspective on duration dependence in social and organizational relationships. *Academy of Management Review, 16,* 442–468.

Foster, L., Haltiwanger, J., & Krizan, C. J. (2001). Aggregate productivity growth: Lessons from microeconomic evidence. In E. Dean, M. Harper, & C. Hulteneds (Eds.), New *developments in productivity analysis*. Chicago: University of Chicago Press.

Fotopoulos, G., & Louri, H. (2000). Location and survival of new entry. *Small Business Economics, 14*(4), 311–321.

Fritsch, M. (2008). How does new business formation affect regional development? Introduction to the special issue. *Small Business Economics, 30*(1), 1–14.

Fritsch, M., & Aamoucke, R. (2013). Regional public research, higher education, and innovative start-ups: An empirical investigation. *Small Business Economics, 41*(4), 865–885.

Fritsch, M., & Mueller, P. (2004). The effects of new business formation on regional development over time. *Regional Studies, 38*(8), 961–975.

Geroski, P. (1995). What do we know about entry? *International Journal of Industrial Organization, 13,* 421–440.

Geroski, P. A., Mata, J., & Portugal, P. (2012). Founding conditions and the survival of new firms. *Strategic Management Journal, 31*(5), 510–529.

Glaeser, E. L., Kerr, W. R., & Ponzetto, G. A. (2010). Clusters of entrepreneurship. *Journal of Urban Economics, 67*(1), 150–168.

Görg, H., & Strobl, E. (2003). Multinational companies, technology spillovers and plant survival. *Scandinavian Journal of Economics, 4*(12), 581–953.

Guiso, L., & Schivardi, F. (2011). What determines entrepreneurial clusters? *Journal of the European Economic Association, 9*(1), 61–86.

Haltiwanger, J., Ron, J., & Miranda, J. (2010). *Who creates jobs? Small vs. Large vs. Young* (NBER Working Paper No. 16300). Cambridge, MA: NBER.

IFC. (2013). *IFC jobs study: Assessing private sector contributions to job creation and poverty reduction*. Washington, DC: IFC.

Jenkins S. P. (2005). *Survival analysis*. Unpublished manuscript, Institute for Social Science and Economic Research, University of Essex, Colchester.

Kalbfleisch, J. D., & Prentice, R. L. (1980). *The statistical analysis of failure time data*. New York: Wiley.

Klapper, L., Amit, R., Guillén, M. F., & Quesada, J. M. (2008). *Entrepreneurship and firm formation across countries* (The World Bank Policy Research Working Paper 4313). Washington, DC: World Bank.

Krugman, P. (1991). Increasing returns and economic geography. *Journal of Political Economy, 99*(3), 483–499.

Kuntchev, V. Ramalho, R. Rodríguez-Meza, J., & Yung, J. (2012). *What have we learned from the enterprise surveys regarding access to finance by SME? Enterprise analysis unit*. Finance and private sector development Vice President, Word Bank Group, Washington, DC.

Landau, S., & Everitt, B. S. (2004). *A handbook of statistical analyses using SPSS*. Boca Raton, FL: Chapman & Hall.

Lee, S., Peng, M., & Barney, J. (2007). Bankruptcy law and entrepreneurship development: A real options perspective. *Academy of Management Review, 32*(1), 257–272.

Li, A., & Guisinger, P. (1991). Comparative business failures of foreign-controlled firms in the United States. *Journal of International Business Studies*, 2nd Quarter, 209–224.

Liedholm, C., & Mead, D. (1987). *Small scale industries in developing countries: Empirical evidence and policy implications* (MSU International Development Paper No. 9, 1978). East Lansing, MI: Department of Agricultural Economics, Michigan State University.

Liedholm, C., & Mead, D. (1995). *The dynamic role of micro and small enterprises in the development process* (GEMINI Action Research Program I, Final Report). Bethesda, MD: GEMINI.

Lijphart. (1971). Comparative politics and the comparative method. *American Political Science Review, 65* (3), 691–693.

Lijphart, (1975). The comparable-cases strategy in comparative research. *Comparative Political Studies, 8* (2), pp. 158–177.

Mata, J., & Portugal, P. (1994). Life duration of new firms. *Journal of Industrial Economics, 42*(3), 227–245.

Mata, J., & Portugal, P. (2002). The survival of new domestic and foreign-owned firms. *Strategic Management Journal, 23*(4), 323–343.

Moretti, E. (2004). Workers' education, spillovers, and productivity: Evidence from plant-level production functions. *American Economic Review, 94*(3), 656–690.

Neumark, D., Wall, B., & Zhang, J. (2011). Do small businesses create more jobs? New evidence for the United States from the National Establishment Time Series. *The Review of Economics and Statistics, 93*(1), 16–29.

OECD. (2013, March). *Assessment of the Kosovo innovation system* (RCI Project Paper). OECD Development.

OECD. (2014). *Young SMEs, growth and job creation*. http://www.oecd.org/sti/young-SME-growth-and-job-creation.pdf.

OECD. (2016a). Overview: 2016 small business act assessment of the Western Balkans and Turkey. In *SME policy index: Western Balkans and Turkey 2016: Assessing the implementation of the small business act for Europe*. Paris: OECD Publishing. http://dx.doi.org/10.1787/9789264254473-4-en.

OECD. (2016b). *Entrepreneurship at a glance 2016*. Paris: OECD Publishing.

OECD. (2016c, 1–2 June). *The productivity-inclusiveness Nexus, meeting of the OECD council at ministerial level*. Paris [C/MIN(2016)3].

OECD. (2017). *Financing SMEs and entrepreneurs 2017: An OECD scoreboard*. Paris: OECD Publishing. http://dx.doi.org/10.1787/fin_sme_ent-2017-en.

Overman, H. G., & Puga, D. (2010). Labour pooling as a source of agglomeration: An empirical investigation. *Agglomeration Economics* (pp. 133–150). Chicago, IL: University of Chicago Press.

Pe'er, A., & Vertinsky, F. (2006a). *The survival value of clusters* (Working Paper). Tuck Business School at Dartmouth.

Pe'er, A., & Vertinsky, F. (2006b). *Who enters, where, and why? The influence of capabilities and initial resource endowments on the location choices of new enterprises* (Working Paper). Tuck Business School at Dartmouth.

Prentice, R., & Gloeckler, L. (1978). Regression analysis of grouped survival data with application to breast cancer data. *Biometrics, 34*, 57–67.

Ragin, C. C. (1987). *The comparative method: Moving beyond qualitative and quantitative strategies*. Berkeley: University of California Press.

Romer, P. (1986). Increasing returns and long-run growth. *Journal of Political Economy, 94*(5), 1002–1037.

Schumpeter, J. (1934). *Theory of economic development*. Cambridge: Harvard University Press.

Schumpeter, J. (1943). *Capitalism, socialism and democracy*. New York: Harper.

Stam, E., Audrutsch, D., & Meijaard, J. (2006). *Renascent entrepreneurship* (ERIM Report Series 17). Rotterdam: Erasmus Research Institute Management, Erasmus University Rotterdam.

Storey, D. J. (1994). *Understanding the small business sector*. London: Routledge.

Sutton, J. (1997). Gibrat's legacy. *Journal of Economic Literature, 35*(1), 40–59.
World Bank. (2008). *Unleashing prosperity productivity growth in Eastern Europe and the Former Soviet Union*. http://siteresources.worldbank.org/ECAEXT/Resources/publications/UnleashingProsperity.pdf.
World Bank. (2015). *World Bank national accounts data* (database). http://data.worldbank.org/. Accessed 26 June 2015.

5
An Analysis of the Business Environment in Kosovo Using Growth Diagnostics Approach

5.1 Introduction

The interest in Chapter 4 was to measure the business demography and dynamics in Kosovo; This chapter focuses on measure the quality of the business or the investment climate in Kosovo. The findings for Kosovo's economy are compared and contrasted to the set of reference countries used in Chapter 4: Estonia, Croatia, Latvia, Lithuania and Slovenia. There is a substantial body of evidence suggesting that a good investment climate provides better opportunities and incentives for entrepreneurs to invest profitably (Rodrik et al. 2004; Dollar et al. 2005; Carlin et al. 2006). The more conducive the country's business environment, the higher the likely levels of private investment and entrepreneurship, and vice versa.

The empirical literature highlights various business environment factors that affect the rates of private investment, survival and growth of firms. Most of these factors belong to one of the following dimensions: human and physical infrastructure; legal and regulatory institutions (interpreted as the rules of the game in which firms engage

F. Sahiti, *The Growth of Firms in Less-Developed Countries*,
https://doi.org/10.1007/978-3-030-14821-8_5

and the organizations that implement these rules and services); and the quality of the financial system (e.g., cost of and access to finance). Evidence that (say) the rule of law in a specific country is a constraint would imply that the incentives for private investment are lower.

Where can we find evidence on which business environment dimensions are constraining? The empirical evidence used to identify business constraints come from two main sources. First, international institutions and organizations (World Bank, EBRD, OECD, IFC, etc.); second, a firm-level survey, conducted by Riinvest Institute in 2017, of 585 firms in Kosovo. International organizations undertake large numbers of firm-level surveys, aimed at measuring the quality of the business or investment climate. The findings obtained from the former sources of data are tested, validated and complemented by data generated from the Riinvest survey. The objective is to build a more reliable picture of the constraints that matter for economic activity as a whole. These complementary datasets allow identification of business environment dimensions matter most. The identification and categorization of the most binding constraints on private investment are the main focuses of this chapter.

The analysis uses the framework and methodology in Hausmann et al. (2008). The authors suggest a method for identifying binding constraints on growth using a simple growth model. The model allows the building of a hierarchy of constraints and provides guidance on how aggregate indicators can be used to highlight the binding constraints in a particular period (Hausmann et al. 2008).

This chapter is organized as follows. Section 5.2 discusses the reason why the growth diagnostics approach is deployed, followed by an outline of this approach. In Sect. 5.4 is provided the theoretical framework used to analyze the data. Section 5.5 discusses the methodology. Sections 5.6, 5.7, and 5.8 examine the symptoms of business environment constraints. Section 5.9 discusses syndromes derived from the symptoms analysis, and Sect. 5.10 offers some concluding remarks.

5.2 Why a Growth Diagnostics Approach and Methodology

As already mentioned, to identify which business environment dimensions are the most constraining in relation to rates of private investment, the growth diagnostics approach and methodology is employed. It is true that such an approach is at the macro level, that is, it seeks to identify macro-level growth constraints. However, according to Hausmann et al. (2008, p. 22), the crucial problem is low levels of private investment and low levels of entrepreneurship. In that respect, growth diagnostics apply a de facto micro-based lens on growth, that is, it assumes that the constraints on growth are essentially at the micro level. Accordingly, growth diagnostics is concerned with what is preventing private firms or private agents from expanding their business activities and why levels of entrepreneurship are low.

Specifically, there are four factors that suggest a growth diagnostics approach to explore firm growth in Kosovo.

(i) growth diagnostics provides a framework for formulating hypotheses about what might be preventing private investors from investing and what is causing the low levels of entrepreneurship. This approach views economic growth as resulting from a restricted optimization process. It seeks to identify those micro-level constraints that are the most binding, in the sense that their removal would create the conditions for firm expansion/growth and higher level of entrepreneurship. It assumes a simple model in which firm growth and entrepreneurship depend on aspects such as physical and human capital, governance quality, institutions, infrastructure and the quality of financial institutions;

(ii) the growth diagnostics approach enables identification of the constraints on firm growth and allows us to rank them according to their importance. It provides a list of the most restrictive factors on firm growth in the case of Kosovo. The underlying idea is that, removing the most significant constraints will have a major impact on growth. This is a more positive approach than those that result in long lists of problems, not ranked by their importance. According to Hausmann et al. (2005, 2008), government reforms should be aimed at removing the most severe constraints, which is in sharp contrast to the traditional approach of trying to remove all distortions simultaneously;

(iii) at the methodological level growth diagnostics tends to be pragmatic with respect to the kind of findings that are evidence of binding constraints. It can be based on national data, comparisons across-countries, among similar proximate countries or among world countries, or on enterprise survey data. Following the decision tree forks (see Fig. 5.3), this framework enables the use of and scrutiny of different types of datasets to identify the most severe constraints on firm growth;

(iv) although in terms of its analytical logic, growth diagnostics is a top-down approach, it is, at the same time, a bottom-up method. Application of the model requires bottom-up survey data, collected at the firm-level, to allow the formulation of a list of costly business environment constraints (Carlin and Seabright 2007). This is complemented by the inclusion of the manager's/owner's perspective (see Fig. 5.4).

5.3 An Outline of the Growth Diagnostics Method

The growth diagnostics framework was developed by Hausmann et al. (2005). It assumes that there can be several reasons why an economy or the firms operating in the economy, do not grow, but for each reason there is a distinctive set of symptoms. These symptoms are the premise for differential diagnosis where the diagnostician tries to distinguish among potential explanations why an economy or the in it do not grow.[1] This theoretical framework is founded on the following three

[1]A decision making model used by clinicians. The clinician uses the information gathered from the patient's medical history and the clinician's physical and mental examinations to develop a list of possible causes of the disorder; this is called a differential diagnosis. On this basis, the clinician decides what tests to order to help to refine the list of causes or identify the specific disease responsible for the patient's symptoms (Encyclopaedia Britannica, 15th ed.).

assumptions. First, while the notion of development is relatively broad, the model of steady economic growth is a major problem faced by developing countries. Second, in trying to promote a particular growth model, the researcher must take account of the circumstances of the specific economic setting. Neglecting this will result in the model generating unintended outcomes. Third, the best growth model may be the one that tries to alleviate some of the binding constraints, rather than resolving all of them.

The authors of the growth diagnostics model maintain that there is a fundamental difference between growth theory and growth diagnostics. Growth theory, typically, uses one or more independent variables to predict growth and poses questions, such as: is variable X (e.g., finance) able to predict firm growth in a typical (average) country and a randomly selected population of firms? In contrast, the research question for those researchers using a growth diagnostics framework would be: in a particular country, at a particular point in time, what are the constraints that hamper firm growth? Although these questions are different, they are not unrelated. They are distinct in the sense that the reasons for weak firm growth in a particular economy are wide ranging. Firm growth can depend on a potentially unknowable set of complex interactions, between many aspects of the focal country and its environment (Hausmann et al. 2008). By implication, while it might be possible to identify what happens, on average, within a sample of countries in a specific population, it might be unclear whether the particular country case is comparable or average within the sample. The list of variables influencing firm growth can be extensive which can make it difficult to identify the most influential in a particular country case. Factors that constrain firm growth can be internal (human capital resources, organizational capabilities, management practices) or external (Carlin and Seabright 2007).[2]

In a growth diagnostics perspective, the explanatory variables are not substitutes, thus, poor performance in one area may be compensated by over-performance in another area. In other words, the impact of

[2]Physical infrastructure, the legal system, the financial system, various aspects of the micro and macro-policy environment such as taxation, regulation, macroeconomic stability, and social factors such as crime and corruption in society.

policy on growth is independent of the level of the other variables. This framework treats the explanatory variables related to growth as complements; their complementary effects may be mutually self-enhancing (Hausmann et al. 2008). This effect has been likened to a barrel structure (see Fig. 5.1). The volume of liquid in the left-hand barrel depends on the width of the staves of the barrel and can be increased by the addition of an extra wooden stave. Similarly, it could be said that the removal or addition of a variable (constraint) in an economic setting will influence growth. In the case of the barrel on the right side in Fig. 5.1, the volume of liquid depends on the height of the shortest stave. Hausmann et al. highlight two implications of this second depiction. First, the impact of a stave on the volume of the barrel depends on whether the stave is or is not a binding constraint. If it is not a binding constraint, then the impact is zero. The second implication is that, if the constraint is binding, the level of impact will depend on the distance between the shortest and the next shortest staves. In other words, they contend that the impact of relaxing a binding constraint is not just an estimated coefficient multiplied by the magnitude of the change; rather, if the change is sufficiently large, the distance to the next binding constraint will matter zero.

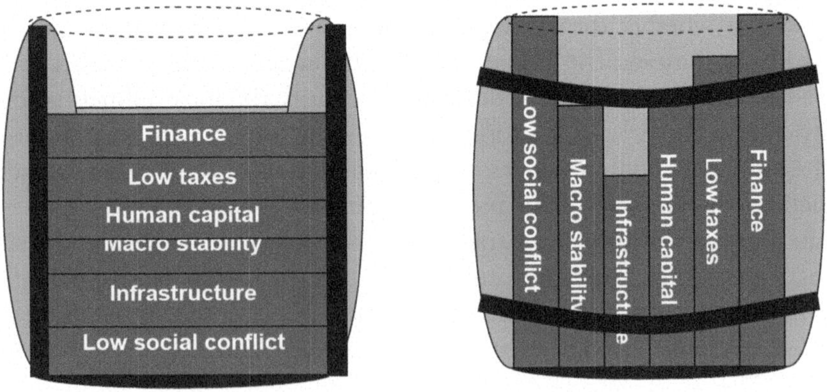

Fig. 5.1 How much will the barrel hold (*Source* Adapted from Hausmann et al. [2008, p. 17])

When analyzing the constraints on growth in a poor economy, such as Kosovo, it is tempting to consider that in such a business environment everything is binding. Hausmann et al. (2008) would agree that the number of constraints in weak economies is large. However, there is no justification for assuming that all of them are simultaneously binding. The infrastructure might be poor, the banks not of the best quality and the education system weak. However, the economy produces some high skilled individuals, although they either leave the country or are forced to undertake menial jobs, such as taxi driving. Also, although the banking system might appear unsophisticated, they may have large stocks of liquidity and may be searching for sound investments/customers to lend money at sensible interest rates (Hausmann et al. 2008).

The central problem from the growth diagnostics perspective, is that it is impossible to know what is the right economic growth model (Haussmann et al. 2008). The process is carried out through a level of ambiguity (Manski 2000; Brock et al. 2003), and the objective is to have a rational prioritization of intervention.

This top-down approach analyzes aggregate outcomes, such as the economic growth rate, and diagnoses the potential constraints that might impede growth (Hausmann et al. 2005). It is aimed a revealing areas that might benefit from policy interventions. It exploits the decision tree model depicted in Fig. 5.2.

This model, like other growth models, is based on the principle that the rate at which the firm grows is a function of the difference between private agents' expected rate of return and the cost of capital. The greater the gap between the expected returns to asset accumulation and the asset acquisition costs, the greater the investment effort (Hausmann et al. 2008, p. 23). Also, the greater the gap, the greater the incentive to accumulate and the higher the growth rate.

Since it was first proposed in 2005, the growth diagnostics approach has been adapted by many researchers. The approach is used, mostly, to investigate binding constraints on economic growth in individual countries.[3]

[3]Hausmann (2005) on Tanzania; Hausmann and Klinger (2007) on *Paraguay and Peru;* Hausmann and Rodrik (2005) on el Salvador; Sen and Kirkpatrick (2009) on Kosovo; Carlin et al. (2006), etc.

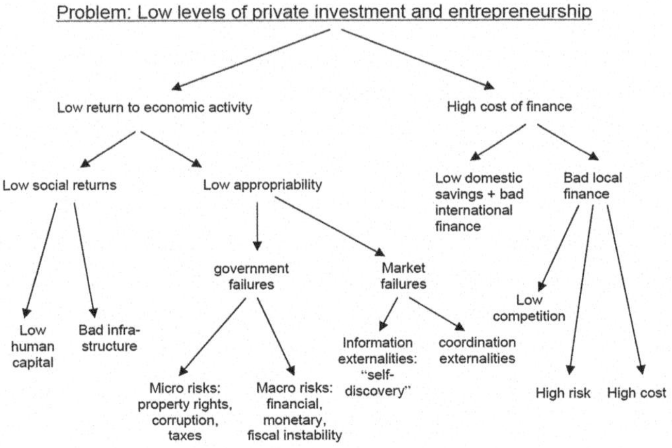

Fig. 5.2 The growth diagnostics decision tree (*Source* Adapted from Hausmann et al. [2008, p. 22])

However, none of this work uses this methodology to investigate binding constraints on firm growth. The only related research study is Carlin et al. (2006).[4] However, their findings mostly contradict the findings from research into how managers perceive binding constraints to firm growth. For instance, Carlin et al. suggest that the telecoms infrastructure is never an important policy priority, which contradicts the results in Dollar et al. (2005). Carlin and co-authors find, also, that transport is important only for some very poor countries, that electricity is the only form of physical infrastructure in some countries in Africa and South Asia while crime and corruption matter in a range of countries, especially in Central and Latin America and weak tax administration matters in CIS. In the case of prosperous countries, labour regulation is a concern. Carlin et al. suggest that more efficient firms are especially constrained by poorly functioning customs regulation and inadequate legal systems. They point out that private rather than state-owned firms are the beneficiaries of improved

[4]The purpose of this paper was to investigate the binding constraints to the growth of firms by using s firm-level data of 20,000 firms for 60 countries. Though the authors have cited the growth diagnostics methodology as one of the methods that provides tools to investigate binding constraints to growth of firms, they in fact use Lagrangian approach to measure the cost of different constraints.

macroeconomic stability and policy predictability, a strong legal system and reduced corruption and crime (Carlin et al. 2006).

Growth diagnostics has been criticized by numerous scholars. Some argue that it is an unscientific framework. For instance Leipziger and Zagha (2006) claim that, growth diagnostics, in contrast to growth regression analysis, only provides a framework allowing the formulation of hypotheses on the binding constraints to growth rather than empirical tools that could be used to test these hypotheses. Also their empirical testing relies on the researcher's ability to create a 'plausible story'. Nobel laureate, Mike Spence, is reported to have described the growth diagnostics framework as more of a 'disciplined art' than a scientific approach, which allows for a more open-ended analysis (Leipziger and Zagha 2006, p. 2). In critiques of the model as being overly concentrated on a single constraint, several authors point out that most countries have more than one constraint hampering their growth. In this context, Rodriguez (2005) argues that, under certain conditions, it is better to reduce the effect of two binding constraints rather than trying to remove one constraint completely. Jeffrey Sachs (cited in Sartor 2007) suggests that this theory might be useful as a tool in a functional economy to investigate binding constraints in an effort to improve growth at the margins. In his view, economies in poor countries are so dysfunctional that marginal improvements to growth by mitigating only the most binding constraints will produce modest returns and fail to deliver the major boost that such countries need. However, other authors maintain that investment does not always lead to economic growth (Fernandez-Arias 2008; Felipe and Usui 2008) while Hausmann et al. (2008) respond, arguing that in a growth diagnostics perspective investigating asset accumulation is useful because problems are often reflected by investment behaviour, regardless of its relative importance to growth. They point to very few cases of countries where distortions result in too high private investment. Lin Justin (2012) acknowledges growth diagnostics as an important advance in growth analysis. However, in his view, the model does not account fully for the notion of binding constraint, and suggests that the variable definitions are rather imprecise, making their operationalization difficult.

To sum up, the growth diagnostics approach and methodology is useful for analyzing the binding constraints on firm growth. By integrating diverse and sometimes disjointed evidence from a variety of sources, this approach provides the basis for a great deal of research. However, it assumes that, once external constraints are removed, the innovative firm will automatically drive economic growth. This chapter claims that this is a rather heroic assumption; it supposes unlimited entrepreneurship given the right external conditions and that the capabilities for firm formation are in place. However, organizations and firms are complex entities which do not grow automatically when external constraints are removed. There are various intra-firm factors that inhibit firm formation and growth and which need to be taken into account. This study argues that an extended growth diagnostics is needed that takes into account of factors external to firm growth and internal to firm formation and growth. To better grasp the factors that constrain firm growth in a developing economy, in this book, the growth diagnostic method is augmented by the addition of an innovative firm theory framework developed by William Lazonick (2013). Lazonick contends that economic models used to analyze economic growth should incorporate the theory of the innovative firm, because this provides researchers with a better understanding of the enablers and constraints on growth. Innovative firm theory puts the main emphasis on the social conditions in the firm's environment. Appropriate social conditions support processes that generate higher quality products at lower unit costs (Lazonick 2012), and vice versa. These social conditions are analyzed in Chapter 7.

5.4 Theoretical Perspective

In providing a theoretical framework for studying the business environment factors that inhibit firm growth, growth diagnostics theory is a useful. It takes full account of the country's specific circumstances and allows a more flexible framework to analyze what restricts firm growth. It is based on the central argument that private investment and entrepreneurial activity are essential for national economic growth. Private investment increases when agents (entrepreneurs) expect high rates of return on assets, and when the funding is available to finance their business projects. Therefore, growth is a function of the difference between the expected rate of return on the capital invested, and the cost of funds to finance business activities. This can be formulated as:

$$\frac{\dot{c}_t}{c_t} = \frac{\dot{k}_t}{k_t} = \sigma[r(1 - \tau) - \rho]$$

where the dot over a variable denotes the rate of change over time, and where c denotes consumption, k is capital, r is the rate of return on capital, τ is the tax rate on actual or expected, and formal or informal capital, ρ is the international interest rate, and σ is the inter-temporal elasticity of consumption. The private return on capital r can be written as

$$r = r(a, \theta, x)$$

where a is an indicator of Total Factor Productivity (TFP), x is the availability of complementary factors of production, such as infrastructure or human capital, and θ is an index of externality (a higher θ means a larger distortion).

According to Hausmann et al. (2008), these two equations summarize the factors that might be affecting growth performance. A growth diagnostics approach consists of review and analysis of these factors to ascertain which constitute the most binding constraints on growth. The problem is identifying those factors (including market distortions and policy wedges) likely to matter most for growth.

This theory provides not only the means to investigate external factors that inhibit growth but also the techniques to identify those that are the most binding at a particular time and for a specific country. There are three classes of variables that need to be considered when investigating the reasons for low rates of private investment. The *first* is related to *low social returns* (geography, low human capital, bad infrastructure). The *second* class is related to *low appropriation* in the form of government failures (corruption, taxes, crime, weak judicial system, political stability, uncertain economic policies, weak regulations), and market failures (information and coordination failures).[5] The *third* class of variables is related to the *costs of finance*, which might result from poor access to international finance (country risks, credit rating), or poor local sources of finance (poor intermediation, access to and cost of finance, low levels of domestic savings).

Thus, the rate of private investment depends on the rate of return on investment and the real interest rate. Assuming that if the rate of expected return on investment is low, the incentive for entrepreneurs to invest is correspondingly low, the important question is what is causing these low rates of return? Is it poor complementary factors such as difficult geography, weak infrastructure or unavailability of human capital? Or, is the low rate of return on investment the result of low levels of appropriation, that is, high levels of corruption, crime, customs rates and taxes, or market failure, that is, information and coordination failures. On the other hand, it might be assumed that entrepreneurs are not short of business ideas, but lack the funds to finance their projects or/and the cost of finance is too high. High finance costs can be related to poor access to international finance (due, primarily, to macro-policy stability) or poor sources of local finance, both of which result in high-interest rates.

The underlying logic for using a growth diagnostics approach is that, despite increasing empirical evidence on the effects of business climate factors on firm growth, derived from different sources; none of them provides conclusive explanations about the factors that constrain firm growth in a particular country (Hausmann et al. 2008). Also, the studies in this area often fail to reach a consensus. This would point to the importance of empirical research be focused and based more on local circumstances as suggested by the logic of the growth diagnostics framework.

The analysis in this chapter investigates the binding constraints on private investment and entrepreneurship in Kosovo and includes examination of:

[5]Information failures are defined as the failure of the firm to 'discover' which products it can produce at sufficiently low cost to be profitable and competitive. Coordination failures are defined as the failure of the market to respond to potential investor demands for a diverse set of services.

a. complementary factors—poor infrastructure and inadequate availability of human capital, market failure manifested through information and coordination externalities;
b. government failures—lack of rule of law, high levels of corruption, crime, taxes, business regulations;
c. cost of finance—poor access to international finance, poor credit rating and sources of local finance, weak intermediation and low levels of domestic savings.

5.5 The Methodology

The methodology employed builds on the growth diagnostics framework proposed by Hausmann et al. (2008), which highlights several reasons for lack of firm growth, each of which produces a specific set of symptoms.[6] These symptoms allow differential diagnosis, based on several sources of empirical evidence which try to distinguish among these problems.[7] The methodology includes strategies and methods to identify (groups of) symptoms or syndromes.

The analysis in this chapter uses the information provided by Chapter 2 which discussed the economic and political profile of Kosovo. These data allow an understanding of the country's overall business environment. This background information, although insufficient for a diagnostic process, identifies some important stylized facts which any potential diagnosis must take into account (Hausmann et al. 2008).

The analytical process includes the use of a decision tree, which was aimed, initially at examining and identifying symptoms. However, Hausmann and colleagues argue that the decision tree is a heuristic device and should not be considered definitive or fundamental. It provides an initial model to frame the argument; it provides a root cause analysis diagram and should be read top down not from side to side

[6]By symptom we mean a feature associated to a specific variable, for instance, a low level of domestic savings could be a symptom of high interest rates.

[7]A syndrome refers to a group of symptoms that occur simultaneously, or to a condition characterized by a set of associated symptoms.

or bottom up (Hausmann et al. 2008). Section 5.2 on the theoretical framework points out that, the central assumption in the diagnostic perspective is that low growth is primarily a function of the low rate of private investments. If this assumption is true, then we need to know why this is the case. To investigate the cause of low rates of private investment requires a diagnosis based on three broad factors: high cost of finance, low appropriation of profits and low provision of complementary factors. In other words, entrepreneurs may not be willing to invest because the cost of capital to start or expand their business is high, because they may perceive low appropriation of profits due to weak complementary factors such as physical infrastructure and human capital resources.[8] All of this assumes that the firm possesses adequate internal capabilities, as crucial for firm growth.

The identification of symptoms enables assessment of the severity of various constraints to firm growth. However, to propose a theory or explanation for the existence of binding constraints, the diagnosis is based on a logically consistent causal chain which accounts, as much as possible, for the observed facts (Hausmann et al. 2008). This is the second step in establishing a cause in the form of a syndrome. The soundness of syndromes is checked by the identification of other symptoms. This process is repeated until there is a final diagnosis based on a well-supported identification of the binding constraints to growth and why they are present (Hausmann et al. 2008, p. 82).

This is a pragmatic methodology with respect to the kind of evidence used in the quest for binding constraints. The empirical evidence used to test the hypotheses comes, basically, from two sources. The first source is information from recent international surveys, which suggest indices to assess the relative importance of countries along an extended set of dimensions.[9] The main purpose is to provide a comparative measure of the country's performance, measured against five reference

[8]By appropriation we mean the environmental factors that govern the firm's ability to capture profits.

[9]Freedom House, the World Economic Forum, Transparency International and the World Bank, OECD, etc.

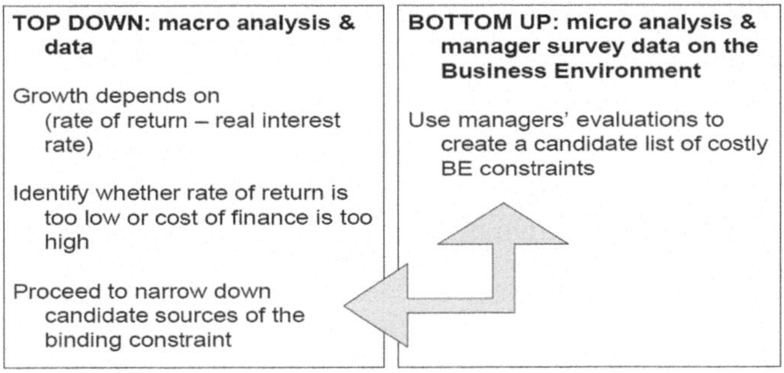

Fig. 5.3 Diagnosing binding constraints, combining growth diagnostics with manager survey data (*Source* Adapted from Carlin and Seabright [2007, p. 18])

countries. This diagnosis provides some useful feedback on national performance in various political and economic indicators relative to what seems feasible (Hausmann et al. 2008). The second source of information is a dataset based on a firm-level survey conducted in April 2017 by the Riinvest Institute in Kosovo. The dataset includes a sample of 585 business firms. The respondents were company owners/managers from all economic sectors, and all Kosovo's regions.

Fundamentally, the growth diagnostics is a top-down approach. However, supplied with the bottom-up firm-level survey data, and by using manager's perceptions on what they view as the growth constraints for their firms, the process of diagnosis enables the creation of a candidate list of costly business environment constraints. Figure 5.3 depicts the combination of these two perspectives:

Although the growth diagnostics approach provides a well-structured methodology to examine the causes of low levels of private investment and entrepreneurship, it has some limitations. The *first* is related to the identification of symptoms/signals. The framework is designed to find symptoms/signals to guide the diagnostics process. It involves searching for price and non-price signals—specifically the resources shadow prices. Measuring shadow prices is not straightforward and may involve resorting to indirect evidence to measure resources scarcity. *Second*, the growth diagnostics approach assumes that the main problem related to lack of growth is low levels of private investment and entrepreneurship. However, growth may depend, also, on public investments

(OECD 2009; Sutherland et al. 2009). *Third*, growth diagnostics is a static methodology. It centres on constraints that may be binding, but may not be in the future. However, the problem in many economies, particularly in developing countries such as Kosovo, is not how to trigger growth, but how to sustain it. We need to investigate the factors of growth primarily from a dynamic perspective, namely, what makes firm growth sustainable.

5.6 Symptoms Analysis Using a Decision Tree

As stated above, the growth diagnostics is based on the assumption that the low rate of growth is the result of low rates of private investment and entrepreneurship. Therefore, the question that emerges logically is what is it that is constraining private agents from making higher investments and constraining entrepreneurship? The analysis starts by searching for the symptoms of these constraints since problems tend to be reflected in investment behaviour. The process of analysis is based on a decision tree. To conduct the symptoms analysis, we make the following assumptions:

1. that private agents have sufficient, privately profitable investment opportunities, but are constrained by finance. So, we need to determine the reasons for this. Is access to finance made difficult by inadequate access to savings, or is the constraint related to problems in mobilizing those savings, that is, inefficient financial intermediation;
2. that there is sufficient availability of finance at a reasonable cost, but private agents are unwilling to invest because of the low level of public goods (poor infrastructure, poor human capital) or because the proportion of the returns they would be able to appropriate is too low. The latter issue is related to private agents' fears that government or market failures will dissipate returns, due to planned or unplanned hold-up problems.

To identify symptoms related to low levels of private investment and entrepreneurship, the analysis examines the right-hand side of the decision tree—see Fig. 5.2.

5.6.1 Diagnosis: The Problems of Finance in Kosovo

Why do access to finance and the cost of finance matter? The ability of firms to invest is important because investment in equipment and new ideas (technology, organizational and managerial capabilities) drives growth. Capital investments allow firms to adopt new technologies, which, in turn, allows them to align their business processes to global best practice. In this context, access to external finance is essential for enterprises to invest, innovate and grow. A developed financial sector and favourable cost of finance support firms to compete effectively in both the local and international marketplace and to anticipate and respond to market changes and to seize new opportunities. In general, alongside the quality of business environment in which firms operate, access to finance and cost of finance play crucial roles in overall levels of private investment and entrepreneurship.

One business environment variable that stands out is the availability and cost of finance. If this restricts the rates of investment and entrepreneurship in the country then it means that economic agents are unable to obtain as much funding as they need. The search for symptoms in this context, is based on the assumption that there are plenty of privately profitable investment opportunities, but the problem is access to finance. We need to search for the symptoms of this problem. *First,* access to finance can be assumed to be a constraint due to inadequate access to savings; *second,* access to finance may be a constraint due to the size of the national financial system and the difficulties related to the capacity to mobilize savings (Hausmann et al. 2008).

We need to find evidence to build a coherent story and argument in relation to the constraint caused by lack of access to finance in Kosovo. As already indicated, an important characteristic of the growth diagnostics framework is the ability to integrate diverse and, at times, disjointed evidence from a variety of sources. The analysis in this chapter uses data from the national bank of Kosovo and the national banks of the five reference countries and international financial institutions such as the World Bank. The symptoms identified by the secondary data are complemented by the responses to the firm-level survey of 585 firms operating in Kosovo which asked managers to indicate the degree to which their firms' activities were constrained by inadequate access to external funds.

Table 5.1 Selected financial sector indicators

	Year	Cro	Est	Lat	Lit	Slo	Kos
Interest - term deposits	2017	0.71	0.83	0.44	0.37	0.25	1.5
Interest - business loans	2017	3.82	2.2	2.14	2.29	2.38	6.8
Interest rate spread	2017	3.11	1.37	1.7	1.92	2.13	5.3
Number of banks	2017	31	16	23	14	18	10
Return on average equity	2016	8.89	11.1	14.34	11.89	7.85	18.5
Savings/GDP (%)*	2017	22.9	28.1	20.5	18.6	27.9	−1
Credit rating**	2017	BB+	AA−	A−	A	A+	n/a

Source Data concerning number of banks, interest rates and banking performance are obtained from respective national banks
*World Bank data https://data.worldbank.org/indicator/NY.GDS.TOTL.ZS
**S&P website https://www.spratings.com

To support the argument of inadequate saving requires identification of several symptoms. In principle, banks should be willing to remunerate saving with high interest rates. If banks reward savers with high levels of interest, then this is a symptom that the banks are unable to capture savings without some coercion. However, if the banks are forced to remunerate savers at a high real rate, this means that other members of society will find it even harder time to access savings. The evidence suggests that the interest rates on deposits in Kosovo are significantly higher than in the reference countries. Table 5.1 shows that deposit interest rates in the reference countries are less than 1%, while in Kosovo, the rate is 1.5% on average.

In addition, access to foreign borrowing must be restricted. To argue that a country has a savings problem requires some evidence that access to foreign borrowing is restricted or expensive and that domestic savings are limited. Hausmann et al. (2008) argue that, in theory, saving can move internationally; if capital mobility was perfect we could expect interest rates to be the same in all countries. Figure 5.4 provides a depiction in which investment and savings are compatible with the international interest rate (points A and B) and the difference is borrowed or invested abroad. In the case that a country has no or very restricted access to international loans, supply and demand has to be balanced locally and, hence, the interest rate is adjusted to a point such as C (Hausmann et al. 2008).

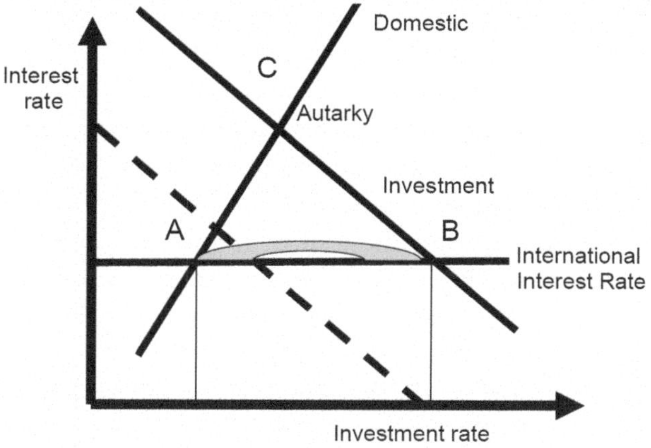

Fig. 5.4 Capital market (*Source* Adapted from Hausmann et al. [2008, p. 62])

Is there a symptom of little or very restricted access to foreign finance in the case of Kosovo? This might be deduced from the country's sovereign risk or credit risk. Kosovo is not included in the credit ratings issued by S&P, Moody's and Fitch, which are the three most prestigious organizations that assess national sovereign risk. Lack of a trustworthy rating for potential investors and credit organizations to measure the investment and credit risk is a major drawback. It is, also, a symptom of Kosovo's limited access to foreign finance and increases the cost of financing from foreign creditors because they are obliged to include a high-risk premium.

The World Bank indicators for government performance ranks Kosovo quite low, indicating a high level of investment risk. Another indicator that might explain the interest rate level is the gross domestic savings trend. Table 5.1 shows that, despite a negative rate after high levels in the current decade, Kosovo continues to have very unfavourable rates of domestic savings compared to the reference countries.

In addition to savings problem, the search for symptoms reveals a financial intermediation problems. The first symptom suggests a wide spread between deposit and lending rates. As described above, Kosovo has the widest spread between deposit and lending rates in the region due to high operating costs, high taxation on financial intermediation, high risks and high profits (Hausmann et al. 2008).

The wide interest rate spread between deposits and lending is considered the result of inefficiencies in the banking sector market including high transaction costs and asymmetric information (Stiglitz and Weiss 1981). The main transaction costs are related to selecting, and analyzing the quality of borrowers and the cost of monitoring them. The greater these inefficiencies, the higher will be the spread between deposits and lending rates. Since 2016, the average operating cost ratio for the three most profitable banks in Kosovo was around 55%.

In terms of the size of the banking system relative to the population, the number of banks operating in the market is the lowest relative to the reference countries and 90% of the market is controlled by four banks based on foreign capital (IMF 2018). These banks have been accused of making excessive profits over a long period of time and enjoy a monopolistic position in the market. Table 5.1 shows that Kosovan banks enjoy higher profits relative to their counterparts, shown by the Returns on Equity (ROE). These figures might infer that the small number of banks and low level of competition are symptoms of the interest rates in Kosovo compared to the reference countries.

5.6.2 Micro Analysis and Manager Survey Findings for Financial Intermediation

Assessments of the binding constraints on firm growth are often based on managers' views about the major obstacles to their business activities. In April 2017, Riinvest Institute conducted a survey of the managers of 585 firms, which asked them to rank a series of business environment constraints on a five-point scale ranging from "no obstacle" to "very severe obstacle". The survey questions referred to 23 different areas.

The survey responses suggest that the major constraints are small market (small demand), corruption, crime and theft, high tax rates and informality. The cost of finance was ranked 6th with the score of 2.82. Among 24 different areas, access to finance was considered problematic and was ranked among the top 10 business binding constraints.

In sum, the findings, both from international surveys and the Riinvest survey suggest that firms find it difficult to access external finance and, also, the cost of finance is a major constraint on firm growth. The most significant symptoms, compared to the reference countries, include:

- significantly higher interest lending rates;
- a significantly higher weighted spread between deposits and lending rate;
- exclusion from the rankings published by the major credit assessment agencies, which restricts access to international finance;
- significantly low rate of domestic savings;
- a smaller financial intermediation system;
- high banking industry profits and a monopolistic financial business environment.

The following section considers the left hand side of the decision tree, that is, complementary factors (infrastructure and human capital) and appropriation factors (government and market failures).

5.7 Diagnosis: The Problems Related to the Institutional Environment in Kosovo

The analysis assumes, next, that finance is not a problem, but that private agents are unwilling to invest because they expect that the proportion of the returns that could be privately appropriated is low. This expectation may be based on the private agent's fears about government failure, planned or unplanned hold-up problems, or market failures, which would dissipate expected returns. We would like to confirm that this is the case with evidence. In the context of government failures, the focus is on microeconomic hold-up problems such as corruption, crime, rule of law (court efficiency), and macroeconomic hold-up problems such as uncertain economic policies, and absence of political, monetary and fiscal stability. Prestigious international institutions publish findings on all of these variables. For instance, the World Bank publishes six indicators of institutional quality that map onto appropriation problems. These indicators include rule of law, voice and accountability, political stability, government effectiveness, regulatory quality and control of corruption.

Figure 5.6, which depicts factors related to institutional quality, shows that, compared to the reference countries, Kosovo is ranked very low.[10] For example, for rule of law and control of corruption Croatia is ranked low, but higher than Kosovo. This can be considered a symptom of the greater sensitivity of Kosovo to poor government performance in most indicators compared to the reference countries. It seems that Kosovo has in place relatively sound policies and regulation allowing and promoting private sector development (World Bank 2012a, b) and that the main problem is legal and regulatory compliance.

In the context of taxation, compared to the reference countries, rates are relatively low. Corporate income tax is significantly lower than in the other countries while value added taxes are slightly higher than most of the reference countries. According to the World Bank/Doing Business Indicators 2017, tax rates are considered one of the least problematic business environment factors in Kosovo. The country is ranked 45th out of over 177 countries for the ease of paying taxes (Table 5.2).

The findings from Riinvest's firm-level survey provide a different picture. Taxation rates and tax administration rules are seen by managers

[10] ***Voice and Accountability (VA)***—capturing perceptions of the extent to which a country's citizens are able to participate in choosing their government, freedom of expression, freedom of association and a free media.

Political Stability and Absence of Violence/Terrorism—measures perceptions of the likelihood of political instability and/or politically-motivated violence including terrorism.

Government effectiveness—captures perceptions of the quality of public services, the quality of the civil service and the degree of its independence from political pressures, the quality of policy formulation and implementation, and the credibility of the government's commitment to such policies.

Regulatory quality—captures perceptions of the ability of the government to formulate and implement sound policies and regulations that permit and promote private sector development.

Rule of law—captures perceptions of the extent to which agents have confidence in and abide by the rules of society, and in particular the quality of contract enforcement, property rights, the police, and the courts, as well as the likelihood of crime and violence.

Control of corruption—captures perceptions of the extent to which public power is exercised for private gain, including both petty and grand forms of corruption, as well as "capture" of the state by elites and private interests.

Table 5.2 Tax rates in Kosovo and comparator countries

Country	Corporate income tax (%)	Value added tax (VAT) (%)	Doing Business Rank (2017)
Croatia	18	25	95
Estonia	20	20	14
Latvia	20	21	13
Lithuania	15	21	18
Slovenia	19	21	58
Kosovo	10	18	45

Source World Bank, Doing Business Indicators 2017

as major obstacles to growth. The tax rate mean is 2.87, that is, 40.2% of respondents consider them an obstacle; the tax administration rules mean is 2.69, that is, 30% of respondents consider tax administration rules to be an obstacle (see Fig. 5.5). Although these results might reflect the subjective nature of the survey responses, there is an association between the above findings and the results for tax administration

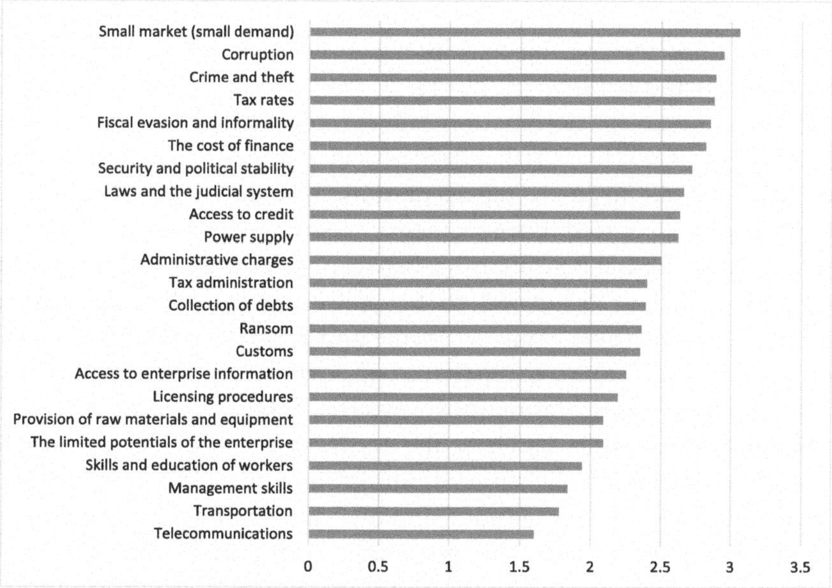

Fig. 5.5 Ranking of business environment constraints according to the perceptions of firm managers (*Source* Riinvest 2017)

Table 5.3 Scores for dimension 5a: Support services for SMEs and start-ups

Dimension 5a	ALB	BIH	KOS	MKD	MNE	SRB	TUR	WBT average
2016 average	2.65	2.42	2.74	2.94	2.95	3.85	4.26	3.12
2012 average	2.48	2.39	1.88	2.61	2.94	3 47	4.32	3.01

Source OECD (2012) and (2016)
Note The scores indicate the regional average of the policy dimension

corruption: when managers were asked to rank the level of corruption in the tax administration. 53% of respondents responded that there is a corruption in the tax administration authority.

The issues related to appropriation are linked not only to government failures but also to market failures such as information externalities (self-discovery) and coordination externalities. Both potentially could constrain firm growth. The structure of exports is unfavourable and has not changed since 2008. This is a sign of lack of self-discovery among firms. However, since Kosovo has a small manufacturing base and is emerging slowly from a war situation, informational externality problems are inevitable. For an economy that is not internationalized, there are no grounds for arguing that informational externality problems are binding (Sen and Kirkpatrick 2011).

In the context of coordination failures, the SME Policy Index published by the OECD (2012, 2016) shows that SMEs in Kosovo have problems related to their representation of interests in government. Despite some reported improvements, government provided support for SMEs and formal consultations between government and the private sector are deficient compared to neighbouring countries. In general, lack of comprehensive, easily accessible and regularly updated information on issues of interest to SMEs is considered a significant constraint for small businesses operating in Kosovo (see Table 5.3).

For the relationship between the business community and central and local government, the survey findings show that 55.5% of respondents do not trust their local government, while 50.1% have no trust in the national government. This is another symptom of the poor coordination and lack of trustful relationships and is a strong indication of lack of coordination between local and central government and the business community in Kosovo.

5.7.1 Micro Analysis of and Manager Survey Findings on Appropriation Problems

Analysis of the data from the firm-level survey suggests that Kosovan entrepreneurs perceive appropriation problems as the greatest barrier. Among the highest ranked barriers, half relate to government performance. For instance, 40% of the managers interviewed perceive corruption as a major obstacle, and crime, theft and informality as severe obstacles (39.6% assess them very high obstacle). Informality is seen as at the root of unfair competition in the market. Although the sources of unfair competition may differ, the survey findings suggest that in Kosovo, it is driven primarily by tax evasion and the informal labour market. According to the survey findings, 34.4% of total sales go untaxed, meaning that firms in Kosovo declare only 65.6% of their sales. In addition, the perception of the surveyed managers is that Kosovan firms report only 63% of their employees to the tax authorities. One explanation for firms corrupt practices in these respects, is the firms' perception of corruption in central and local government, the judicial system and the tax administration. Asked whether they considered these institutions to be corrupt, 52% believed central government was corrupt, 48% believed the same about local government, and 64% thought that the judicial system was corrupt and 53% considered the tax administration to be corrupt.[11]

In sum, the symptoms of appropriation factors include:

[11]Corruption in this study is defined as he misuse or abuse of public office for private gain and emerges in various forms and in a wide array of illicit behaviours including bribery, extortion, fraud, nepotism, graft WHAT DOES GRAFT MEAN, speed money WHAT IS THIS, pilfering, theft, misappropriation, falsification of records, kickbacks, influence peddling WHAT DOES THISMEAN and campaign contributions.

See Robert Klitgaard, 'Strategies Against Corruption', http://www.clad.org.ve/klit3.htm.p.1.

- difficulties related to identifying which products/services can be produced at low enough cost to be profitable and competitive. Bearing in mind the country's small manufacturing base and the recent transition phase, problems related to informational externalities are unavoidable. It could be argued that the constraints related to information externalities are not binding, but this does not apply to coordination externalities. There are clear signs that government has failed to provide the necessary SME services. An important finding is that the relationship between the business community and government at both levels is poor. Consequently, it can be argued that there is weak coordination between government/s and the private sector (OECD 2012, 2016);
- in terms of micro-level government failures, there is clear evidence that the business environment is heavily constrained by ineffective and inefficient government institutions. As a result, corruption is uncontrolled, crime is seen as lucrative, there are high levels of tax evasion and the informal economy and unfair competition/practices are severe constraints. Also, and rule of law is weak. Firm-level survey findings and findings from other sources are consistent with the perception of a low level of investment by the private sector as a function of government failures.[12]

5.8 Diagnosis: The Problems Related to Human Capital in Kosovo

According to the decision tree, geography can be a reason why firms do not grow. However, in the case of Kosovo, this is difficult to argue since it is located in a Southeast European region close to the European Union market, which suggests Kosovo's geographical location should not be a binding constraint (Fig. 5.6).

[12]Worldwide Governance Indicators, Transparency International, Doing Business Indicators.

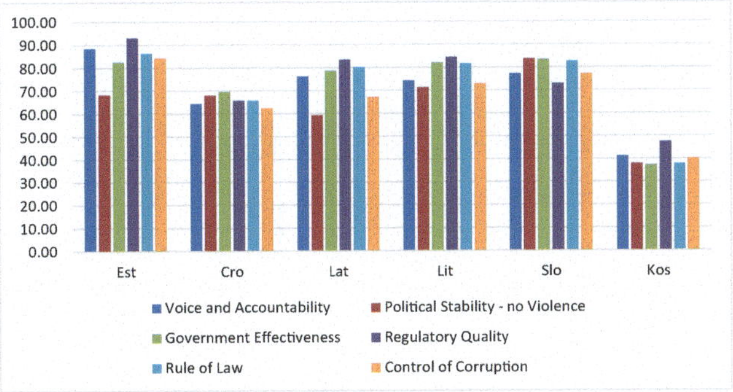

Fig. 5.6 Six indicators of institutional quality—Kosovo and the reference countries, 2016 (*Source* World Bank 2016)

Kosovo's infrastructure has improved since 2013. Major government spending has been concentrated on improving its road infrastructure. However, other infrastructural remain poor. Kosovo has an out-dated power system, which is inadequate and unreliable and poses significant challenges to economic growth; frequent outages hamper investment and disrupt manufacturing, education and health services (World Bank 2012a, b). The managers surveyed ranked power supply 11th in the list of major constraints. However, compared to what governance performance indicators would suggest, these complementary factors are considered by managers to be less binding (see Fig. 5.7).

An important variable related to complementary factors is the quality of human capital. Both economic theory and the empirical evidence show that in the long run, human capital is a critical input for growth (Mincer 1958). Although human capital is not ranked by managers as among the most important constraints, there are other symptoms that emerge from other data, which indicate that human capital could be a binding constraint on firm growth. Hausmann et al. (2008) argue that one way to assess the restrictiveness of weak human capital is to use the Mincerian returns to human capital model. According to this, if the returns from education are high, this implies that human capital is a binding constraint. However, in countries, such as Kosovo,

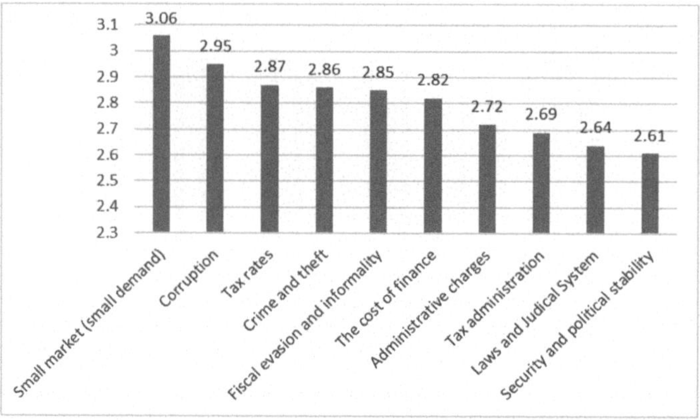

Fig. 5.7 Top ten obstacles according to firm managers' rankings (*Source* Riinvest 2017)

characterized by very high unemployment rates for unskilled workers and slow growth in less skill-intensive tradable activities, including manufacturing, it is difficult to argue that high returns from education signal that human capital is a binding constraint on growth (Rodrik 2010). Some studies show that the returns from education in Kosovo are low. However, this might be due to the high levels of unemployment when workers tend to trade off lower wages against more secure employment (Hoti 2011).

There are other signs that might shed light on the human capital conditions in Kosovo. Assuming that profits are appropriable, government provides decent services to firms, there are no market failures and access to finance is not a problem, would this infer that the education system in place generates human capital aligned to market demand?

Various international reports indicate that the Kosovan education system is not properly aligned to labour market needs. This misalignment results in low employability of graduates and a significant skills premium (European Commission 2018; OECD 2016). A 2013 OECD report claims that a major issue related to human capital and, specifically, the education system in Kosovo, is its structure. For example, only 5.6% of university students are enrolled in natural and mathematical sciences and only 3.4% are studying electrical and computer engineering. Other unfavourable signs include the relationship between universities and firms and weak use of apprenticeships to tackle the problem of low/intermediate skills. Firms believe that graduates from both private and public universities in Kosovo lack practical skills (OECD 2013).[13] Although the country produces relatively large numbers of students, it spends considerably less per student than some neighbouring countries on primary and secondary education.[14] According to the European Commission (2018), the wage bill dominates spending on education. In terms of enrolment rates in education, the findings suggest that early childcare and pre-school enrolment rates are very low at 4.4 and 33.9% respectively, well below the EU target of 95% by 2020. However, enrolment in primary and secondary education is relatively high (96 and 88.1%). Enrolment in tertiary level education is also high with 120,000 students enrolled in public or private higher education institutions in 2017. However, low PISA scores and high levels of unemployment among higher education graduates (26.7% in Q3 2017) are an indication of the poor quality of education in general and its misalignment with labour market needs (European Commission 2018).[15]

In the context of development of intermediate skills, around half of all students in upper secondary education choose vocational programmes.[16] However, VET courses do not teach practical and applied skills and their link to the labour market remains weak (European Commission 2018).

---

[13]There are 18 private universities and colleges and 5 public universities in Kosovo (OECD 2013).

[14]The number of students in higher education is nearly double the EU average compared to the population. However, completion rates are low and there is a high level of unemployment among university degree holders (25%), suggesting a mismatch between higher education programmes and labour market needs (European Commission 2018).

[15]According to the 2015 OECD PISA assessment Kosovo is ranked 3rd bottom in a list of over 70 systems tested.

[16]http://ask.rks-gov.net/media/1658/statistikat-e-arsimit-n%C3%AB-kosov%C3%AB-2015-2016-m%C3%AB-30062016-versioni-i-fundit.pdf.

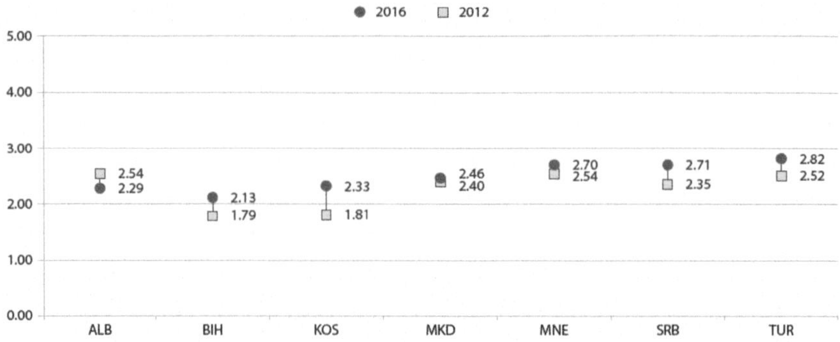

Fig. 5.8 Entrepreneurship learning and training in the Western Balkans and Turkey (*Source* OECD 2016)

OECD (2016) assesses Kosovo in relation to its application of the SBA principles for Europe 2008.[17] One of these is related to entrepreneurship learning and training. Specifically, the report assesses the ability of various countries to build coherent entrepreneurship skills through the national education system. It found that Kosovo has not managed to establish a specific policy framework to promote entrepreneurship learning in higher education. The report argues, also, that Kosovo has not established a link between universities and firms. The comparative analysis shows that, in terms of entrepreneurship learning and inclusion of entrepreneurship in the education system, the country lags behind many Western Balkans countries (see Fig. 5.8).

[17]The SBA was implemented in June 2008 and the European Commission's political will to recognize the central role of SMEs in the EU economy and puts in place a comprehensive SME policy framework for the EU and member states http://ec.europa.eu/enterprise/policies/sme/small-business-act.

The findings from the Riinvest firm-level survey provide a slightly different picture. From the list of 23 business environment factors included in the questionnaire, recruitment of educated and skilled employees and management skills is ranked quite low as a constraint, with respective means of 1.95 and 1.84 (see Fig. 5.7). However, this might be due to managers' considering only current requests rather than ongoing ones.

Based on European Commission, World Bank, OECD data, and the findings from firm-level survey, there seem to be few symptoms indicating lack of adequate human capital. The findings in OECD (2012, 2016) demonstrate the country's education system is not oriented towards promoting entrepreneurship learning. There is lack of a well-structured relationship between private sector firms and universities and there are no formal government initiatives for implementing the principles set out in the SBA 2008.

The above analysis was aimed at identifying symptoms that constrain firm growth. The results provide signals which can be translated into a structured list of the kinds of tests that help discriminate between different explanations. The objective is to match symptoms with the relative tightness of constraints. The columns in Table 5.4 present constraints and the rows present the number of symptoms identified in the second step of the analysis.

There are two possible interpretations: one is related to the situation when the cost of finance is high, and possible reasons for the high interest rates identified. In situation when aggregate savings are a problem, it would be expected to see a high deposit rate, because money is scarce. In addition, foreign borrowing could be limited, and consequently the interest rate will be high. Second interpretation presents a scenario where lending is available and cheap, but promotes little investment. The columns on the right side of the Table 5.4 provide symptoms related to government and market failures and complementary factors such as infrastructure and human capital.

Table 5.4 The matrix of tests

Binding finance		Binding social returns					
				Low appropriability			Coordination
		Lack of complementary factors		Government failure			Market failure
Low aggregate savings	Bad finance			Ex ante	Ex post		
		Human Capital	Infrastructure and public goods (geography?)	Ex ante risks	Tax	Low property rights, crime and corruption	Low R&D low self discovery
High lending interest rate		Low lending interest rate					
Low net cash flow from banks		High net cash flow from banks (dC/C - i)					
Investment elastic to interest rate		Lack of investment response to interest rate change					
Access to external finance is low (high country risk, high credit risk attributed to country)		Number of people with high educational level is lower than in comparator countries				Corruption is uncontrolled	Low R&D Low Innovation and therefore Low self discovery
Short loan duration, credit rationing		Significantly more students enrolled in social sciences rather than natural, mathematical, engineering, and computer sciences than in comparator countries	Complamantory factors (roads) are comparable to comparator countries	Political risk, social risk	Corruption at tax administration authority	Crime is seen as a lucrative area	
High deposit interest rate	High spread						
Low domestic savings	Interest rates on loans are significantly higher than those in comparator countries	No relationship between private sector firms and universities	The only symptom emerged is related to power sypply which was more emphesised by international surveys than by micro- manager survey (2017)		Rampant tax evasion and informality in the economy	Unfair competition/ practices	Unfavourable export structure
	Profits in banking industry are quite high, giving an indication that banks operate in a relatively monopolistic business environment	Entrepreneurship learning/ training is not part of national education system		High expectation of losing future profits		Rule of law is highly defective	There is no coordination, no relationship between business community and governments (central and local)
The size of intermediation system in the country is smaller than in comparator countries						Uncertain economic policies	
					Cost of doing business		

Source Author

5.9 From Symptoms to Syndromes

The previous two steps were aimed at assessing the degree of constraint on growth of different symptoms/signals. The aim of the next step is to organize the findings and propose an explanation for these syndromes/constraints.

5.9.1 Syndrome Number 1: Institutional Quality

For firms to grow, it is necessary to have good quality institutions with predictable rules and regulations. Data from various sources indicate that countries with better economic performance, on average, tend to report less severe constraints on firm performance (Djankov et al. 2006; Kaufmann et al. 2007). The statistical relation between growth and institutional quality could be caused by less severe constraints on the availability of public goods, all other things being equal, and improved performance for other reasons may also lead the country to have an improved availability of the relevant public goods (Carlin et al. 2006, p. 4). Long-term private investment requires a stable institutional environment that allows investors to manage risk over long periods of time. Institutional stability is fostered by a predictable policy framework. Failure to create these conditions undermines investment and is a serious impediment to growth. There is a large body of research that argues that it is institutional weakness (government failure) that hampers the rapid catch up of transition countries (see, e.g., Rodrik 2006).

The above evidence suggests that Kosovo has failed to create an enabling environment in a number of areas important for growth. The institutional instability in Kosovo is compounded by other factors. World Bank reports on Kosovo provide governance indicators that are low compared to comparator countries (see Fig. 5.6). For instance, Kosovo is ranked relatively low for control of corruption, which in line with the Transparency International Corruption Perceptions Index and the findings from a firm-level survey conducted by Riinvest in 2017.[18]

[18]http://www.transparency.org/country#KOS.

The survey shows that 40% of respondents perceive corruption, crime and theft, and the informal sector to constitute the most binding constraints on growth.

Alleviation of appropriation constraints (rule of law, corruption, informality, etc.) could have positive effects on other constraints. *First*, less tax evasion and better governance could induce fairer competition in the marketplace. *Second*, stronger rule of law and less corruption would improve the country's credit risk rating. *Third*, an improved credit risk score and a reduction in other risks would increase the access to foreign finance. *Fourth*, as a consequence of all these improvements, the cost of finance would potentially decrease.

In summary, based on the evidence, it can be inferred that low appropriation—government failures—represent the biggest problem related to doing business in Kosovo. More specifically, lack of law and order is reflected in high levels of informality, uncontrolled corruption, court inefficiency and governance effectiveness.

5.9.2 Syndrome Number 2: Access to Finance

Fostering a supportive environment for private investment is crucial for dynamic and productive firms and availability of finance is essential to support investment. It enables firms to compete effectively in the regional and global marketplaces and helps them to anticipate and respond to changing markets and opportunities. Some studies of Kosovo consider access to external finance as the biggest problem (Sen and Kirkpatrick 2009). Sen and Kirkpatrick's study highlights various finance related bottlenecks that deter private investment. Some of these symptoms are correlated and suggest that finance is one of the constraints faced by firms in Kosovo's business environment.

First, the retail banking sector in Kosovo is monopolized (90%) by four banks with foreign capital (IMF 2018). Retail banks in Kosovo earn significantly higher profits compared to the reference countries (illustrated by the ROE which are higher in Kosovo than in the comparator countries—see Table 5.1). As a result of the concentration in retail banking, competition in the country's banking sector is significantly lower than in the reference countries.

Second, potential investors and credit organizations have no trustworthy benchmarks against which to measure investment and credit risk in Kosovo. This is a symptom of Kosovo's limited access to foreign finance and increases the cost of funding by foreign creditors, which are obliged to apply a high-risk premium.

Third, it appears that interest rates on business loans and the weighted interest rate spread in Kosovo are significantly higher than those in the comparator countries.

This evidence converges with managers' perceptions collected in the 2017 survey. Although the cost of and access to finance are not ranked higher than governance-related factors, managers still perceive them as a significant constraint.

Addressing these problems is not easy. Credit rating issues, which are related to the political and overall economic structure, are long-term in nature and structural issues are beyond the scope of this chapter. However, there might be some short-term measures that contribute to improving the situation in the banking sector.

One measure, which could have long-lasting benefits, would be fostering competition in the retail banking sector, which would reduce the concentration in the banking sector. Liberalizing bank entry conditions, including speeding up the process for obtaining a banking licence, is essential. Increased competition in Kosovo's banking sector would bring various benefits. It would encourage banks to search for more profitable lending opportunities and could stimulate relationship lending as retail banks focus on more mundane finance.

Another action would be to create a business bank whose remit would be provision of loans to SMEs, especially manufacturers, exporters and high-growth firms. The rationale would be that a business bank would be able to access funds on more favourable terms than commercial banks, which would lower the cost of capital. In particular, a business bank would be able to take a wider perspective on (the benefits of) investment in certain sectors. It could focus on lending for innovation investments by new and growing firms, which are those that suffer the most acute financial market failures and where externalities will be greatest.

Business bank operations in the context of Kosovo would be risky. To be effective, the bank's governance would have to be free from political pressures and operate according to clearly defined economic objectives. A business bank might need to be managed by an independent (possibly international) board to oversee operational decisions. It would need to operate according to a charter setting out its mission and ensuring its fulfilment. To avoid the perennial abolition, reinvention and rebranding process, which characterizes much of Kosovo's government policy in the past, the business bank would need to be a long-term operation, supported by all stakeholders including the business community, political entities and government.

5.9.3 Syndrome Number 3: Human Capital

Complementary factors such as infrastructure (roads, power supply, water supply) and human capital, the evidence shows that human capital has more symptoms to be treated as the third binding constraint. Having said that, it does not mean that infrastructure is the best. Specifically it could be said that infrastructure in the country is improving and as such is more comparable with other countries in the region. This is not the case with the factor of human capital. Several symptoms point out that the education system is in a poor state.

In relation to supply of human capital, there is a systemic failing in Kosovo's education system based on its structure. The education sector is not aligned to labour market needs, resulting in low employability of graduates and a significant skills premium. Students receive very broad and theoretical knowledge and there is no requirement for practical work in the form of internships. Although half of upper secondary education students choose vocational education, it lacks practical and applied courses. Vocational education and training are out of line with market needs. Kosovo has started to apply the SBA principles for Europe, it has no policy framework for promoting entrepreneurship learning in higher education. The results in OECD (2016) indicate that Kosovo is lagging behind many Western Balkans countries for entrepreneurship learning and inclusion of entrepreneurship in the education system.

It is clear that the education system suffers from many deficiencies. The long tail of poorly performing schools and students compared to other countries (based on PISA results) needs to be addressed. Although resolving these fundamental problems is not easy, the education system urgently needs restructuring to be aligned to market needs. Some of the measures, which could produce significant improvement in the objective function, would include the following: *first*, in order to improve the performance of schools a strict and consistent inspection regime will be needed. This would improve governance, leadership and management at all levels in education institutions. *Second*, floor standards should be implemented to address the poor performance of schools and teachers. Performance targets should be specific and aligned to the strategy defined in the framework for school inspections. *Third*, teacher quality should be improved through well-designed entry and exit conditions. The teacher recruitment process must be depoliticized and mainstream teacher recruitment should focus on the best universities and schools. Teachers should be employed based upon a probation period of, say, two to four years. The implementation of these proposal will require a dedicated strategy, transparent communication and financial and non-financial incentives.

5.10 Conclusions

This chapter has discussed the binding constraints to firm growth in a less-developed economic setting. The focus was on those aspects of the business environment not controlled by business, but which affect the expense, ease and reliability of doing business in Kosovo. The investigation was conducted by applying a growth diagnostics approach and methodology. This model provides methodological principles to identify the most binding externalities on firm growth in a particular economy, by taking account of the country's institutional context and socio-economic realities. The empirical data used throughout the analysis were from rankings and surveys conducted by various international organizations, and the subjective evaluations of constraints by of 585 firms operating in Kosovo. The conclusions below are derived from a top-down growth diagnostics approach combined with bottom-up survey data from managers.

Among a set of business economic factors, appropriation (government failures) is a binding external constraint. There is compelling evidence that the biggest problem related to firm growth in Kosovo is low appropriation in the form of government failures such as serious deficiencies in the rule of law, unfair competition and high levels of corruption.

Under the assumption that internal business capabilities exist, the findings indicate that the higher the risk of appropriation of returns, the lower will be the interest of private agents in investing and, consequently, the lower the capital accumulation and growth rate of firms. On the other hand, the higher the government failures (rule of law, unfair competition, corruption), the higher will be the cost of capital, the scarcer the investible resources and the lower the amount of investment that can be financed (Rodrik 2010). It could be argued that the relaxation of this constraint would have a greater effect on growth than changes to the costs of finance or human capital.

The results of the analysis also suggest that the cost of capital in Kosovo is the second most important constraint on firm growth. This constraint is related, in part, to macro and governance factors. The greater the government failures, the lower the levels of appropriation and, consequently, the higher the cost of capital. The findings indicate that scarcity of investible resources originates also from low levels of domestic savings, poor domestic intermediation, monopolistic behaviours by the banks and poor access to international finance.

The reason for the low rate of private returns in Kosovo's economy may also be related to complementary factors, primarily human capital. There is evidence suggesting that the country's current education system suffers from many distortions including: an inadequate link between market needs and university graduates; no link between higher education and research and innovation activities; and poor labour skills (OECD 2013). All these symptoms contribute to a syndrome, which needs to be addressed to ensure sufficient growth.

If the central argument of growth diagnostics theory is that private investment and entrepreneurial activity is essential for any country to experience growth, then, based on the evidence presented in this chapter, it could be inferred that the current investment climate in Kosovo provides little incentive for firm growth. Growth is a function of private investment, which increases only when agents (entrepreneurs) expect a high rate of return on asset accumulation and when there are available funds to finance their business projects. The findings show that private investors perceive the business environment in Kosovo as unfavourable; characterized by high microeconomic risks, with high costs of capital, and scarce complementary factors in the form of human capital.

This is not to suggest that other external constraints are trivial or unimportant. This chapter explored the sequence of binding constraints that firms in Kosovo currently face. It should be treated as a work in progress, because changes in the business environment occur constantly, new data and evidence may become available, and updates to the list of binding constraints may be necessary. In sum, this work should be considered as working hypotheses to be challenged and extended by further research.

References

Brock, W., Durlauf, S., & West, K. (2003). *Policy evaluation in uncertain economic environments* (NBER Working Papers, No. W10025).

Carlin, W., & Seabright, P. (2007). *Bring me sunshine: Which parts of the business climate should public policy try to fix?* (Unpublished manuscript). Available at http://www.worldbank.org.

Carlin, W., Schaffer, M., & Seabright, P. (2006). *Where are the real bottlenecks? A Lagrangian approach to identifying constraints on growth from subjective survey data* (CEPR Discussion Paper 5719).

Djankov S., La Porta R., Lopez-de-Silanes F., & Shleifer A. (2006). *The law and economics of self-dealing* (Working Paper). World Bank.

Dollar, D., Hallward-Driemeier, M., & Mengistae, T. (2005). Investment climate and firm performance in developing economies. *Economic Development and Cultural Change, 54,* 1–31.

European Commission. (2018). *Kosovo2018 Report.* Commission staff working document. Strasburg. https://ec.europa.eu/neighbourhood-enlargement/sites/near/files/20180417-kosovo-report.pdf.

Felipe, J., & Usui, N. (2008, February). *Rethinking the growth diagnostics approach: Questions from the practitioners.* Asian Development Bank. Version of February.

Fernández-Arias, E. (2008). Living with debt: How to limit the risks of Sovereign finance. Inter-American Development Bank.

Hausmann, R. (2005). Tanzania comments. In *Growth path workshop* (pp. 1–2). Washington, DC: The World Bank.

Hausmann, R., & Rodrik, D. (2005). *Self-discovery in a development strategy for El Salvador*. Brainstorming on Growth Analysis Methodology (GAM). Washington, DC: Inter-American Development Bank.

Hausmann, R., & Klinger, B. (2007). *Growth diagnostic: Belize*. Cambridge: Centre for International Development.

Hausmann, R., Rodrik, D., & Velasco, A. (2005). *Growth diagnostics*. Cambridge, MA: Harvard University, mimeo.

Hausmann, R., Klinger, B., & Wagner, R. (2008). *Doing growth diagnostics in practice: A mindbook* (Harvard University Centre for International Development Working Paper 177).

Hoti, A. (2011). Returns for education in Kosovo: Estimates of wage and employment premia. *South East European Journal of Economics and Business, 6*(1), 71–84.

IMF. (2018). *Republic of Kosovo; Selected Issues* (IMF Country Report No. 18/31).

Kaufmann, D., Aart, K., & Mastruzzi, M. (2007). *Governance matters VI: aggregate and individual governance indicators for 1996–2006* (World Bank Policy Research Working Paper No. 4280). Washington, DC.

Lazonick, W. (2012). *The innovative enterprise and the developmental state: Toward an economics of organizational success*. Paper prepared for the annual conference of the Institute for New Economic Thinking, Breton Woods, NH, April 8–11, 2011, and revised for the conference on Finance, Business Models, and Sustainable Prosperity, Ford Foundation, New York.

Lazonick, W. (2013). The theory of innovative enterprise: Methodology, ideology, and institutions. In Jamee K. Moudud, Cyrus Bina, & Patrick L. Mason (Eds.), *Alternative theories of competition: Challenges to the orthodoxy* (pp. 127–159). London and New York: Routledge.

Leipziger, D., & Zagha, R. (2006). Getting out of the rut. *Finance and Development (IMF), 43*(1), 16.

Lin, J. (2012). *New structural economics: A framework for rethinking development and policy*. Washington: World Bank. http://siteresources.worldbank.org/DEC/Resources/84797-1104785060319/598886-1104951889260/NSE-Book.pdf.

Mincer, J. (1958). Investment in human capital and personal income distribution. *The Journal of Political Economy, 66*(4), 281–302.

Manski, C. (2000). Identification problems and decisions under ambiguity: Empirical analysis of treatment response and normative analysis of treatment choice. *Journal of Econometrics, 95*(2), 415–442.

OECD. (2009). *Strategies for aligning stimulus measures with long-term growth.* Paris: OECD.

OECD. (2012). *SME policy index: Western Balkans and Turkey 2012: Progress in the implementation of the small business act for Europe.* Paris: OECD Publishing. http://dx.doi.org/10.1787/9789264178861-en.

OECD. (2013, March). *Assessment of the Kosovo innovation system* (RCI Project Paper). OECE Development.

OECD. (2016). Overview: 2016 small business act assessment of the Western Balkans and Turkey. In *SME policy index: Western Balkans and Turkey 2016: Assessing the Implementation of the Small Business Act for Europe.* Paris: OECD Publishing. http://dx.doi.org/10.1787/9789264254473-4-en.

Riinvest. (2017). *Business environment in Kosovo: From SMEs perspective.* Prishtina.

Rodriguez, F. (2005). Comment on Hausmann and Rodrik. *Journal of the Latin American and Caribbean Economic Association, 6*(1), 101–110.

Rodrik, D. (2006). *Why we learn nothing from regressing economic growth on policies.* Cambridge, MA: Harvard University, mimeo.

Rodrik, D. (2010). Diagnostics before prescription. *Journal of Economic Perspectives, 24*(3), 33–44.

Rodrik, D., Subramanian, A., & Trebbi, F. (2004). Institutions rule: The primacy of institutions over geography and integration in economic development. *Journal of Economic Growth, 9*(2), 131–165.

Sartor, O. (2007). An outline and critique of growth diagnostics as a response to the policy vacuum left by the Washington consensus. Seminar Paper in Development Economics, Institute of Public Economics, Humboldt University, Berlin.

Sen, K., & Kirkpatrick, C. (2009). A diagnostic approach to economic growth and employment policy in low income economies: The case of Kosovo. *Journal of International Development, 23*(1), 132–154.

Sen, K., & Kirkpatrick, C. (2011). A diagnostics approach to economic growth and employment policy in low income economies: The case of Kosovo. *Journal of International Development, 23*(1): 132–154.

Stiglitz, J., & Weiss, A. (1981). Credit rationing in markets with imperfect information. *American Economic Review, 71*(3), 393–409.

Sutherland, D., Sonia, A., Balázs, É., & Tomasz, K. (2009). *Infrastructure investment: Links to growth and the role of public policies* (Economics Department Working Paper No. 686 ECO/WKP [2009]27).

World Bank. (2012a). *World Bank—Kosovo partnership: Country program snapshot*. Pristina: The World Bank Country Office in Kosovo.

World Bank. (2012b). *Implementation status and results: Kosovo institutional development for education project*. Washington, DC: The World Bank.

World Bank. (2016). *Worldwide governance indicators*. https://databank.worldbank.org/data/source/worldwide-governance-indicators.

6

Resources, Capabilities and Managerial Practices of Firms in Less-Developed Economies: Evidence from Kosovo Manufacturing Firms

6.1 Introduction

From a Schumpeterian and evolutionary perspective, economic growth is driven by firm growth; firms accumulate capabilities and generate variety, leading to greater division of labour and higher income. However, the firm centred view of growth is an undeveloped area, although numerous research studies highlight various internal capabilities that enable and/or constrain firm growth (Hallak 2006; Sutton and Trefler 2016). Most studies focus on developed economies and there is comparatively much less evidence on the specifics of firms' internal capabilities in the context of less-developed economies. There is large body of work that takes a Schumpeterian approach to the process of technological capabilities building in developed economies (Bell and Pavitt 1993; Kim 1997; Dutrénit 2004) and this inspired the present work. However, this literature does not include process of internal capabilities building in the recent period and is focused strongly on technological capabilities, overlooking the full range of firm growth.

Why should analysis of the factors that drive firm growth in less-developed economies be important? It might be expected that more

F. Sahiti, *The Growth of Firms in Less-Developed Countries*,
https://doi.org/10.1007/978-3-030-14821-8_6

differentiating factors, such as organizational capabilities, are less important for these economies and that their growth is driven by the availability of 'factors of production' or resources (inputs) rather than by unique organizational capabilities and managerial practices.

This chapter investigates the differentiating capabilities for two groups of firms: gazelles, which are firm that have grown by more than 20% in the previous three years, and firms that have grown less than 20% over the same period. The aim is to distinguish factors such as level of inputs, organizational capabilities and management practices that drive growth.

The data were gathered from in-depth, semi-structured interviews with the managers of 44 selected manufacturing firms operating in Kosovo. The number of variables used during the interviewing process greatly exceeds the number of cases with the result that the interviews provided a huge amount of detail on a small number of firms.

The contribution of this chapter to the literature on firm growth is twofold. *Firstly*, although we have a good empirical understanding of the relationship between internal resource capabilities and firm growth, most research focuses on developed economies. There is comparatively less evidence on this relationship for less-developed economies. In providing evidence about the impact of different internal groups of factors on performance variabilities in less-developed countries, this research tries to fill this gap in the literature. *Secondly*, our research combines different theoretical perspectives. The conventional micro-economic approach, which focuses on resources (inputs), ignores the firm as organizational entity and assumes that the key to growth is the market as the allocator of resources (inputs). Previous studies focus mostly on one dimension of internal growth enablers/constraints, with a resource-based theory perspective. However, there is an emerging literature that adopts a management practices approach. The research in this chapter combines all three approaches to firm growth.

The empirical results suggest that management practices (although still underdeveloped in less-developed economies such as Kosovo) are important in relation to performance differences while the impact of organizational capabilities seem more truncated. Some of these organizational capabilities, such as marketing and teamwork, seem to have a smaller effect on performance compared to networking or dynamic capabilities. We find less evidence supporting a micro-economic approach.

The chapter is organized as follows. Section 6.2 discusses some economic theories related to firm growth and Sect. 6.3 describes the theoretical frameworks used for this research. Section 6.4 discusses the similarities and differences between resources, capabilities and managerial practices and Sect. 6.5 describes our methodology. Section 6.6 presents the empirical results and Sects. 6.7 and 6.8 provide the Mann–Witney U Test and factors analysis results. Section 6.9 provides a summary of empirical results, while Sect. 6.10 provides the conclusions.

6.2 Economic Theories of Firm Growth

There are several determinants of firm growth and productivity. Understanding the factors underling these processes has occupied the minds of economists for hundreds of years and resulted in various theories, ranging from Adam Smith's focus on specialization and the division of labour, to the neoclassical economists' emphasis on investment in physical capital and infrastructure (Schumpeter 1943; Solow 1957).

In the conventional approach, the firm's main objective is profit maximization and how to increase revenue by minimizing production costs. It assumes that markets are fully competitive with many small firms being price takers; therefore, firms are not free to set sales prices if they want to avoid consumers turning to their competitors. Firms have to accept the market price and, consequently, need to focus on cost minimization. Those that are more successful at minimizing costs, make higher profits while those that are less successful will achieve reduced profit and, eventually, will exit the market. Therefore, the focus in conventional analyses is on the production function; in conventional approaches, production is treated as a black box. Here, we model production as a function that turns inputs into output: $q = f(k, l)$.[1]

[1]Where: q: output; k: capital input; l: labour input; $f(k, l)$: production function.

Endogenous growth theory focuses on R&D and empiricists are interested in the relationship between Total-Factor Productivity (TFP) and innovation, measured by R&D, patents and/or more direct proxies for innovation and diffusion (e.g., Information and Communication Technology—ICT). This body of work provides robust evidence on the causal importance of hard technology for productivity growth. Bloom et al. (2016) point out that there are at least two major problems related to a focus on these aspects of technical change as the sole drivers of productivity. First, even after controlling for a wide range of observable measures of hard technologies, there remains a large residual in measured TFP. Second, many studies find that the impact of technology on productivity varies widely across firms and countries.

In contrast, the Resourced-based View (RBV) argues that it is not inputs per se, but the way they are utilized that produces growth variation between firms (Collis and Montgomary 1995). The longstanding interest in understanding the concept of firm capabilities is rooted in Penrose's (1959) seminal work on firm growth. Her ideas were taken forward by Barney (1991), who argues that firms within the same industry are heterogeneous in terms of the strategic resources they control, which are not perfectly mobile across firms. According to this framework, firms possess a number of resources that support or constrain their growth (Cantwell 2000; Jacobides and Winter 2005). These resources cannot be purchased on the open market; they can only be created internally. They have some idiosyncratic features: they are able to bring value to the firm; they are rare, imperfectly imitable and non-substitutable. Firms endowed with heterogeneous resources can attain competitive advantage, based essentially on the relative productivity of a bindingly scarce resource. It is not scarcity per se, but the capability that lies behind the resource that allows firms to capture higher economic value (Leiblein 2011).

In his empirical work, Sutton (2000, 2005, 2012) distinguishes between two firm capability concepts. First, there is the firm's underlying capability ("the set of elements of 'know-how' or 'working practices' held collectively by the group of individuals comprising the firm"; Sutton 2005, p. 3). Second, there is the firm's revealed capability, which is the observable (and performance-relevant) outcomes reflecting the firm's productive capacities in terms of both quality and productivity.

Although conceptual models related to firm capabilities vary, there are some common characteristics highlighted by empirical studies. For example, capabilities are primarily internal, firm-specific, knowledge-based and not easily replicable. These knowledge capabilities are manifested in routines, management practices, specialized departments or assets acquired firms internally or externally, which can be measured and result from investment in learning and knowledge accumulation over time (Sutton 2005). In this framework productivity and innovation are considered to be combinative capabilities to generate new applications from existing knowledge (Kogut and Zander 1996) or the produce of a change to established routines (Nelson and Winter 1982).

There is a strand of literature that examines whether the management styles in different firms and countries play a role in firm growth heterogeneity. Are there specific managerial practices that influence firm performance regardless of the industry or country? Conventional management theories emphasize that the practices the firm establishes are contingent on number of factors (e.g. firm size, firm structure, industry) that make the firm unique (Bloom et al. 2016). Also, relative to other inputs, such as capital, the firm's management practices should be easier to change. In other words, as new best practice emerges, it can be adopted by the firm to reduce differences over time.

Nicholas Bloom from Stanford University and John Van Reenen from the London School of Economics and Political Science have challenged this conventional view. They argue that there are some basic management practices that act similar to a new technology and, like advanced machinery, can help companies increase their output (Bloom and Van Reenen 2007). They suggest, also, that managerial processes are as important as other inputs to production and can create significant competitive advantage. These authors used a new survey methodology to survey a large random sample of companies to understand how well best practices are being used. The surveys were administered by telephone, in interviews with company managers who were asked

18 questions, which fell into three categories. The first category dealt with the monitoring of their production processes and how they collected data on what happened on the shop floor. The second group of questions asked about how the firm used that data in meetings and how it set targets—from upper management to frontline workers. The third category was related to human resources and how workers are hired, trained and motivated to produce their best work. The responses scored from 1 to 5 depending on the non-adoption to full adoption of a specific practice. The raw average scores across all these questions provided a score for the firm's management a one to five scale.

6.3 The Theoretical Framework Applied in This Study

To investigate the specifics of the internal factors affecting performance variability among firms operating in Kosovo, we used a three perspective framework. *First*, the conventional micro-economic perspective considers firm growth as driven primarily by differences in the quantity of inputs or resources and the efficiency of their use. *Second*, the RBV extends the focus by interpreting differences between firms based not on inputs or resources, but on the services employed (Penrose 1959). *Third*, it includes managerial practices which have been shown to be an important differentiator of firm performance.

We expect the potential for superior performance, in a specific situation, to be a function of the firm's resources (inputs), organizational capabilities and managerial practices. The emphasis on expectations within this theoretical framework refers to the perceived degree of probability that a 'causal relationship' exists between the above-mentioned variables and superior firm performance. This generalized expectancy construct is seen as an "internal locus of control" where the firm expects that, by developing specific and unique resources, organizational capabilities and managerial practices, superior performance will follow. Inputs/resources, organizational capabilities and managerial practices are defined as follows (Fig. 6.1).

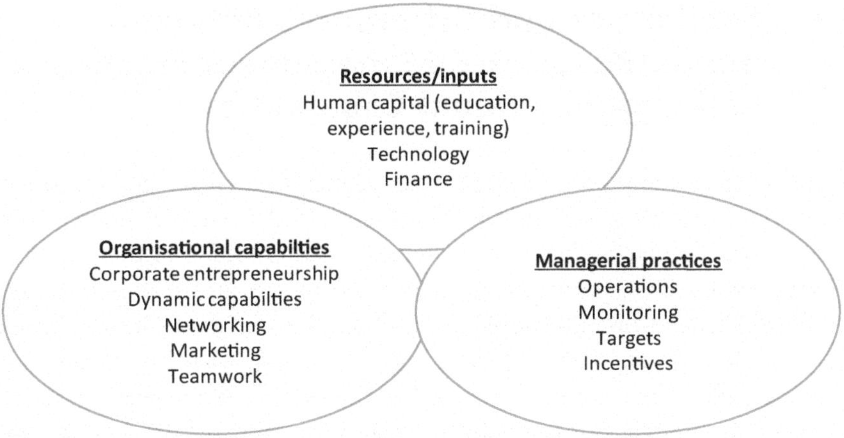

Fig. 6.1 Organizational success triangle (*Source* Author)

1. Resources are the inputs used by the firm to conduct its business operations (Grant 2002). They can be technological, financial or human capital.
2. Organizational capabilities are defined as complex patterns of coordination between people (human capital) and other resources (Grant 2002). The variables related to organizational capabilities include: corporate entrepreneurship, dynamic capabilities, networking, marketing and team working.
3. Managerial practices are defined as a bundle of operating, monitoring, target and incentive practices (Bloom and Van Reenen 2007).

Bearing in mind that organizational success is vital to firm and industry upgrading, which is critical for growth, these three categories are considered essential to understand organizational success (Lazonick 2013). They need to be considered in the business environment context with which they interact.

Using this theoretical framework, this chapter addresses the following question: *do high-growing firms differ from low-growing firms in terms of the resources, organizational capabilities and managerial practices employed in the Kosovo economy?*

6.4 Similarities and Differences Between Inputs/Resources, Management Practices and Organizational Capabilities

An important question is to what extent these internal factors are similar to, overlap with or are different from each other? An essential element that makes them similar is that they all represent internal levers that can lead to superior business performance. However, inputs and resources clearly are different from organizational capabilities. Resources are more focused on tangible aspects, such as technology, or people with knowledge and working skills. They can be purchased in the market. Managerial practices are more intangible, but differ from organizational capabilities in dealing with internal processes, procedures and systems established internally by the firm. However, are these systems unique, or, can they be transferred? By deploying specific management practices, firms are able to manage their internal resources. These practices are transferable and adaptable and constitute a form of organizational technology, a set of techniques, systems, rules, principles and typologies that provide the most rational and efficient management model. Firms are able to adapt to certain operating, monitoring, targeting and incentivising techniques based on their functionality. Organizational capabilities differ in being unique and idiosyncratic. They are path dependent and cannot be purchased in the market. They constitute working routines which are difficult for competitors to replicate due to their path dependence, causal ambiguity, social complexity and non-substitutability. In Table 6.1 presents an overview of the features and attributes of these three components.

6.5 Methodology and Data

The methodology used draws on the SAPPHO[2] model used to study industrial innovation and management innovation in two science-based industries: chemicals and scientific instruments. The SAPPHO project

---

[2]SAPPHO—Scientific Activity Predictor from Patterns with Heuristic Origins.

Table 6.1 Attributes that differentiate three components

	Organizational capabilities	Managerial capabilities	Resources
Attributes	Rareness	Generic	Generic
	Causal ambiguity	Replicable	Identical
	Path dependency	Mimetic	Changeable
	Social complexity	Technical by nature	Purchasable
	Due to organizational culture, internally generated	Adaptable	Physical
	Non-substitutability	Substitutable	Substitutable

Source Author

aimed to identify and evaluate factors that distinguish between profitably commercial innovations and unsuccessful innovations. The methodology suggests that, to achieve market success depends on more than the technological components and requires an understanding of user needs, marketing, organization, external knowledge sources and leadership (SPRU 1972; Rothwell et al. 1974; Freeman 1997). By employing a similar logic and methodology, this chapter provides new empirical evidence to show that technology (equipment) is not the only requirement for good performance from manufacturing firms operating in a less-developed economy. Good performance requires organizational capabilities and good managerial practices, also.

The dataset used for this study is based on the responses to a survey carried out in 2018. The survey questionnaire was based on the AEGIS survey and the survey used by Bloom and Van Reenen (2007).[3] The sample includes 44 manufacturing firms operating in the Kosovo economy. Data were collected through a survey via in-depth semi-structured interviews with managers/owners of selected firms. The selection of sectors is in line with those covered in the AEGIS survey and includes all

[3]AEGIS stands for advancing knowledge-intensive entrepreneurship and innovation for growth and social well-being in Europe. The AEGIS project studies Knowledge-Intensive Entrepreneurship (KIE), its defining characteristics, boundaries, scope and incentives in high technology as well as in low-technology sectors and in services. KIE is perceived here as a core interface between two interdependent systems: the knowledge generation and diffusion system, on the one hand, and the productive system, on the other. More information on AEGIS is available at: http://cordis.europa.eu/result/rcn/57920_en.html.

manufacturing firms employing between 20 and 250 workers. The classification of sectors is based on NACE C10–C30.

Through in-depth semi-structured interviews, many performance measurement indicators were used; with each of them designed to throw light on the factors that enable higher business growth. The factors measured include tangible resources (physical, financial), human capital (education, training and experience), organizational capabilities (corporate entrepreneurship, marketing, teamwork, dynamic, and networking capabilities) and management practices (operating, monitoring, targeting, and incentive practices). This methodology identifies the factors that enable or constrain firm growth.

To assess the characteristics of each group of firms, we constructed 48 groups of indicators or variables for tangible and human resources, organizational capabilities and management practices. The questionnaire included 173 variables and 44 cases, which allowed us to obtain very detailed data on this small number of firms.

There are numerous indicators of high-growth firms. We use the Eurostat/OECD (2008, p. 61) definition of a growing firm as a firm with 'average annualized growth (in terms of sales/turnover) greater than 20 per cent per annum'. The survey questionnaire asked managers specifically whether the firm had experienced a huge increase in sales (higher than 20%), a significant increase (10–19%), a slight increase (5–9%), a slowdown (1–4% increase) or a decline (up to −3%) in the period 2015–2017.

The descriptive analysis summarizes the main findings from the survey. It provides the statistical summary of the empirical findings. The second part of the analysis investigates factors that differentiate the two groups of firms. A Mann–Whitney *U* test was employed to differentiate high-growing firms from low growing firms. This statistical technique is used to test for differences between two independent groups on a continuous measure. In our case, we are interested in the differences between high-growing firms and low-growing firms in terms of their resources, organizational capabilities and managerial practice. The Mann–Whitney *U* test is a non-parametric alternative to the t-test for independent samples. Instead of comparing means of the two groups, as in the case of the t-test, the Mann–Whitney technique compares medians. It converts the scores on the continuous variables to rank two groups and evaluates whether the ranking differ significantly.

To test differences between two groups, the dataset must meet at least three conditions. First, groups must be randomly drawn from the target population, which implies the absence of measurement and sampling errors (Robert and Casella 2004).[4] Second, each observation must correspond to a different participant, meaning that, in statistical terms, there is independence within groups and mutual independence between groups (Mann and Whitney 1947). Third, the data measurement scale must be an ordinal or continuous type, that is, the observation values are ordinal, relative or absolute scale types.

The Mann-Whitney *U* statistics can be defined by the following *U* equations, for each group:

$$\begin{aligned} U_x &= n_x n_y + ((n_x(n_x + 1))/2) - R_x(1) \\ U_y &= n_x n_y + ((n_y(n_y + 1))/2) - R_y(2) \end{aligned} \tag{6.1}$$

where n_x is the number of observations in the first group, n_y is the number of observations in the second group, R_x is the sum of the ranks assigned to the first group and R_y is the sum of the ranks assigned to the second group. In other words, both *U* equations can be understood as the number of times observations in one sample follow observations in the other sample when all the scores from one group are placed in ascending order.

Following calculation of the *U* test and determination of an appropriate statistical threshold (α), the statement that there is difference between two groups in terms of resources, capabilities, and managerial practices can be rejected or not. Before the test was performed, a threshold value or significance level was chosen as $< 5\%$, denoted as α.

To explain correlations among multiple outcomes as being the result of one or more underlying explanations or factors, we performed a factor analysis. This technique involves data reduction since it attempts to represent a set of variables by a smaller number. In addition,

[4]Note that there can be small sampling and measurement errors.

factor analysis reveals unexplained factors that influence the co-variation among multiple observations (Bartholomew et al. 2011). These factors represent underlying concepts that cannot be measured adequately using a single variable (Rummel 1970). For example, various measures of firm heterogeneity may be influenced by one or more underlying factors.

Several methods are available, but principle component analysis is the most common. It uses mathematical procedures to simplify interrelated measures to discover patterns in a set of variables (Child 2006). In the principle component analysis mathematical model, *p* is the number of variables ($X_1, X_2, \ldots, X_p$) and *m* is the number of underlying factors ($F_1, F_2, \ldots, F_m$). Xj is the variable for latent factors. Hence, this model assumes that there are *m* underlying factors and each observed variables is a linear function of these factors together with a residual variate. The model is intended to reproduce the maximum correlations. Explicitly, the principal component variables are obtained from $x_1, \ldots, x_q$ as follows:

$$X_j = a_{j1}F_1 + a_{j2}F_2 + \cdots + a_{jm}F_m + e_j \tag{6.2}$$

where $j = 1, 2, \ldots, p$.

The factor loadings are $a_{j1}, a_{j2}, \ldots, a_{jm}$ meaning that a_{j1} is the factor loading of the *jth* variable on the 1st factor, while the specific or unique factor is denoted e_j. The factor loadings give an idea of how much the variable contributes to the factor; the larger the factor loading, the more the variable has contributed to that factor (Harman 1976). Factor loadings are similar to weights in multiple regression analysis and represent the strength of the correlation between the variable and the factor (Kline 1994).

Since names may not accurately reflect the variables within the factor, one of the limitations of this technique is that naming the factors can be problematic. Also, because some of the variables may load onto more than one factor, known as split loadings, their accurate interpretation can be difficult. As Tabachnick and Fidell (2007) point out, variables may correlate with each other to produce a factor despite having little underlying meaning for the factor.

To be suitable for factor analysis the dataset should meet two criteria related to sample size and strength of the relationship among the variables. There is little agreement among authors about sample size, but it is generally recommended that two statistical measures should be generated to assess the factorability of the data: Bartlett's (1954) test of sphericity and the Kaiser–Meyer–Olkin (KMO) measure of sampling adequacy (Kaiser 1970, 1974). The former should reach a statistical significance not greater than 0.05 ($p < .05$), while the suggested minimum value of the KMO index is 0.6 for a good factor analysis. With regard to the strength of relationship between variables, Tabachnick and Fidell (2007) recommend inspection of the correlation matrix for evidence of coefficients greater than 0.3.

6.6 Empirical Findings on Inputs, Organizational Capabilities and Management Practices

6.6.1 Descriptive Statistics on Human Resources

The first section of the survey questionnaire, part A, captures some general information about the firm. The purpose was to collect data on number of employees; educational levels of founders and employees; occupation and area of expertise of founders before firm establishment; and training activities undertaken by the firm in the previous 12 months.

In terms of number of employees, the results show that the majority, that is, 51.52%, are small firms with less than 50 employees, 33% of firms employ up 100 people, and around 16% employ 100–250 employees. The educational level of the workforce can be considered high, since two-thirds of the firms have employees with university degrees, and 19% of firms have doctoral graduate employees. Employee educational levels tend to be higher in high-growing compared to the other group of firms.

The questionnaire also asked about the characteristics of the founding team and, if where there was more than one founder, one of the founders responded to the questionnaire. The firm founders are important for subsequent firm growth. In this survey we followed the definition of a new venture founding team in Almer-Jarz et al. (2008, p. 164): "a founder team has to consist of at least two individuals, all team members have to be shareholders (bearing risks), they must participate actively in the venture (work together) and make concerted decisions (corporative goals)".

The larger the founding team, the more heterogeneous it might be in terms of competences, knowledge, wisdom and experience, and the better able to deal with everyday problems. The founding team might provide psychological benefits (Bird 1989) and mutual support structures, which can increase the satisfaction and performance of team members (Janz et al. 1997). However, there is some evidence of negative aspects of multi-founder ventures related to monitoring, shirking, distributing incentives (e.g. Mosakowski 1998) and group conflict (Amason and Sapienza 1997). Apart from solo ventures, two person founding teams are the most common (Shane 2008). The survey results show that this is true for both groups of firms.

The education attainment of founders is considered to be a generic component of the founder's human capital and is related to the knowledge acquired through formal education. This variable is generally positively related to the likelihood of new firm survival and firm growth (Reagans et al. 2005). Table 6.2 shows that 40.9% of firm founders do not have a university degree, 4.5% have a post-graduate degree, none have a doctoral degree. The share of founders without a university education does not differ across firms, although it is slightly higher in low-growing firm (50.5%).

Prior industry experience is relevant because team members are likely to share their experience, knowledge and information with the entire team, making knowledge of industry practices and routines available to everyone. This type of knowledge can differ from the type of knowledge that individual team member can accumulate directly (Reagans et al. 2005). According to Shane and Stuart (2002), the founder's prior experience can increase start-up capital, speed the transition of a prospective new venture a liquidity event and avoid outright failure of the new firm. Hsu (2004) points out that entrepreneurs with prior founding experience may have an increased likelihood of receiving venture capital funding for their venture compared to those with no previous experience in the focal industry.

Table 6.2 shows that approximately 40% of founders were former employees in a firm in a different industry, 20.5% worked previously in a firm in the same industry, 22.7% of owners had worked in a firm that closed down and 13.6% were current firm owners.

The main areas of expertise of firm founders are related to the specific knowledge and skills acquired during their formal education and

Table 6.2 Resources/inputs—human capital

	High growing firms	Low growing firms	Total
Formal education of the founders			
Secondary education	50	27.8	40.9
Higher education BA	38.5	66.7	50.1
Higher education BS	3.8	5.6	4.5
Masters PhD	7.7	0	4.5
	100	100	100
Occupation of the founders before they started actual business			
Owner of a firm still in existence	11.5	16.7	13.6
Owner of a firm that has ceased operations	11.5	38.9	22.7
Employee of a firm in the same Industry	19.2	22.2	20.5
Employee of a firm in a different industry	53.8	22.2	40.9
None of above	3.8		2.3
	100	100	100
Area of expertise of the founders			
Technical and engineering knowledge	26.9	23.5	25
General management	69.2	70.6	70.4
Marketing	1.9	2.9	2.3
Finance	1.9	2.9	2.3
	100	100	100

Source Survey 2018

in the course of their previous employment and entrepreneurial experience. The majority of founders have expertise in general management (70.4%) followed by technical and engineering knowledge (20%). Equal shares of them have marketing (2.3%) and finance expertise (2.3%). Technical and engineering knowledge is the most important area of expertise across high-growth firms (27%) compared to low-growth firms (22%).

Training is relevant and facilitates upgrading and updating of know-how, knowledge and skills. Winter (1987) suggests that firm-specific training can increase the managers' and workers' competencies to make them a 'strategic asset'. Continuous training activities allows the building of "bundles" of routines that are difficult for competitors to imitate and allow the firm to increase its competitive advantage and achieve superior performance (Koch and McGrath 1996).

The results of the survey show that most firms conduct training activities: 53.1% of firms indicated that they provide training. Around 67% of beverages and wood sub-sectors firms confirmed that they organize in-house training although industries, such as those that produce styropor (*polystyrene*) do not consider training important and do not offer in-house training. None of the firms interviewed had received the support of a university or collect and EU agencies provide training only for firms operating in the food industry (6%).

6.6.2 Descriptive Statistics on New Technology Investment and Sources of Finance

The survey asked about investment in physical technology, especially production technology, information technology. The responses show that 91.8% of firms had purchased production technology in the previous three years and 46.9% had invested in information technology (Table 6.3).

In relation to sources of finance, 97% of respondents used internal resources augmented by bank loans (97%) to purchase their technology. Six percent of respondents reported receiving EU funding to purchase new technology and 3% reported receiving government funding. Three out of the 44 firms used bank loans to purchase their technology while 10 out of the 44 firms used only internal funds.

Table 6.3 Investment in last three years in technology

	High growing firm		Low growing firm		Total	
	Yes	No	Yes	No	Yes	No
Over the past three years the firm invested in new technology	96.2	3.8	94.4	5.6	95.5	4.5
Over the past three years the firm invested in new information technology	61.5	38.5	44.4	55.6	54.5	45.5
Over the past three years the firm invested in other new technology	3.8	96.2	3.8	96.2	3.8	96.2

Source Survey 2018

6.6.3 Corporate Entrepreneurship and Innovation Capabilities

This section of the questionnaire examined the firm's capacity to coordinate, put into productive use and shape inputs into innovative outputs (Collis 1994). It includes specific questions about process innovations, which involve all those new or significantly improved production and delivery methods, and other additional support activities aimed at decreasing unit costs or increasing product quality. Organizational innovations are related, primarily, to new or significant changes to the firm structure and the implementation of new management methods to improve in-house use of knowledge, the quality of goods and services and work flow efficiency.

Figure 6.2 depicts the share of firms that implemented (blue bar) or not (red bar) specific process and organizational innovations. Half of the surveyed firms had introduced new or significantly improved manufacturing methods, while approximately 31.3% of firms had introduced new or significantly improved knowledge management systems or changes to their managing structure. A quarter of firms had introduced process support activities (such as maintenance systems or purchasing, accounting and computing systems). Changes to supply chain and distribution activities had been implemented by 37.5% of firms.

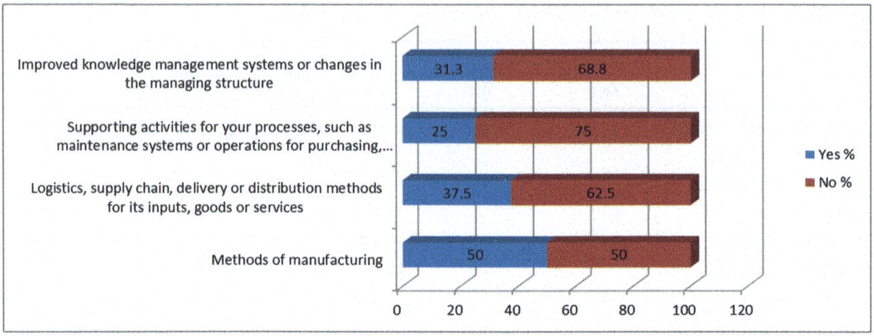

Fig. 6.2 Introduction of new methods of production and processes (*Source* Survey 2018)

With responses based on a five point Likert-scale, one part of the questionnaire asked about the specific sources of knowledge firms used to explore new business opportunities. The aim was to identify and evaluate the significant of linkages in the innovation process.

Table 6.4 shows that customers are the most important source of knowledge. More than 34% of respondents rated them 4 or 5, with a mean of 3.28. The second most important source of knowledge is exhibitions, with the mean of 3.03 followed by competitors with a mean of 2.84 and scientific journals and other trade or technical publications with a mean of 2.22.

Risk-taking is considered to be a significant aspect of corporate entrepreneurship capability. This capability is linked to the firm's ability to use resources effectively, exploit new opportunities and launch projects with uncertain outcomes and uncertain returns on investment (Scheepers et al. 2008). A majority (71.9%) of firms reported having introduced a new product, service or process in the previous three years, which eventually had been unsuccessful. This shows that most firms are risk takers.

6.6.4 Dynamic Capabilities

This section identifies ow firms recognize and exploit opportunities, the sources of knowledge used and the formal or informal mechanisms employed to achieve the best business results.

Table 6.4 Sources of knowledge for exploring new business opportunities

	Mean	Std. Dev.	% of firms that responded	
			Not (that) important[a]	Important/very important[b]
Clients or customers	3.28	1.68	18.2	34.2
Suppliers	1.63	0.75	90.7	9.3
In-house (know how, R&D laboratories in your firm)	1.25	0.984	46.9	25
Competitors	2.84	1.221	46.9	25
Trade fairs, conferences and exhibitions	3.03	1.47	43.8	43.8
Scientific journals and other trade or technical publications	2.22	1.408	54.7	24.9
Universities	1.06	3.54	96.1	3.1
Public research institutes	1.13	0.707	96.9	3.1
External commercial labs/R&D firms/technical institutes	1.03	1.77	96.9	3.1

[a]Responses of 1 or 2 in a 1–5 Likert scale [b]Responses of 4 or 5 in a 1–5 Likert scale
Source Survey 2018

The findings indicate that respondents tend to evaluate their performance very positively: 55% of firms agreed or strongly agreed with 6 out of the 11 items. First ranked with observance and adoption of the best practice in their sector with a mean of 3.99, followed by frequent sharing of practical experience among employees with a mean of 3.88 and changing practices based on customer feedback with a mean of 3.78. Recognizing new opportunities to respond better to customers' needs was ranked equally highly (3.72). These types of organizational capabilities are related to identifying market opportunities and the ability to be continuously aware of client needs. As already mentioned, almost 70% of firms responded that their employees share their practical experiences. This is considered an important aspect of human capital capabilities (Protogerou et al. 2011). In contrast, existence of a formal R&D department and a formal engineering and technical studies department received the lowest scores; most firms have no formal R&D or engineering department (Table 6.5).

Table 6.5 Recognizing and seizing opportunities

	Mean	Std. Dev.	% of firms that responded	
			Disagree/ strongly disagree	Agree/ strongly disagree
We change our practices based on customer feedback	3.78		35.5	62.5
Our firm responds rapidly to competitive moves	3.66	0.92	44.8	56.3
Our firm actively observes and adopts the best practices in our sector	3.99	0.818	32.2	68.8
We quickly understand new opportunities to better serve our customers	3.72	0.924	9.3	68.7
Our firm regularly considers the consequences of changing market demand in terms of new products and services	3.47	0.718	53.2	46.9
Our firm is quick to recognize shifts in our market (e.g. competition, regulation, demography)	3.63	0.707	37.6	62.6
There is a formal R&D department in our firm	1.06	2.46	6.3	93.8
There is a formal engineering and technical studies department in our firm	1.03	0.177	3.1	96.9
Design activity is important in introducing new products/services to the market	2.81	1.595	40.6	40.7
We implement systematic internal and external personnel training	2.84	1.394	40.7	28.2
Employees share practical experiences on a frequent basis	3.88	1.04	9.4	68.8

Source Survey 2018

6.6.5 Networking Capabilities

An important organizational capability is business networking. Owners/managers were asked to evaluate how much their business network(s) helped them to improve their operations and achieve and maintain competitive advantage in the market. This part of the questionnaire explores the importance of interpersonal and inter-organizational relationships for specific firm operations. These relationships are seen as providing means of access to a variety of resources including market trends, market changes, demand changes, etc. (Protogerou et al. 2011).

The most important outcome of networking activity is the establishment of lasting relationships with customers and stakeholders such as suppliers, banks, headhunting companies, tax authorities, etc. The ultimate aim of business networking activity should be to increase the client base. Networking activities provide greater rewards in a context of reduced information asymmetries (Protogerou et al. 2011). It is important for the firm to obtain precise and reliable information on possible suppliers and their advantages before testing their capabilities to deliver (Protogerou et al. 2011). Networking provides various information relevant to the development of firm strategy.

Among the ten items related to these activities, three were ranked quite high—see Table 6.6. The highest score was given to managing production and operations. This is related to the fact that most firms are new producers and good relations with technology producers are considered crucial. In contrast, exploring export opportunities was not ranked highly perhaps because most firms did not aim to export their production. Also, networking internationally is more difficult. The results for finance may be explained by better access to external funding is important. In the section that asked about funding sources, the responses show that 74% of firms financed their projects using bank loans. Several of the managers interviewed said it was not straightforward to obtain a bank loan. The lowest ranked items (lowest mean/average scores) were for advertising and promotion (2.84), recruiting skilled labour, developing new products, assistance with taxation and legal issues (3.31) and exploring export opportunities (3.34).

6.6.6 Marketing Capabilities of Firms

Marketing capabilities are considered an important driver of superior performance (Day 1994). According to Kotler (2004), firms benefit from the development of good marketing capabilities. An efficient

Table 6.6 Contribution of the network to successful activities

	Mean	Std. Dev.	%of firms that responded	
			Not (that) important[a]	Important/very important[b]
Selecting suppliers	4.22	0.975	25.1	75
Recruiting skilled labour	3.31	0.965	59.4	40.6
Collecting information about competitors	3.44	0.84	9.4	40.6
Accessing distribution channels	4.03	0.861	24.9	77.2
Assistance in obtaining business loans/attracting funds	3.97	1.121	12.5	71.9
Advertising and promotion	2.84	1.247	43.8	25
Developing new products	3.31	1.203	31.3	53.1
Managing production and operations	4.13	7.93	12.6	87.6
Assistance in arranging taxation or other legal issues	3.31	1.091	15.7	34.2
Exploring export opportunities	3.34	1.45	31.2	53.1

[a]Responses of 1 or 2 in a 1–5 Likert scale
[b]Responses of 4 or 5 in a 1–5 Likert scale
Source Survey 2018

marketing strategy facilitates the identification and selection of markets and distribution channels, and helps the firm to position its products in terms of price relative to competitors. It identifies the most appropriate advertising channels and branding strategy.

Very few of the sample firms had formal marketing systems in place. Most of the means for marketing activities are below 3. Among 29 variables included in the model, only 4 had means of between 3 and 3.38. This suggests that the marketing capabilities of firms in less-developed economies such as Kosovo are underdeveloped or are neglected by firm managers (Table 6.7).

6.6.7 Teamwork Capabilities of Firms

Many authors, such as Nonaka and Takeuchi (1995), consider teamwork to be a relevant variable that facilitates competitive advantage.

Table 6.7 Contribution of marketing activities to growth as perceived by owner/managers

	Mean	Std. Dev.	% of firms that responded	
			Not (that) important[a]	Importart/ veryimportant[b]
Marketing implementation				
Translating marketing strategies into action	2.66	1.153	56.3	17.8
Executing marketing strategies quickly	2.41	1.341	65.6	21.9
Monitoring marketing performance	1.97	1.332	71.9	18.8
Service responsiveness				
Ability to provide rapid response to clients	3.16	0.987	28.1	31.3
Superior levels of service customization	2.97	1.15	34.4	28.1
Rapid response to customer complaints	2.75	1.191	40.6	18.8
Pricing				
Using pricing skills and systems to respond quickly to market changes	2.16	1.051	75	9.4
Knowledge of competitors' pricing tactics	2.03	1.15	71.9	9.4
Monitoring competitors' pricing and pricing changes	2	1.295	75	18.8
Marketing communication				
Sales management skills	2.63	1.338	62.5	21.9
Giving the salespeople the training they need to be effective	2.19	1.355	75	18.8
Providing effective sales support to the sales force	2.03	1.356	75	18.8
Developing and executing advertising programs	1.94	1.318	73.1	18.8
Customer performance				
Customer satisfaction	3.38	0.942	6[a]	37.5
Customer loyalty/retention	3.03	1.062	37.5	25
Added value provided to customers	2.56	0.948	65.6	12.5
Adaptation to customer preferences	3	0.916	31.3	21.9

(continued)

Table 6.7 (continued)

	Mean	Std. Dev.	% of firms that responded	
			Not (that) important[a]	Importart/ veryimportant[b]
Improved communication with customers	2.63	1.07	56.3	21.9
Reduction in the number of customer complaints	2.56	1.134	68.8	18.8
Improved customers' perceived image of the firm	2.78	0.975	46.9	21.9
Retained most-valued customers	2.56	1.162	59.1	15.6

[a]Responses of 1 or 2 in a 1–5 Likert scale
[b]Responses of 4 or 5 in a 1–5 Likert scale
Source Survey 2018

Teamwork allows the workforce to interact socially and is difficult for other firms to imitate. Penrose (1959) suggested that an organizational team is more than a collection of individuals and Barney (1995) characterizes teamwork as something idiosyncratically creative that is difficult to imitate and, therefore, can be a causally ambiguous source of heterogeneity, which leads to sustained competitive advantage.

Table 6.8 shows that 44% of firms responded that they used team working fairly regularly, 40% operated solely on team working and 16% used it occasionally. The size of firm teams varied, mostly 3 and 5—with 48.5%, followed by 1–3 with 30.3%. In response to a question about whether teams were organized autonomously, 68.8% of respondents responded positively and the remainder responded negatively. In response to a question about how much teams are expected to make decisions on

Table 6.8 Contribution of teamwork capabilities to growth as perceived by owners/managers

	Frequency	Percentage
Applies entirely	18	41
Generally applies	19	43
Partially applies	7	16
Total	44	100

Source Survey 2018

their own, most firms (90.6%) responded that teams are responsible for their results, but that these are reviewed by non-team members.

6.6.8 Descriptive Statistics of Managerial Practices

Work on developed and developing economies suggests that management quality is important for firm performance. Bloom and Van Reenen (2011) found large differences in management practices across firms and countries, and found, also, that management quality is strongly associated to firm-level productivity and other performance measures such as profitability and survival rates. This body of work suggests that the differences are higher among firms in the same country than across countries, suggesting that firm and sector-specific factors are at least as important as the firm's general business environment for firm performance. There is some empirical evidence showing that differences in management practices are correlated to competition, labour market flexibility, education, ownership structure, etc. (Friebel and Schweiger 2012; Bloom et al. 2011).

As in the model proposed by Bloom and Van Reenen (2010), management practices were grouped into four areas: operations, monitoring, targets and incentives. The questions related to operations focused primarily on how the firm handles a process problem such as a machinery breakdown. Questions related to monitoring covered issues such as collection, monitoring, revision and use of production performance indicators. Targets focused on production time-scales and incentives refers to promotion criteria, practices for addressing poor employee performance and rewarding achievement of production targets.

In the context of firm operations, managers were asked whether, during the previous three years, the firm had introduced any modern manufacturing techniques including just-in-time delivery from suppliers, automation, flexible manpower, support systems, attitudes and behaviour. For the majority (81.8%) the average score was 1.38. This might be because firms in developing countries do not belong to global value chains. When asked why they had introduced a new manufacturing technique, most said it was other firms have done so or because

Table 6.9 Management practices—operational area

	Mean	Std. Dev.	% of firms that responded		
			Score 1	Score 3	Score 5
Introduction of modern manufacturing techniques	1.38	0.942	81.8	12.5	3.1
Rational for introduction of modern manufacturing techniques	2.94	1.48	28.1	46.9	25
Process problem documentation	2.25	1.589	56.3	25	18.8
Total	2.19		55	28.13	15.63

Source Survey 2018

they wanted to reduce costs. In relation to the tracking of problems and managing process improvements, that is, whether the firm makes continuous process improvements or make them only if problems arise, the average score was 2.25. This suggests that firms make process improvements only if a problem arises. Managers answered that, in most cases, problems and their tracking are not recorded (Table 6.9).

Monitoring was considered important to track, review and communicate performance to the workforce and requires an appropriate internal process. When asked wither tracking and communication with staff were ad hoc or continuous, the majority indicated that it was ad hoc and that many processes are not tracked (mean score 1). Good management practice requires continuous tracking and communication of firm performance either formally or informally, to all staff using a range of visual management tools.

How managers review workforce performance was scored 2.31, which suggests reviews are infrequent and occur, typically, only if there is a particular success or failure, or are periodic, but do not include follow up to adopt performance. Modern management models include continuous performance reviews based on clear indicators, whose results are communicated to all staff to ensure continuous improvement. Table 6.10 shows that most managers provide no formal performance feedback to their workforce or provide it verbally and unbacked by data. Modern monitoring models include regular review/performance conversations, focused on problem solving. They address root causes of

Table 6.10 Management practices—monitoring area

	Mean	Std. Dev.	% of firms that responded		
			Score 1	Score 3	Score 5
Is tracking ad hoc and incomplete, or is performance continually tracked and communicated to all staff?	2.19	1.512	62.5	28.1	9.4
Is performance reviewed infrequently and only on a success/failure scale, or is performance reviewed continually with an expectation of continuous improvement?	2.31	1.306	43.8	43.8	12.5
In review/performance conversations, to what extent is the purpose, data, agenda, and follow-up steps (like coaching) clear to all parties?	2.13	1.238	53.1	40.6	6.3
To what extent does failure to achieve agreed objectives carry consequences, which can include retraining or reassignment to other jobs?	2.81	1.176	9.4	78.1	12.5
Are performance measures ill-defined, poorly understood, and private, or are they well-defined, clearly communicated, and made public?	2.06	1.343	59.4	34.4	6.3
Total	2.3	1.315	45.64	45	9.4

Source Survey 2018

problems and allow for constructive feedback and coaching. The average score for this question was 2.13.

Managers were asked how they deal with the potential consequences following a performance review. The average score was 2.81, indicating that failure to achieve agreed results is tolerated for certain time before action is taken. The final question on monitoring practices aimed to identify how well firms formulate performance measures and whether measures are clearly communicated to and understood by the workforce. The average score of 2.06 indicates that performance measures are ill-defined, complex and not clearly understood by those being evaluated. Also, individual performance is not made public. This contrasts with management best practice, which ensure that performance measures are well-defined, easy to understand and clearly communicated, and that performance is made transparent to induce constructive competition.

The average scores for *targets* are similar to those for the other areas analyzed. For whether management sets financial/operational targets or whether targets are balanced against other non-financial targets, around 68% of respondents answered that targets are based predominantly on accounting and financial figures. The average score was relatively low—1.94. The second question referred to the interconnection of targets between upper and lower levels in the firm and to individual performance. This received the lowest average score—1.31. The third question

Table 6.11 Management practices—targeting area

	Mean	Std. Dev.	% of firms that responded		
			Score 1	Score 3	Score 5
Are the goals exclusively financial, or is there a balance of financial and non-financial targets	1.94	1.523	68.8	15.6	15.6
Are goals based on accounting value, or are they based on shareholder value in a way that works through business units and ultimately is connected to individual performance expectations?	1.31	0.896	87.5	9.4	3.1
Does top management focus mainly on the short term, or does it visualize short-term targets as a "staircase" toward the main focus on long-term goals?	2.75	1.666	40.6	31.3	28.1
Are goals too easy to achieve, especially for some "sacred cows" areas of the firm, or are goals demanding but attainable for all parts of the firm?	2.94	1.795	40.6	21.9	37.5
Total	2.24	1.47	59.37	19.55	21.1

Source Survey 2018

scored 3 (with mean 2.75) suggesting that all units had short and long term goals that are not necessarily linked. The final question scored 2.94 on average, meaning that the firms' management set targets based on solid economic rationale, but there were few 'sacred cows' and rigorous standards (Table 6.11).

The final area of management practices is related to incentives. The aim was to investigate practices related to good and poor performers, that is, whether poor performers are helped to achieve expected levels of performance, the criteria for promotion, etc. Compared to other management practices, three out of five had means greater than 3. The only one with a mean below 2 was for how firms reward high performers. In most cases, firms have no formal procedures for rewarding good performance (Table 6.12).

6.6.9 Comparing Management Practices in Kosovo with Other Countries

Bloom et al. (2012) found that management practices in many developed and developing countries are used also in less-developed countries like Kosovo. Figure 6.3 depicts average management practice scores across countries. It shows that the highest management practices scores, on average, are in the US followed by Japan and Germany. Among the developed countries, Greece and Spain are at the bottom of the rankings along with the developing countries of China and India. For ease of comparison, overall management scores are separated into three broad categories: monitoring, targets and incentives. Kosovo, a developing country, is lagging behind other countries for monitoring and targeting management practices, but scores better for management incentives than some developed and developing countries. The incentives dimension is high ranked in the US, followed by Canada and Germany. Note that management incentive practices are ranked higher in some other developing countries, such as India and China, than other management practices. In Kosovo, the management incentive score is 2.86, on average, which is higher than China, India or Greece. It might be that

Table 6.12 Management practices—incentive area

	Mean	Std. Dev.	% of firms that responded		
			Score 1	Score 3	Score 5
To what extent are people in the firm rewarded equally irrespective of performance level, or is performance clearly related to accountability and rewards?	1.81	0.998	59.4	40.6	0
Are poor performers rarely removed, or are they retrained and/or moved into different roles or out of the company as soon as the weakness is identified?	2.88	1.176	21.9	65.6	12.5
Are people promoted mainly on the basis of tenure, or does the firm actively identify, develop and promote its top performers?	3.38	0.871	6.3	81.3	12.5
Do competitors offer stronger reasons for talented people to join their companies, or does a firm provide a wide range of reasons to encourage talented people to join?	3.19	7.8	3.1	84.4	12.5
Does the firm do relatively little to retain top talent, or do whatever it takes to retain top talent when they look likely to leave?	3.06	1.076	12.5	71.9	15.6
Total	2.86		20.64	68.76	10.62

Source Survey 2018

developing countries have less strict labour market regulations (as is the case in the US) which makes it easier to get rid of poor performing staff and to reward high performers. The findings show that in developed countries (US, Germany, Japan, UK, Sweden, etc.) there is more similarity in the distribution of scores. The distribution is small in China which applies, also, to Kosovo. This can be explained by the fact that firms in China (and Kosovo) are very young and there is less variation in managerial practices among firms.

As mentioned in the theoretical framework section, firms in Kosovo lack both market demand and business environment factors and, also,

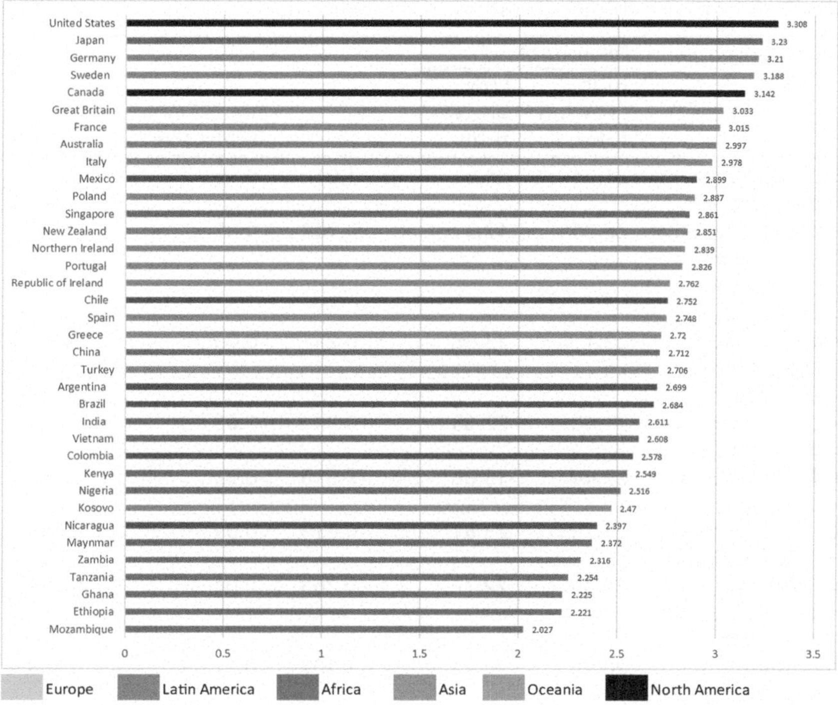

Fig. 6.3 Average management scores by country (*Source* Scores for other countries are taken from the paper "Management as a Technology" published by Bloom et al. [2016], while scores for Kosovo from Survey 2018 conducted by the author)

organizational factors such management practices. This can be seen from the survey findings where the average score for comparator countries is 2.99 and 2.47 for Kosovo. The difference is higher for monitoring and targeting managerial practices compared to incentive practices.

6.7 The Mann–Witney *U* Test Results

6.7.1 Resources

The outcomes pf the Mann–Whitney *U* test reveal that resources such as technology (new equipment) do not play a role in distinguishing the

Table 6.13 Mann–Whitney *U* test results of resources

Significance of variables	Mean rank				
	High growing firms	Low growing firms	*z*	Effect size −*r*	*p* <0.10
Formal education of founders	21.04	24.61	−1.01	0.15	0.313
Occupation of the founders before they started actual business	26.04	17.39	−2.303	0.35	0.021
Working experience of the founders	22.1	23.08	−0.251	0.05	0.8
Area of expertise of the founders	21.58	22.65	−0.34	0.05	0.733
In firm provision of training	27.44	19.08	−2.518	0.39	0.012
In industry provision of training	21.73	23.61	−0.619	0.09	0.536
Investment in new production technology	22.35	22.72	−0.265	0.04	0.791
Investment in new information technology	20.96	24.72	−1.107	0.17	0.268

Source Survey 2018

two groups of firms. In relation to whether firms invested in new technology in the previous three years, 94% responded positively. In the case of other inputs, two variables related to human capital represent a differentiating factor between firms. Among eight variables, the Mann–Whitney *U* Test indicates that only the founders more recent employment and provision of in-house training are statistically significant for firm growth—see Table 6.13.

6.7.2 Organizational Capabilities

Corporate entrepreneurship capabilities are considered a core constituent of capitalism and a driving force of the market system (Baumol 1993). These competences are embedded in the enterprise culture, which contributes to building and renewing the firm's competitive advantage (Morrow et al. 2007). They are related to the firm's articulation of a long-term vision and achievement of higher growth through the introduction of innovative products, technologies and processes (Foss et al. 2008). The results of the Mann–Whitney *U* test indicate that, among the 15 variables included in the model, only one represents a differentiating factor between the two groups of firms. More specifically, the test shows that high-growing firms differ from the other group in terms of how they explore new ideas, technology and markets (see Table 6.14).

Outcomes suggest that dynamic capabilities play a crucial role in differentiating firms. These capabilities refer to the firm's ability to recognize and exploit new market opportunities. From the 11 variables included in the model, 5 are statistically significant. High-growing firms differ from the other group in observing and adopting market best practice and change their practices based, mostly, on feedback from customers. High-growth firms excel in activities related to adapting to changes in market demand. Better dynamic capabilities are reflected in firms' implementation of training activities; high-growth firms implement systematic in-house and external training sessions. This is in line with the previous variable, which indicates that high-growth firms provide continuous in firm training. This variable is the most robust and statistically significant among the group of human capital indicators. Another variable that differentiates groups is how employees share their practical experience with the organization. The means are higher for high-growth firms compared to other firms—see Table 6.13.

In the case of business networking capabilities, the results indicate that high-growth firms select suppliers more carefully than the other firm group. The differences are statistically significant, also, for recruiting skilled labour; high-growth firms put more emphasis on business networks for recruiting skilled labour. The findings show that firms differ also in terms of the relevance they give to assistance obtaining business loans and attracting investors. The high-growth firms report that this variable is significantly less relevant (mean rank = 19.4 vs. 26.97). This can probably be explained by the fact that high-growth firms are

Table 6.14 Mann–Whitney *U* test results of organizational capabilities

Significant variables	Mean rank		*z*	Effect size –*r*	*p* <0.05
	High growing firms	Low growing firms			
Entrepreneurship and innovation capabilities					
Exploring new ideas, technologies and markets through clients	26	17.44	−2.276	0.34	0.023
Dynamic capabilities					
Our firm actively observes and adopts the best practices in our sector	26.17	17.19	−2.426	0.37	0.015
We change our practices based on customer feedback	26.1	17.31	−2.326	0.35	0.02
Our firm regularly considers the consequences of changing market demand	26.06	17.36	−2.311	0.35	0.021
We implement systematic internal and external personnel training	26.77	16.33	−2.741	0.41	0.006
Employees share experiences on a frequent basis	25.73	17.83	−2.13	0.32	0.033
Networking					
Selecting suppliers	26.46	16.78	−2.826	0.43	0.005
Recruiting skilled labour	27.35	15.5	−3.132	0.47	0.002
Assistance in obtaining business loans/attracting funds	19.4	26.97	−2.014	0.3	0.044
Marketing					
Customer satisfaction	26.83	16.25	−2.836	0.43	0.005
Customer loyalty/retention	26.6	16.58	−2.645	0.4	0.008

Source Survey 2018

less dependent on external funds, compared to the other group of firms, which need more external funding to run their business activities.

The results show that marketing capabilities are the least significant for differentiating high-growth and other firms. Among 21 variables, only two are statistically significant—customer satisfaction and customer loyalty/retention. One reason why firms do not consider marketing a key capability might be because the majority (65%) do not view market demand as an obstacle. Another reason could be that most of the sample firms are relatively young. Embedding marketing-based processes in firm competences takes time (Teece et al. 1997).

The findings are similar for teamwork capabilities. Among the seven variables considered, none was statistically significant. This may be due to the structure of the firms included in the sample whose production processes require fewer teamwork activities.

6.7.3 Management Practices

The previous evidence suggests that the generation of higher rents is a function of managerial practice (Bloom and Von Reenen 2010). The survey results show that management practices seem to have the highest effect on performance variability between high-growing and low growing firms. Among the 18 indicators tested, half are statistically significant for explaining the difference between high-growth and low growth firms.

The outcomes show that, statistically, there is no significant difference between groups in terms of operations. The difference relates, mostly, to how managers implement monitoring practices, set up business targets and deal with incentive systems. Among the five indicators for monitoring practices, three are important for performance variability. High-performing firms apply better management practices in terms of performance tracking, performance dialogue and consequence management (see Table 6.15).

In the context of management practices related to targets, high-growing firms show differences in relation to three fundamental elements. They use more sophisticated management practices related to long term targets and, as well as in the way the targets are stretched and interlinked throughout the organizational units. It seems that high-growing firms employ better managerial practices in relation to making senior managers responsible for attracting, retaining and developing talent in the organization (see Table 6.15).

The results for management practices related to incentives are interesting and support some of the findings for other management areas.

Table 6.15 Mann–Whitney *U* test results of organizational capabilities

Significant variables	Mean rank		*z*	Effect size −*r*	*p* <0.05
	High growing firms	Low growing firms			
Management practices on how business processes are monitored					
Performance Tracking	25.92	17.56	−2.308	0.35	0.021
Performance dialog	25.35	18.39	−1.967	0.3	0.049
Consequence Management	26.77	16.33	−3.224	0.49	0.001
Management practices in setting up business targets					
Target time horizon	25.5	18.17	−1.977	0.3	0.048
Targets are stretching	26	17.44	−2.316	0.35	0.021
Managing human capital	26.42	16.83	−2.607	0.39	0.009
Management practices on how staff is motivated and promoted					
Removing poor performers	25.62	18	−2.304	0.35	0.021
Promoting high performers	25.75	17.81	−2.469	0.37	0.014
Attracting human capital	26.6	16.58	−3.282	0.5	0.001

Source Survey 2018

As indicated above, one of the main reasons why high-growth firms excel is their human capital management. Half of the six incentive management indicators are statistically significant. High-performing firms are distinguished in terms of how they get rid of poor performers, how they promote high performers and the models employed to attract human capital.

6.8 Factor Analysis of Resources, Capabilities and Managerial Practices

In Sect. 6.7, the Mann–Whitney *U* test was applied to investigate the variables that differentiate the two groups of firms. Among all of the survey variables, only 22 are statistically significant for explaining heterogeneous firm growth. In the next section, these variables are used to construct a statistical model to observe regularities variables, and their covariance structure, in terms of the number of underlying latent 'factors'. The factors are considered broad concepts or ideas that describe how the variables included in the model are grouped.

We conducted Principal Components Analysis (PCA) to the 22 variables in the three categories (resources, organizational capabilities, managerial practices) after assessing the suitability of the data for factor analysis. The Kaiser–Meyer–Olkin value was 0.772, exceeding the recommended value of 0.6 (Kaiser 1970, 1974) and Bartlett's (1954) Test of Sphericity reached statistical significance ($p < 0.000$), supporting the factorability of the correlation matrix. In addition, inspection of the correlation matrix revealed the presence of many coefficients of value .3 or above. We checked the internal reliability and constituents of the variables used in the model. Cronbach's alpha was used to measure internal consistency that is, how closely related a set of items are as a group. The alpha coefficient for all factors was higher than 0.70, suggesting that the items have considerably high internal consistency.

The analysis generated five factors, explaining a total 70.184% of the variation in the latent variables, with the first factor (component) accounting for 41.96%, the second for 9.27%, the third for 7.01%, the fourth for 6.18% and the fifth for 5.75%. The factors identified are presented in Table 6.16, which also provides the practices associated to specific loadings.

The first factor is related to six variables, four of which belong to managerial practices. It seems that these practices form the main component of firm capabilities. Since factor one contributes 41.96% to the total variation in the latent variables, managerial practices are key capabilities influencing firm growth heterogeneity. Practices that load highly on this factor are performance tracking (0.819) and dialogue (0.802), and promotion of high performers (0.648). Note that, firms that review their business performance continually in the expectation of continuous improvement, and those that engage in regular review/performance conversations, are more likely to experience higher business growth. In addition, these firms are more likely to employ advanced management systems that enable them to identify and promote top performers.

Table 6.16 The extracted factors and their loadings

	Factors					Communalities
	1	2	3	4	5	
Performance tracking	0.819					0.789
Performance dialogue	0.802					0.791
Promoting high performers	0.648					0.545
Targets are stretching	0.586					0.609
Our firm actively observes and adopts the best practices in our sector	0.541					0.568
We change our practices based on customer feedback		0.830				0.769
Exploring new ideas, technologies and markets through clients		0.772				0.664
Customer loyalty/retention		0.626	0.504			0.733
Customer satisfaction		0.563	0.560			0.778
Removing poor performers			0.710			0.745
Consequence management			0.694			0.642
Our firm regularly considers the consequences of changing market demand	0.486		0.623			0.641
Attracting human capital		0.412	0.449			0.537
Recruiting skilled labour				0.793		0.789
Selecting suppliers		0.548		0.651		0.803
We implement systematic internal and external personnel training				0.544		0.685
Target time horizon					0.878	0.812
Employees share practical experiences on a frequent basis					0.610	0.688
Managing human capital	0.437		0.472		0.476	0.748

Note Extraction method: Principal component analysis. Rotation method: Varimax with Kaiser normalization
Source Survey 2018

Although their loadings are lower, there are two dynamic capability variables (capability to observe and adopt best practices in the sector, and ability of the firm to react to market demand) that help to explain the variation in the latent variables—with loadings of 0.541 and 0.486 respectively.

The second factor (9.27%) also includes six variables, but, compared to the first factor, it is dominated by organizational capability variables. The items with the highest loadings are dynamic capabilities (changes to the organization based on customer feedback with loading 0.830), and corporate entrepreneurship (exploration of new ideas, technology an new markets through client with loading 0.772), followed by marketing capabilities (customer loyalty/retention with 0.626, and customer satisfaction with 0.563).

Three remaining factors are dominated by managerial practices variables, which is not surprising since, as previously mentioned, among 22 items included in the model, 9 (41%) belong to this category of factors. Variables with the highest loadings are related to managerial practices such as target time horizon (0.878), removing poor performers (0.710), etc.

6.9 Main Findings

The outcomes show that, statistically, there is no evidence to infer that three of the factors included in the model have the same impact on the firm heterogeneity. More specifically, among these three factors, resources/inputs seem to have the least influence. The model includes six variables, only two of which contribute to firm growth differentiation. The outcomes of the factor analysis indicate that none of them contributes to the five factors.

With respect to organizational capabilities, the findings indicate that among five sets of capabilities, dynamic and business networking capabilities have the greater influence on firm performance heterogeneity. Specifically, there is significant evidence suggesting that high-growing firms apply more sector best practices, adapt their practices based on customer feedback, and provide regular training to update and improve the knowledge and skills of their employees. They consider supplier selection to be important and see networking as important for recruiting a skilled and experienced workforce. Marketing capabilities (2 variables customer satisfaction and customer loyalty) contribute to performance variability and the results suggest that implementation of team working does not seem to have an influence.

The results show that managerial practices in Kosovo (an underdeveloped country), are important for firms' performance variability. These results support evidence that indicates that there is not just a single management practice that explains the statistical correlation between management practices and performance (Bloom and Van Reenen 2007). The findings suggest that firms that "better" management practices translate into better performance, that is, higher sales.

While there is no significant differences among firms in the area of operations, monitoring practices seem to be important for performance variability. The findings suggest that the way managers deal with non-achievement of targets is important, that is, the actions managers implement to retrain staff or move to them to other job positions.

In the context of setting and communicating business targets, the evidence shows that high-growth firms consider short term goals which are considered stepping stones to long-term goals. The evidence indicates, also, that high-growth firms are better able to link departmental goals and overall firm goals.

Incentives are a new managerial practice. The results show that high-performing firms assign more importance to labour incentives than low growth firms. Among five variables for incentives, three are statistically significant. Also the outcome of from factor analysis indicates that attracting human capital and management systems to promote good performers and remove poor performers are the most significant predictors of performance variability.

6.10 Conclusions

This chapter used a theoretical framework combining three different firm growth theories to explore whether resources (inputs), organizational capabilities and managerial practices have an effect on performance variability among firms operating in a less-developed economy (Kosovo).

While there is insufficient evidence to argue that inputs/resources are significant for the performance variation among firms, this does not apply to organizational capabilities and managerial practices. Overall, our results support resource-based theory linking organizational capabilities to firm's performance variability. However, consistent with the RBV that inter-firm performance variation can be explained by firms' distinctive and unique capabilities, the findings from this chapter suggest that some organizational capabilities have a greater impact on firm performance differences, than others. For instance, capabilities such as entrepreneurship, innovation and networking, seem to be more strongly associated to high-performing firms compared to marketing and team working capabilities. We found less evidence to support the predictions that marketing and teamwork capabilities play a role in firm performance variability. In the case of marketing capabilities, the explanation might be that the firms are operating in a business environment where market demand for their products is not considered an obstacle and marketing capabilities are not considered vital for overall performance. Similarly, team-working is used less in manufacturing sector firms.

We also investigated managerial practices. The empirical evidence shows that the quality of the managerial practices applied by manufacturing firms matter. Indeed, much performance variation seems to be due to the presence or absence of various managerial factors. Managerial indicators related to monitoring, targeting and incentive practices were more statistically influential on performance variability than indicators related to operations. It could be argued that the better management practices in high-performing firms facilitates their higher market share and consequent higher sales volumes.

Although the evidence obtained from this study could be used as grounds to argue that managerial practices explain the performance variability among firms, the quality of these practices in Kosovo is much lower than in the developed countries.

Our results indicate that there is no substantial empirical evidence to support the prediction that performance variability among firms is due to the capability to invest in new technology (equipment): 95% of the firms in the sample reported investing in new equipment in the previous three years. There is also no statistically significant evidence to argue that performance variability is the result of the source of funding, that is, whether new technology acquisitions were financed entirely by the firm or augmented by government, EU or other funding sources. However, the findings show that human capital in the form of education, experience and training, explains some of the performance variations among firms. More specifically, variables such as founder's occupation before current firm establishment and training activities, contribute significantly to the performance variations among firms.

In general, the findings in this chapter confirm the RBV and managerial practices approach to factors that differentiate firms' performance. Therefore, based on these findings, we can conclude: *first*, business inputs do not seem to be a differentiating factor in relation to firm performance. *Second*, the empirical evidence indicates that managerial practices (though still underdeveloped in Kosovo) play a crucial role in performance variability and seem equivalent to production capabilities in that regard. *Third*, organizational capabilities appear to be differentiating factors for performance variability, but are more truncated. Some of these organizational capabilities have a significant effect while others do not. This is because some of the elements related to organizational capabilities, such as marketing and teamwork, seem to have considerably less effect on the variation in firm performance for companies operating in less-developed economies.

References

Almer-Jarz, D. A., Schwarz, E. J., & Breitenecher, B. J. (2008). New venture teams: The relationship between initial team characteristics, team processes and performance. In H. Landstrom, H. Crijns, E. Laveren, & D. Smallbone (Eds.), *Entrepreneurship sustainable growth and performance: Frontiers in European entrepreneurship research*. Cheltenham: Edward Elgar Publishing.

Amason, A. C., & Sapienza, H. J. (1997). The effects of top management team size and interaction norms on cognitive and affective conflict. *Journal of Management, 23,* 495–516.

Barney, J. B. (1991). Firm resources and sustained competitive advantage. *Journal of Management, 17,* 99–120.

Barney, J. (1995). Looking inside for competitive advantage. *Academy of Management Executive, 9*(4), 49–61.

Bartholomew, D., Knotts, M., & Moustaki, I. (2011). *Latent variable models and factor analysis: A unified approach* (3rd ed.). West Sussex, UK: Wiley.
Bartlett, M. S. (1954). A note on the multiplying factors for various x2 approximation. *Journal of the Royal Statistical Society*, Series B16, 296–298.
Baumol, W. J. (1993). Formal entrepreneurship theory in economics: Existence and bounds. *Journal of Business Venturing, 3,* 197–210.
Bell, M., & Pavitt, K. (1993). Accumulating technological capability in developing countries. *Proceedings of the World Bank Annual Conference on Development Economics*, 1992 (pp. 57–81). Washington, DC: World Bank.
Bird, B. (1989). *Entrepreneurial behaviour*. Glenview, IL: Scott Foresman.
Bloom, N., & Van Reenen, J. (2007). Measuring and explaining management practices across firms and countries. *Quarterly Journal of Economics, 122*(4), 1351–1408.
Bloom, N., & Van Reenen, J. (2010). Why do management practices differ across firms and countries? *Journal of Economic Perspectives, 24*(1), 203–224.
Bloom, N., & Van Reenen, J. (2011). Human resource management and productivity. In O. Ashenfelter & D. Card (Eds.), *Handbook of labor economics volume 4B* (Chapter 19, pp. 1697–1769). Amsterdam: Elsevier..
Bloom, N., Schweiger, H., & Van Reenen, J. (2011). *The land that lean manufacturing forgot? Management practices in transition countries* (National Bureau of Economic Research Working Paper Series, No. 17231).
Bloom, N., Genakos, C., Sadun, R., & Van Reenen, J. (2012). Management practices across firms and countries. *The Academy of Management Perspectives, 26,* 12–33.
Bloom, N., Sadun, R., & Van Reenen, J. (2016). *Management as a technology* (NBER Working Paper No. 22327).
Cantwell, J. A. (2000). A survey of theories of international production. In C. N. Pitelis & R. Sugden (Eds.), *The nature of the transnational firm* (pp. 10–56). London: Routledge.
Child, D. (2006). *The essentials of factor analysis* (3rd ed.). New York, NY: Continuum International Publishing Group.
Collis, D. J. (1994). Research note: How valuable are organizational capabilities? *Strategic Management Journal, 15,* 143–152.
Collis, D. J., & Montgomery, C. A. (1995). Competing on resources: Strategy in the 1990s. *Harvard Business Review, 73*(4), 118–128.
Day, G. S. (1994). The capabilities of market driven organizations. *Journal of Marketing, 58,* 37–52.
Dutrénit, G. (2004). Building technological capabilities in latecomer firms: A review essay. *Science Technology & Society, 9*(2), 209–241.

Eurostat/OECD. (2008). *Manual on business demography statistics*. http://ec.europa.eu/eurostat/ramon/statmanuals/files/KS-RA-07-010-EN.pdf.
Foss, N. J., Klein, P. G., Kor, Y. Y., & Mahoney, J. T. (2008). Entrepreneurship, subjectivism, and the resource based view: Toward a new synthesis. *Strategic Entrepreneurship Journal, 2,* 73–94.
Freeman, C. (1997). Success and failure in industrial innovation. In C. Freeman & L. Soete (Eds.), *Economics of Industrial Innovation* (p. 198). London and New York: Routledge.
Friebel, G., & Schweiger, H. (2012). *Management quality, firm performance, and market pressure in Russia* (European Bank for Reconstruction and Development Working Papers, 144), 1–29.
Grant, R. M. (2002). *Contemporary strategy analysis: Concepts, techniques, applications* (4th ed.). Malden, MA: Blackwell.
Hallak, J. (2006). Product quality and the direction of trade. *Journal of International Economics, 68*(1), 238–265.
Harman, H. H. (1976). *Modern factor analysis* (3rd ed. revised). Chicago, IL: University of Chicago Press.
Hsu, D. H. (2004). What do entrepreneurs pay for venture capital affiliation? *Journal of Finance, 59,* 1805–1844.
Jacobides, M. G., & Winter, S. G. (2005). The co-evolution of capabilities and transaction costs: Explaining the institutional structure of production. *Strategic Management Journal, 26*(5), 395–413.
Janz, B. D., Colquitt, J. A., & Noe, R. A. (1997). Knowledge worker team effectiveness: The role of autonomy, interdependence, team development, and contextual support variables. *Personnel Psychology, 50,* 877–904.
Kaiser, H. (1970). A second generation Little Jiffy. *Psychometrika, 35,* 401–415.
Kaiser, H. (1974). An index of factorial simplicity. *Psychometrika, 39,* 31–36.
Kim, L. (1997). *Imitation to innovation. The dynamics of Korea's technological learning*. Boston: Harvard Business School Press.
Kline, P. (1994). *An easy guide to factor analysis*. New York, NY: Routledge.
Koch, M. J., & McGrath, R. G. (1996). Improving labour productivity: Human resource management policies do matter. *Strategic Management Journal, 17,* 335–354.
Kogut, B., & Zander, U. (1996). What firms do? Coordination, identify, and learning. *Organization Science, 7,* 502–518.
Kotler, A. (2004). *Principles of marketing*. Hoboken, NJ: Pearson Education.

Lazonick, W. (2013). The theory of innovative enterprise: Methodology, ideology, and institutions. In J. K. Moudud, C. Bina, & P. L. Mason (Eds.), *Alternative theories of competition: Challenges to the orthodoxy* (pp. 127–159). London and New York: Routledge.

Leiblein, M. J. (2011). What do resource and capability theories propose? *Journal of Management, 37*(4), 909–932.

Mann, H. B., & Whitney, D. R. (1947). On a test of whether one of two random variables is stochastically larger than the other. *Annals of Mathematical Statistics, 18,* 50–60.

Morrow, J. L., Sirmon, D. G., Hitt, M. A., & Holcomb, T. R. (2007). Creating value in the face of declining performance: Firm strategies and organisational recovery. *Strategic Management Journal, 28,* 271–283.

Mosakowski, E. (1998). Entrepreneurial resources, organizational choices, and competitive outcomes. *Organization Science, 9*(6), 625–643.

Nelson, R., & Winter, G. (1982). *An evolutionary theory of economic change.* Cambridge, MA: Belknap Press/Harvard University Press.

Nonaka, I., & Takeuchi, H. (1995). *The knowledge-creating company.* New York: Oxford University Press.

Penrose, E. T. (1959). *The growth of the firm.* New York: Wiley.

Protogerou, A., Caloghirou, Y., & Lioukas, S. (2011). Dynamic capabilities and their indirect impact on firm performance. *Industrial Corporate Change, 21*(3), 615–647.

Reagans, R., Argote, L., & Brooks, D. (2005). Individual experience and experience working together: Predicting learning rates from knowing who knows what and knowing how to work together. *Management Science, 51*(6), 869–881.

Robert, C. P., & Casella, G. (2004). *Monte carlo statistical methods* (2nd ed.). New York: Springer-Verlag.

Rothwell, R., Freeman, C., Horlsey, A., Jervis, V. T. P., Robertson, A. B., & Townsend, J. (1974). SAPPHO updated: Project SAPPHO phase II. *Research Policy, 3,* 258–291.

Rummel, R. J. (1970). *Applied factor analysis.* Evanston, IL: Northwestern University Press.

Scheepers, M. J., Hough, J., & Bloom, J. Z. (2008). Nurturing the corporate entrepreneurship capability. *Southern African Business Review, 12*(3), 50–75.

Schumpeter, J. (1943). *Capitalism, socialism and democracy.* New York: Harper.

Shane, S. (2008). *Illusions of entrepreneurship.* New Haven, CT: Yale University Press.

Shane, S., & Stuart, T. (2002). Organizational endowments and the performance of university start-ups. *Management Science, 48,* 154–170.
Solow, R. (1957). Technical change and the aggregate production function. *Review of Economics and Statistics, 39*(3), 312–320.
SPRU. (1972). *Success and failure in industrial innovation, report on Project SAPPHO by Science Policy Research Unit, University of Sussex*. Report prepared by C. Freeman, A. Robertson, B. Achilladelis, P. Jervis, R. Curnow, A. Horsley, C. Tudway, & J. Fuller. Published by the Centre for the Study of Industrial Innovation, printed by Bishop and Sons Ltd., Edinburgh.
Sutton, J. (2000). *Rich trades, scarce capabilities: Industrial development revisited,* Keynes Lecture in Economics, British Academy, London.
Sutton, J. (2005). *Competing in capabilities: An informal overview*. Washington, DC: World Bank.
Sutton, J. (2012). *Competing in capabilities: The globalization process*. Oxford, UK: Oxford University Press.
Sutton, J., & Trefler, D. (2016). Capabilities, wealth, and trade. *Journal of Political Economy, 124*(3), 826–878.
Tabachnick, B. G., & Fidell, L. S. (2007). *Using multivariate statistics* (5th ed.). Boston, MA: Allyn & Bacon.
Teece, D. J., Pisano, G., & Shuen, A. (1997). Dynamic capabilities and strategic management. *Strategic Management Journal, 18*(7), 509–533.
Winter, S. (1987). Knowledge and competence as strategic assets. In D. J. Teece (Ed.), *The competitive challenge*. Cambridge, MA: Ballinger.

7

Social and Economic Conditions and Firm Growth

7.1 Introduction

While internal factors, such as organizational capabilities and good management practices, may affect the firm's ability to innovate, the wider economic and social conditions in which companies operate can also enable or/and deter innovation efforts. To expand the number of firms with innovation capacity requires the appropriate wider social conditions for innovation. However, understanding which social conditions can spur or stifle innovation efforts and how to influence them can be difficult.

Based on evidence from Kosovo firms, this chapter discusses the social conditions affecting firms' capacities to innovate. It examines those social conditions that enable or deter the emergence of innovative firms. While several research studies investigate the relationship between innovative activity and the benefits of innovation for the economy, this chapter focuses on assessing the social conditions in which firms operate. This is important since social conditions are variables that can be influenced by government policies and managers.

F. Sahiti, *The Growth of Firms in Less-Developed Countries*,
https://doi.org/10.1007/978-3-030-14821-8_7

The methodology employed consists of two steps. In the first step, we examine the macro level social conditions and in the second step, we investigate the social conditions internal to business firms. The analysis is conducted utilizing diverse data and information from different sources. Social conditions at the national level are examined using data from various national and international sources; social conditions at the firm level are analysed using a firm-level dataset based on the responses to two different surveys. The unit of analysis are Small and Medium size Enterprises (SMEs).

The findings indicate that Kosovo's economy provide a comparatively poor social environment for firm innovation. While the country has managed to establish a business institutional framework, which largely is compatible with developed countries, the implementation of this framework in practice is a major issue. Further, the outcomes suggest that there are sets of internal social factors that matter for the emergence of innovative firms.

This chapter makes two contributions. First, it is clear that the literature has significantly improved our empirical understanding of the determinants of firm innovation. However, most research focuses on developed economies and there is less evidence on the innovation determinants in less-developed economies. By providing new evidence on the impact of social conditions on firm innovation in less-developed economies, the findings in this chapter help to fill this gap in the literature on firm innovation. Second, this study is one of the first to use the theory of innovative enterprise as an organizing framework to assess the impact of social conditions on firm innovation. To our best knowledge, apart from the empirical study conducted by Lazonick et al. (2013) on Apple's changing business model, there is no other published research that provides empirical support for the propositions made by this theory.

The rest of the chapter is organized as follows. Section 7.2 discusses the rational for using the theory of innovative enterprises and the theoretical perspective applied in analysis. Section 7.3 discusses the methods and datasets used to study the social conditions of firm innovation. Sections 7.4 and 7.5 present and discuss the empirical results at the national and firm levels. Finally, Sect. 7.6 concludes.

7.2 Why the Theory of the Innovative Enterprise

According to Lazonick (2013), the theory of innovative enterprise is an approach that considers the operation, performance and regulation of the business enterprise as central to a prosperous economy. The fundamentals of this theory are based on two ideas. First, the theory stems from the idea that innovation is a key condition for a prosperous economy; second, the innovative enterprise is its main driver. Innovation tends to be collective and cumulative process. It involves several people, funds and periods of time. It often involves the government. Developed industries in advanced economies are successful because government has invested in the knowledge base, the basic infrastructure for entrepreneurs and firms. Without such investment, industry would not survive.

The theory of innovative enterprises draws on the limitations in two theories: neoclassical theory and transaction cost theory. Neoclassical theory takes technologies and markets as given constraints and, as a result, cannot differentiate from its equally 'perfect' competitors. In innovative enterprise theory, firms endowed with innovative capabilities make investments to transform technologies and access markets that, potentially, can give them a competitive advantage in the market. Similarly, transaction cost theory assumes that firms operate under 'bounded rationality', 'opportunism' and 'asset specificity'. The theory of the innovative firm argues that, based on its investment strategy and organizational structure, the innovative firm can transform asset specificity, bounded rationality and opportunism rather than using these conditions as given constraints to its activities (Lazonick 2013).

The neoclassical and transaction cost theories of the firm lack any theory of value creation or what Lazonick calls, a 'theory of innovative enterprise'. The value-creation process takes place within a specific social context. Any analysis of the conditions that enable or constrain the emergence of innovative firms should take account of two classes of variables. First, variables related to the social conditions at the national level represented by government institutions (governance, employment, investment), and the second is related to the social conditions at the firm level represented by strategic control, organizational integration and financial commitment. The functions of the government institutions of specific countries can support or undermine the types of strategic control, organizational integration and financial commitment that produce high-quality products at low unit costs (i.e., innovative enterprise).

A key question is how do the functions of government institutions affect the conditions of innovative enterprise? The answer to this is that an important national differentiator is the social and economic institutions that enable and proscribe firms' activities, while, overtime, distinctive elements of these institutions become embedded in the ways that which firms function (Lazonick 2012). In this context, of particular importance for influencing the social conditions of innovative enterprise are the economic institutions related to governance, employment and investment. However, the firm's activities influence the characteristics of these economic institutions through the rules and norms applicable to economic activities; these institutions exist and persist independently of these firms.

Governance institutions determine how productive resources are allocated and imposes restrictions on their development and utilization. Employment institutions determine how society develops the capabilities of its present and future labour force and levels of employment and working conditions and remuneration. We know that a successful economy requires government investment in education, knowledge, basic infrastructure, etc. Finally, the investor institutions determine how much financial resources will be available, on a continuing basis, to sustain the development of productive capabilities. These economic institutions influence the emergence of firms endowed with innovative capabilities.

The ability of firms to deliver higher quality products at lower unit compared to competitors is not straightforward. It requires innovation capabilities. Lazonick highlights three distinctive attributes inherent in the innovation processes. Innovation is uncertain because if we knew how to produce a higher quality product at the time of the investment, it would not require an innovation. Innovation is a collective activity and requires the commitment of many people involved in the organizational learning process. Finally, innovation is a cumulative activity and, since it is also collective, this learning takes time, and what is learned today determines what can be learned tomorrow.

The creation of innovative capabilities requires three types of social conditions, related to the above innovation attributes. Innovation requires strategy, organization and finance. So, to address uncertainty, innovation requires a strategy. Who exercises strategic control matters? This component is linked to the set of relations within the business organization, which give the decision-makers power to allocate the firm's resources to deal with uncertainty by transforming technologies and accessing markets to generate higher quality, lower cost products. Organization is related to the collective work related to innovation and the set of relations that create the incentives for people to apply their skills and efforts to engage in collective learning. Finally, since the innovation process takes time, it requires secure funding until it is able to generate financial returns.

By being able to generate higher quality and lower cost products, the innovative enterprise allows all the economic actors to gain. For instance, employees receive higher pay and have better working conditions; financial institutions have more available funding and achieve more secure loans; shareholder receives higher dividends and share prices are higher; government receives more taxes; companies have stronger balance sheets; and consumers obtain higher quality and lower cost products.

In summary, according to Lazonick, innovative firms are central to a prosperous economy. They are the key drivers of economic growth. To increase the number of firms equipped with innovation capabilities requires the right social conditions for innovation. The theory of the innovative enterprise provides a comprehensive organizing framework to analyse the social and economic conditions that enable and/or constrain the emergence of innovative firms in Kosovo. This chapter investigates the social and economic conditions, at both the macro and micro levels, that influence the emergence of firms with innovative capabilities. The indicators used to investigate the social and economic environment in the country are operationalized into specific variables, which are presented in Table 7.1.

Table 7.1 List of indicators and variables

Indicators	Variables	Themes	Proxies used
Social conditions at national level	Governance institutions	Involves issues related to the regulatory framework	The enterprise/firm law, and tax laws
	Employment institutions	Covers aspects related to employability	Employment law, labour market flexibility, easiness to hire or lay-off employees, and reward systems
	Investment institutions	Covers aspects related to the system which ensures that sufficient financial resources are available on a continuing basis to sustain the development of innovative capabilities	External financing through equity, and external financing through debt
Social conditions at firm level	The strategic control	Covers a set of relations that give power to those that take decisions to allocate the firm's resources to confront the technological, market, and competitive uncertainties inherent to innovation process	– Structure and characteristics of the ownership – Relationship between owners and managers – Concentration of ownership (minorities and majority owners) – Interactions between managers and owners – Abilities of those who have power to take decisions (educational attainment of decision-makers, experiences collected over the years, and training received)

Indicators	Variables	Themes	Proxies used
	The organisational integration	Covers relations that enable firms to transform inputs into innovative outputs	– Learning sources, i.e. learning from supplier, competitors, consumers – Internal learning from the experience of workers – The way how the innovation process is organised, i.e. innovation processes organised independently or in collaboration with other external entities (academic institutions and research institutions, business associations) – How the labour- management relationships are administered, i.e. the way how organisations create incentives for people with different hierarchical responsibilities and functional capabilities
	Investment capabilities	Covers aspects related to availability of financial resources to commit during the innovation processes	– Amount of investments committed by firms in last three years – The investment funds raised from banks, and – The terms and conditions in which funds were raised from banks

Source Author

7.3 Methodology and Data

Before reviewing the methodology and data, we need to clarify the concept of innovation in the context of this study. The innovation perspective is deliberately broad, suggested by OECD/Eurostat (2005, p 46): '*an innovation is the implementation of a new or significantly improved product (good or service), or process, a new marketing method, or a new organizational method in business practices, workplace organization or external relations*'. This broad definition of an innovation encompasses a wide range of possible inventions. The minimum requirement for an innovation is that the product, process, marketing method or organizational method must be new (or significantly improved) to the firm. This includes the products, processes and methods that firms are the first to develop and those that have been adopted from other firms or organizations.

In the absence of data related directly to an investigation of Kosovan firms' innovation activities, exporting is used to proxy for innovation. Innovation is treated as those products and processes new to the firm, but not necessarily new to the national or international markets. So, innovation is a firm and market-driven activity that is quite close to the firm's daily activities and, in the case of Kosovo, generally does not involve major R&D efforts. The unit of analysis is SMEs. In this chapter, exporting is understood as outward international trade in goods and/or services, conducted directly or through a third party (Jones 2001). The entrepreneurship literature links exporting capabilities to firms' innovation capabilities. The findings suggest that exporting firms create sustainable competitive advantages based on unique technologies and innovation, which they leverage worldwide (Almor and Hashai 2004; Almor 2006). There is evidence that exporting firms typically are endowed with higher innovation capabilities, suggesting that innovation improves the quality of products and boosts the profitability of exporting (Anderton 1999). Other variables linked to innovation include human capital and labour quality; the hypothesis is that the quality of the workforce reflects the quality of the good or service produced and, hence, is related positively to export entry (Bernard and Jensen 2001).

According to Ayyagari et al. (2007, p 19), exporters are more likely to upgrade product lines, introduce new technology, open new plants and enter joint ventures or licensing agreements.

The data analysis is conducted by identifying and assessing similarities and differences between two groups of firms: exporters and non-exporters. Specifically, the aim is to identify more general patterns and regularities that are different between two sample groups. The process of investigation consists of two steps. First, in the discussion of national social conditions, the analysis is descriptive. In the discussion of micro (firm) level social conditions, the aim is to examine how much the business environment in Kosovo promotes or constrains the emergence of innovative enterprises. The analysis is conducted using various data and information reported by national and international institutions—the World Bank, OECD, UNESCO and official institutions and agencies in Kosovo.

Second, the analysis of national social conditions at the micro level, is based on two types of data generated from firm-level surveys. The first dataset was obtained from the Business Support Centre of Kosovo (BSCK). The survey was carried out in December 2012, on (a sample of 500 SMEs). We used data from the responses to questions about intra-firm labour–management relationships to generate a survey that was administered by the author in December 2018.[1]

To distinguish patterns that are more general from those that are specific, we created dummy variables for the two separate groups of firms. One group consists of exporting firms and the other of non-exporting firms. Following a data statistical description to identify which social factors are more likely to differentiate the two groups of firms, a logistic regression technique is applied.

Logistic regression analysis is a statistical method that is similar to linear regression analysis except the outcome is dichotomous (e.g., success/failure, yes/no). It makes use of mathematical models to describe relationships. It is an approach aimed at predicting a

[1]More information on this dataset is provided in Chapter 6 which analyses organizational capabilities and managerial practices.

dichotomous outcome. In essence, the objective of logistic regression analysis is to examine the odds of an outcome occurring (or not) and, by using the natural log of the odds of the outcome as the dependent variable, the relationships can be linearized and treated much like multiple linear regression (Cabrera 1994; Hosmer and Lemeshow 2000). The outcome of logistic regression analysis is often coded 0 or 1, where 1 indicates presence and 0 indicates absence of the outcome of interest (Austin et al. 1992). If p is defined as the probability that the outcome is 1, the multiple logistic regression model can be written as follows:

$$\hat{p} = \frac{\exp\left(b_0 + b_1X_1 + b_2X_2 + L + b_pX_p\right)}{1 + \exp\left(b_0 + b_1X_1 + b_2X_2 + L + b_pX_p\right)} \tag{7.1}$$

where $\hat{p}$ is the expected probability that the outcome is present; X_1 through X_p are distinct independent variables; and b_0 through b_p are the regression coefficients. In some cases, the multiple logistic regression model can be written differently. In the following form, the outcome is the expected log of the odds of the outcome being present,

$$\begin{aligned} &\ln\left(\frac{\hat{p}}{(1-\hat{p})}\right): \\ &\ln\left(\frac{\hat{p}}{(1-\hat{p})}\right) = b_0 + b_1X_1 + b_2X_2 + \cdots + b_pX_p \end{aligned} \tag{7.2}$$

Note that the right hand side of the above equation resembles a multiple linear regression equation. However, the technique for estimating the regression coefficients of a logistic regression model is different from that used to estimate the regression coefficients of a multiple linear regression model. In logistic regression, the coefficients of the model (e.g., b_1) indicate the change in the expected log odds relative to a one unit change in X_1, holding all other predictors constant. Therefore, the antilog of an estimated regression coefficient, $\exp(b_i)$, produces an odds ratio.

7.4 Empirical Results at the National Level

The national level social conditions can support or limit the emergence of innovative firms. Building the social conditions conducive to innovation is not straightforward. It requires multiple inputs some of which may be scarce in less-developed economies such as Kosovo (World Bank 2013).

To investigate the social conditions, we use Lazonick's analytical theory of innovative enterprise framework. This framework pairs governance institutions with strategic control, national employment institutions with organizational integration, and investment institutions with financial commitment. It should be noted that we do not try to provide an exhaustive analysis of these interactions. Rather, based on the available data, we are interested in the state of current social conditions in Kosovo and whether they provide a foundation for the emergence of innovative firms.

The following analysis examines the set of social conditions related to governance institutions (firm regulatory framework, tax laws), followed by employment institutions (employment law, labour market flexibility, ease of hiring and firing staff and reward systems), and the social conditions related to investment institutions.

7.4.1 Governance Institutions

According to Lazonick (2013, p. 30), 'nations differ in their institutions which enable and proscribe the activities of firms'. Overtime, elements typical of these institutions become embedded in the ways firms function. In this context, of particular importance for influencing firm innovation, are those economic institutions related to governance. This element of the social conditions determines how a society assigns rights and responsibilities to different groups of people over the allocation of its productive resources and how it imposes restrictions on the development and utilization of these resources. More specifically, this element of the social conditions is related to the enterprise/firm, regulatory framework, governance elements and tax laws.

Kosovo is a relatively young independent country. Since, for over a decade, the country was a UN and EU protectorate, whose experts assisted in the drafting of laws, Kosovo's firm regulatory framework is quite modern and compatible with European and international standards (EBRD 2013). Although new laws and secondary legislation is needed to address certain gaps, overall, the main issue is the gap between the legislation and its implementation. The country has relatively modern laws regulating business activity, including the Law on Business Organizations, the Law on Publicly-Owned Enterprises, the Law on Banks, Microfinance Institutions and Non-Bank Financial Institutions, the Law on Accounting, Financial Reporting and Audits and the Law on Tax. Special emphasis is placed on the legal framework with respect to corporate governance.

Governance institutions influence the level of strategic control. This component of the social conditions determines how a society assigns rights and responsibilities to different groups of people over the allocation of its productive resources, and how it imposes restrictions on the development and utilization of these resources. More specifically, this component of social conditions is related to the regulatory framework for firms, governance elements and tax laws.

The concept of corporate governance is relatively new in the Kosovo context. Although there are some established bodies that supervise corporate governance, according to some international reports, political influence in both the appointment of board members and decisions about company policies are major problems (EBRD 2013). More specifically, members of the boards of publicly owned enterprises are elected on the basis of their political affiliation rather than their merits and expertise.

In the context of indirect taxation, the rate of Value-Added Tax (VAT) is broadly in line with EU legislation. It is applied at the standard rate of 18% and the reduced rate of 8% in line with the rules on rates set out in the EU Directive on the Common System of VAT, although the reduced rather than the standard rate is applied to supplies and imports of IT equipment. In relation to direct taxation, the

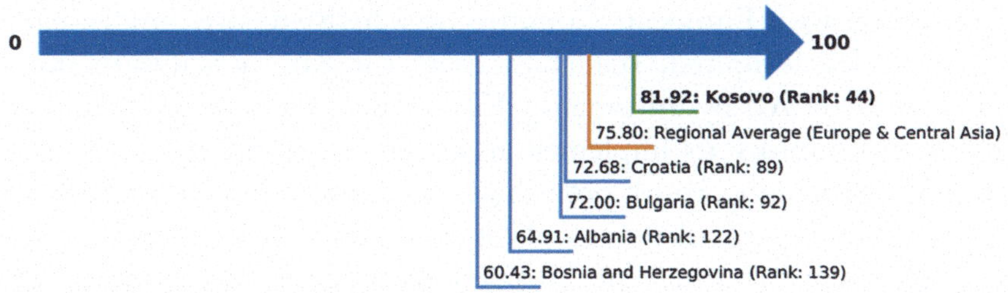

Fig. 7.1 Paying taxes in Kosovo and comparator economies—ranking and score (*Source* Doing business database)

transfer pricing between enterprises under common ownership or control is addressed by the Law on Corporate Income Tax, in line with OECD guidelines for agreements on the elimination of double taxation. Kosovo is ranked 44th among 189 economies for ease of paying taxes (Fig. 7.1).

7.4.2 Employment Institutions and Human Resource Development

The second aspect of social conditions at the national level is related to the creation of employment institutions. This is an important factor that determines how a society develops the capabilities of its present and future labour forces and the working and remuneration conditions. Employment institutions are involved in aspects related to employment law, labour market flexibility, easiness of hiring and firing employees and the reward system.

Kosovo has adapted legislation related to employment and labour relations, in line, generally, with EU standards. This law represents a major milestone in labour relations and contributes to codifying employer–employee relationship in the country. More specifically, the law on labour ensures four fundamental principles: (a) freedom of association and recognition of the right to collective negotiations; (b) elimination of any kind of forced or violent labour; (c) elimination of child labour; and (d) elimination of discrimination at work. The application of this law is the responsibility of the Labour Inspectorate.

According to a European Commission (2018) report, implementation of this law is limited. The labour market in Kosovo is dysfunctional and is characterized by informality. Kosovo needs to amend its Law on Labour and improve its implementation. The small number of inspectors and the lengthy court procedures undermine implementation of the law which is particularly complicated and difficult in the private sector. Child labour continues to be a serious concern, with around 11% of children involved in work and this percentage is higher (up to 17%) among some minority groups (Roma and Ashkali). World Bank (2010) indicates that, although the process of hiring and firing of the workforce is relatively easy, the legislation has significant limitations in relation to flexible working arrangements. For instance, there are restrictions on fixed-term contracts, part-time work, working from home, alternative work schedules, overtime and night work.

The fundamental element of this part of the social conditions is related to the ability of the society to develop an educated and skilled labour force. The development of human capital is considered fundamental for innovating firms because a well-educated and skilled workforce can generate new ideas and knowledge that foster innovation. This applies to both the workplace and society more generally (OECD 2011). There are some empirical findings that support this. For instance, Carlino and Hunt (2009) find that the presence of an educated and a trained workforce is decisive for inventive output in American cities: a 10% increase in the share of the workforce with at least a college degree increases (quality-adjusted) patenting per capita by about 10%. Although the economy of Kosovo cannot be described as skill-intensive, there are signs that demand for skills is increasing and the nature of the skills required is changing towards more general skills that allow workers (and firms) to survive and adapt quickly to changes to demand (World Bank 2010).

In relation to employees with a university degree, BEEPS results indicate that the share of employees with a university degrees or post graduate qualification in Kosovo is only half that in SEE (7% compared to 15%), while compared with the Europe and Central Asia (ECA) region, it is three times lower (7% compared to 24%) (Fig. 7.2).

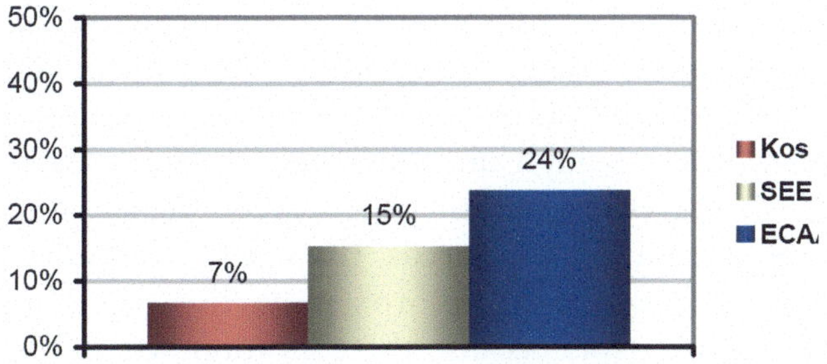

Fig. 7.2 Professionalism of labour (*Source* World Bank BEEPS 2010)

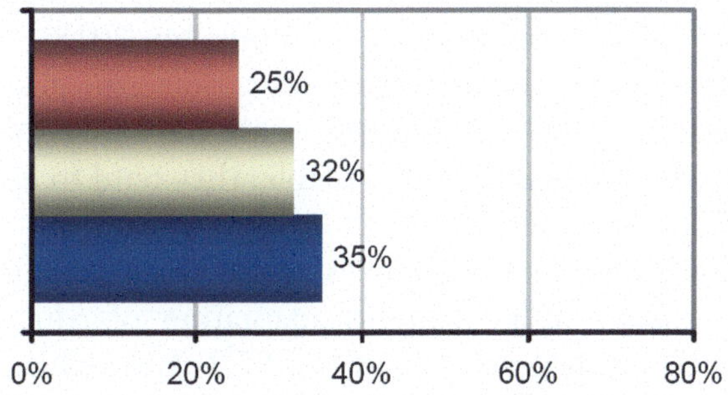

Fig. 7.3 Provision of formal training (*Source* BEEPS 2010)

The BEEPS (2010) report provides data on the training activities organized by firms. It indicates that business firms in Kosovo are less likely to offer training to their employees. Only 25% of firms in Kosovo offer training for their employees compared to 32% in SEE and 35% in the ECA region. The number of employees that participate in training in the production sector of firms that operate in Kosovo is significantly lower at only 9%, compared to SEE with 46%, and ECA with 36% (World Bank 2010) (Fig. 7.3).

Low levels of public spending on education and how it is managed are among the reasons for the level of human capital in Kosovo. Public spending on education (4.7% of GDP) is significantly lower than in the comparator countries (see Table 4.10, Ch. 3). In addition, a recent European Commission (2018) report indicates that the budget allocated to education is not managed efficiently to provide a modern and good quality education for the comparatively large number of young Kosovans. While the number of students in higher education is nearly double the EU average for its population size, completion rates are poor. There is high unemployment among university degree holders (25%), suggesting a mismatch between higher education programmes and labour market needs (European Commission 2018). Students that graduate from Kosovo's universities, both private and public, lack applied skills because the education system, especially in the public universities, is predominantly theoretical. The implementation of a curriculum reform has been hampered by the lack of qualified teaching staff, teaching materials and supplies, and an underdeveloped student assessment system (European Commission 2018). A teacher training system to improve the quality of education is in place, but has to bear fruit. Practical work and internships are not obligatory for students and even where internships are available, they tend to last for only a few weeks (OECD 2013b).

Vocational education is considered as enabling the creation of an entrepreneurship culture and facilitates adaptation of education outcomes to market needs. Kosovo passed the VET Law, which purports to regulate formal vocational education. The Institutional framework of vocational education and training is similar to the rest of the region. However, the evidence shows that, enrolment of the younger generation in vocational training in Kosovo is significantly lower than in neighbouring countries. In Kosovo, 43% of students entered vocational schools in 2009/2010, which is low compared to 71% in Croatia and 61% in FYR Macedonia (OECD 2013a).

According to the World Bank (2010), vocational education in Kosovo has various weaknesses. For instance, VET is predominantly school-based, meaning that the education programmes are not aligned to the needs of an emerging market economy, there is not enough practical training in business companies, the private sector does not participate systematically in planning and implementing vocational training, etc. It seems that the links between the labour market and the education structure are poor or non-existent. Business entities are not involved in the development of workforce strategies, making it impossible to provide skilled workers and technicians.

In relation to research and innovation institutions, the findings show that there is almost no spending on research: only 0.1% of GDP goes to research activity, which is significantly lower than in the comparator countries such as Croatia (0.84%) and Slovenia (2.2%)—see Table 4.10. In addition, there are very few research and innovative institutions in Kosovo and those that do exist suffer from lack of research capacity and very weak links between academic institutions and the private sector (European Commission 2018).

These poor social conditions are related, in part, to the low level of investment in the creation of a supportive environment conducive to the emergence of innovative firms. This third element of the social conditions is discussed below.

7.4.3 Investment Institutions

The third element of the macro level social conditions is related to investment institutions, which govern how society ensures that sufficient financial resources are available, on a continuing basis, to sustain the development of its productive capabilities (Lazonick 2013).

The investment environment in Kosovo is based exclusively on financial institutions, that is, the banking system. The country has no financial institutions that trade equity/shares. According to the report issued by Central Bank of Kosovo in 2017, the financial sector is well capitalized, with ample liquidity buffers. Regulatory capital to risk-weighted assets in the banking sector in December 2017 was 18%, which is above the regulatory minimum of 12%. The proportion of non-performing loans is the lowest in the region, with 3.1% as of December 2017. This was due to stronger credit growth, strong economic performance and improvements to bankruptcy and insolvency procedures. The financial sector recorded high profitability in 2017. Return on average equity was 21.3%, 17.6% and 17.7% for the banking sector, micro-financial institutions and the insurance sector, respectively. Total assets in the banking sector grew by 6.6% in 2017 to 61.3% of GDP. The average interest rate on loans decreased in 2017 to 6.8% from 7.5% in 2016, but still remains above the regional average.

More detailed data investment and financial condition in the country are provided in Chapters 2 and 3.

The above evidence shows that, with regard to the regulatory framework for business firms, Kosovo has instituted laws, which, in general, are compatible with modern EU standards. However, it seems that, overall, the major problem is poor implementation of these institutions in practice. This is especially evident in the case of legislation related to employment and labour relations, labour market flexibility, easiness of hiring and firing employees, reward systems, corporate governance practices, etc. Another important finding is related to the capability of institutions to provide the population with high quality and modern education, training and access to research. The outcomes suggest that the education system suffers from numerous weaknesses, related mainly to the inability of the young generation to acquire real life working skills. Due to the absence of applied training and soft skills, graduates struggle to find jobs after graduation. The entire higher education system in Kosovo is characterized by the marginalization of scientific research. Kosovo has quite low levels of investment in R&D activities. The existing research institutions suffer from lack of research capacity and applied research is under-developed. Although the financial system seems stable and well-regulated, the evidence shows that the cost of finance is higher than in comparator countries.

The constraints related to institutional governance and lack of human resources may be related, in part, to the financial capability of firms to implement their business projects. Despite a stable and well-regulated financial system, the finance provided is costly relative to comparator countries.

7.5 Empirical Results at the Firm Level

The basic function of a business entity is to transform its inputs into goods and services, which, when sold, generate rents (Coase 1937). The theory of the innovative firm explains this process according to three generic business activities: strategic control, organizational integration and financial commitment. In the following section, these three activities are analysed using the datasets described in Sect. 7.3. The survey questionnaires addressed different aspects related to strategic control (founding team size, concentration of ownership, educational level of founders), organizational integration (innovation processes in firms) and how firms obtain external finance to manage their business activities.

The descriptive statistics indicate that only 5.9% of firms are exporting/innovating. In terms of ownership structure, 89% of firms are sole-owned, 5% are partnerships and 5.9% are limited liability companies. In terms of sectors, the findings show that around 13% of firms belong to the manufacturing sectors, while the majority of them belong to trading (57.9%) and other service sectors (29.4%).

7.5.1 Empirical Results for Strategic Control Factors

For firms to innovate requires strategic allocation of resources. According to Lazonick (2013), this aspect of the social conditions involves a set of relations that gives decision-makers power to allocate the firm's resources and manage the technological, market and competitive uncertainties inherent in the innovation processes. These decision-makers must have the abilities and incentives to allocate resources according to innovative investment strategies. Their abilities require good education, knowledge, experience and training and their incentives depend on whether the interests of strategic decision-makers are in line with the interests of the firms they are managing. Therefore, from the perspective of the theory of the innovative firm, it is important to understand who owns the firm, who manages it and how their interests are aligned to the firm strategy.

The questionnaires include questions about the characteristics of the firm founding team and were completed by (one of) the firm's founders. Specifically, the questionnaire gathered information on the ownership structure, the relationships among owners (in the case of more than one owner) and the owner's formal education and previous working experience.

Several proxies are used to investigate the strategic control relations, such as structure and characteristics of firm ownership, relationship between owners and managers, concentration of ownership (minority and majority owners), interactions between managers and owners. In the case of the capabilities of those with decision power to allocate internal resources to innovation activities strategically, the proxies used include education attainment of decision-makers, experience accumulated over the years and training received.

Empirical studies suggest that the characteristics of the firm owners/founders are central to firm growth. The number of founders involved at firm founding has been discussed in the literature. Larger founding teams are considered more likely to bring valuable resources such as human capital or financial resources. A larger number of founders, also, are assumed to mean the firm is better placed to evaluate and recognize business opportunities in the market. In particular, the empirical evidence suggests that the larger the founding team, the more heterogeneous the firm's competences, knowledge, wisdom and experience and, therefore, the more effective its handling of everyday problems (Janz al. 1997). Other studies suggest that there can be negative aspects related to multi-founder ventures, related to monitoring, shirking, distributing incentives (Mosakowki 1998) and group conflict (Amason and Sapienza 1997).

Our empirical findings show that most firms are single owner (87.1%) and this applies also to non-exporting firms. Table 6.2 shows that exporting-based firms differ from other firms: 52% have more than two owners.

With regard to power concentration, the results indicate that, in the vast majority of firms, strategic control is concentrated in one person. In the area of decision-making control, the questionnaire asked whether strategic business decisions were made by the owner or by the managers of the firm. In most cases (80%), it is the owner with the remaining 20% made by managers. The findings are different for exporting firms: 74.1% of exporting firms are managed by their managers compared to only 20.2% of non-exporting firms. It seems that power distribution distinguishes exporting from non-exporting firms.

Education attainment is a basic component of the founder's human capital. Human capital includes the knowledge acquired during formal education, training and working experience. In general, this variable is positively related to the likelihood of firm survival and has a positive impact on growth. Table 7.1 shows the differences between the two groups of firms: 81.5% of exporting firms are owned by owners with higher education (at least a university degree), but this falls to 37% for non-exporting firms.

The entrepreneurship literature considers working experience in the same economic activity to be a very important factor. Founders with previous experience in the same industry are more likely to share knowledge and information, with the result that all firm members with having a better knowledge of industry practices and routines (Shane and Stuart 2002). The outcomes indicate that the majority of founders (55.8%) have no or little prior experience in the same industry. Prior experience has a significant impact on the capability to export. Table 6.1 shows that 48.1% of founders reported having prior experience in the focal industry compared to 40.1% for those not involved in exporting and who reported prior experience in the focal industry.

The findings show, also, that in-house training shows some differences among the two groups of firms. Only 37.2% of firms provide managerial training but there are more exporting firms that provide management training—70.4% compared to 27.9% for non-exporting firms. In terms of firm size (measured as numbers of employees) and the relation to ownership, the evidence suggests that 51.9% of SMEs are owned by more than two shareholders while among micro firms over 90% of are sole owned (Table 7.2).

We employed direct logistic regression to assess the impact of the strategic control variables on the likelihood of greater exporting success. The model was tested to check that it met the requirements for this specific statistical technique. The model includes four independent variables-ownership concentration, power distribution, educational attainment and training activities. The full model, containing all the predictors, is statistically significant, $\chi 2$ (4, $N = 500$) = 50.937, $p < .000$, indicating that the model distinguishes between exporting and non-exporting firms. Overall, the model explains between 15.41% (Cox and Snell R^2) and 36.3% (Nagelkerke R^2) of the variance in exporting and correctly classified 96.5% of cases.

Table 7.2 Descriptive statistics on strategic control indicators (*N*: 500)

Variable		Total sample	Exporting	Non-exporting
Ownership structure	One owner	87.1	48.0	90.3
	More than two owners	12.9	52.0	9.7
Power distribution	Owner	80.0	25.9	79.8
	Manager	20.0	74.1	20.2
Experience before starting business	Experience	44.2	48.1	37.2
	Non-experience	55.8	51.9	62.8
Formal education	University degree holder	29.2	81.5	37.0
	Secondary school	70.8	18.5	63.0
Management training	Training	37.2	70.4	27.9
	No training	62.8	29.6	72.1

Source BSCK (2012)

Table 7.3 shows that, among five variables four make a unique statistically significant contribution to the model. In summary, the results of the regression exercise indicate that ownership structure, distribution of power, educational attainment and organization of training sessions for managers are significant predictors of higher business success. More specifically, the ownership structure and the power distribution in the firm seem to have the most robust impact on the differences between the two groups of firms. Knowledge, and other working skills are shown to be crucial for enhancing firm performance. Specific firm training—for example, management training—can increase the competencies of managers and workers such that they become a strategic asset. Previous experience of training allows the building of 'bundles' of routines which are difficult to imitate (Koch and McGrath 1996). This can increase competitive advantage and lead to superior performance.

7.5.2 Empirical Results for Organizational Integration Factors

According to the theory of the innovative firm, if business entities are endowed with strategic control factors, these can translate into specific innovative activities. Innovative activities require organization, that is, the social conditions integrating different hierarchical responsibilities

Table 7.3 Logistic regression results on strategic factors

	B	S.E	Wald	df	Cox and Snell R^2 Nagelkerke R^2	p	Odds ratio	90% C.I. for Odds	
								Lower	Upper
Ownership structure	1.665	.500	11.095	1		.001	5.284	1.984	14.073
Power distribution	1.399	.516	7.366	1		.007	4.052	1.475	11.128
Formal education	1.122	.560	4.015	1	36.3	.045	3.072	1.025	9.211
Management training	1.281	.511	6.273	1	96.5	.012	3.600	1.321	9.810
Working experience	.023	.501	.002	1		.963	1.023	.384	2.730
Constant	−.605	.465	1.694	1		.193	.546		

Source BSCK (2012)

and functional capabilities, which result in higher quality production and lower cost products and services (Lazonick 2012). More specifically, this element of the social conditions includes a set of relations that enable firms to transform inputs into innovative outputs. Lazonick (2013) suggests that the need for organizational integration derives from the developmental complexity of the innovation process—that is, the need for organizational learning. In this context, compensation in the form of work incentives are important for integrating individuals into the organization. How labour relations are managed can motivate employees as individuals to engage in collective learning.

Several proxies are used to investigate the sources of organizational learning, namely, whether firms learn mostly from the market (supplier, competitors and consumers) or from the experience of their workers and the ideas generated inside the organization. Business plan is used to proxy for whether the firm's business activities are based on advance strategic planning. We also use business collaboration with international companies as another proxy for differentiation of exporting and non-exporting firms. The second category of proxies is related to the way the innovation process is organized, namely whether the innovation process is organized independently or in collaboration with other external entities (academic research institutions, business associations), and risk-taking abilities. This last variable includes labour–management relationships, that is, how organizations create incentives for people with different hierarchical responsibilities and functional capabilities.

Table 7.4 shows that only 23% of firms organize their business activities according to a formal written business plan. This does not apply to exporting firms: 70.4% of exporting firms report that business activates are organized based on previously codified business plans. The percentage for non-exporting firms is significantly lower at 29.3%. A business plan can be used as a means of discipline to encourage the firm to formulate a rigorous business strategy and conduct appropriate market research (Gruber 2007).

In relation to how firms generate knowledge, the outcomes indicate that 44% of firms view the market (competitors, suppliers, customers) as a most valuable source of new knowledge, with higher a percentage obtained by exporting firms, 70.4% versus 41.6% for non-exporting

Table 7.4 Descriptive statistics on organizational indicators (*N*: 500)

Variable		Total sample	Exporting	Non-exporting
Business plan	Yes	23.3	70.4	29.3
	No	76.7	29.6	70.7
Collaboration	Yes	45.6	52.6	44.5
	No	54.4	47.4	55.5
Market as source of learning	Important	44.2	70.4	41.6
	Not important	55.8	29.6	58.4
Staff's ideas as source of learning	Important	39.5	51.9	39.3
	Not important	60.5	48.1	60.7
Risk taking	Yes	13.9	44.4	6.5
	No	86.1	55.6	93.5
Change of marketing strategy	Yes	13.5	22.2	9.5
	No	86.5	77.8	90.5
Foreign partners	Yes	11.6	51.9	10.3
	No	88.4	48.1	89.7

Source BSCK (2012)

firms. In terms of how the innovation process is organized, the results indicate that 52% of firms organize the innovation process based exclusively on their own resources, 14.6% of firms reported organizing the innovation process in collaboration with other local firms and 31.4% of firms reported licensing of patents and brands from other firms to launch their products in the market. The results indicate only a small contribution of academic research institutions to the innovation process: only 1.5% of firms reported innovation collaboration with academic research institutions in the country.

The outcomes suggest that only a few firms are prepared to take business risks. Only 13.9% of firms reported trying, but failing to innovate. There is a significant difference between exporting and non-exporting firms. For instance, while the percentage of exporting firms that reported innovation failure is 44.4, the percentage of non-exporting firms is only 6.5. Exporting and non-exporting firms differ, also, in the changes they make to their marketing strategies (see Table 7.4).

Establishing a global network can facilitate the development of new capabilities which firms can leverage across national and international markets (Autio et al. 2000). Businesses linkages with foreign partners provide access to the knowledge and skills required for product and process innovation. Innovation relationships with international partners improve the firm's domestic competitiveness and its ability to compete internationally. In the context of international business linkages, the questionnaire asked whether the firm had business partnerships with foreign firms. Only 12.7% of the sample had established some kind of business collaboration with a foreign firm. The outcomes are significantly different for exporting firms: 52% of them have established formal partnership relationships with a foreign firm compared to only 10% of non-exporting firms.

The results of the logistic regression exercise shows the model used is statistically significant, χ^2 (5) = 60.982, $p < .0000$, explaining 37.0% (Nagelkerke R^2) of the difference between exporting and non-exporting firms and correctly classifying 93.9% of cases. Table 7.5 shows that, among the five variables included in the model, four make a unique statistically significant contribution to the model. The strongest predictor seems to be risk-taking, with an odds ratio of 7.7, followed by ability of the firm to link with a foreign partner, with an odds ratio of 6.2. Organizing business activities based on a business plan, with an odds ratio of 5.8, is also a significant predictor. The evidence suggests that exporting firms are 2.6 times more likely than non-exporting firms to report the market as a source of learning. The smallest effect on the variance between two groups of firms seems to be the ability of the firm to change its marketing strategy to respond to market demands (Table 7.5).

The empirical outcomes obtained of both exercises indicate that risk-taking capability is a significant factor. This suggests that exporting firms effectively organize their strategic resources, exploit new opportunities and launch projects with uncertain outcomes and uncertain returns on investment (Scheepers et al. 2008). It is expected that new projects involve risks, which can be minimized either by the knowledge residing in the firm, by its unique capabilities or by collaboration with other firms, specifically foreign partners. Collaboration with foreign partners is another differentiating factor that emerged from the analysis. Collaboration with foreign partners allows the firms to share resources including ideas, know-how technologies and staff in order to solve a given problem (Lawton Smith and Dickson 2003). Also, collaboration

Table 7.5 Logistic regression results on organizational integration

	B	S.E	Wald	df	Cox and Snell R^2 Nagelkerke R^2	*p*	Odds ratio	90% C.I. for Odds	
								Lower	Upper
Business plan	1.753	.511	11.785	1		.001	5.774	2.122	15.713
Market as source of learning	.961	.502	3.671	1		.055	2.615	.978	6.989
Attempting to innovate but failed	2.047	.510	16.110	1	0.15	. 000	7. 743	2.850	21.035
Change of marketing strategy	−.421	.600	.491	1	0.37	.483	.657	.202	2.129
Foreign partners	1.829	.469	15.206	1		.000	6.230	2.484	15.625
Constant	−1.233	.636	3.754	1		.053	.291		

Source BSCK (2012)

and partnerships with foreign firms can minimize the risks related to testing the market and allow the accumulation of risk-taking capabilities which render them more successful (Scheepers et al. 2008).

7.5.3 Empirical Results on the Labour–Management Relations

An important part of organization integration is linked to labour–management relations. Modes of compensation in the form of work incentives are important instruments for integrating individuals into the organization. How labour–management relations are governed can motivate employees as individuals to engage in collective learning (Lazonick 2012).

Organizational integration is analysed using data from the survey conducted in 2018. The analysis examines three areas of managerial practice: monitoring, the way business targets are set and incentive practices. These three areas of managerial practice address labour–management relations directly. Monitoring includes issues related to how managers supervise the firm's employees (performance tracking, reviewing, dialogue with them, consequences of poor performance and clarity of communication). Targets include production target timescales and their difficulty and employees' awareness of them. Incentives include how managers deal with promotion, practices for addressing poor employee performance and how good performance is rewarded.

Monitoring is considered important to allow managers to track, review and communicate firm performance to the workforce. One of the questions asked whether tracking was ad hoc and incomplete or continuous and communicated to all staff. Most indicated that it was ad hoc or non-existent. The best managerial practice requires managers to monitor the work of employees on a continuous basis and to communicate their business performance clearly. This practice should be carried out formally and informally, for all staff members, using a range of visual management tools (Bloom and Van Reenen 2010).

The findings show that workers' performance is reviewed infrequently, typically when a success or failure is spotted, or periodically,

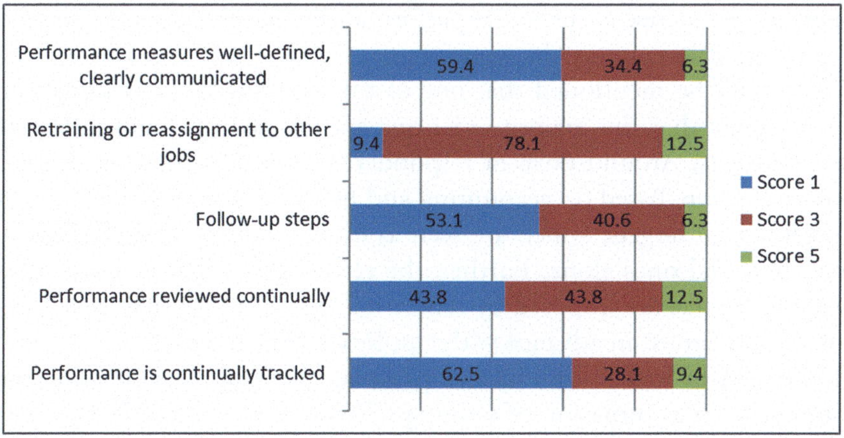

Fig. 7.4 Labour—management practices—monitoring area (*Source* Survey 2018)

but without a clear follow-up plan. Modern models of managerial practice require regular performance reviews and clear indicators. Also, the results to be communicated to all staff to ensure continuous improvement. Another relatively poor score was obtained for how feedback on performance is provided to the workforce. Figure 7.4 shows that performance feedback is either non-existent or focuses on issues unrelated to business improvements. Again, modern monitoring models require managers to provide regular review/performance conversations focused on problem solving and aimed at addressing root causes. Moreover, the ultimate aim of feedback should be not to penalize workers, but to offer opportunities for constructive conversations and coaching. The average score for this question is 2.13, while the best score is 5.

Another important aspect that sheds light on the relationship between managers and employees is the potential consequences of a performance review. The average score is 2.81, indicating that failure to achieve agreed results is tolerated for a period before action is taken.

The final question related to monitoring practices referred to how managers formulate performance measures and whether these measures are communicated clearly and understood by the workforce. The results indicate that performance measures are ill-defined, are quite complex and are not clearly understood by those being evaluated. The best managerial practice ensures that performance measures induce constructive competition among the workforce.

It should be mentioned that one of the findings for how targets are set, suggests that the majority of firms are focused on financial/operational targets. Around 66% of respondents responded that targets predominantly are based on accounting and financial figures rather than on non-financial targets, which are seen as more inspiring and challenging than financial ones alone. Further, the results show that in most cases, business targets are imposed by senior managers, rather than being discussed and agreed in advance with employees (Fig. 7.5).

The area of incentives includes practices for dealing with poor performers, such as provision of training to allow the expected level of performance or firing. It also includes the lengths to which companies go to retain talent. It is surprising that, compared to other management practices, three out of the five practices in this area have a mean greater than 3. The only practice with a mean below 2 is how firms reward high performers. In most cases, firms have no formal procedure for rewarding good performance (Fig. 7.6).

Though these managerial practices do not directly investigate managerial–worker relationships in the context of innovation activities, the quality of these practices may be an indication of this relationship. However, as Bloom et al. (2011) argue, it remains an open question whether high/low scores on the management practices grid are

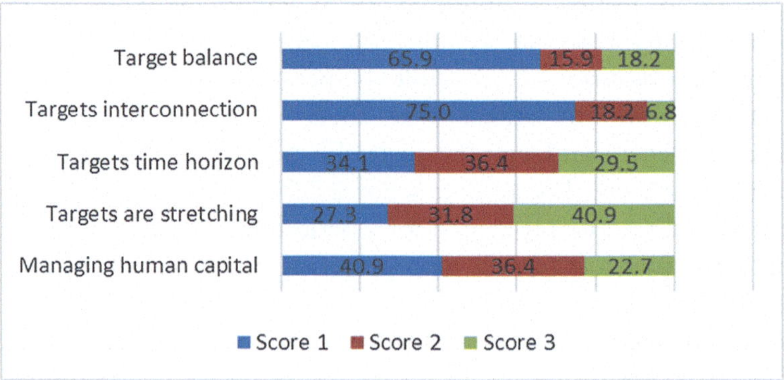

Fig. 7.5 Labour—management practices—targets area (*Source* Survey 2018)

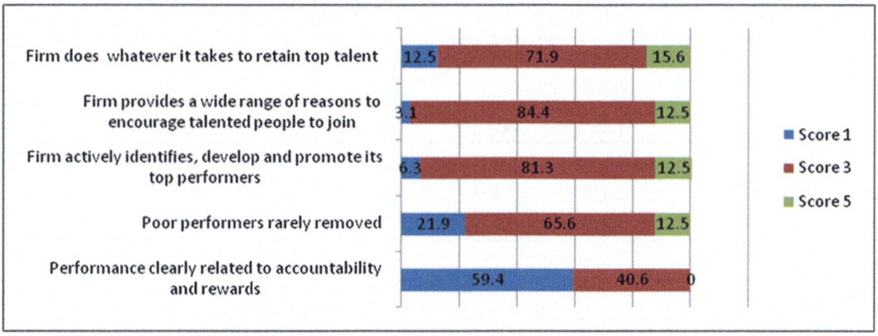

Fig. 7.6 Management practices—incentive area (*Source* Survey 2018)

beneficial, neutral or detrimental to innovation (the generation of new goods and services). These authors emphasize that good management practices may complement innovation since efficient organization of the research team is likely to lead to more 'bang' for every 'R&D buck' spent.

7.5.4 Empirical Results on Investment Commitment

As indicated in the theoretical framework section, the innovation process is not an activity, but rather is a process that is cumulative over time (Lazonick 2013). Thus, it needs sustained commitment of financial resources for its evolution. This is an essential social condition that enables a cumulative innovation process until it becomes profitable. Lazonick maintains that, implementing innovative projects based on internal finance is risky and that internal funds often need to be supplemented by external sources. Section 7.4.3 showed that a major weakness of investment institutions at the national level is related to the absence of an equity market. Hence, the only source of external finance is bank loans.

On the question of whether firms have invested in new projects in the last three years, 61% responded negatively. However, 65% of exporting firms responded positively. For sources of the funds, 77% of firms responded that most projects were financed by internal funds and

Table 7.6 Statistical summary of investment commitment variables

	Invested in last three years		Loans from financial		Time duration of loans	
	Yes (%)	No (%)	Yes (%)	No (%)	<3 years	>3 years
Total firms	55.3	44.7	53.8	46.2	78	22
Exporting firms	65.4	34.6	59.3	40.7	66.7	33.3
Non-exporting firms	35.9	64.1	27	73	76.1	23.9

Source BSCK (2012)

the rest indicated bank loans. 70% of firms considered the conditions for financial loans to be unfavourable.

The generally short time duration and the high interest rates indicate that the financial social conditions are unfavourable. 83% of respondents mentioned lack of collateral as the main reason for being unable to obtain a bank loan. It seems that banks' perception of risk is high and they require large collateral in order to provide a loan. In relation to whether the firms received support (subsidies) from the EU, central government or local governments, 1.4% responded having received EU funding, while 99.7% reported no support from central or local government (Table 7.6).

These findings are generally in line with those in the World Bank enterprise survey (BEEPS 2013) in relation to how firms obtain the funds necessary to finance their operations and the characteristics of their financial transactions. Figure 7.4 shows that, around 73% of business activities are financed by internal funds, 17% by bank loans, 5% by equity and sales of stocks and the remainder by other sources. According to these figures, firms in Kosovo use internal sources to finance their investments more than do other countries in Europe and the ECA region, and less than do other low-income countries (Fig. 7.7).

The main findings from the analysis of social conditions at firm level are as follows:

- Exporting firms seems to differ significantly from non-exporting firms in their ownership concentration. The majority of exporting firms tend to have more than one owner and be managed by the firm's managers rather than its owners. The separation of these

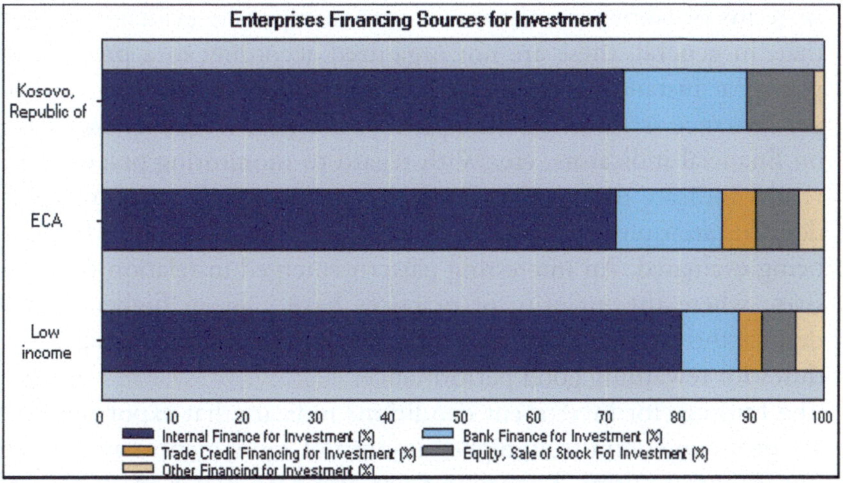

Fig. 7.7 Source of finance for investment purposes in Kosovo and comparator countries (*Source* World Bank BEEPS 2013)

two functions leads to professionalization of management and most likely leads to greater business success. Furthermore, owners and managers that manage exporting firms are better educated, which could translate into higher innovation capacity, but not necessarily a higher number of innovations. Results show that 80% of managers in exporting firms hold a university degree versus 37% in the case of non-exporting firms. In addition, exporting firms seem to consider management training as important for business success. The findings show that the relationship between shareholders and owners' prior experience seems not to differ significantly between the two groups of firms.

- In relation to organizational integration, factors such as establishing business collaboration with foreign partners and readiness to take risks in business activities have the strongest impact on differentiating exporting from non-exporting firms. Other factors, such as possession of a business plan and the market as a source of organizational learning, are likely to have a positive influence on the firm's capability to transform inputs into innovative outputs.

- In terms of labour–management relationships, the evidence suggests that, in general, these are not organized according to a predesigned plan. For instance, tracking of working activities is ad hoc, workers' performance is reviewed infrequently, business targets are set based on financial indicators, etc. With regard to monitoring practices, the results indicate that performance measurement indicators are poorly defined, are quite complex and are not clearly understood by those being evaluated. An interesting pattern emerged in relation to incentives, where the majority of practices have a mean higher than 3, despite the fact that, in most cases, the firms have no formal procedures for rewarding good performance.
- The findings for investment conditions indicate that exporting firms are prone to committing higher amount of investments compared to non-exporting firms. Exporting firms also have better access to bank loans than the other group of firms. The banks' lending conditions seem to have similar negative effects for both types of firms.

7.6 Concluding Remarks

This chapter investigated the social conditions that enable and/or constrain the emergence of firms endowed with innovative capabilities. The analysis was carried out using the conceptual framework proposed by Lazonick (2013). The outcomes show that a business firm is a social structure that is embedded in a broader institutional environment involving governance, employment and investment institutions. The outcomes suggest, also, that the social conditions within firms, embodied by strategic control, organizational integration and financial commitments have a significant impact on developing the human and physical capabilities that enable the firm to compete in product/service markets.

The evidence provided in this chapter suggests that the institutional environment in Kosovo suffers from many deficiencies. Although some less-developed countries have managed to establish legal structures compatible with the developed countries, there is a major problem related to their application in practice. The findings show that, although Kosovo has managed to establish an institutional framework which is mostly in line with EU standards, its implementation is problematic. This legal framework addresses important issues related to business operations such as enterprise law, tax law, regulations related to employment, corporate governance, etc. Kosovo also has created and adopted a modern institutional framework which includes aspects such as human capital development. Nevertheless, the findings indicate that the current education system is not addressing labour market needs. There is a poor coordination between market needs and graduate programmes, vocational schools and universities. High youth unemployment (51.6%) shows that there is a clear misalignment between education system outcomes and labour market needs. In other words, there is a mismatch between students' qualifications and skills and what is needed in the job market. In terms of investment institutions, the findings suggest that the financial system is quite stable, but the cost of loans seems to be higher than in comparator countries.

The results provided in this chapter point to the relevance of the social conditions within firms. They indicate that they affect the decision-makers' power to allocate the firm's resources and compete in the market. The results show that, in Kosovo, the percentage of firms endowed with the conditions for strategic control that enable the emergence of innovative firms is small. They show, also, that the conditions in which firms organize and integrate their business operations have a significant impact on the emergence of innovative capabilities. These conditions contribute significantly to explaining the emergence of innovative firms. Finally, it would seem that the financial conditions are a major constraint for both types of firms, regardless of their endowment of innovation capabilities.

In sum, the theory of the innovative enterprise provides a good framework for understanding the dynamic interactions between the organizational conditions of the firm and the institutional environment in which it operates. This theory offers a hybrid framework, able to capture external as well as internal variables related to the firm's business setting. The theory of the innovative enterprise differs from growth diagnostics and resource-based theory and the management practice approach, all of which are focused on static issues such as how the firm can operate successfully using a given technology. In contrast, the innovative enterprise concept asks what factors enable or inhibit firms from improving their technological capabilities. Further, the results of this study show that the social conditions include distinctive sets of factors that must be considered in an analysis of the business factors related to firm growth and not just their current operations. Finally, the methodological and theoretical foundations of the innovative firm theory could serve as a fertile and exciting framework for future empirical research.

References

Almor, T. (2006). *Conceptualizing path of growth for the born global firms*. Paper presented at the ACCS Annual Conference, Berlin.

Almor, T., & Hashai, N. (2004). Competitive advantage and strategic configuration of knowledge-intensive small and medium sized multinationals: A modified resource based view. *Journal of International Management, 10*(4), 479–500.

Amason, A. C., & Sapienza, H. J. (1997). The effects of top management team size and interaction norms on cognitive and affective conflict. *Journal of Management, 23,* 495–516.

Anderton, B. (1999). UK trade performance and the role of product quality, innovation and hysteresis: Some preliminary results. *Scottish Journal of Political Economy, 46,* 570–595.

Austin, J. T., Yaffee, R. A., & Hinkle, D. E. (1992). Logistic regression for research in higher education. *Handbook of Theory and Research, 8,* 379–410.

Autio, E., Sapienza, H. J., & Almeida, J. G. (2000). Effects of age at entry, knowledge intensity, and imitability on international growth. *Academy of Management Journal, 43,* 909–924.

Ayyagari, M., Thorsten, B., & Demirgüç-Kunt, A. (2007). Small and medium enterprises across the globe: A new database. *Small Business Economics, 29*(4), 415–434.

Bernard, A. B., & Jensen, J. B. (2001). *Why some firms export?* (NBER Working Paper No. 8349). Cambridge: National Bureau of Economic Research.

Bloom, N., & Van Reenen, J. (2010). Why do management practices differ across firms and countries? *Journal of Economic Perspectives, 24*(1), 203–224.

Bloom, N., Schweiger, H., & Van Reenen, J. (2011). *The land that lean manufacturing forgot? Management practices in transition countries* (National Bureau of Economic Research Working Paper Series No. 17231). Cambridge: National Bureau of Economic Research.

BSCK. (2012). *Entrepreneurship and small business development in Kosovo: Research report*. http://www.bsckosovo.org/publikimet/20121108044632244.pdf.

Cabrera, A. F. (1994). Logistic regression analysis in higher education: An applied perspective. *Higher Education: Handbook of Theory and Research, 10,* 225–256.

Carlino, G., & Hunt, R. (2009). What explains the quantity and quality of local inventive activity? In G. Burtless & J. R. Pack (Eds.), *Brookings-Wharton papers on urban affairs*. Washington, DC: Brookings Institution Press.

Central Bank of Kosovo. (2017). *Annual report 2017*. Retrieved from https://bqk-kos.org/repository/docs/2018/CBK_AR_2017.pdf.

Coase, R. H. (1937). The nature of the firm. *Economica, 4,* 386–405.

EBRD. (2013). *Commercial Laws of Kosovo*, an assessment by EBRD. http://www.ebrd.com/downloads/sector/legal/kosovo.pdf. Accessed 22 March 2014.

European Commission. (2018). *Kosovo 2018 report*. Commission staff working document. Strasburg. https://ec.europa.eu/neighbourhood-enlargement/sites/near/files/20180417-kosovo-report.pdf.

Gruber, M. (2007). Uncovering the value of planning in new venture creation: A process and contingency perspective. *Journal of Business Venturing, 22*(6), 782–807.

Hosmer, D. W., Jr., & Lemeshow, S. (2000). *Applied logistic regression* (2nd ed.). New York: Wiley.

Janz, B. D., Colquitt, J. A., & Noe, R. A. (1997). Knowledge worker team effectiveness: The role of autonomy, interdependence, team development, and contextual support variables. *Personnel Psychology, 50,* 877–904.

Jones, M. V. (2001). First steps in internationalisation: Concepts and evidence from a sample of small high-technology firms. *Journal of International Management, 7*(3), 191–210.

Koch, M. J., & McGrath, R. G. (1996). Improving labour productivity: Human resource management policies do matter. *Strategic Management Journal, 17,* 335–354.

Lawton Smith, H., & Dickson, K. (2003). Critical factors in inter-firm collaboration. *International Journal of Technology Management, 25*(1/2), 34–50.

Lazonick, W. (2012). *The innovative enterprise and the developmental state: Toward an economics of organizational success*. Paper prepared for the annual conference of the Institute for New Economic Thinking, Breton Woods, NH, 8–11 April 2011, and revised for the conference on Finance, Business Models, and Sustainable Prosperity, Ford Foundation, New York.
Lazonick, W. (2013). The theory of innovative enterprise: Methodology, ideology, and institutions. In J. K. Moudud, C. Bina, & P. L. Mason (Eds.), *Alternative theories of competition: Challenges to the orthodoxy* (pp. 127–159). London: Routledge.
Lazonick, W. H., Mazzucato, M., & Tulum, İ. (2013). Apple's changing business model: What should the world's richest company do with all those profits? *Accounting Forum, 37,* 249–267.
Mosakowski, E. (1998). Entrepreneurial resources, organizational choices, and competitive outcomes. *Organization Science, 9*(6), 625–643.
OECD. (2011). *Skills for innovation and research* (p. 96). Paris: OECD.
OECD. (2013a, March). *Assessment of the Kosovo innovation system* (RCI Project Paper). OECD Development.
OECD. (2013b). *Skills development and training in SMEs*. Paris: OECD Publishing.
OECD/Eurostat. (2005). *Oslo manual, guidelines for collecting and interpreting innovation data*. Paris: OECD.
Scheepers, M. J., Hough, J., & Bloom, J. Z. (2008). Nurturing the corporate entrepreneurship capability. *Southern African Business Review, 12*(3), 50–75.
Shane, S., & Stuart, T. (2002). Organizational endowments and the performance of university start-ups. *Management Science, 48,* 154–170.
World Bank. (2010). *BEEPS At-A-Glance 2008 Kosovo, Business Environment and Enterprise Performance Survey (BEEPS IV)*. Washington, DC: World Bank.
World Bank. (2013). *BEEPS 2013, Kosovo, Business Environment and Enterprise Performance Survey (BEEPS IV)*. Washington, DC: World Bank. http://www.enterprisesurveys.org/~/media/GIAWB/EnterpriseSurveys/Documents/Profiles/English/kosovo-2013.pdf.

8

Conclusions on the Growth of Firms in Less-Developed Countries

8.1 Introduction

This chapter summarizes the overall empirical evidence on firm growth presented in the different chapters of this book. The book set out to examine the external and internal factors that enable or/and constrain the growth of SMEs in less-developed economies. The focus of analysis was firms operating in Kosovo's economy. Four different approaches and methodologies were employed to assess four distinct but interrelated aspects of firm growth. The four approaches used were: (a) firm dynamics and their role in firm growth; (b) the role played by resources (inputs), organizational capabilities and managerial practices in firm growth; (c) the business environment factors that affect firm growth; and (d) the social and economic conditions in Kosovo and their impact on the emergence of firms with innovative capabilities. The book provides empirical evidence based on a sample of Kosovo firms that responds to the research objectives of providing new empirical evidence on the factors that enable and constrain firm growth and the aspects that explain firm growth in a less-developed economic setting.

F. Sahiti, *The Growth of Firms in Less-Developed Countries*,
https://doi.org/10.1007/978-3-030-14821-8_8

This concluding chapter discusses the enablers and barriers to the achievement of higher, sustained and shared growth by firms in Kosovo and presents the main findings from the four aspects to firm growth investigated in the seven chapters constituting this volume.

This chapter is organized as follows. Section 8.2 provides a summary of the main findings from each chapter; Sect. 8.3 discusses the constraints of the analysis, and directions and opportunities for future research.

8.2 Summary of the Main Findings

The first area investigated was related to whether firm churn (entry and exit rates) in less-developed economies has any impact on firm growth. The literature review highlighted especially that developed market economies exhibit high rates of firm churn, which promote the reallocation of inputs from less productive to more productive business firms (Bartelsman et al. 2009). In other words, the previous findings indicate that firms in healthy economies operate under conditions of 'creative destruction' where new firms enter and, it is assumed, put pressure on incumbent firms due to their new technologies, new working methods and new managerial practices. This pressure forces the incumbent firms either to adapt to the new conditions or exit the market.

The evidence presented in Chapter 4 shows that the rate of firm churn in Kosovo is considerably lower than in the reference countries. The findings indicate that Kosovo's economy is characterized by a low level of firm dynamics. While the sectoral structure of firms in Kosovo is fairly comparable to that in other reference countries, average firm size is significantly different. Most firms in the business economy in Kosovo are micro firms, employing less than four people. This applies particularly to firms in the manufacturing sector. For instance, while a typical EU country manufacturing firm employs 13 people on average, the same type of firm in Kosovo employs an average of 4 individuals. Another significant difference between Kosovo and the comparator countries can be found in the service subsector. Kosovo's service firms are dominated by wholesale and retail activities, which account for 54.5% of firms; in the reference countries, this proportion ranges between 25.7 and 35.2%.

Kosovo differs, also, with respect to the structure of new firms entering the market. Overall, small firm entry is comparable to the entry of small firms in the reference countries; however, this differs in the case of large firms. Large firm entry in Kosovo is significantly lower relative to the reference countries. This suggests that the overall business environment in Kosovo does not favour the entry of larger firms.

Also interesting are the findings related to firm survival. The results indicate that the survival prospects for firms in Kosovo aged one-four years are comparable to the survival prospects of firms in the reference countries. However, after four years, the survival probability for firms in Kosovo increases significantly relative to the reference countries. Industry sector firms whose production tends to be more capital-intensive and larger firms can exploit increasing returns to scale, firm survival is consistently higher than in other sectors. These higher survival prospects are not necessarily correlated to growth; rather they tend, primarily, to be due to the less severe impact of market selection compared to developed countries. Although we found no direct evidence of this trend, it can be inferred that firms in Kosovo are not solely economic institutions, but are also social organizations. For families in poor countries such as Kosovo with very high rates of unemployment, firms represent the only means of survival and revenue generation (DeSoto 1989; Naudé 2010a, b). Therefore, firms in less-developed countries operate according to different profitability and loss metrics.

Previous empirical work suggests there is a connection between firm dynamics and various macroeconomic business indicators (Klapper et al. 2008; Geroski et al. 2012). An efficient and inclusive business environment can boost firm dynamics, and vice versa. What are the barriers to higher firm churn in less-developed countries such as Kosovo? We identified a range of factors that either encourage or inhibit higher entry or ease exit of unproductive firms. There are at least two doing business dimensions linked to firm churn and Kosovo performs very poorly in both these dimensions relative to the reference countries.

Evidence on firm dynamics suggests that contract enforcement and resolution of insolvency are associated to the firm birth, death and survival rates (Stam et al. 2006). Other business environment factors in which Kosovo differs significantly from the reference countries are access to finance and level of human capital/ the education system. Access to finance, specifically the cost of loans in Kosovo, remains a major issue for Kosovo firms. Finally, the findings suggest that the education system in Kosovo lacks the capabilities to generate the type of human capital that is required by the local market and is compatible with modern global market requirements.

Overall terms, the empirical evidence provided in Chapter 4 suggests that the firm dynamics in Kosovo are particularly low. The outcomes suggest that the behaviour of firms that operate in this type of business environment generates less turbulence; firm churn is significantly lower than in developed economies and, consequently, the effects of firm dynamics are much less growth-enhancing than in developed economies.

The second investigation focused on the business environment factors that deter higher investment by private agents, and entrepreneurship. Chapter 5 provides a critical appraisal of growth diagnostic theory and comprehensive evidence on those business environment factors that potentially constrain firm growth in the Kosovo economy. The findings for Kosovo were compared to conditions in the reference countries.

Outcomes show that the principal constraint is related to the appropriation of profit. It can be inferred that the proportion of returns that can be appropriated by investors is not sufficiently high. In other words, private agents are apprehensive that government failures will result in dissipation of their returns due to planned or unplanned hold-up problems. There are several indications that the Kosovo government is failing to provide crucial public goods. This can be seen in relation to microrisk factors such as unfair competitive practices, weak rule of law and high levels of corruption. We argued that improving appropriability would produce substantial change in the objective function.

The second binding constraint is the high cost of finance and is related to some macro and microeconomic risk factors. The high cost of finance is a particular constraint. The evidence indicates that the low level of domestic savings, monopolistic behaviour by the banks and poor access to international finance increase the costs of finance. The third binding constraint is related to complementary factors, particularly t poor availability of human capital.

Overall, these findings suggest that the quality of the business environment dominating Kosovo's economy provides few incentives for higher private investment and higher levels of entrepreneurship. The responses to both the international and firm-level surveys provide evidence of this. Private investors have a very poor perception of the quality of the business environment in Kosovo. They perceive it as characterized by high micro-risks (government failures), high cost of capital (relative to comparator countries in the region), and complementary factors such as scarce human capital.

The third is of investigation looked at the factors that differentiate manufacturing firms' performance. In Chapter 6 of the book, three theoretical approaches are combined to enable an investigation into whether resources/inputs, organizational capabilities and managerial practices influence the performance variability between two groups of firms. The findings indicate that firms differ more in terms of their organizational capabilities and managerial practices than the resources/inputs used.

Overall, the results show that there are no significant differences among firms in terms of inputs, that is, their investment in new technology and the financial resources obtained to purchase that technology, are similar. However, the findings for inputs show that high-growth firms differ from low growth firms in the amount of internal training that is provided and the previous occupation of the firm founders. It seems that the business environment is unlikely to affect firm performance, that is, firms less constrained by business environment factors do not necessarily perform better.

Although the quality of the managerial practices applied in Kosovo is poor compared to developed countries, the findings from the analysis suggest that managerial practices still play a crucial role in the performance variability and appear to be equivalent to production capabilities.

In the context of organizational capabilities, the findings reveal that their impact on performance variability is more truncated. This is due primarily to the fact that some organizational capabilities, such as marketing and teamwork, have far less effect on performance variability relative to entrepreneurship and innovation capabilities, dynamic capabilities and networking capabilities.

The fourth line of our investigation, was tackled using a theoretical approach that assumed that innovation was the key condition required for a prosperous economy and that firms endowed with innovative capabilities are the main drivers of growth. The focus in this part of the book was on assessing the social and economic institutions that enable or constrain the rise of innovative firms. Some of these elements overlap with the second and third area of investigations. However, in Chapter 7, the emphasis was on both the macro and micro factors that lead to innovation. We defined innovation as a product/service or a process that is new to the firm, but not necessarily new to the local or international market.

Our findings suggest that Kosovo has managed to establish an institutional framework largely in line with EU standards. Specifically, the institutional framework related to how firms function is similar to that of neighbour countries and other countries more generally. The problem for Kosovo is the implementation of its institutions. Further, the legal structure that, potentially, enables the development of human capital is in line with EU standards, but the outcomes indicate that the alignment between market demand and the structure and quality of the human resources produced by the education system in Kosovo, is deficient. There is no evidence of a link between universities, vocational schools and market needs. In the case of investment institutions, as already noted, the findings suggest that Kosovo has a stable financial system, but that the cost of investment is significantly higher than in the comparator countries. The evidence for this is provided in Chapter 5.

Our examination of the firm-level social conditions suggests that the number of firms with innovation capabilities is very small (5.9%). This is the result of firms' external conditions and firm-level strategies and organizational integration factors. The analysis of the social conditions related to strategic control suggests that most innovative firms are multi-owned (at least 2 owners) and that firm ownership and firm management are separated. The small number of innovative firms tends to be owned by well-educated individuals and run by managers who receive regular training.

The analysis of organizational integration indicates that managing according to a formal business plan, readiness to take risks, collaboration with foreign business partners and ability to learn from market feedback are pivotal to business growth and firm innovation. It provided evidence that labour–management relationships could be much improved and that business targets are based predominantly on financial indicators. This contrasts with modern management practices, which use both financial and non-financial indicators. We found, also, that monitoring of job activities is ad hoc and reviews of workers' performance are infrequent. Finally, performance measures are ill-defined, complex and not clearly understood by those being evaluated.

In summary, organizational integration, as a precondition for innovative activity, suffers important weaknesses related to management practices. The findings for the third social condition, that is, investment conditions, show that these, also, are unfavourable. Kosovo lacks an equity market that could be a source of investment funds, and the cost of loans is high, with the result that firms rely mostly on internal financial resources.

The analysis to identify and assess the factors that enable or/and constrain firm growth in the less-developed economic setting of Kosovo, was based on a combination of different firm growth approaches and methodologies. Firm dynamics was used as an outcome variable in the research in this book. This approach was aimed at investigating the rate of firm churn in Kosovo and estimating firms' propensities to enter, survive and grow in the Kosovan context. The findings show that larger firms, limited liability firms, firm operating in the manufacturing and construction sectors and firms located in the capital of the country, have better chances of surviving and growing.

To understand the factors that are likely to affect firm growth, we employed the following approaches. A resource-based theory and managerial practices approach was applied to examine internal growth factors and a growth diagnostics methodology was used to investigate external factors. The social conditions of innovative enterprises in Kosovo were investigated using a method that combined parts of the first and second methodologies (i.e., uses some of the same variables) (see Fig. 8.1). However, the meaning of these variables differs in these different approaches. Growth diagnostics is concerned with the current state of the firm and not necessarily whether or not it is innovative or has the potential to grow. This approach assumes that the existence of a good infrastructure, good supply of and human capital, adequate public goods (rule of law, low levels of corruption, etc.), and easy access to reasonably priced finance will result in firm growth. Similarly, resource-based theory and managerial practices approach focuses on the internal factors that constitute a successful firm, and those factors that distinguish firms. However, neither of these approaches examines firm growth dynamically or investigates the factors that increase innovativeness.

The theory of the innovative enterprise is a more comprehensive approach. It focuses not on what enables or constrains current firm growth, but on what facilitates or hampers their long-term growth and,

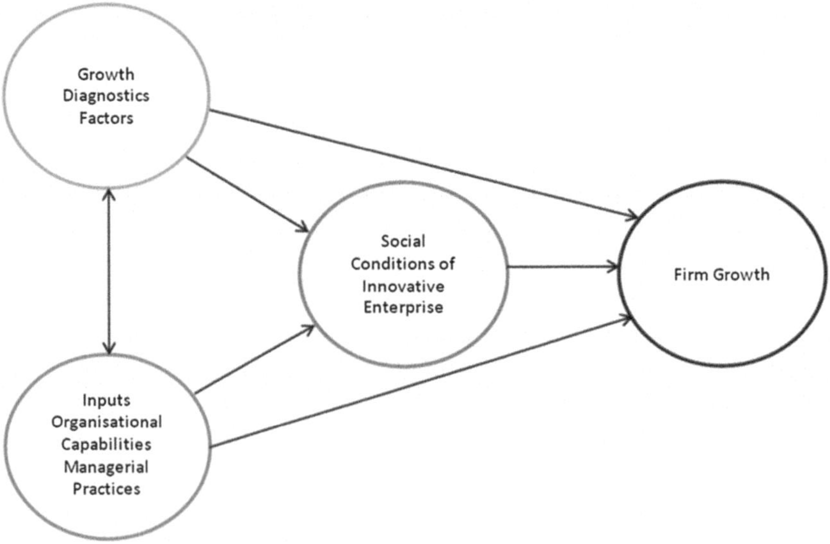

Fig. 8.1 The integration of three frameworks (*Source* Author)

particularly, what increases the capability for innovation. The theory of the innovative enterprise examines what facilitates the emergence of innovative firms, which are crucial for a prosperous economy. This approach lies somewhere between the organizational capabilities and managerial practices approaches, which focus on internal factors, and the growth diagnostics approach which focuses on external factors. The social and economic conditions are additional variables to those considered in the resource-based theory, managerial practices and growth diagnostics approaches. The variables included in the social conditions of innovative firm approach are complementary to the variables included in the other approaches.

The first conclusion that emerges from the results of this study is that firm growth in economic environments such as Kosovo cannot be explained only by the first or/and second dimensions. Firm growth is more complex and is a function of factors involved in all three theoretical frameworks. In other words, the outcomes show that the drivers of firm growth derive from the interaction between micro and macro factors. This is because firm growth is not an exclusively macro or micro issue, but is based on their interaction. Table 8.1 presents the factors associated most directly to business growth.

To summarize, the findings in this book suggest that firm growth in less-developed economies, such as Kosovo, is hampered by some specific constraints whose examination requires a particular approach. Conventional approaches focus on macro aspects (business environment factors) or micro aspects (internal factors). Firm growth cannot be assigned to one or other of these categories: it is based on the interaction among macro and micro issues. External factors, such as rule of law, cost of finance and appropriate human capital have an impact on firm growth. However, it cannot be assumed that if these conditions are favourable, firm growth will follow. The results indicate that successful firms are led by entrepreneurs with higher education and solid experience, who account of feedback from clients, are risk takers, apply better management practices, etc.

So how do change and growth occur? The conventional view would highlight the most important external constraints. However, the findings in this book suggest that firm-level factors are of equal if not higher

Table 8.1 Statistically significant variables obtained from three frameworks

Growth diagnostics	Social factors at national level	Organisational capabilties	Management practices
Unfair competition High level of corruption **Rule of law** **High cost of finance** Low level of human capital	**Implementation of adapted legal structures** Development of human capital **High cost of finance** **Social factors at firm-level:** Ownership structure Relationship between owners Power distribution **Formal education** **Management trainings** Business plan **Market as a source of learning** **Risk taking** Change of marketing strategy Collaboration with foreign partners	**Finding and keeping skilled labour** Introduction of new products Introduction of new manufacturing methods **Learning through customers** **Risk taking ability** Observing skills Changing based on market demand and customers' feedback **Implementation of internal trainings** Sharing experience among labours Selecting suppliers Recruiting skilled labour Assistance in obtaining loans and tax advices Customer satisfaction and retention Finding and keeping skilled labour	Performance tracking Performance dialog Consequence management Performance clarity and comparability Targets time horizon Targets stretching **Managing human capital** Removing poor performance Promoting high performers **Attracting human capital**

Source Author

importance; some are affected by external factors, others are entirely internal in nature. What is key is that growth and catch up require the emergence of innovative firms that are able to overcome the external constraints to growth by either internalizing or externalizing them. The success of such firms will help to change the existing business environment. The underlying assumption is that there is a co-evolutionary and mutual process between firm-level dynamics and the business environment.

8.3 Constraints and Future Research Programmes

The empirical evidence presented in this book provides important insights into the factors that enable or constrain firm growth in less-developed economic settings. They show that the drivers of firm growth are complex and cannot be reduced to either external or internal factors, but, rather, derive from interactions among them.

The analysis in this book has some limitations, which suggest directions for future research on this topic. Future research will depend on the availability of firm-level data to allow more thorough examination of firm growth factors.

One of the shortcomings of the research presented in this book is that it does not provide in depth study of the factors driving productivity growth in Kosovo. This would require productivity growth to be decomposed further, which would require more firm-level data. This would allow an examination of the interaction between newborn firms and exits of unproductive firms and how this affects the longevity of existing firms. By analysing the production factors that constitute the building blocks to productivity growth, it would be possible to deconstruct industry productivity to show the contributions made by continuing firms, new entrants and exiting firms (reallocation of resources). Each of these production factors is related to a specific source of productivity growth. Analysis of continuing firms would explain the productivity growth of incumbent firms, based on changes to their efficiency and the intensity of the inputs used for production, while an analysis of new entrants would explain the aggregate firm churn effect on total productivity growth. An investigation of the reallocation of resources would help to explain the gains deriving from high-productivity firms that acquire market share or low-productivity firms that lose market share (World Bank 2008). These issues should be part of a future research agenda; their investigation will depend on the availability of appropriate data.

A second research opportunity is related to analysis of a larger sample that includes different types of firms and data on inputs, organizational capabilities and managerial practices. A survey to collect these data could include the whole range of the firms operating in the market. To explore the profiles of the organizational capabilities and management practices (configurations) and identify those associated to high-growth firms might require qualitative comparative analysis to enhance the quality of the findings (Ragin 1987, 2000).

Finally, our investigation of the social and economic institutions that support or constrain the emergence of innovative firms was based on data not designed specifically for this purpose. A survey questionnaire based on semi-structured questions, would allow more comprehensive information gathered from owners and managers of wide range of firms. This would allow us to gather information on their tacit perceptions and understanding related to the social conditions of their daily business operations. For instance, interviews with owners and managers would provide more detailed information on the relationship between principals (owners) and agents (managers), the concentration of ownership (majority or minority owners), etc. Interviews would also allow the gathering of more detailed information on industrial relations and the interactions between managers and workers, which, in part, are specific to each country and in part are firm-specific, that is firms in similar institutional environment may have quite different intra-firm labour–management relations. Another way to improve the present study might be use of case studies. Qualitative data would provide better insights into how firms organize their industrial relations or interactions between managers and labour.

Thus, more work is needed to explore the enablers and constraints to firm growth in developing economies through a well-designed and specific survey that integrates the variables from all three of the frameworks used in the present work. That would enable a model to be proposed that might be more consistent and more comprehensive and, more importantly, might reduce the inconsistencies and other limitations related to the research in this book. A future research objective is the construction of a more consistent and comprehensive research programme, combining the approaches used in this study.

References

Bartelsman, E., Haltiwanger, J., & Scarpetta, S. (2009). Measuring and analyzing cross-country differences in firm dynamics. In T. Dunne, J. B. Jensen, & M. J. Roberts (Eds.), *Producer dynamics*. Chicago, IL: University of Chicago Press for the NBER.

De Soto, H. (1989). *The other path: The invisible revolution in the third world*. New York: Harper Row.

Geroski, P. A., Mata, J., & Portugal, P. (2012). Founding conditions and the survival of new firms. *Strategic Management Journal, 31*(5), 510–529.

Klapper, L., Amit, R., Guillén, M. F., & Quesada, J. M. (2008). *Entrepreneurship and firm formation across countries* (The World Bank Policy Research Working Paper 4313).

Naudé, W. A. (2010a). *Entrepreneurship and economic development*. Basingstoke: Palgrave Macmillan.

Naudé, W. A. (2010b). Entrepreneurship is not a binding constraint on growth and development in the poorest countries. *World Development, 39*(1), 33–44.

Ragin, C. C. (1987). *The comparative method. Moving beyond qualitative and quantitative strategies*. Berkeley: University of California Press.

Ragin, C. C. (2000). *Fuzzy-set social science*. Chicago and London: University of Chicago Press.

Stam, E., Audrutsch, D., & Meijaard, J. (2006). *Renascent entrepreneurship* (ERIM Report Series 17). Erasmus Research Institute Management, Erasmus University Rotterdam.

World Bank. (2008). Unleashing prosperity productivity growth in Eastern Europe and the former Soviet Union. http://siteresources.worldbank.org/ECAEXT/Resources/publications/UnleashingProsperity.pdf.

References

Acemoglu, D., Johnson, S., & Robinson, J. A. (2001). The colonial origins of comparative development: An empirical investigation. *American Economic Review, 91*(5), 1369–1401.

Acemoglu, D., Aghion, P., & Zilibotti, F. (2002). *Distance to frontier, selection, and economic growth* (NBER Working Paper No. 9066).

Aghion, P., & Howitt, P. (1998). *Endogenous growth theory*. Cambridge: MIT Press.

Aghion, P., Howitt, P., & Mayer-Foulkes, D. (2005). The effect of financial development on convergence: Theory and evidence. *Quarterly Journal of Economics, 120*(1), 173–222.

Aghion, P., Blundell, R., Bloom, N., Griffith, R., & Howitt, P. (2005). Competition and innovation: An inverted-U relationship. *Quarterly Journal of Economics, 120*(2), 701–728.

Aghion, P., Akcigit, U., & Howitt, P. (2014). What do we learn from Schumpeterian growth theory? In *Handbook of economic growth* (1st ed., Vol. 2, Chapter 1, pp. 515–563). Amsterdam: Elsevier.

Ahmad, N. (2008). A proposed framework for business demography statistics. In *Measuring Entrepreneurship*, Springer US, pp. 113–174.

Ahn, S. (2001). *Firm dynamics and productivity growth: A review of micro evidence from OECD countries* (OECD Economics Department Working Paper 297). Paris: OECD.

F. Sahiti, *The Growth of Firms in Less-Developed Countries*,
https://doi.org/10.1007/978-3-030-14821-8

Aidis, R., & Estrin, S. (2006). *Institutions, networks and entrepreneurship development in Russia: An exploration* (Discussion Paper 2161). Bonn: Institute for Study of Labour-IZA.

Aidis, R., & Mickiewicz, T. (2006). Entrepreneurs, expectations and business expansion: Lessons from Lithuania. *Europe-Asia Studies, 58,* 855–880.

Aidt, T. (2009). Corruption, institutions, and economic growth. *Oxford Review of Economic Policy, 25*(2), 271–291.

Aidt, T. (2011). Corruption and sustainable development. In S. Rose-Ackerman & T. Søreide (Eds.), *International handbook on the economics of corruption, volume 2.* Cheltenham, UK: Edward.

Almer-Jarz, D. A., Schwarz, E. J., & Breitenecher, B. J. (2008). New venture teams: The relationship between initial team characteristics, team processes and performance. In H. Landstrom, H. Crijns, E. Laveren, & D. Smallbone (Eds.), *Entrepreneurship sustainable growth and performance: Frontiers in European entrepreneurship research.* Cheltenham: Edward Elgar.

Almor, T. (2006). *Conceptualizing path of growth for the born global firms.* Paper Presented at the ACCS Annual Conference, Berlin.

Almor, T., & Hashai, N. (2004). Competitive advantage and strategic configuration of knowledge-intensive small and medium sized multinationals: A modified resource based view. *Journal of International Management, 10*(4), 479–500.

Amason, A. C., & Sapienza, H. J. (1997). The effects of top management team size and interaction norms on cognitive and affective conflict. *Journal of Management, 23,* 495–516.

Anderton, B. (1999). UK trade performance and the role of product quality, innovation and hysteresis: Some preliminary results. *Scottish Journal of Political Economy, 46,* 570–595.

Araujo, A., Rafael, V., & Funchal, B. (2012). The Brazilian bankruptcy law experience. *Journal of Corporate Finance, 18*(4), 994–1004.

Arbia, G., Cella, P., Espa, G., & Giuliani, D. (2015). A micro spatial analysis of firm demography: The case of food stores in the area of Trento (Italy). *Empirical Economics, 48*(3), 923–937.

Audretsch, D. B. (1995). Innovation, growth and survival. *International Journal of Industrial Organization, 13,* 441–457.

Audretsch, D. B., & Mahmood, T. (1994). The rate of hazard confronting new firms and plants in US manufacturing. *Review of Industrial Organization, 9,* 41–56.

Audretsch, D. B., Santarelli, E., & Vivarelli, M. (1999). Start-up and industrial dynamics: Some evidence from Italian manufacturing. *International Journal of Industrial Organization, 17,* 965–983.

Audretsch, D. B., Houweling, P., & Thurik, A. R. (2000). Firm survival in the Netherlands. *Review of Industrial Organization, 16,* 1–11.

Audretsch, D. B., Lehmann, E., & Warning, S. (2005). University spillovers and new firm location. *Research Policy, 34,* 1113–1122.

Audretsch, D. B., Belitski, M., & Desai, S. (2014, February 20–21). *Multidimensional business environment and entrepreneurship in European cities*. Paper Presented at the Conference: Doing Business: Past, Present and Future of Business Regulations, Washington, DC.

Austin, J. T., Yaffee, R. A., & Hinkle, D. E. (1992). Logistic regression for research in higher education. In *Handbook of theory and research* (Vol. 8, pp. 379–410). New York: Agathon Press.

Autio, E., Sapienza, H. J., & Almeida, J. G. (2000). Effects of age at entry, knowledge intensity, and imitability on international growth. *Academy of Management Journal, 43,* 909–924.

Ayyagari, M., Beck, T., & Demirgüç-Kunt, A. (2003). *Small and medium enterprises across the globe: A new database* (WPS3127). World Bank Publications.

Ayyagari M., Demirgüç-Kunt A., & Maksimovic, V. (2006). *How important are financing constraints? The role of finance in the business environment* (World Bank Policy Research Working Paper, WPS3820).

Ayyagari, M., Thorsten, B., & Demirgüç-Kunt, A. (2007). Small and medium Enterprises across the globe: A new database. *Small Business Economics, 29*(4), 415–434.

Ayyagari, M., Demirgüç-Kunt, A.,& Maksimovic, V. (2011). *Small vs. young firms across the world—Contribution to employment, job creation, and growth* (Policy Research Working Paper 5631). The World Bank Development Research Group.

Baldwin, J., Bian, L., Dupuy, R., & Galletly, G. (2000). *Failure rates of new Canadian firms: New perspectives on entry and exit.* Ottawa: Statistics Canada.

Banerjee, A. V., & Duflo, E. (2007). The economic lives of the poor. *Journal of Economic Perspectives, 21*(1), 141–167.

Bardhan, P. (1997). Corruption and development: A review of issues. *Journal of Economic Literature, 35,* 1320–1346.

Bardhan, P. (2005). *Scarcity, conflicts, and cooperation: Essays in political and institutional economics of development.* Cambridge: MIT Press.

Barney, J. B. (1991). Firm resources and sustained competitive advantage. *Journal of Management, 17,* 99–120.

Barney, J. B. (1995). Looking inside for competitive advantage. *Academy of Management Executive, 9*(4), 49–61.

Barney, J. B., Ketchen, D. J., & Wright, M. (2011). The future of resource-based theory: Revitalization or decline. *Journal of Management, 37*(5), 1299–1315.

Barr, H., Koppel, I., Reeves, S., Hammick, M., & Freeth, D. (2005). *Effective inter-professional education: Assumption, argument and evidence*. London: Blackwell.

Bartelsman, E. J., & Doms, M. (2000). Understanding productivity: Lessons from longitudinal microdata. *Journal of Economic Literature, 38,* 569–594.

Bartelsman, E., Haltiwanger, J., & Scarpetta, S. (2004). *Microeconomic evidence of creative destruction in industrial and developing countries* (The World Bank Policy Research Working Paper Series 3464).

Bartelsman, E., Haltiwanger, J., & Scarpetta, S. (2009). Measuring and Analyzing cross-country differences in firm dynamics. In T. Dunne, J. B. Jensen, & M. J. Roberts (Eds.), *Producer dynamics*. Chicago, IL: University of Chicago Press for the NBER.

Bartholomew, D., Knotts, M., & Moustaki, I. (2011). *Latent variable models and factor analysis: A unified approach* (3rd ed.). West Sussex, UK: Wiley.

Bartlett, M. S. (1954). A note on the multiplying factors for various x2 approximation. *Journal of the Royal Statistical Society, Series B16,* 296–298.

Bartlett, W. (1985). Social services and local democracy in Yugoslavia. *Community Development Journal, 20*(1), 18–23.

Bartlett, W., & Bukvic, B. (2001). Barriers to SME growth in Slovenia. *Most Economic Policy in Transition Economies, 11*(2), 177–195.

Bartlett, W., & Bukvič, V. (2002). What are the main barriers to SME growth and development in South-East Europe. In W. Bartlett, M. Bateman, & M. Vehovec (Eds.), *Small enterprise development in South-East Europe: Policies for sustainable growth* (pp. 17–38). Boston: Kluwer.

Baumol, W. J. (1990). Entrepreneurship: Productive, unproductive and destructive. *Journal of Political Economy, 98,* 893–921.

Baumol, W. J. (1993a). Formal entrepreneurship theory in economics: Existence and bounds. *Journal of Business Venturing, 3,* 197–210.

Baumol, W. J. (1993b). *Entrepreneurship, management, and the structure of payoffs*. Cambridge: MIT Press.

Baumol, W. J. (2002). *The free-market innovation machine: Analyzing the Growth miracle of capitalism*. Princeton: Princeton University Press.

Baysinger, B. D., & Hoskisson, R. E. (1989). Diversification strategy and R&D intensity in large multi-product firms. *Academy of Management Journal, 32,* 310–332.

Beaver, G. (2002). *Small business, entrepreneurship and enterprise development*. London: Pearson Education.

Becattini, G. (1990). The Marshallian industrial districts as a socio-economic notion. In F. Pyke, et al. (Eds.), *Industrial districts and inter-firm co-operation in Italy* (pp. 37–51). Geneva: International Institute for Labour Studies.

Bell, M., & Pavitt, K. (1993). Accumulating technological capability in developing countries. In *Proceedings of the World Bank Annual Conference on Development Economics 1992* (pp. 57–81). Washington, DC: World Bank.

Benhabib, J., & Spiegel, M. M. (1994). The role of human capital in economic development: Evidence from aggregate cross-country data. *Journal of Monetary Economics, 34*(2), 143–174.

Berglund, E., & Brännäs, K. (1996). Entry and exit of plants: A study based on Swedish panel count data for municipalities. In *Yearbook of the Finnish statistical society 1995* (pp. 95–111). Helsinki: Springer.

Berglund, E., & Brännäs, K. (2001). Plants' entry and exit in Swedish municipalities. *The Annals of Regional Studies, 35,* 431–448.

Bernard, A. B., & Jensen, J. B. (2001). *Why some firms export?* (NBER Working Paper No. 8349). Cambridge: National Bureau of Economic Research.

Bernard, A. B., & Sjöholm, F. (2003). *Foreign owners and plant survival* (NBER Working Paper No. 10039).

Berner, E., Gomez, G., & Knorringa, P. (2008). *Helping a large number of people becoming a little less poor: The logic of survival entrepreneurs.* UNU-WIDER Workshop on Entrepreneurship and Economic Development, Helsinki, Finland.

Bevan, A., & Estrin, S. (2004). The determinants of foreign direct investment into European transition economies. *Journal of Comparative Economics, 32*(4), 775–787.

Bharadwaj, S. G., Varadarajan, R. P., & Fahy, J. (1993). Sustainable competitive advantage in service industries: A conceptual model and research propositions. *Journal of Marketing, 57*(10), 83–99.

Birch, D. L. (1979). *The job generation process.* MIT Program on Neighborhood and Regional Change, Cambridge, MA (mimeo).

Birch, D. L. (1981). Who creates jobs? *The Public Interest, 65*, 3.

Bird, B. (1989). *Entrepreneurial behaviour*. Glenview, IL: Scott, Foresman.

Birkinshaw, J. (2003). The paradox of corporate entrepreneurship. *Strategy and Business, 30*, 46–57.

Bishop, J. H. (1991). *The impact of previous training in schools and on job on productivity, require OJT, and turnover of new hires* (Unpublished manuscript). Centre for Advanced Human Resource Studies, Cornell University (cited in Cappelli and Singh, 1992).

Bloom, N., & Van Reenen, J. (2007). Measuring and explaining management practices across firms and countries. *Quarterly Journal of Economics, 122*(4), 1351–1408.

Bloom, N., & Van Reenen, J. (2010). Why do management practices differ across firms and countries? *Journal of Economic Perspectives, 24*(1), 203–224.

Bloom, N., & Van Reenen, J. (2011). Human resource management and productivity. In O. Ashenfelter & D. Card (Eds.), *Handbook of labor economics, volume 4B* (Chapter 19, pp. 1697–1769). Amsterdam: Elsevier.

Bloom, N., Raffaella S., & Van Reenen, J. (2009a). *The organization of firms across countries* (National Bureau of Economic Research Working Paper Series No.15129). Retrieved from http://www.nber.org/papers/w15129.pdf.

Bloom, N., Sadun, R., & Van Reenen, J. (2009b). Do private equity-owned firms have better management practices? In A. Gurung & J. Lerner (Eds.), *The global economic impact of private equity report 2009* (pp. 1–23). Geneva, Switzerland: World Economic Forum. Available from http://www.weforum.org/pdf/cgi/pe/Full_Report2.pdf.

Bloom, N., Schweiger, H., & Van Reenen, J. (2011). *The land that lean manufacturing forgot? Management practices in transition countries* (National Bureau of Economic Research Working Paper Series No. 17231). Cambridge: National Bureau of Economic Research.

Bloom, N., Genakos, C., Sadun, R., & Van Reenen, J. (2012). Management practices across firms and countries. *The Academy of Management Perspectives, 26,* 12–33.

Bloom, N., Sadun, R., & Van Reenen, J. (2016). *Management as a technology* (NBER Working Paper No. 22327).

Bohata, M., & Mladek, J. (1999). The development of the Czech SME sector. *Journal of Business Venturing, 14*(5), 461–473.

Bosma, N. S., Jones, K., Autio, E., & Levie, J. (2008). *Global entrepreneurship monitor 2007 executive report.* London: Global Entrepreneurship Research Association.

Bouchard, V. (2001). *Exploring corporate entrepreneurship: A corporate strategy perspective.* Paper presented at the European Entrepreneurial Learning Conference.

Box, T. M., White, M. A., & Barr, S. H. (1993). A contingency model of new manufacturing firm performance. *Entrepreneurship Theory and Practice, 18*(2), 31–45.

Bratkowski, A., Grosfeld, I., & Rostowski, J. (2000). Investment and finance in de novo private firms: Empirical evidence from the Czech Republic, Hungary and Poland. *Economics of Transition, 8*(1), 101–116.

Bresciani, S., Thrassou, A., & Vrontis, D. (2013). Change through innovation in family businesses: Evidence from an Italian sample. *World Review of Entrepreneurship, Management and Sustainable Development, 9*(2), 195–215.

Bripi, F. (2013). *The role of regulations on entry: Evidence from the Italian provinces* (Working Paper 932, B). Rome.

Brock, W., Durlauf, S., & West, K. (2003). *Policy evaluation in uncertain economic environments* (NBER Working Papers No. W10025).

Brown, J. D., & Earle, J. S. (2008). *Understanding the contributions of reallocation to productivity growth: Lessons from a comparative firm-level analysis* (Upjohn Institute Staff Working Paper, No. 08-141).

Brown, M. E., Trevino, L. K., & Harrison, D. A. (2005). Ethical leadership: A social learning perspective for construct development and testing. *Organizational Behaviour and Human Decision Processes, 97,* 117–134.

Brown, J., Earle, S., & Telegdy, A. (2006). The productivity effects of privatization: Longitudinal estimates from Hungary, Romania, Russia, and Ukraine. *Journal of Political Economy, 114*(1), 61–99.

Brüderl, J., & Schussler, R. (1990). Organizational mortality: The liabilities of newness and adolescence. *Administrative Science Quarterly, 35,* 530–547.

Bruderl, J., Preisendorfer, P., & Ziegler, R. (1992). Survival chances of newly founded business organizations. *American Sociological Review, 57*(2), 227–242.

Brunetti, A., Gregory, K., & Weder, B. (1997). *Institutional obstacles to doing business: Region-by-region results from a worldwide survey of the private sector* (World Bank PRD Working Paper 1759).

Brunswicker, S., & Vanhaverbeke, W. (2011). Beyond open innovation in large enterprises: How do small and medium-sized enterprises (SMEs) open up to external innovation sources? https://papers.ssrn.com/sol3/papers.cfm?abstract_id=1925185.

Brush, C. G., & Hisrish, R. D. (1991). Antecedent influences on women-owned businesses. *Journal of Management Psychology, 6*(2), 9–16.

BSCK. (2012). *Entrepreneurship and small business development in Kosovo: Research report.* http://www.bsckosovo.org/publikimet/20121108044632244.pdf.

Burstein, A., & Monge-Naranjo, A. (2009). Foreign know-how, firm control, and the income of developing countries. *Quarterly Journal of Economics, 124*(1), 149–195.

Caballero, R. (2006). *The macroeconomics of specificity and restructuring.* Cambridge: The MIT Press.

Cabrera, A. F. (1994). Logistic regression analysis in higher education: An applied perspective. In *Higher education: Handbook of theory and research* (Vol. 10, pp. 225–256). New York: Agathon Press.

Calderón, C., & Servén L. (2004). *The effects of infrastructure development on growth and income distribution* (Working Papers No. 270). Central Bank of Chile.

Cantwell, J. A. (2000). A survey of theories of international production. In C. N. Pitelis & R. Sugden (Eds.), *The nature of the transnational firm* (pp. 10–56). London: Routledge.

Cao, M., & Zhang, Q. (2011). Supply chain collaboration: Impact on collaborative advantage and firm performance. *Journal of Operations Management, 29*(3), 163–180.

Capron, L., & Hulland, J. (1999). Redeployment of brands, sales forces, and general marketing management expertise following horizontal acquisitions: A resource-based view. *Journal of Marketing, 63*(2), 41–54.

Carlin, W., & Seabright, P. (2007). *Bring me sunshine: Which parts of the business climate should public policy try to fix?* (Unpublished manuscript). Available at http://www.worldbank.org.

Carlin, W., Schaffer, M., & Seabright, P. (2006). *Where are the real bottlenecks? A Lagrangian approach to identifying constraints on growth from subjective survey data* (CEPR Discussion Paper 5719).

Carlino, G., & Hunt, R. (2009). What explains the quantity and quality of local inventive activity? In G. Burtless & J. R. Pack (Eds.), *Brookings-Wharton papers on urban affairs*. Washington, DC: Brookings Institution Press.

Carter, N. M., William, B., Gatwoood, E. J., & Shaver, K. G. (2003). The career reasons of nascent entrepreneurs. *Journal of Business Venturing, 18*(1), 13–39.

Castanias, R. P., & Helfat, C. E. (1991). Managerial resources and rents. *Journal of Management, 17*(1), 155–177.

Caves, R. E. (1998). Industrial organization and new findings on the turnover and mobility of firms. *Journal of Economic Literature, 36*(4), 1947–1982.

Central Bank of Kosovo. (2017). *Annual report 2017*. Retrieved from https://bqk-kos.org/repository/docs/2018/CBK_AR_2017.pdf.

Chatterji, A., Glaeser, E. L., & Kerr, W. R. (2013). *Clusters of entrepreneurship and innovation* (NBER Working Paper Series No. 19013). Cambridge, MA: National Bureau of Economic Research. www.nber.org/papers/w19013.pdf.

Child, D. (2006). *The essentials of factor analysis* (3rd ed.). New York, NY: Continuum International Publishing Group.

Chilosi, A. (2001). Entrepreneurship and transition. *Economic Policy in Transitional Economies, 11*(4), 327–357.

Cirmizi, E., Klapper, L., & Uttamchandani, M. (2010). *The challenges of bankruptcy reform* (Policy Research Working Paper 5448). Washington, DC: World Bank.

Classen, N., Van Gils, A., Bammens, Y., & Carree, M. (2012). Accessing resources from innovation partners: The search breadth of family SMEs. *Journal of Small Business Management, 50*(2), 191–215.

Clement, K., Wang, K., & Ang, B. (2004). Determinants of venture performance in Singapore. *Journal of Small Business Management, 42*(4), 347–363.

Coase, R. H. (1937). The nature of the firm. *Economica, 4,* 386–405.

Coff, R., & Kryscynski, D. (2011). Drilling for microfoundations of human capital-based competitive advantage. *Journal of Management, 37*(5), 1429–1443.

Collier, D. (1998). Comparative method in the 1990s. *American Political Science Association–Comparative, 9*(1), 1–2, 4–5.

Collis, D. J. (1994). Research note: How valuable are organizational capabilities? *Strategic Management Journal, 15,* 143–152.

Collis, D. J., & Montgomery, C. A. (1995). Competing on resources: Strategy in the 1990s. *Harvard Business Review, 73*(4), 118–128.

Commander, S., & Svejnar, J. (2007). *Do institutions, ownership, exporting and competition explain firm performance. Evidence from 26 transition countries* (Discussion Paper 2637). Institute for the Study of Labour (IZA).

Cooney, R. (2010). Exploring skill ecosystems in the Australian meat processing industry: Unions, employers and institutional change. *Economic and Labour Relations Review, 21*(2), 121–138.

Cooper, A. C. (1981). Strategic management: New ventures and business performance. *Long Range Planning, 14*(5), 39–45.

Covin, J. G., & Slevin, D. P. (1988). The influence of organization structure on the utility of an entrepreneurial top management style. *Journal of Management Studies, 25,* 217–234.

Cox, D. R. (1975). Partial likelihood. *Biometrica, 60,* 269–276.

Criscuolo, C., Gal, P. N., & Menon, C. (2014). *The dynamics of employment growth: New evidence from 18 countries* (OECD Science, Technology and Industry Policy Papers No. 14). Paris: OECD Publishing. https://doi.org/10.1787/5jz417hj6hg6-e.

Čučković, N., & Bartlett, W. (2007). Entrepreneurship and competitiveness: The Europeanization of small and medium-sized enterprise policy in Croatia. *Southeast European and Black Sea Studies, 7*(1), 37–56.

Cummings, T. G. (1981). Self-regulating work groups: A sociotechnical synthesis. *Academy of Management Review, 3*(3), 625–634.

Dallago, B., & Uvalic, M. (1998). The distributive consequences of nationalism: The case of former Yugoslavia. *Europe-Asia Studies, 50*(1), 519–543.

Davidsson, P., & Honig, B. (2003). The role of social and human capital among nascent entrepreneurs. *Journal of Business Venturing, 18,* 301–331.

Day, G. S. (1994). The capabilities of market driven organizations. *Journal of Marketing, 58*, 37–52.

Day, D. V. (2000). Leadership development: A review in context. *Leadership Quarterly, 11*, 581–613.

De Kok, J. M. P., Vroonhof, P., Verhoeven, W., Timmermans, N., Kwaak, T., Snijders, J., et al. (2011). *Do SMEs create more and better jobs?* Report prepared by EIM for the European Commission DG Enterprise and Industry, Brussels.

De Soto, H. (1989). *The other path: The invisible revolution in the third world.* New York: Harper Row.

De Soto, H. (2000). *The mystery of capital: Why capitalism triumphs in the west and fails everywhere else.* New York: Harper & Row.

Delgado, M., Porter, M. E., & Stern, S. (2010). Clusters and entrepreneurship. *Journal of Economic Geography, 10*(4), 495–518.

Delgado, M., Porter, M. E., & Stern, S. (2014). Clusters, convergence, and economic performance. *Research Policy, 43*(10), 1785–1799. https://doi.org/10.1016/j.respol.2014.05.007.

Deshpande, R., Farley, J. U., & Webster, F. E., Jr. (1993). Corporate culture, customer orientation, and innovativeness in Japanese firms: A quadrad analysis. *Journal of Marketing, 57*(1), 23–37.

Dierickx, I., & Cool, K. (1989). Asset stock accumulation and sustainability of competitive advantage. *Management Science, 35*(12), 1504–1511.

DiMatteo, L., & Rich, B. (2006). A consent theory of unconscionability: An empirical study of law in action. *Florida University Law Review, 33*, 1067–1118.

Djankov, S., La Porta, R., Lopez-de-Silanes, F., & Shleifer, A. (2003). Courts. *Quarterly Journal of Economics, 118*, 453–518.

Djankov S., La Porta R., Lopez-de-Silanes F., & Shleifer, A. (2006). *The law and economics of self-dealing* (Working Paper). World Bank.

Djankov, S., Hart, O., McLiesh, C., & A, Shleifer. (2008). Debt enforcement around the world. *Journal of Political Economy, 116*(6), 1105–1149.

Dollar, D., Hallward-Driemeier, M., & Mengistae, T. (2005). Investment climate and firm performance in developing economies. *Economic Development and Cultural Change, 54*, 1–31.

Down, S. (1999). Owner-manager learning in small firms. *Journal of Small Business and Enterprise Development, 6*(3), 267–280.

Drucker, P. F. (1993). *Postcapitalist society.* New York: HarperCollins Publishers.

Dunne, T., Roberts, M., & Samuelson, L. (1988). Patterns of firm entry and exit in US manufacturing industries. *Journal of Economics, 19*(4), 495–515.

Dunne, T., Klimek, S., & Roberts, M. J. (2005). Exit from regional manufacturing markets: The role of entrant experience. *International Journal of Industrial Organization, 23,* 399–421.

Duranton, G., & Diego, P. (2001). Nursery cities: Urban diversity, process innovation, and the life cycle of products. *American Economic Review, 91*(5), 1454–1477.

Dutrénit, G. (2004). Building technological capabilities in latecomer firms: A review essay. *Science, Technology and Society, 9*(2), 209–241.

EBRD. (2013). *Commercial Laws of Kosovo.* An assessment by EBRD. http://www.ebrd.com/downloads/sector/legal/kosovo.pdf. Accessed 22 March 2014.

Edwards, C. (2009). Freedom of contract and fundamental fairness for individual parties: The tug of war continues. *University of Kentucky Law Review, 77,* 569–646.

Eisenhardt, K. M., & Martin, J. A. (2000). Dynamic capabilities: what are they? *Strategic Management Journal, 21*(10–11), 1105–1121. Special Issue.

EIU—Economist Intelligence Unit. (2010). SMEs in Japan: A new growth driver. *The Economist.* http://viewswire.eiu.com/report_dl.asp?-mode=fi&fi=1227698307.PDF.

Ericson, R., & Pakes, A. (1989). *An alternative theory of firm and industry dynamics* (Discussion Paper No. 445). New York: Columbia University.

Ericson, R., & Pakes, A. (1995). Markov-perfect industry dynamics: A framework for empirical work. *The Review of Economic Studies, 62*(1), 53–82.

Estrin, S., Hanousek, J., Kočenda, E., & Svejnar, J. (2009). Effects of privatization and ownership in transition economies. *Journal of Economic Literature, 47*(3), 699–728.

European Commission. (2006, February). *Communication from the Commission to the Council, the European Parliament, the European Economic and Social Committee and the Committee of the Regions—Implementing the Community Lisbon Programme: Fostering entrepreneurial mindsets through education and learning.* Brussels: European Commission.

European Commission (EC). (2010). *Internationalisation of European SMEs.* Directorate-General for Enterprise and Industry, Brussels [Online]. http://www.ec.europa.eu/enterprise/policies/sme/market-access/files/internationalisation_of_european_smes_final_en.pdf. Accessed 12 July 2012.

European Commission. (2012). *Entrepreneurship in the EU and beyond.* Flesh Eurobarometer 354, European Commission, Brussels. http://ec.europa.eu/public_opinion/flesh/fl_354_en.pdf.

European Commission. (2018). *Kosovo 2018 report.* Commission staff Working Document. Strasburg. https://ec.europa.eu/neighbourhood-enlargement/sites/near/files/20180417-kosovo-report.pdf.

European Commission and the World Bank. (1999, November 3). *Toward stability and prosperity*. Pristina. https://reliefweb.int/sites/reliefweb.int/files/resources/7DC58861A1B9C11685256824006EE9FF-ecwb-kosovo.pdf.

Eurostat. (2014). *Patent statistics at Eurostat. Mapping the contribution of SMEs in EU patenting*. Eurostat Manuals and Guidelines, Luxembourg. http://ec.europa.eu/eurostat/documents/3859598/6064260/KS-GQ-14-009-EN-N.pdf/caa6f467-11f8-43f9-ba76-eb3ccb6fab6d.

Eurostat/OECD. (2008). *Manual on business demography statistics*. http://ec.europa.eu/eurostat/ramon/statmanuals/files/KS-RA-07-010-EN.pdf.

Feldman, D. C., & Bolino, M. C. (2000). Career patterns of the self-employed: Career motivations and career outcomes. *Journal of Small Business Management, 38*(3), 53–67.

Felipe, J., & Usui, N. (2008). *Rethinking the growth diagnostics approach: Questions from the practitioners*. Asian Development Bank. Version of February, 2008.

Fernández-Arias, E. (2008). *Living with debt: How to limit the risks of sovereign finance*. Inter-American Development Bank.

Fichman, M., & Levinthal, D. (1991). Honeymoons and the liability of adolescence: A new perspective on duration dependence in social and organizational relationships. *Academy of Management Review, 16*, 442–468.

Filatotchev, I., & Mickiewicz, T. (2006). Private benefits of control and debt financing. In T. Mickiewicz (Ed.), *Corporate governance and finance in Poland and Russia* (pp. 159–176). Houndmills: Palgrave Macmillan.

Forum 2015. (2008). *Privatization and post-privatization in Kosova: Glass half empty of half full?* Pristina: Riinvest Institute.

Forum 2015. (2009). *Dilemmas and backwards in a fast track: Privatization of POEs in Kosovo*. Pristina. http://kfos.org/wp-content/uploads/2011/10/Privatization_ENG.pdf.

Foss, N. J., Klein, P. G., Kor, Y. Y., & Mahoney, J. T. (2008). Entrepreneurship, subjectivism, and the resource based view: Toward a new synthesis. *Strategic Entrepreneurship Journal, 2*, 73–94.

Foster, L., Haltiwanger, J., & Krizan, C. J. (2001). Aggregate productivity growth: Lessons from microeconomic evidence. In E. Dean, M. Harper, & C. Hulteneds (Eds.), *New developments in productivity analysis*. Chicago: University of Chicago Press.

Foster, L., Haltiwanger, J., & Krizan C. J. (2002). *The link between aggregate and micro productivity growth: Evidence from retail trade* (NBER Working Paper).

Fotopoulos, G., & Louri, H. (2000). Location and survival of new entry. *Small Business Economics, 14*(4), 311–321.

Fowler, S. W., Wilcox King, A., Marsh, S. W., & Victor, B. (2000). Beyond products: New strategic imperatives for developing competencies in dynamic environments. *Journal of Engineering and Technology Management, 17*(3–4), 357–377.

Freel, M. S. (2005). Patterns of innovation and skills in small firms. *Technovation, 25*(4), 123–134.

Freeman, C. (1997). Success and failure in industrial innovation. In C. Freeman & L. Soete (Eds.), *Economics of industrial innovation* (pp. 198–226). Cambridge: MIT Press.

Freeman, J., Styles, C., & Lawley, M. (2012). Does firm location make a difference to the export performance of SMEs? *International Marketing Review, 29*(1), 88–113.

Friebel, G., & Schweiger, H. (2012). *Management quality, firm performance, and market pressure in Russia* (European Bank for Reconstruction and Development Working Papers, 144), pp. 1–29.

Fritsch, M. (2008). How does new business formation affect regional development? Introduction to the special issue. *Small Business Economics, 30*(1), 1–14.

Fritsch, M., & Aamoucke, R. (2013). Regional public research, higher education, and innovative start-ups: An empirical investigation. *Small Business Economics, 41*(4), 865–885.

Fritsch, M., & Mueller, P. (2004). The effects of new business formation on regional development over time. *Regional Studies, 38*(8), 961–975.

Geroski, PA. (1995). What do we know about entry? *International Journal of Industrial Organization, 13,* 421–440.

Geroski, P. A., Mata, J., & Portugal, P. (2012). Founding conditions and the survival of new firms. *Strategic Management Journal, 31*(5), 510–529.

Giavazzi, F., & Tabellini, G. (2004). *Economic and political liberalizations* (NBER Working Paper No. 10657).

Glaeser, E. L., LaPorta, R., Lopez-de-Silanes, F., & Shleifer, A. (2004). Do institutions cause growth? *Journal of Economic Growth, 9*(3), 271–303.

Glaeser, E. L., Kerr, W. R., & Ponzetto, G. A. (2010). Clusters of entrepreneurship. *Journal of Urban Economics, 67*(1), 150–168.

Golovko, E., & Valentini, G. (2011). Exploring the complementarity between innovation and export for SMEs' growth. *Journal of International Business Studies, 42*(3), 362–380.

Görg, H., & Strobl, E. (2003). Multinational companies, technology spillovers and plant survival. *Scandinavian Journal of Economics, 4*(12), 581–953.

Gort, M., & Klepper, S. (1982). Time paths in the diffusion of product innovations. *Economics Journal, 92*(3), 153–158.

Grant, R. M. (1991). The resource-based theory of competitive advantage: Implications for strategy formulation. *California Management Review, 33*(3), 114–135.

Grant, R. M. (1996). Toward a knowledge-based theory of the firm. *Strategic Management Journal, 17,* 109–122.

Grant, R. M. (2002). *Contemporary strategy analysis: Concepts, techniques, applications* (4th ed.). Maiden, MA: Blackwell.

Greenbank, P. (2000). Training micro-business owner-managers: A challenge to current approaches. *Journal of European Industrial Training, 24*(7), 403.

Greene, F. J., Mole, K. F., & Storey, D. J. (2004). Does more mean worse? Three decades of enterprise policy in the Tees Valley. *Urban Studies, 41*(7), 1207–1228.

Greenwald, B. (2004). The good life: How managers made the modern world. *Hermes*. Retrieved from 18 March 2008, http://www2.gsb.columbia.edu/hermes/winter2004/article_greenwald.cfm.

Griffith, R., Redding, S., & Van Reenen, J. (2004). Mapping the two faces of R&D: Productivity growth in a panel of OECD industries. *Review of Economics and Statistics, 86*(4), 883–895.

Gruber, M. (2007). Uncovering the value of planning in new venture creation: A process and contingency perspective. *Journal of Business Venturing, 22*(6), 782–807.

Grunert, K. G., Jensen, B. B., Sonne, A. M., Brunsø, K., Byrne, D. V., Clausen, C., et al. (2008). User-oriented innovation in the food sector: relevant streams of research and an agenda or future work. *Trends in Food Science and Technology, 19,* 590–602.

Guiso, L., & Schivardi, F. (2011). What determines entrepreneurial clusters? *Journal of the European Economic Association, 9*(1), 61–86.

Gust-Bardon, N. I. (2014). Regional development in the context of an innovation processes. *International Journal of Innovation and Regional Development, 5*(4/5), 349–366.

Hallak, J. (2006). Product quality and the direction of trade. *Journal of International Economics, 68*(1), 238–265.

Haltiwanger, J., Ron, J., & Miranda, J. (2010). *Who creates jobs? Small vs. large vs. young* (Working Paper No. 16300). Cambridge, MA: NBER.

Harman, H. H. (1976). *Modern factor analysis* (3rd ed. Revised). Chicago, IL: University of Chicago Press.

Harris, R., & Trainor, M. (1995). Innovations and R&D in Northern Ireland manufacturing: A Schumpeterian approach. *Regional Studies, 29*(7), 593–604.

Hashi, I. (2001). Financial and institutional barriers to SME growth in Albania: Results of an enterprise survey. *MOST: Economic Policy in Transitional Economies, 11*(3), 221–238.

Hashi, I., & Stojcic, N. (2010). The impact of innovation activities on firm performance using a multi-stage model: Evidence from the Community Innovation Survey 4. *Research Policy, 42*(4), 353–366.

Hashi, I., & Krasniqi, B. (2011). Entrepreneurship and SME growth in transition: Evidence from advanced and laggard transition economies. *International Journal of Entrepreneurial Behaviour & Research, 17*(5), 456–487.

Hausmann, R. (2005). *Tanzania comments. Growth path workshop* (pp. 1–2). Washington, DC: The World Bank.

Hausmann, R., & Rodrik, D. (2005). *Self-discovery in a development strategy for El Salvador.* Brainstorming on Growth Analysis Methodology (GAM). Washington, DC: Inter-American Development Bank.

Hausmann, R., & Klinger, B. (2007). *Growth diagnostic: Belize.* Cambridge: Centre for International Development.

Hausmann, R., Rodrik, D., & Velasco, A. (2005). *Growth diagnostics.* Harvard University (mimeo).

Hausmann, R., Klinger, B., & Wagner, R. (2008). *Doing Growth diagnostics in practice: A mindbook* (Working Paper 177). Harvard University Centre for International Development .

He, Z. L., & Wong, P. K. (2012). Reaching out and reaching within: A study of the relationship between innovation collaboration and innovation performance. *Industry and Innovation, 19*(7), 539–561.

Helfat, C. E. (1994). Firm specificity in corporate applied R&D. *Organization Science, 5*(2), 173–184.

Helfat, C. E., & Lieberman, M. B. (2002). The birth of capabilities: Market entry and the importance of pre-history. *Industrial and Corporate Change, 11*(4), 725–760.

Helfat, C., & Peteraf, M. (2003). The dynamic resource-based view: Capability lifecycles. *Strategic Management Journal, 24*(10), 997–1010.

Helfat, C., Finkelstein, S., Mitchell, W., Peteraf, M., Singh, H., Teece, D., & Winter, S. (2007). *Dynamic capabilities: Understanding strategic change in organisations.* Malden: Blackwell Publishing.

Helpman, E., Marc, J., & Stephen, R. (2004). Export versus FDI with heterogeneous firms. *American Economic Review, 94*(1), 300–316.

Herrmann, A. M., & Peine, A. (2011). When 'national innovation system' meet 'varieties of capitalism' arguments on labour qualifications: On the skill types and scientific knowledge needed for radical and incremental product innovations. *Research Policy, 40*(5), 687–701.

Hethy, L. (2002). Labour law for Kosovo South East Europe. *Review for Labour and Social Affairs, 5*(3), 65–77.

Hewitt-Dundas, N., & Roper, S. (2009). Output additionality of public support for innovation: Evidence for Irish manufacturing plants. *European Planning Studies, 18*(1), 107–122.

Hitt, M. A., & Ireland, R. D. (1985). Corporate distinctive competence, strategy, industry and performance. *Strategic Management Journal, 6*(3), 273–293.

Hitt, M. A., Bierman, L., Shimizu, K., & Kochhar, R. (2001). Direct and moderating effects of human capital onstrategy and performance in professional service firms: A resource-based perspective. *Academy of Management Journal, 44,* 13–28.

Holmes, P., Stone, I., & Braidford, P. (2000). New firm survival: An analysis of UK firms using hazard function. In *Proceedings: The Royal Economic Society 2000 Conference.* St Andrews, Scotland: University of St Andrews.

Hosmer, D. W., Jr., & Lemeshow, S. (2000). *Applied logistic regression* (2nd ed.). New York: Wiley.

Hoti, A. (2004). *Human capital and unemployment in transition: The case of Kosova*. Pristina: Riinvest.

Hoti, A. (2011). Returns for education in Kosovo: Estimates of wage and employment premia. *South East European Journal of Economics and Business, 6*(1), 71–84.

Howitt, P. (2000). Endogenous growth and cross-country income differences. *American Economic Review, 90,* 829–846.

Howitt, P., & Mayer-Foulkes, D. (2005). R&D, implementation and stagnation: A Schumpeterian theory of convergence clubs. *Journal of Money, Credit and Banking, 37,* 147–177.

Hoxha, D. (2009). The performance of micro firms in Kosova: Size, age and educational implications. *International Journal of Globalisation and Small Business, 3*(1). https://doi.org/10.1504/ijgsb.2009.021568.

Hsu, D. H. (2004). What do entrepreneurs pay for venture capital affiliation? *Journal of Finance, 59,* 1805–1844.

IFC. (2010). *The SME banking knowledge guide*. Washington, DC: IFC.

IFC. (2013). *IFC jobs study: Assessing private sector contributions to job creation and poverty reduction*. Washington, DC: IFC.

IMF. (2018). *Republic of Kosovo: Selected issues* (IMF Country Report No. 18/31).

Jacobides, M. G., & Winter, S. G. (2005). The co-evolution of capabilities and transaction costs: Explaining the institutional structure of production. *Strategic Management Journal, 26*(5), 395–413.

Janz, B. D., Colquitt, J. A., & Noe, R. A. (1997). Knowledge worker team effectiveness: The role of autonomy, interdependence, team development, and contextual support variables. *Personnel Psychology, 50,* 877–904.

Jaworski, B. J., & Kohli, A. K. (1993). Market orientation: Antecedents and consequences. *Journal of Marketing, 57*(3), 53–70.

Jenkins, S. P. (2005). *Survival Analysis* (Unpublished manuscript). Institute for Social Science and Economic Research, University of Essex, Colchester.

Johnson, S., Kaufmann, D., McMillan, J., & Woodruff, C. (2000). Why do firms hide? Bribes and unofficial activity after communism. *Journal of Public Economics, 76*(3), 495–520.

Jones, M. V. (2001). First steps in internationalisation: Concepts and evidence from a sample of small high-technology firms. *Journal of International Management, 7*(3), 191–210.

Jovanovic, B. (1982). Selection and the evolution of industry. *Econometrica, 50*(3), 649–670.

Jovanovic, B., & MacDonald, G. (1994). The life cycle of a competitive industry. *Journal of Political Economy, 102*(2), 322–347.

Kaiser, H. (1970). A second generation Little Jiffy. *Psychometrika, 35,* 401–415.

Kaiser, H. (1974). An index of factorial simplicity. *Psychometrika, 39,* 31–36.

Kalbfleisch, J. D., & Prentice, R. L. (1980). *The statistical analysis of failure time data.* New York: Wiley.

Kanter, R. M. (2000). When a thousand flowers bloom: Structural, collective, and social conditions for innovation in organizations. In B. Staw & R. Sutton (Eds.), *Research in organizational behavior* (Vol. 22). Amsterdam, The Netherlands: Elsevier Science.

Kara, A., Lonial, S., Tarım, M., & Zaim, S. (2005). A paradox of service quality in Turkey: The seemingly contradictory relative importance of tangible and intangible determinants of service quality. *European Business Review, 17,* 5–20.

Kaufmann, D., Aart, K., & Mastruzzi, M. (2007). *Governance matters VI: Aggregate and individual governance indicators for 1996–2006* (World Bank Policy Research Working Paper No. 4280). Washington, DC.

Kelliher, F., & Henderson, J. B. (2006). A learning framework for the small business environment. *Journal of European Industrial Training, 30*(7), 512–528.

Keupp, M. M., Palmié, M., & Gassmann, O. (2012). The strategic management of innovation: A systematic review and paths for future research. *International Journal of Management Reviews, 14*(4), 367–390.

Kim, L. (1997). *Imitation to innovation. The dynamics of Korea's technological learning*. Boston: Harvard Business School Press.

Klapper, L., & Love, I. (2011). The impact of the financial crisis on new firm registration. *Economics Letters, 113*, 1–4.

Klapper, L., & Richmond, C. (2009). *Patterns of business creation, survival, and growth: Evidence from a developing country*. Development Research Group, World Bank, Washington, DC and Anderson School of Management, University of California, Los Angeles.

Klapper, L., Laeven, L., & Rajan, R. (2004). *Business environment and firm entry: Evidence from international data* (Working Paper No. 10380). Cambridge, MA: NBER.

Klapper, L., Amit, R., Guillén, M. F., & Quesada, J. M. (2008). *Entrepreneurship and firm formation across countries* (The World Bank Policy Research Working Paper 4313).

Klepper, S. (2001). Employee start-ups in high-tech industries. *Industrial and Corporate Change, 10*, 639–674.

Klepper, S., & Simons K. L. (1993). *Technological change and industry shakeouts*. Carnegie Mellon University (mimeo).

Kline, P. (1994). *An easy guide to factor analysis*. New York, NY: Routledge.

Knight, G. A. (1997). Cross-cultural reliability and validity of a scale to measure firm entrepreneurial orientation. *Journal of Business Venturing, 12*(3), 213–225.

Koch, M. J., & McGrath, R. G. (1996). Improving labour productivity: Human resource management policies do matter. *Strategic Management Journal, 17*, 335–354.

Kogut, B., & Zander, U. (1996). What firms do? Coordination, identify, and learning. *Organization Science, 7*, 502–518.

Kosovo Statistics Agency (KSA). (2015). *Statistical yearbook of the Republic of Kosovo*. Pristina. http://ask.rks-gov.net/media/1303/statistical-yearbook-of-the-republic-of-kosovo-2015-08102015.pdf.

Kosovo Trust Agency (KTA). (2004). *Draft strategy of the privatisation department of the Kosovo Trust Agency*. https://www.esiweb.org/pdf/bridges/kosovo/11/1.pdf.

Kostoff, R. N. (2003). Stimulating innovation. In L. V. Shavinina (Eds.), *The international handbook on innovation* (pp. 388–400). London: Pergamon.

Kotler, A. (2004). *Principles of marketing*. Hoboken, NJ: Pearson Education.

Kraiser, H. (1958). The varimax criterion for analytic rotation in factor analysis. *Psychometrika, 23,* 187–200.

Krasniqi, B. (2007). Barriers to entrepreneurship and SME growth in transition: Case of Kosova. *Journal of Developmental Entrepreneurship, 12*(1), 71–94.

Krasniqi, B. (2012). Building an expanded small firm growth model in a transitional economy: Evidence on fast growing firms. *Journal of East West Business, 18*(3), 231–273.

Kreiser, P. M., Marino, L. D., & Weaver, K. M. (2002). Assessing the psychometric properties of the entrepreneurial orientation scale: A multi-country analysis. *Entrepreneurship Theory and Practice, 26,* 71–94.

Krugman, P. (1991). Increasing returns and economic geography. *Journal of Political Economy, 99*(3), 483–499.

Kuntchev, V. Ramalho R., Rodríguez-Meza J., & Yung, J. (2012). *What have we learned from the enterprise surveys regarding access to finance by SME? Enterprise analysis unit.* Finance and Private Sector Development Vice President, World Bank Group, Washington, DC.

Kutlaca, D. (2002). Small and medium sized enterprises in Yugoslavia: A driving force in the catching-up process. *Small Firms and Entrepreneurship in Central and Eastern Europe, 14,* 157–178.

Kutllovci, E., Shala, V., & Troni, B. (2012). *Business strategy, the key determinants of SME growth in Kosovo* [Data file]. Retrieved 15 June 2013, from the University of Prishtina site www.managementjournal.info.

Lambson, V. (1991). Industry evolution with sunk costs and uncertain market conditions. *International Journal of Industrial Organization, 9*(2), 171–196.

Landau, S., & Everitt, B. S. (2004). *A handbook of statistical analyses using SPSS.* Boca Raton, FL: Chapman & Hall.

Lawton Smith, H., & Dickson, K. (2003). Critical factors in inter-firm collaboration. *International Journal of Technology Management, 25*(1/2), 34–50.

Lazonick, W. (2012). *The innovative enterprise and the developmental state: Toward an economics of organizational success.* Paper Prepared for the Annual Conference of the Institute for New Economic Thinking, Breton Woods, NH, April 8–11, 2011, and Revised for the Conference on Finance, Business Models, and Sustainable Prosperity, Ford Foundation, New York.

Lazonick, W. (2013). The theory of innovative enterprise: Methodology, ideology, and institutions. In J. K. Moudud, C. Bina, & P. L. Mason (Eds.),

Alternative theories of competition: Challenges to the orthodoxy (pp. 127–159). London and New York: Routledge.
Lazonick, W. H., Mazzucato, M., & Tulum, Ì. (2013). Apple's changing business model: What should the world's richest company do with all those profits? *Accounting Forum, 37,* 249–267.
Lee, C., Lee, K., & Pennings, J. M. (2001). Internal capabilities, external networks, and performance: A study on technology-based ventures. *Strategic Management Journal, 22,* 615–640.
Lee, S., Peng, M., & Barney, J. (2007). Bankruptcy law and entrepreneurship development: A real options perspective. *Academy of Management Review, 32*(1), 257–272.
Lee, R. P., Naylor, G., & Chen, Q. (2011). Linking customer resources to firm success: The role of marketing program implementation. *Journal of Business Research, 64,* 394–400.
Leiblein, M. J. (2011). What do resource and capability theories propose? *Journal of Management, 37*(4), 909–932.
Leiponen, A. (2005). Skills and innovation. *International Journal of Industrial Organization, 23*(5/6), 303–323.
Leipziger, D., & Zagha, R. (2006). Getting out of the rut. *Finance and Development (IMF), 43,* 1.
Lewis, E. G. (2005, May). *Immigration, skill mix, and the choice of technique* (Federal Reserve Bank of Philadelphia Working Paper No. 05-8).
Li, A., & Guisinger, P. (1991). Comparative business failures of foreign-controlled firms in the United States. *Journal of International Business Studies, 22*(2), 209–224.
Li, S., & Wu, J. (2010). Why some countries thrive despite corruption: The role of trust in the corruption-efficiency relationship. *Review of International Political Economy, 17*(1), 129–154.
Lichtenthaler, U., & Muethel, M. (2012). The impact of family involvement on dynamic innovation capabilities: Evidence from German manufacturing firms. *Entrepreneurship Theory and Practice, 36*(6), 1235–1253.
Liedholm, C., & Mead, D. (1987). *Small scale industries in developing countries: Empirical evidence and policy implications* (MSU International Development Paper No. 9, 1978). East Lansing: Department of Agricultural Economics, Michigan State University.
Liedholm, C., & Mead, D. (1995). *The dynamic role of micro and small enterprises in the development process* (GEMINI Action Research Program I, Final Report). Bethesda, MD: GEMINI.
Lijphart, A. (1971). Comparative politics and the comparative method. *American Political Science Review, 65*(3), 691–693.

Lijphart, A. (1975). The comparable-cases strategy in comparative research. *Comparative Political Studies, 8*(2), 158–177.

Lin, J. (2012). *New structural economics: A framework for rethinking development and policy*. Washington: World Bank. http://siteresources.worldbank.org/DEC/Resources/84797-1104785060319/598886-1104951889260/NSE-Book.pdf.

Lizal, L., & Svejnar, J. (2002). Investment, credit rationing, and the soft budget constraint: Evidence from Czech panel data. *The Review of Economics and Statistics, 84*(2), 353–370.

Love, I., & Mylenko, N. (2003). *Credit reporting and financing constraints* (World Bank Policy Research Working Paper 3142).

Love, J., & Roper, S. (2013). *SME innovation, exporting and growth, enterprise research center* (White Paper No. 5).

Love, J. H., Roper, S., & Du, J. (2009). Innovation, ownership and profitability. *International Journal of Industrial Organization, 27*(3), 424–434.

Lucas, R. E. (1988). On the mechanics of economic development. *Journal of Monetary Economics, 22,* 3–42.

Lumpkin, G. T., & Dess, G. G. (1996). Clarifying entrepreneurial orientation construct and linking it to performance. *Academy of Management Review, 2*(1), 135–172.

Mahoney, J. T. (1995). The management of resources and the resource of management. *Journal of Business Research, 33,* 91–101.

Makadok, R. (2001). Toward a synthesis of the resource-based and dynamic-capability views of rent creation. *Strategic Management Journal, 22*(5), 387–401.

Mankiw, N. G., Romer, D., & Weil, D. (1992). A contribution to the empirics of economic growth. *Quarterly Journal of Economics, 107*(2), 407–437.

Mann, H. B., & Whitney, D. R. (1947). On a test of whether one of two random variables is stochastically larger than the other. *Annals of Mathematical Statistics, 18,* 50–60.

Manski, C. (2000). Identification problems and decisions under ambiguity: Empirical analysis of treatment response and normative analysis of treatment choice. *Journal of Econometrics, 95*(2), 415–442.

Mata, J., & Portugal, P. (1994). Life duration of new firms. *Journal of Industrial Economics, 42*(3), 227–245.

Mata, J., & Portugal, P. (2002). The survival of new domestic and foreign-owned firms. *Strategic Management Journal, 23*(4), 323–343.

Mata, J., Portugal, P., & Guimaraes, P. (1995). The survival of new plants: Start-up conditions and post-entry evolution. *International Journal of Industrial Organization, 13,* 459–481.

Mauro, P. (1995). Corruption and growth. *Quarterly Journal of Economics, 110*(3), 681–712.
McMillan, J., & Woodruff, C. (1999). Inter-firm relationships and informal credit in Vietnam. *Quarterly Journal of Economics, 114*(4), 1285–1320.
McMillan, J., & Woodruff, C. (2002). The central role of entrepreneurs in transition economies. *Journal of Economic Perspectives, 16*(3), 153–170.
Medjad, K. (2004). The fate of the Yugoslav model: A case against legal conformity. *The American Journal of Comparative Law, 52*(1), 287–319.
Melkas, H., & Pekkarinen, S. (2016). SMEs and regional design services for innovation: Experienced and expected impacts on users and non-users. *International Journal of Innovation and Regional Development, 7*(3), 222–236.
Méon, P. G., & Weill, L. (2010). Is corruption an efficient grease? A cross-country aggregate analysis. *World Development, 38*(3), 244–259.
Mickiewicz, T. (2005). *Economic transition in Central Europe and the Commonwealth of Independent States*. Houndmills: Palgrave Macmillan.
Mincer, J. (1958). Investment in human capital and personal income distribution. *The Journal of Political Economy, 66*(4), 281–302.
Mises, L. V. (1949). *Human action: A treatise on economics*. New Haven, CT: Yale University Press.
Moorman, C., & Rust, R. T. (1999). The role of marketing. *Journal of Marketing, 63*, 180–197.
Moorman, C., & Slotegraaf, R. J. (1999). The contingency value of complementary capabilities in product development. *Journal of Marketing Research, 36*(2), 239–257.
Moretti, E. (2004). Workers' education, spillovers, and productivity: Evidence from plant-level production functions. *American Economic Review, 94*(3), 656–690.
Morris, M. H., & Kuratko, D. F. (2002). *Corporate entrepreneurship*. Mason, OH: South-Western College Publishers.
Morrow, J. L., Sirmon, D. G., Hitt, M. A., & Holcomb, T. R. (2007). Creating value in the face of declining performance: Firm strategies and organisational recovery. *Strategic Management Journal, 28*, 271–283.
Mosakowski, E. (1998). Entrepreneurial resources, organizational choices, and competitive outcomes. *Organization Science, 9*(6), 625–643.
Murphree, M., Tang, L., & Breznitz, D. (2016). Tacit local alliance and SME innovation in China. *International Journal of Innovation and Regional Development, 7*(3), 184–202.
Naudé, W. A. (2007). *Peace, prosperity, and pro-growth entrepreneurship* (WIDER Discussion Paper 2007/02). Helsinki: UNU-WIDER.

Naudé, W. A. (2010a). *Entrepreneurship and economic development*. Basingstoke: Palgrave Macmillan.

Naudé, W. A. (2010b). Entrepreneurship is not a binding constraint on growth and development in the poorest countries. *World Development, 39*(1), 33–44.

Naudé, W. A. (2012). *Entrepreneurship and economic development: Theory, evidence and policy* (Discussion Paper No. 7507). Bonn, Germany: University of Maastricht.

Naudé, W. A., Amorós, E., & Cristi, O. (2013). *Surfeiting the appetite may sicken: Entrepreneurship and the happiness of nations*. Small Business Economics (Early Online).

Nelson, R. R., & Phelps, E. (1966). Investment in humans, technology diffusion and economic growth. *American Economic Review, 56*(2), 69–75.

Nelson, R., & Winter, G. (1982). *An evolutionary theory of economic change*. Cambridge, MA: Belknap Press/Harvard University Press.

Neumark, D., Wall, B., & Zhang, J. (2011). Do small businesses create more jobs? New evidence for the United States from the National Establishment Time Series. *The Review of Economics and Statistics, 93*(1), 16–29.

Nichter, S., & Goldmark, L. (2009). Small firm growth in developing countries. *World Development, 37*(9), 1453–1464.

Nonaka, I. (1991). The knowledge-creating company. *Harvard Business Review, 69*(6), 96–104.

Nonaka, I., & Takeuchi, H. (1995). *The knowledge-creating company*. New York: Oxford University Press.

North, D. C. (1981). *Structure and change in economic history*. New York: W. W. Norton.

North, D. C. (1990). *Institutions, institutional change and economic performance*. Cambridge: Cambridge University Press.

O'Dwyer, M., & Ryan, E. (2002). Management development—A model for retail business. *Journal of European Industrial Training, 26*(9), 420–429.

OECD. (2009). *Strategies for aligning stimulus measures with long-term growth*. Paris: OECD.

OECD. (2010). *SMEs, entrepreneurship and innovation*. Paris: OECD Publishing.

OECD. (2011). *Skills for innovation and research* (p. 96). Paris: OECD.

OECD. (2012). *SME Policy Index: Western Balkans and Turkey 2012: Progress in the implementation of the Small Business Act for Europe*. Paris: OECD Publishing. https://doi.org/10.1787/9789264178861-en.

OECD. (2013a, March). *Assessment of the Kosovo innovation system*. RCI Project Paper, OECE Development.

OECD. (2013b). *Skills development and training in SMEs*. Paris: OECD Publishing.

OECD. (2014). *Young SMEs, growth and job creation*. http://www.oecd.org/sti/young-SME-growth-and-job-creation.pdf.

OECD. (2016a). Overview: 2016 Small Business Act assessment of the Western Balkans and Turkey. In *SME Policy Index: Western Balkans and Turkey 2016: Assessing the implementation of the Small Business Act for Europe*. Paris: OECD Publishing. https://doi.org/10.1787/9789264254473-4-en.

OECD. (2016b). *Entrepreneurship at a Glance 2016*. Paris: OECD Publishing.

OECD (2016c, June 1–2). *The productivity-inclusiveness nexus, meeting of the OECD Council at Ministerial Level*. Paris [C/MIN(2016)3].

OECD. (2017a). *Financing SMEs and entrepreneurs 2017: An OECD scoreboard*. Paris: OECD Publishing. https://doi.org/10.1787/fin_sme_ent-2017-en.

OECD. (2017b). *Increasing productivity in small traditional enterprises: Programmes for upgrading management skills and practices*. OECD Working Party on SMEs and Entrepreneurship [CFE/SME(2016)6].

OECD/Eurostat. (2005). *Oslo manual, guidelines for collecting and interpreting innovation data*. Paris: OECD.

Østergaard, C. R., Timmermans, B., & Kristinsson, K. (2011). Does a different view create something new? The effect of employee diversity on innovation. *Research Policy, 40*(3), 500–509.

Overman, H. G., & Puga, D. (2010). Labour pooling as a source of agglomeration: An empirical investigation. *Agglomeration Economics* (pp. 133–150). Chicago, IL: University of Chicago Press.

PAK. (2015). *Annual activity report of Privatization Agency of Kosovo*. http://www.pak-ks.org/repository/docs/150130_FINANCIAL_STATEMENTS_OF_KOSOVO_BUDGET_Jan_-_Dec_2014_ENG.compressed.PDF.

Palairet, M. (2001). The economic consequences of Slobodan Milosevic. *Europe-Asia Studies, 53*(6), 309–323.

Pallant, J. (2016). *SPSS survival manual: A step by step guide to data analysis using SPSS program* (6th ed.). London, UK: McGraw-Hill Education.

Pe'er A., & Vertinsky, F. (2006a). *The survival value of clusters* (Tuck Business School at Dartmouth Working Paper).

Pe'er, A., & Vertinsky, F. (2006b). *Who enters, where, and why? The influence of capabilities and initial resource endowments on the location choices of new enterprises* (Tuck Business School at Dartmouth Working Paper).

Pellegrino, G., Piva, M., & Vivarelli, M. (2009). *How do young companies innovate?* (Discussion Paper IZA DP No. 4301) [Online]. http://www.ftp.iza.org/dp4301.pdf. Accessed 12 April 2013.

Penrose, E. T. (1959). *The growth of the firm*. New York: Wiley.

Perritt, H. (2005). Resolving claims when countries disintegrate: The challenge of Kosovo. *Chicago-Kent Law Review, 80*(119). https://scholarship.kentlaw.iit.edu/cklawreview/vol80/iss1/8.

Peteraf, M. (1993). The cornerstones of competitive advantage: A resource-based view. *Strategic Management Journal, 14*(3), 179–191.

Pettifer, J. (2002, January). *Kosovo economy and society after 1945—Some observations*. Conflict Studies Research Centre, Royal Military Academy, Surrey.

Piech, K. (2004). *The knowledge-based economy in transition countries: Selected issue*. London: University College London—School of Slavonic and East European Studies.

Pissarides, F. (1999). Is the lack of funds the main obstacle to growth? EBRD's experience with small and medium-sized businesses in Central and Eastern Europe. *Journal of Business Venturing, 14*, 519–539.

Pissarides, F., Singer, M., & Svenjar, J. (2003). Objectives and constraints of entrepreneurs: Evidence from small and medium-sized enterprises in Russia and Bulgaria. *Journal of Comparative Economics, 31*(3), 503–531.

Polanyi, M. (1962). *Personal knowledge—Towards a post-critical philosophy*. London: Routledge and Kegan Paul.

Prahalad, C. K., & Hamel, G. (1990). The core competence of the corporation. *Harvard Business Review, 68*(3), 79–91.

Prentice, R., & Gloeckler, L. (1978). Regression analysis of grouped survival data with application to breast cancer data. *Biometrics, 34*, 57–67.

Protogerou, A., Caloghirou, Y., & Lioukas, S. (2011). Dynamic capabilities and their indirect impact on firm performance. *Industrial Corporate Change, 21*(3), 615–647.

Pula, B. (2004). The emergence of the Kosovo parallel state 1988–1992. *Nationalities Papers, 32*(4), 79–91.

Radosevic, S., & Mickiewicz, T. (2003). *Innovation capabilities in seven candidate countries: An assessment* (Vol. 2.8). Brussels: Enterprise Directorate General, CEC.

Ragin, C. C. (1987). *The comparative method. Moving beyond qualitative and quantitative strategies*. Berkeley: University of California Press.

Ragin, C. C. (2000). *Fuzzy-set social science*. Chicago and London: University of Chicago Press.

Rajan, R., & Zingales, L. (2003). The great reversal: The politics of financial development in the 20th century. *Journal of financial economics, 69*(1), 5–50.

Ramet, S. P. (2006). *The three Yugoslavias. State-building and legitimating, 1918–2005*. Washington, DC: The Woodrow Wilson Centre Press and Bloomington: Indian University Press.

Reagans, R., Argote, L., & Brooks, D. (2005). Individual experience and experience working together: Predicting learning rates from knowing who knows what and knowing how to work together. *Management Science, 51*(6), 869–881.

Reinikka, R., & Svensson, J. (2004). Local capture: Evidence from a central government transfer program in Uganda. *The Quarterly Journal of Economics, 119*(2), 679–705.

Resende, M., Cardoso, V., & Façanha, L. O. (2015). Determinants of survival of newly created SMEs in the Brazilian manufacturing industry: An econometric study. *Empirical Economics, 50*(4), 1255–1274.

Reuveny, R., & Li, Q. (2003). Economic openness, democracy and income inequality: An empirical analysis. *Comparative Political Studies, 36*(5), 575–601.

Richter, A., & Schaffer, M. (1996). The performance of de novo private firms in Russian manufacturing. In S. Commander, Q. Fan, & M. Schaffer (Eds.), *Enterprise Restructuring Economic Policy in Russia*. Washington, DC: EDI/The World Bank.

Riinvest. (2001). *SOEs and their privatization/transformation, in cooperation with Centre for International Private Enterprise*. Washington, supported by the United States Agency for International Development (USAID), Pristina.

Riinvest. (2004). *Privatization in Kosova: Forwards and backwards*. Pristina.

Riinvest. (2017). *Business environment in Kosovo: From SMEs perspective*. Prishtina.

Robbins, V. K. (1996). *Exploring the texture of the texts: A guide to socio-rhetorical interpretation*. Harrisburg, PA: Trinity Press International.

Robert, C. P., & Casella, G. (2004). *Monte carlo statistical methods* (2nd ed.). New York: Springer-Verlag.

Roberts, K., & Weitzman, M. L. (1981). Funding criteria for research, development, and exploration projects. *Econometrica, 49*(5), 1261–1288.

Rock, M. T., & Bonnet, H. (2004). The comparative politics of corruption: Accounting for the East Asian Paradox in empirical studies of corruption, growth and investment. *World Development, 32*, 999–1017.

Rodriguez, F. (2005). Comment on Hausmann and Rodrik. *Journal of the Latin American and Caribbean Economic Association, 6*(1), 101–110.

Rodríguez, J. C., Navarro-Chávez, L., & Gómez, M. (2014). Regional innovation systems in emerging economies: Evidence of system failures for innovation. *International Journal of Innovation and Regional Development, 5*(4/5), 384–404.

Rodrik, D. (2006). *Why we learn nothing from regressing economic growth on policies*. Harvard University (mimeo).

Rodrik, D. (2010). Diagnostics before prescription. *Journal of Economic Perspectives, 24*(3), 33–44.

Rodrik, D., Subramanian, A., & Trebbi, F. (2004). Institutions rule: The primacy of institutions over geography and integration in economic development. *Journal of Economic Growth, 9*(2), 131–165.

Roll, R., & Talbott, J. (2003). Political freedom, economic liberty, and prosperity. *Journal of Democracy, 4,* 75–89.

Romer, P. (1986). Increasing returns and long-run growth. *Journal of Political Economy, 94*(5), 1002–1037.

Rosen, H. S. (2005). *Public finance*. New York: McGraw-Hill/Irwin.

Rothwell, R., Freeman, C., Horlsey, A., Jervis, V. T. P., Robertson, A. B., & Townsend, J. (1974). SAPPHO updated: Project SAPPHO phase II. *Research Policy, 3,* 258–291.

Ruben, R., Slingerland, M., & Nijhoff, H. (2006). Agro-food chains and networks for development—Issues, approaches and strategies. In R. Ruben, M. Slingerland, & H. Nijhoff (Eds.), *Agro-food chains and networks for development*. Dordrecht, The Netherlands: Springer.

Ruekert, R. W. (1992). Developing a market orientation: An organizational strategy perspective. *International Journal of Research in Marketing, 9*(3), 225–245.

Rumelt, R. (1991). How much does industry matter? *Strategic Management Journal, 12,* 167–185.

Rummel, R. J. (1970). *Applied factor analysis*. Evanston: Northwestern University Press.

Sachs, J., & Warner, A. (1995). *Natural resource abundance and economic growth* (National Bureau of Economic Research Working Paper 5398). Cambridge, MA.

Sala-i-Martin, X. (1997). I just ran two million regressions. *American Economic Review, 87,* 178–183.

Sartor, O. (2007). *An outline and critique of growth diagnostics as a response to the policy vacuum left by the Washington Consensus.* Seminar Paper in Development Economics, Institute of Public Economics, Humboldt University, Berlin.

Scarpetta, S., Hemmings, P., Tressel, T., & Woo, J. (2002). *The role of policy and institutions from productivity and firm dynamics: Evidence from micro and industry data* (OECD Economics Department Working Papers 329).

Scheepers, M. J., Hough, J., & Bloom, J. Z. (2008). Nurturing the corporate entrepreneurship capability. *Southern African Business Review, 12*(3), 50–75.

Schiefer, J., & Hartmann, M. (2008). Determinants of competitive advantage for German food processors. *Agribusiness, 24*(3), 306–319.

Schiffer, M., & Weder, B. (2001). *Firm size and the business environment: Worldwide survey results* (IFC Discussion Paper Number 43).

Schmitz, H. (1995). Collective efficiency: Growth path for small scale industry. *Journal of Development Studies, 31*(4), 529–666.

Schrör, H. (2005). *Business demography in Europe: Results from 1997 to 2002, Eurostat statistics in focus: Industry.* Trade and Services, 36/2005. Luxembourg: Eurostat.

Schumpeter, J. (1934). *Theory of economic development.* Cambridge: Harvard University Press.

Schumpeter, J. (1943). *Capitalism, socialism and democracy.* New York: Harper.

Schutjens, A., & Wever, E. (2000). Determinants of new firm success. *Papers in Regional Science, 79*(2), 135–159.

Sen, K., & Kirkpatrick, C. (2009). A diagnostic approach to economic growth and employment policy in low income economies: The case of Kosovo. *Journal of International Development, 23*(1), 132–154.

Sen, K., & Kirkpatrick, C. (2011). A diagnostics approach to economic growth and employment policy in low income economies: The case of Kosovo. *Journal of International Development, 23*(1): 132–154.

Senge, P., Roberts, C., Ross, R., Smith, B. J., & Kleiner, A. (1994). *The fifth discipline fieldbook.* London: Century.

Senge, P., Kleiner, A., Roberts, C., Roth, G., & Ross, R. (1999). The dance of change: The challenges of sustaining the learning organization. New York, NY: Doubleday.

Shane, S. (2008). *Illusions of entrepreneurship.* New Haven, CT: Yale University Press.

Shane, S., & Stuart, T. (2002). Organizational endowments and the performance of university start-ups. *Management Science, 48,* 154–170.

Shapira, P., Youtie, J., & Kay, K. (2011). Building capabilities for innovation in SMEs: A cross-country comparison of technology extension policies and programmes. *International Journal of Innovation and Regional Development, 3*(3/4), 254–272.

Simpson, M., & Taylor, N. (2002). The role and relevance of marketing in SMEs: Towards a new model. *Journal of Small Business and Enterprise Development, 9*(4), 370–382.

Sirmon, D. G., Hitt, M. A., & Ireland, R. D. (2007). Managing firm resources in dynamic environments to create value: Looking inside the black box. *Academy of Management Review, 32*(1), 273–292.

Smallbone, D., & Welter, F. (2001). The role of government in SME development in transition economies. *International Small Business Journal, 19*(4), 63–76.

Sobel, R. (2008). Testing Baumol: Institutional quality and the productivity of entrepreneurship. *Journal of Business Venturing, 23,* 641–655.

Solow, R. (1957). Technical change and the aggregate production function. *Review of Economics and Statistics, 39*(3), 312–320.

Spillan, J., & Parnell, J. (2006). Marketing resources and firm performance among SMEs. *European Management Journal, 24,* 236–245.

SPRU. (1972). *Success and failure in industrial innovation, Report on Project SAPPHO by Science Policy Research Unit.* University of Sussex, Report prepared by C. Freeman, A. Robertson, B. Achilladelis, P. Jervis, R. Curnow, A. Horsley, C. Tudway, & J. Fuller. Published by the Centre for the Study of Industrial Innovation, printed by Bishop and Sons Ltd., Edinburgh.

Stam E., Audrutsch D., & Meijaard, J. (2006). *Renascent entrepreneurship* (ERIM Report Series 17). Erasmus Research Institute Management, Erasmus University Rotterdam.

Steiner, M. P., & Solem, O. (1988). Factors for success in small manufacturing firms. *Journal of Small Business Management, 26*(1), 51–56.

Stephan, J. (2011). The role of human capital and managerial skills in explaining productivity gaps between East and West. *Eastern European Economics, 46*(6), 5–24.

Stevenson, H., & Jarillo, J. (1990). A paradigm of entrepreneurship: Entrepreneurial management. *Strategic Management Journal, 11,* 17–27. Special Issue.

Stiglitz, J., & Weiss, A. (1981). Credit rationing in markets with imperfect information. *American Economic Review, 71*(3), 393–409.

Stinchcombe, A. L. (1965). Social structure and organizations. In J. G. March (Ed.), *Handbook of organizations* (pp. 142–193). Chicago: Rand McNally & Co.

Storey D. J., & Greene, F. J. (2010). *Small business and entrepreneurship*. Harlow: Prentice Hall.

Storey, D. J. (1985). Problems facing new firms. *Journal of Management Studies, 22*(3), 327–345.

Storey, D. J. (1994). *Understanding the small business sector*. London: Routledge.

Sutherland, D., Sonia, A., Balázs, É., & Tomasz, K. (2009). *Infrastructure investment: Links to growth and the role of public policies* (Economics Department Working Paper No. 686 ECO/WKP (2009)27).

Sutton, J. (1997). Gibrat's legacy. *Journal of Economic Literature, 35*(1), 40–59.

Sutton, J. (2000). *Rich trades, scarce capabilities: Industrial development revisited*. Keynes Lecture in Economics, British Academy, London.

Sutton, J. (2005). *Competing in capabilities: An informal overview*. Washington, DC: World Bank.

Sutton, J. (2012). *Competing in capabilities: The globalization process*. Oxford, UK: Oxford University Press.

Sutton, J., & Trefler, D. (2016). Capabilities, wealth, and trade. *Journal of Political Economy, 124*(3), 826–878.

Svejnar, J. (2002). Transition economies: Performance and challenges. *Journal of Economic Perspectives, 16*(1), 3–28.

Svensson, J. (2005). Eight questions about corruption. *Journal of Economic Perspectives, 19*(3), 19–42.

Switzer, L., & Huang, Y. (2007). How does human capital affect the performance of small and mid-cap mutual funds? *Journal of Intellectual Capital, 8*(4), 666–681.

Syverson, C. (2004). Product substitutability and productivity dispersion. *Review of Economics and Statistics, 86*(2), 534–550.

Tabachnick, B. G., & Fidell, L. S. (2007). *Using multivariate statistics* (5th ed.). Boston, MA: Allyn & Bacon.

Tanzi, V. (1998). Corruption around the world: Causes, consequences, scope, and cures. *IMF Staff Papers, 45*(4), 559–594. Republished in V. Tanzi (2000), *Policies, institutions and the dark side of economics*. Chellenham: Edward Elgar and in G. T. Abed & S. Gupta (Eds.) (2002), *Governance, corruption and economic performance*. Washington, DC: The International Monetary Fund.

Teece, D. J. (2000). *Managing intellectual capital: Organizational, strategic, and policy dimensions*. Oxford: Oxford University Press.

Teece, D. J. (2007). Explicating dynamic capabilities: The nature and microfundations of (sustainable) enterprise performance. *Strategic Management Journal, 28*(13), 1319–1350.

Teece, D. J. (2012). Dynamic capabilities: Routines versus entrepreneurial action. *Journal of Management Studies, 49*(8), 1395–1401.

Teece, D. J. (2014). The foundations of enterprise performance: Dynamic and ordinary capabilities in an (economic) theory of firms. *Academy of Management Perspectives, 28*(4), 328–352.

Teece, D. J. (2016). Dynamic capabilities and entrepreneurial management in large organizations: Toward a theory of the (entrepreneurial) firm. *European Economic Review, 86,* 202–216.

Teece, D. J., & Pisano, G. (1994). The dynamic capabilities of firms: An introduction. *Industrial and Corporate Change, 3*(3), 537–556.

Teece, D. J., Pisano, G., & Shuen, A. (1997). Dynamic capabilities and strategic management. *Strategic Management Journal, 18*(7), 509–533.

Treisman, D. (2007). What have we learned about the causes of corruption from ten years of cross-national empirical research? *Annual Review of Political Science, 10,* 211–244.

Ughetto, E. (2008). Does internal finance matter for R&D? New evidence from a panel of Italian firms. *Cambridge Journal of Economics, 32*(6), 907–925.

UNESCO. (2012). *Data Centre, UNESCO Institute for Statistics website.* http://stats.uis.unesco.org/unesco/TableViewer/document.aspx?ReportId=136&IF_Language=eng&BR_Topic=0. Accessed on 25 November 2012.

United Nations Development Programme (UNDP). (2007). *Energy for development: Kosovo human development report.* Pristina.

Vossen, R. W. (1998). Relative strengths and weaknesses of small firms in innovation. *International Small Business Journal, 16*(3), 88–95.

Wacziarg, R., & Welch, K. H. (2003). *Trade liberalization and growth: New evidence* (NBER Working Paper 10152). Cambridge, MA: National Bureau of Economic Research.

Wei, Y., & Wang, Q. (2011). Making sense of a market information system for superior performance: The roles of organizational responsiveness and innovation strategy. *Industrial Marketing Management, 40*(2), 267–277.

Winter, S. (1987). Knowledge and competence as strategic assets. In D. J. Teece (Ed.), *The competitive challenge*. Cambridge, MA: Ballinger.

Woodward, S. (1995). *Socialist unemployment: The political economy of Yugoslavia, 1945–1990.* Princeton, NJ: Princeton University Press.

World Bank. (1999). *Kosovo—Building peace through sustainable growth: The economic and social policy agenda*. Washington, DC: World Bank.

World Bank. (2004). *World development report: A better investment climate for everyone.* Washington, DC: World Bank.

World Bank. (2008). *Unleashing prosperity productivity growth in Eastern Europe and the former Soviet Union*. http://siteresources.worldbank.org/ECAEXT/Resources/publications/UnleashingProsperity.pdf.
World Bank. (2010). *BEEPS At-A-Glance 2008 Kosovo, Business Environment and Enterprise Performance Survey (BEEPS IV)*. Washington, DC: World Bank.
World Bank. (2012a). *World Bank—Kosovo partnership: Country program snapshot*. Pristina: The World Bank Country Office in Kosovo.
World Bank. (2012b). *Implementation status and results: Kosovo institutional development for education project*. Washington, DC: The World Bank.
World Bank. (2013). *BEEPS 2013, Kosovo, Business Environment and Enterprise Performance Survey (BEEPS IV)*. Washington, DC: World Bank. http://www.enterprisesurveys.org/~/media/GIAWB/EnterpriseSurveys/Documents/Profiles/English/kosovo-2013.pdf.
World Bank. (2014). *Country snapshot on Kosovo*. http://www.worldbank.org/content/dam/Worldbank/document/eca/Kosovo-Snapshot.pdf.
World Bank. (2015). *World Bank national accounts data* (database). http://data.worldbank.org/. Accessed 26 June 2015.
World Bank. (2016). *Worldwide governance indicators*. https://databank.worldbank.org/data/source/worldwide-governance-indicators.
World Bank. (2017). *Doing business indicators*. http://www.doingbusiness.org/content/dam/doingBusiness/media/Annual-Reports/English/DB17-Report.pdf.
World Bank. (2018). *Country snapshot*. http://pubdocs.worldbank.org/en/423771524155944422/Kosovo-Snapshot-Spring2018.pdf.
Wright, M., Filatotchev, I., Hoskisson, R. E., & Peng, M. W. (2005). Strategy research in emerging economies: Challenging the conventional wisdom. *Journal of Management Studies, 42,* 1–33.
Wymenga, P., Spanikova, V., Derbyshire, J., & Barker, A. (2011). *Are EU SMEs recovering from the crisis? Annual report on eu small and medium-sized enterprises 2010/11*. Report for the European Commission.
Xheneti, M. (2006, November 22–24). *SME development in Albania—An empirical investigation of business growth*. Paper Presented at the RENT XX Conference, Brussels, Belgium.
Youndt, M., Subramaniam, M., & Snell, S. A. (2004). Intellectual capital profiles: An examination of investments and returns. *Journal of Management Studies, 2,* 335–361.
Yudaeva, K., Melentieva, N., & Ponomareva, N. (2003). Does foreign ownership matter? The Russian experience. *Economics of Transition, 11*(3), 383–409.

Yusuf, A. (1995). Critical success factors for small business: Perceptions of South Pacific entrepreneurs. *Journal of Small Business Management, 32*(3), 68–73.

Zahra, S. A., & Covin, J. G. (1995). Contextual influences on the corporate entrepreneurship performance relationship: A longitudinal analysis. *Journal of Business Venturing, 10*(1), 43–58.

Zahra, S. A., Sapienza, H. J., & Davidsson, P. (2006). Entrepreneurship and dynamic capabilities: A review, model and research agenda. *Journal of Management Studies, 43*(4), 917–955.

Zelenyuk, V., & Zheka, V. (2006). Corporate governance and firms efficiency: The case of transitional country, Ukraine. *Journal of Productivity Analysis, 25*(1), 143–169.

Zingales, L. (1998). Survival of the fittest or the fattest? Exit and financing in the trucking industry. *Journal of Finance, 53*(3), 905–938.

Zollo, M., & Winter, S. (2002). Deliberate learning and the evolution of dynamic capabilities. *Organization Science, 13*(3), 339.

Index

F. Sahiti, *The Growth of Firms in Less-Developed Countries*,
https://doi.org/10.1007/978-3-030-14821-8

The manufacturer's authorised representative in the EU is Springer Nature Customer Service Centre GmbH, Europaplatz 3, 69115 Heidelberg, Germany. If you have any concerns regarding our products, please contact ProductSafety@springernature.com

Printed and bound by CPI Group (UK) Ltd, Croydon, CR0 4YY

01/10/2026

02225974-0007